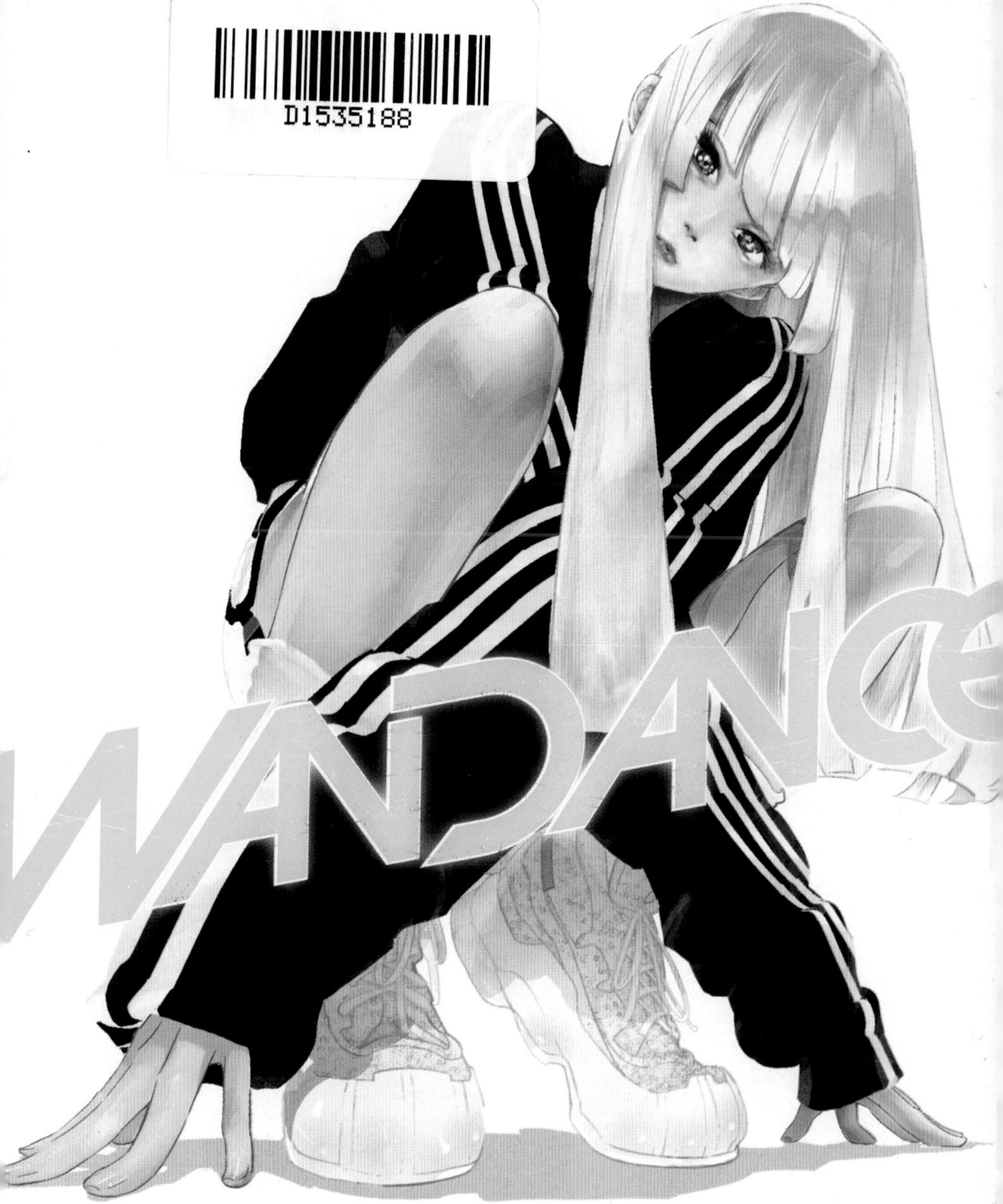
WANDANCE

CONTENTS

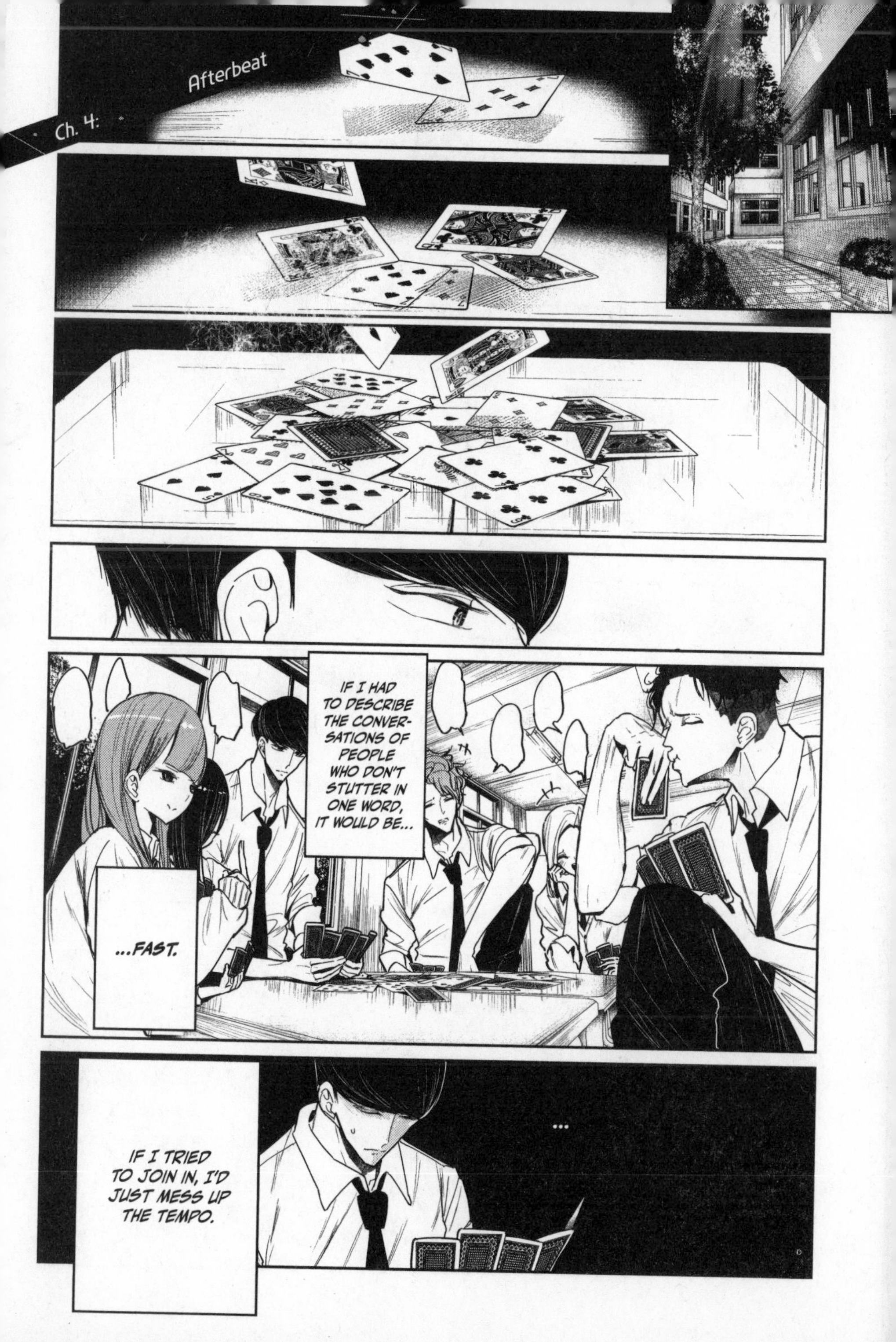

Ch. 4: Afterbeat
IF I HAD TO DESCRIBE THE CONVERSATIONS OF PEOPLE WHO DON'T STUTTER IN ONE WORD, IT WOULD BE...
...FAST.
...
IF I TRIED TO JOIN IN, I'D JUST MESS UP THE TEMPO.

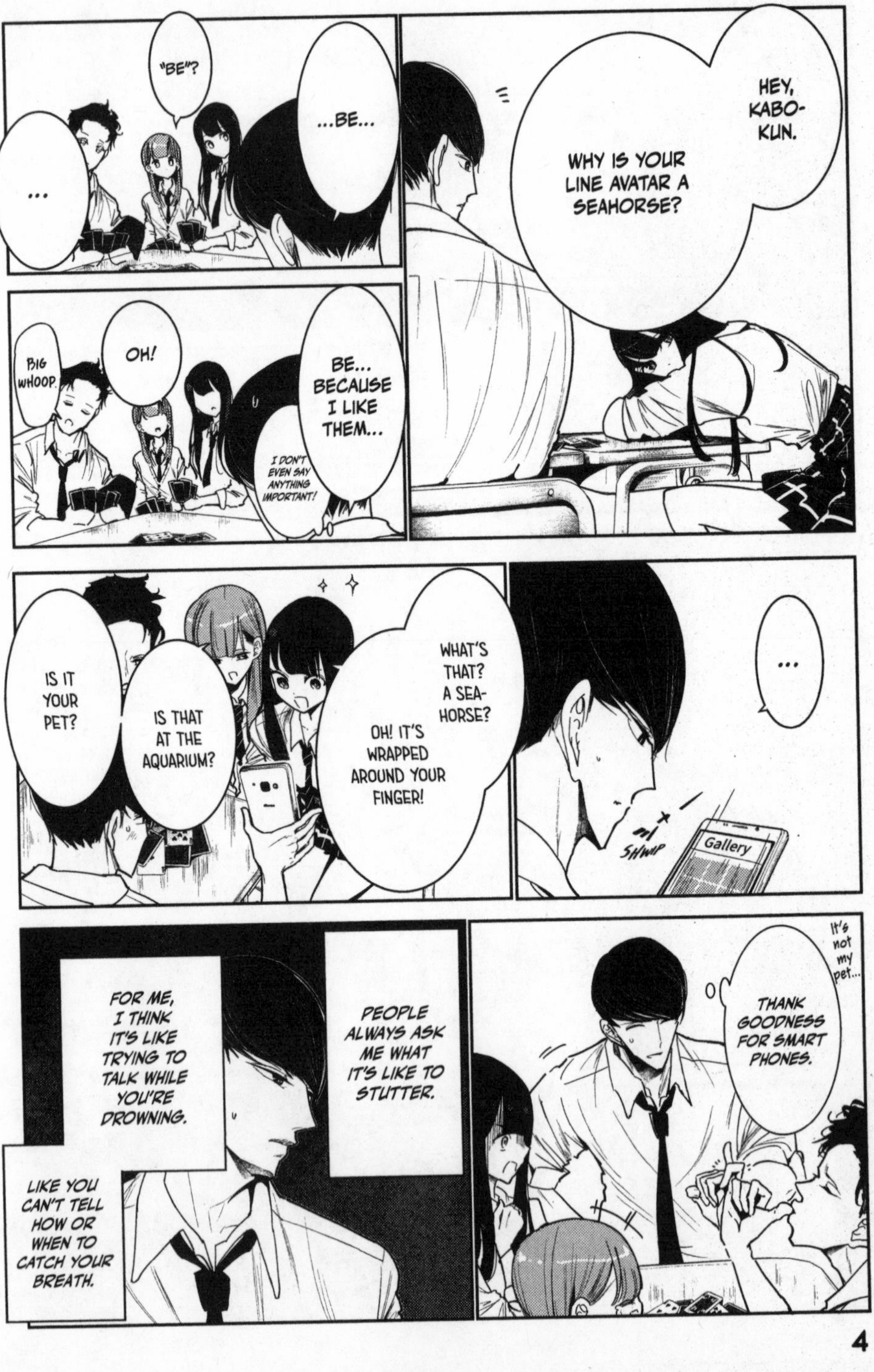
HEY, KABO-KUN.
WHY IS YOUR LINE AVATAR A SEAHORSE?
...BE...
"BE"?
...
BE... BECAUSE I LIKE THEM...
I DON'T EVEN SAY ANYTHING IMPORTANT!
OH!
BIG WHOOP.
...
SHWIP
Gallery
WHAT'S THAT? A SEA-HORSE?
OH! IT'S WRAPPED AROUND YOUR FINGER!
IS THAT AT THE AQUARIUM?
IS IT YOUR PET?
It's not my pet...
THANK GOODNESS FOR SMART PHONES.
PEOPLE ALWAYS ASK ME WHAT IT'S LIKE TO STUTTER.
FOR ME, I THINK IT'S LIKE TRYING TO TALK WHILE YOU'RE DROWNING.
LIKE YOU CAN'T TELL HOW OR WHEN TO CATCH YOUR BREATH.

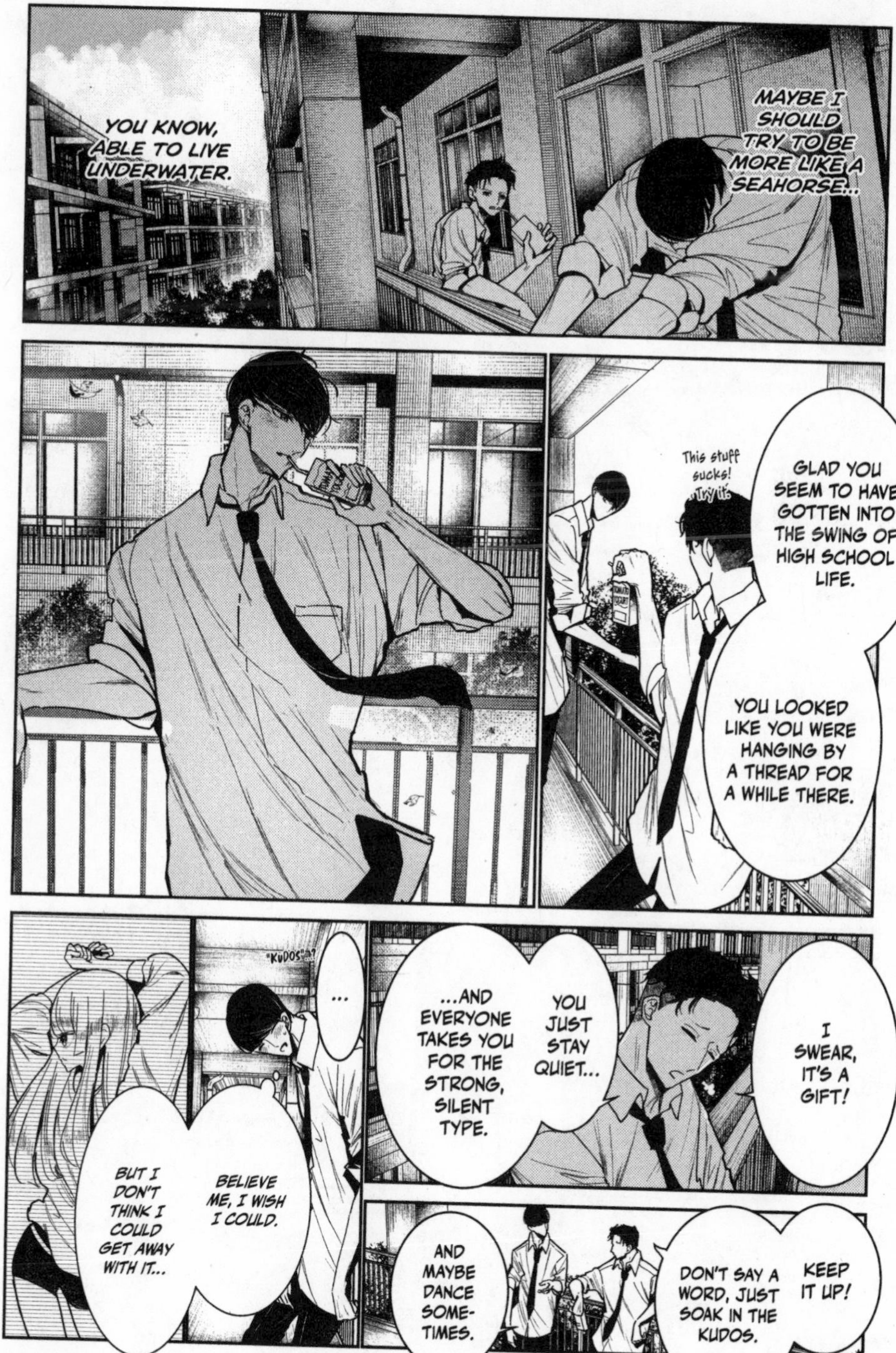
MAYBE I SHOULD TRY TO BE MORE LIKE A SEAHORSE...
YOU KNOW, ABLE TO LIVE UNDERWATER.
GLAD YOU SEEM TO HAVE GOTTEN INTO THE SWING OF HIGH SCHOOL LIFE.
This stuff sucks! Try it.
YOU LOOKED LIKE YOU WERE HANGING BY A THREAD FOR A WHILE THERE.
I SWEAR, IT'S A GIFT!
YOU JUST STAY QUIET...
...AND EVERYONE TAKES YOU FOR THE STRONG, SILENT TYPE.
KEEP IT UP!
DON'T SAY A WORD, JUST SOAK IN THE KUDOS.
AND MAYBE DANCE SOME-TIMES.
"KUDOS"?
...
BELIEVE ME, I WISH I COULD.
BUT I DON'T THINK I COULD GET AWAY WITH IT...

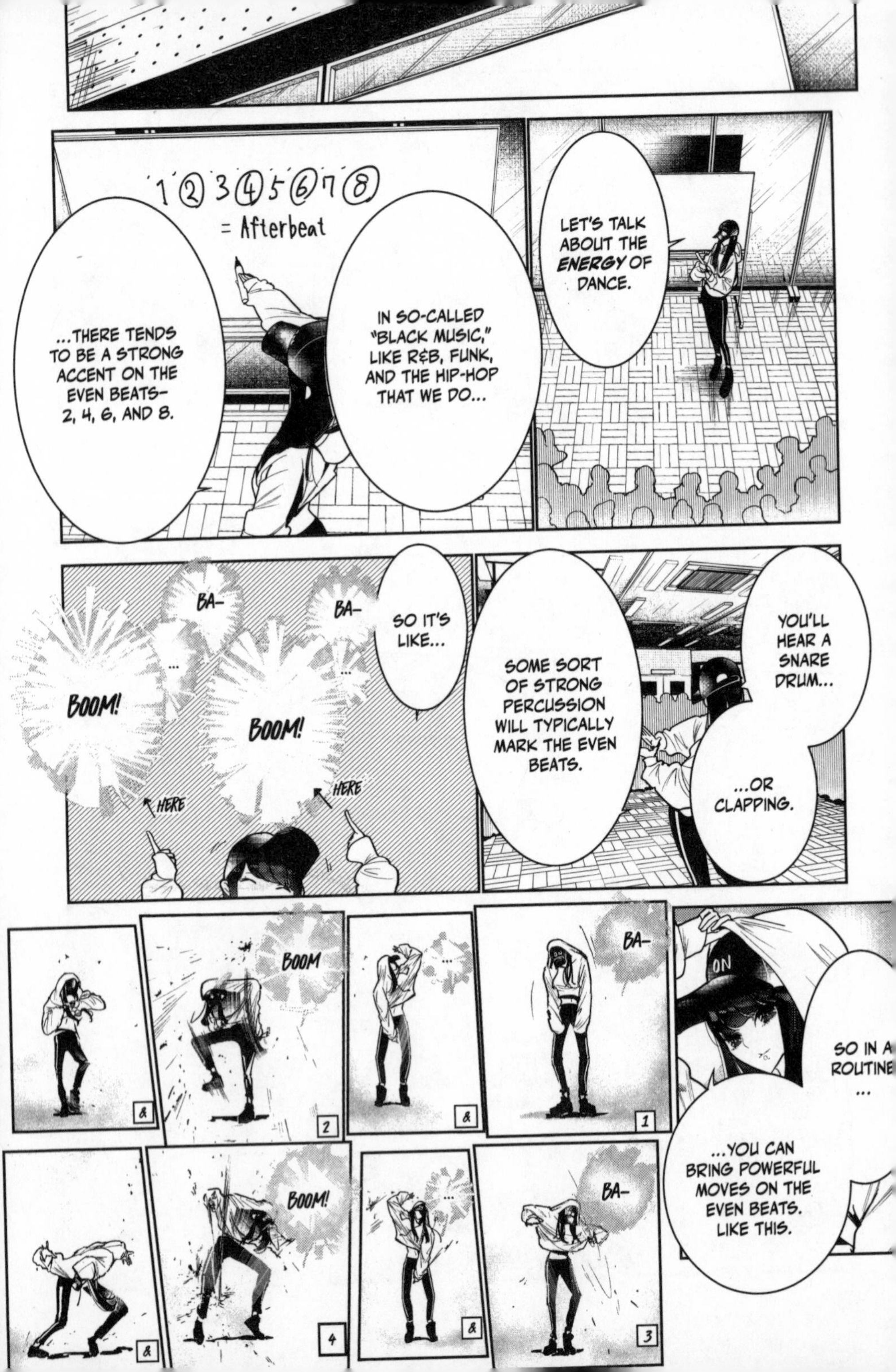
LET'S TALK ABOUT THE *ENERGY* OF DANCE.
1 2 3 4 5 6 7 8
= Afterbeat
IN SO-CALLED "BLACK MUSIC," LIKE R&B, FUNK, AND THE HIP-HOP THAT WE DO...
...THERE TENDS TO BE A STRONG ACCENT ON THE EVEN BEATS– 2, 4, 6, AND 8.
SOME SORT OF STRONG PERCUSSION WILL TYPICALLY MARK THE EVEN BEATS.
YOU'LL HEAR A SNARE DRUM...
...OR CLAPPING.
SO IT'S LIKE...
BA-
...
BOOM!
HERE
BA-
...
BOOM!
HERE
SO IN A ROUTINE...
...YOU CAN BRING POWERFUL MOVES ON THE EVEN BEATS. LIKE THIS.
BA-
1
...
&
BOOM
2
&
BA-
3
...
&
BOOM!
4
&

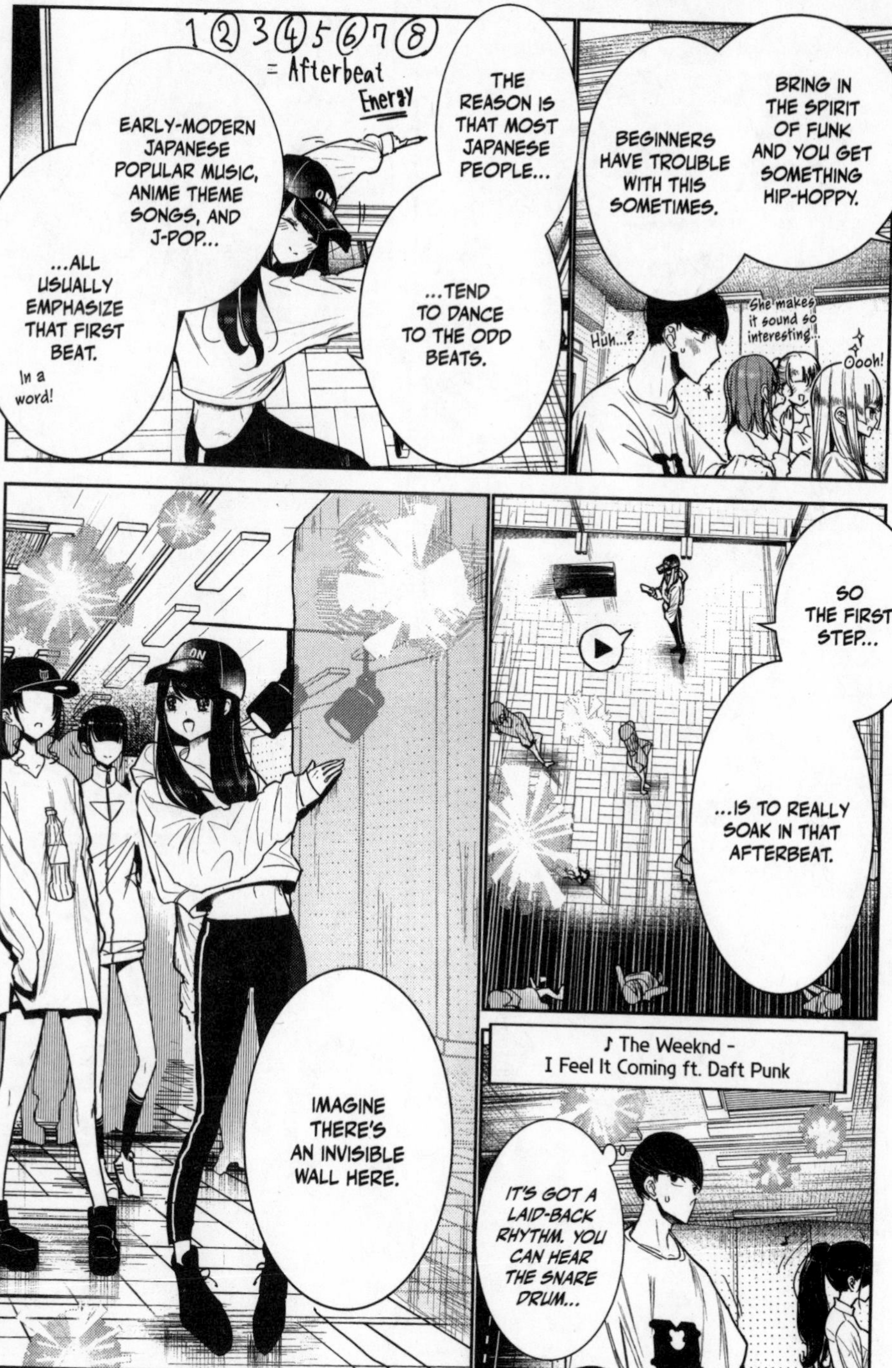
BEGINNERS HAVE TROUBLE WITH THIS SOMETIMES.
BRING IN THE SPIRIT OF FUNK AND YOU GET SOMETHING HIP-HOPPY.
She makes it sound so interesting!!
Huh...?
Oooh!
1 2 3 4 5 6 7 8
= Afterbeat
Energy
THE REASON IS THAT MOST JAPANESE PEOPLE...
...TEND TO DANCE TO THE ODD BEATS.
EARLY-MODERN JAPANESE POPULAR MUSIC, ANIME THEME SONGS, AND J-POP...
...ALL USUALLY EMPHASIZE THAT FIRST BEAT.
In a word!
SO THE FIRST STEP...
...IS TO REALLY SOAK IN THAT AFTERBEAT.
♪ The Weeknd - I Feel It Coming ft. Daft Punk
IT'S GOT A LAID-BACK RHYTHM. YOU CAN HEAR THE SNARE DRUM...
IMAGINE THERE'S AN INVISIBLE WALL HERE.

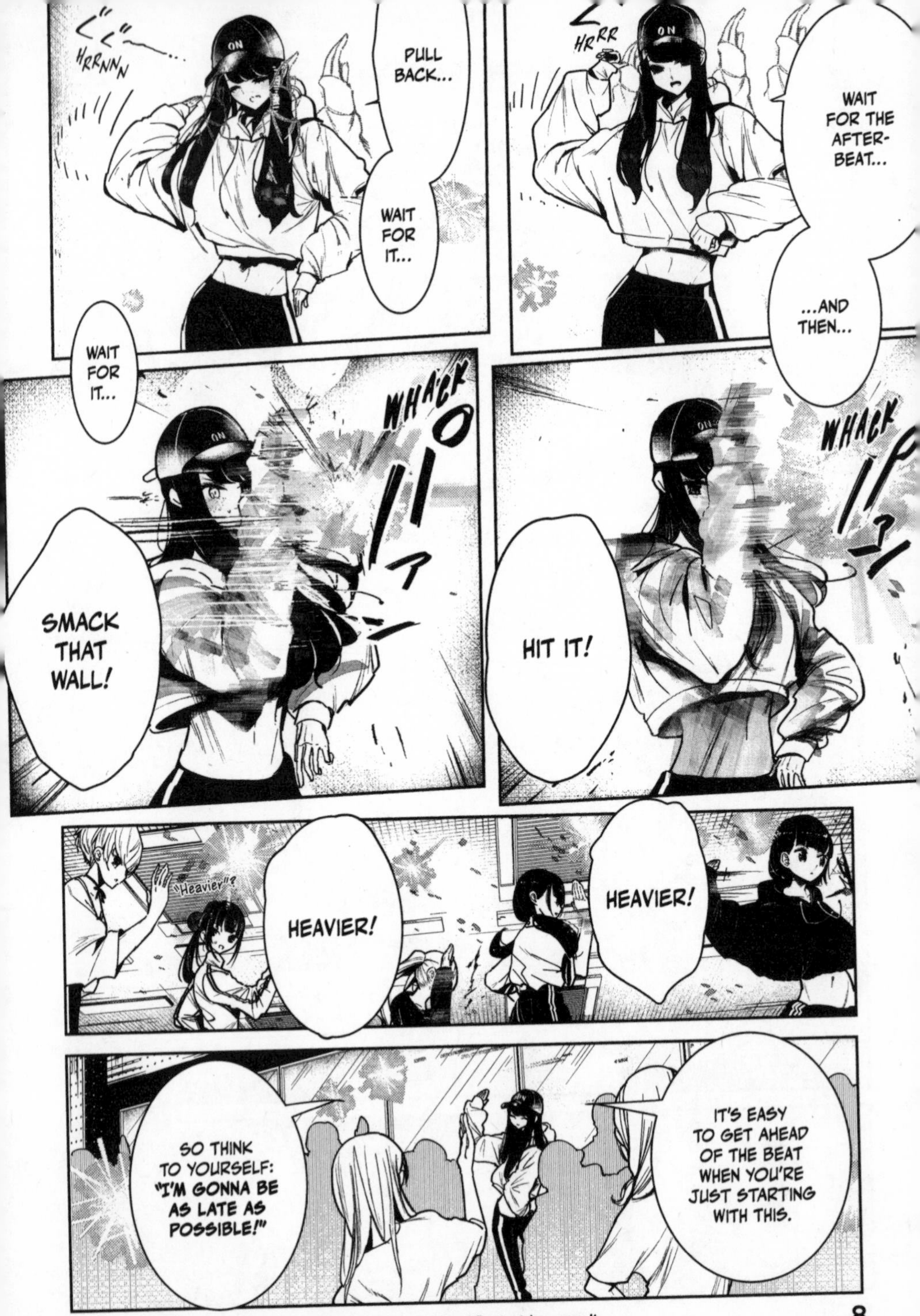
HRRR
WAIT FOR THE AFTER-BEAT...
...AND THEN...
HRRNNN
PULL BACK...
WAIT FOR IT...
WAIT FOR IT...
WHACK
HIT IT!
WHACK
SMACK THAT WALL!
HEAVIER!
HEAVIER!
"Heavier"?
IT'S EASY TO GET AHEAD OF THE BEAT WHEN YOU'RE JUST STARTING WITH THIS.
SO THINK TO YOURSELF: "I'M GONNA BE AS LATE AS POSSIBLE!"

This is an exercise they actually did at Uenomiya Senior High School, which has a killer street dance group. It was so shockingly effective that I thought to myself, "I wish I'd had this when I was a teen..." You start with the arms, which are easy to feel, then move on to the legs, neck, chest, and hips.

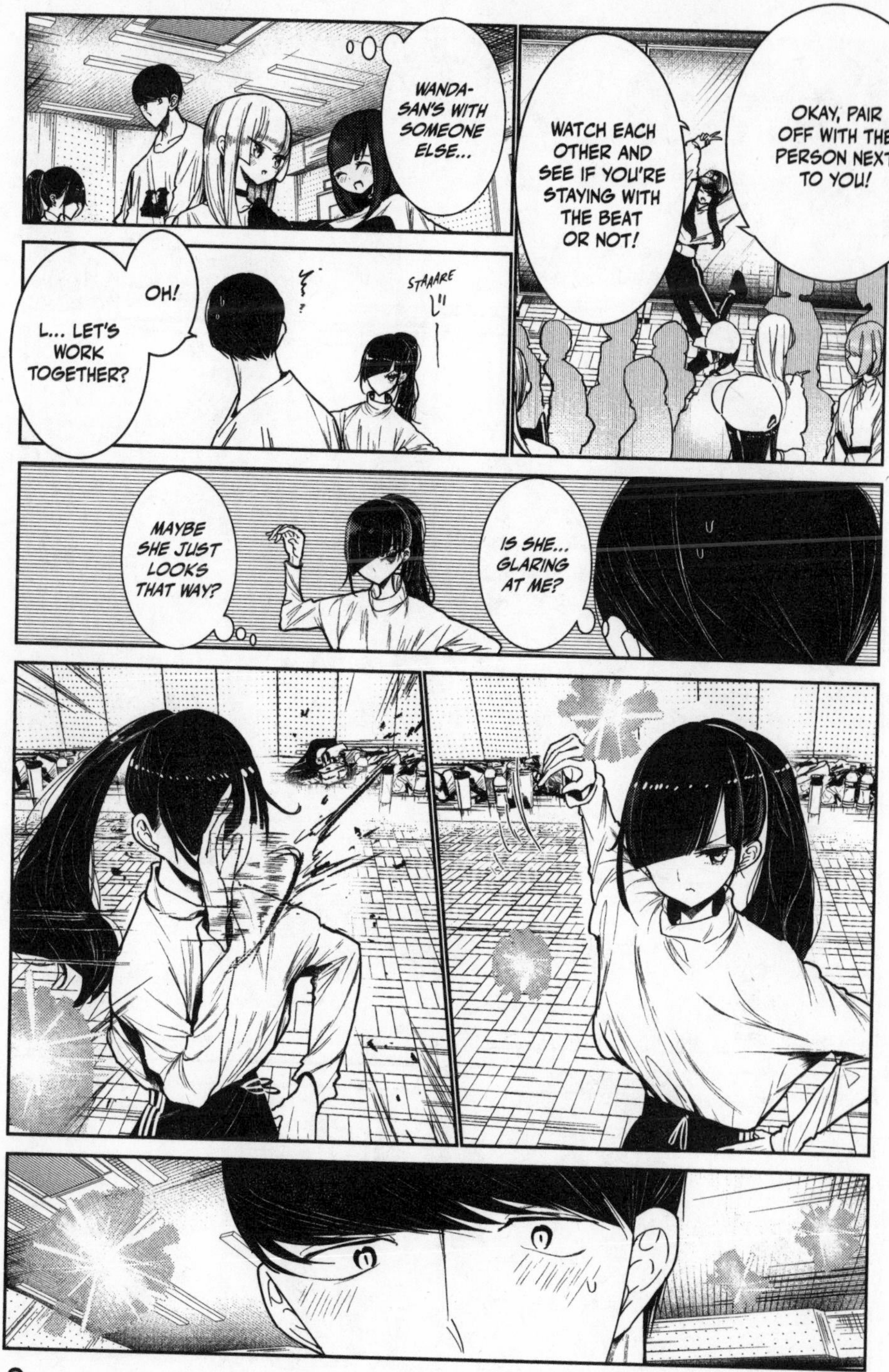
OKAY, PAIR OFF WITH THE PERSON NEXT TO YOU!
WATCH EACH OTHER AND SEE IF YOU'RE STAYING WITH THE BEAT OR NOT!
WANDA-SAN'S WITH SOMEONE ELSE...
STAAARE
OH!
L... LET'S WORK TOGETHER?
IS SHE... GLARING AT ME?
MAYBE SHE JUST LOOKS THAT WAY?

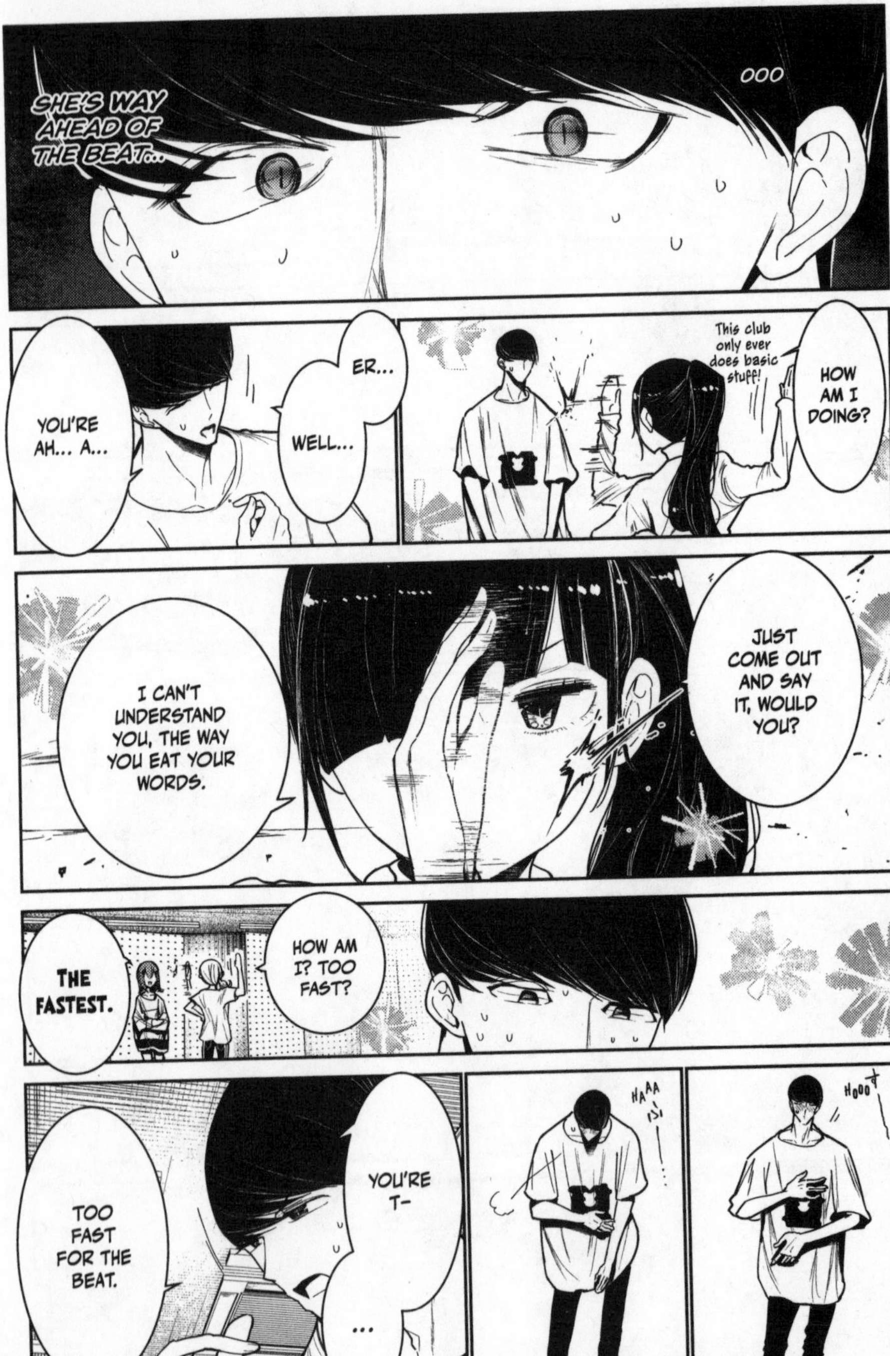

OOO
SHE'S WAY AHEAD OF THE BEAT...
HOW AM I DOING?
This club only ever does basic stuff!
ER... WELL...
YOU'RE AH... A...
JUST COME OUT AND SAY IT, WOULD YOU?
I CAN'T UNDERSTAND YOU, THE WAY YOU EAT YOUR WORDS.
HOW AM I? TOO FAST?
THE FASTEST.
HOOO
HAAA
YOU'RE T- ...
TOO FAST FOR THE BEAT.

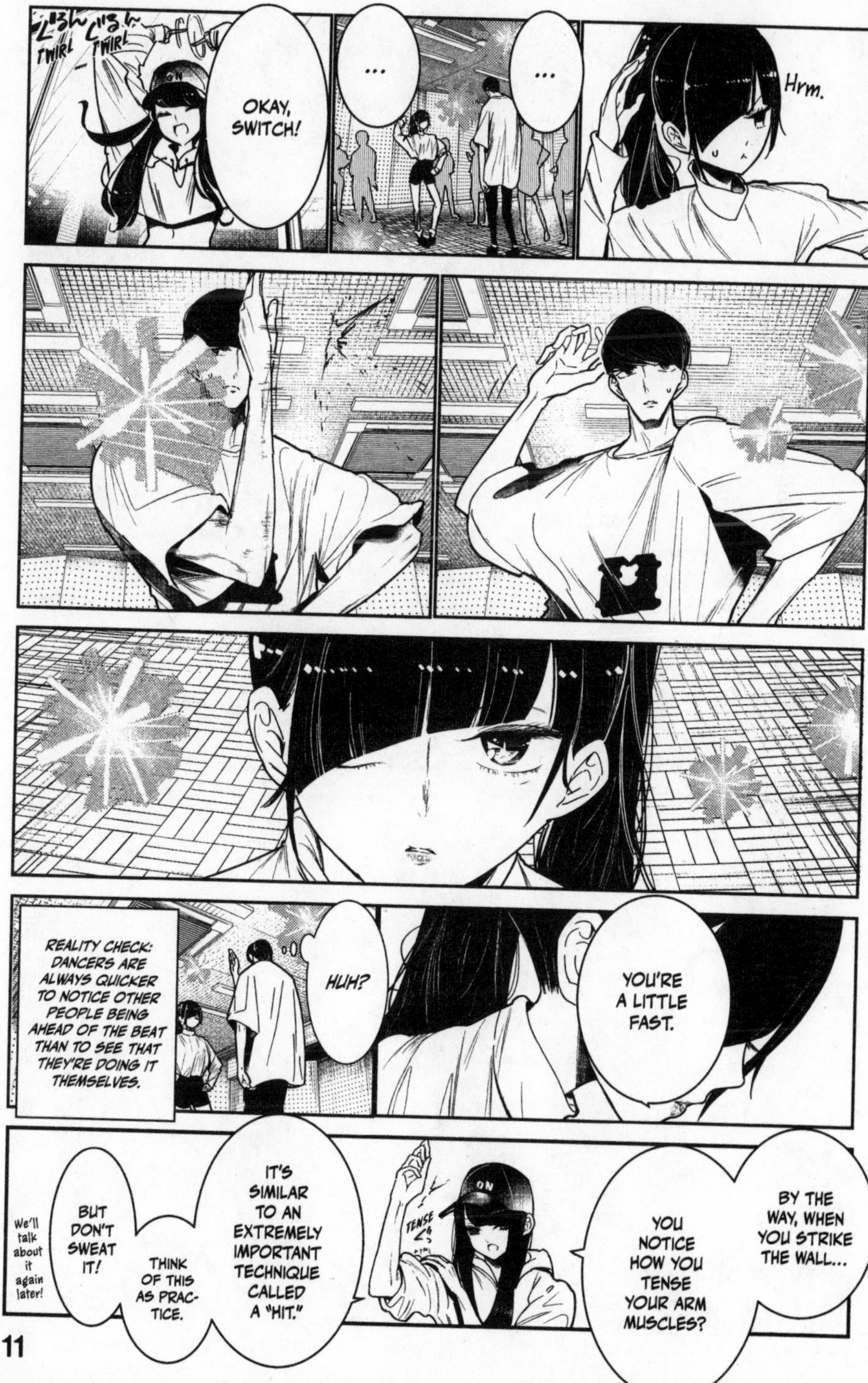
Hrm.
...
...
OKAY, SWITCH!
TWIRL TWIRL
YOU'RE A LITTLE FAST.
HUH?
REALITY CHECK: DANCERS ARE ALWAYS QUICKER TO NOTICE OTHER PEOPLE BEING AHEAD OF THE BEAT THAN TO SEE THAT THEY'RE DOING IT THEMSELVES.
BY THE WAY, WHEN YOU STRIKE THE WALL...
YOU NOTICE HOW YOU TENSE YOUR ARM MUSCLES?
TENSE
IT'S SIMILAR TO AN EXTREMELY IMPORTANT TECHNIQUE CALLED A "HIT."
THINK OF THIS AS PRAC- TICE.
BUT DON'T SWEAT IT!
We'll talk about it again later!

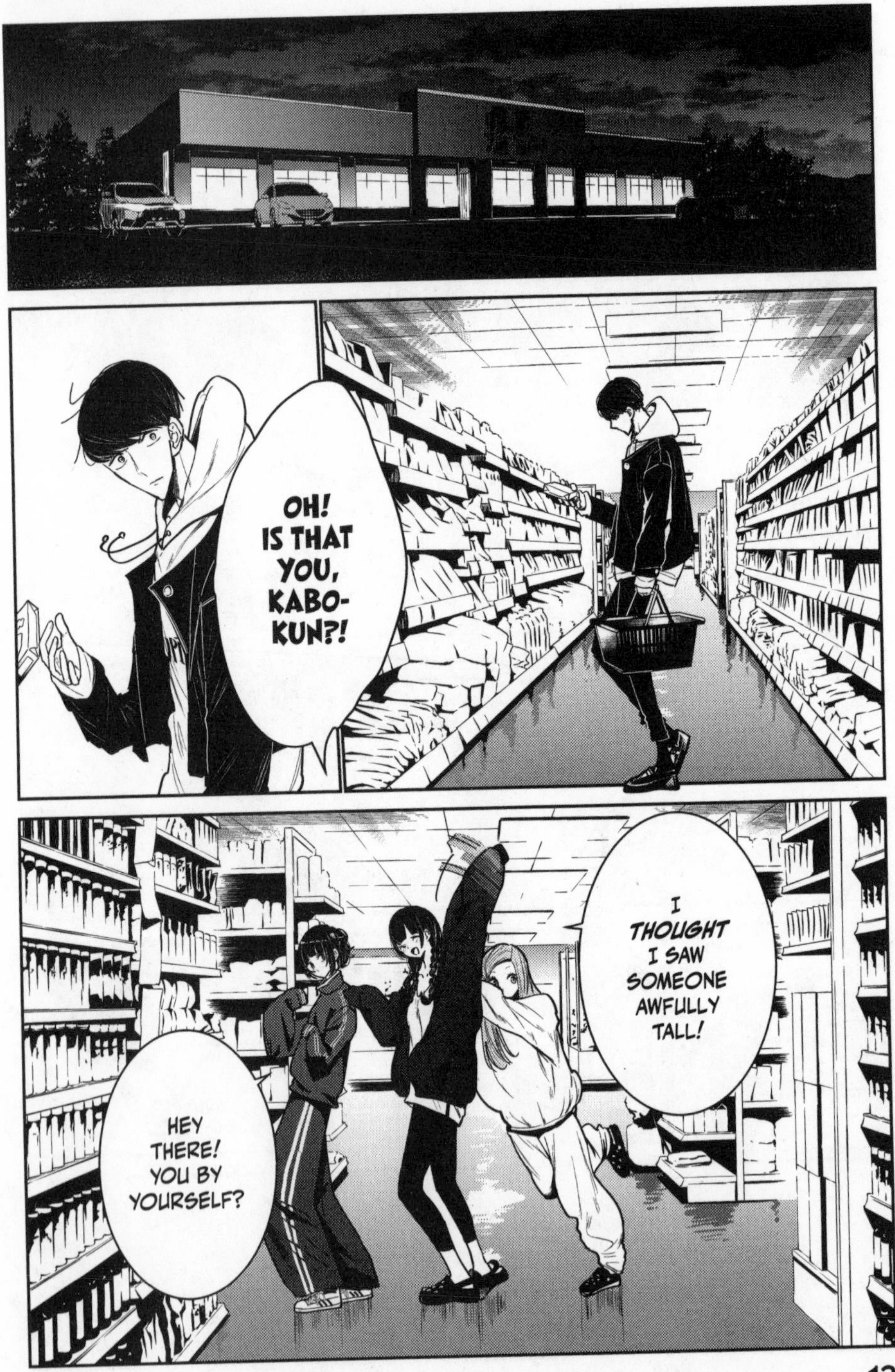
OH! IS THAT YOU, KABO-KUN?!
I THOUGHT I SAW SOMEONE AWFULLY TALL!
HEY THERE! YOU BY YOURSELF?

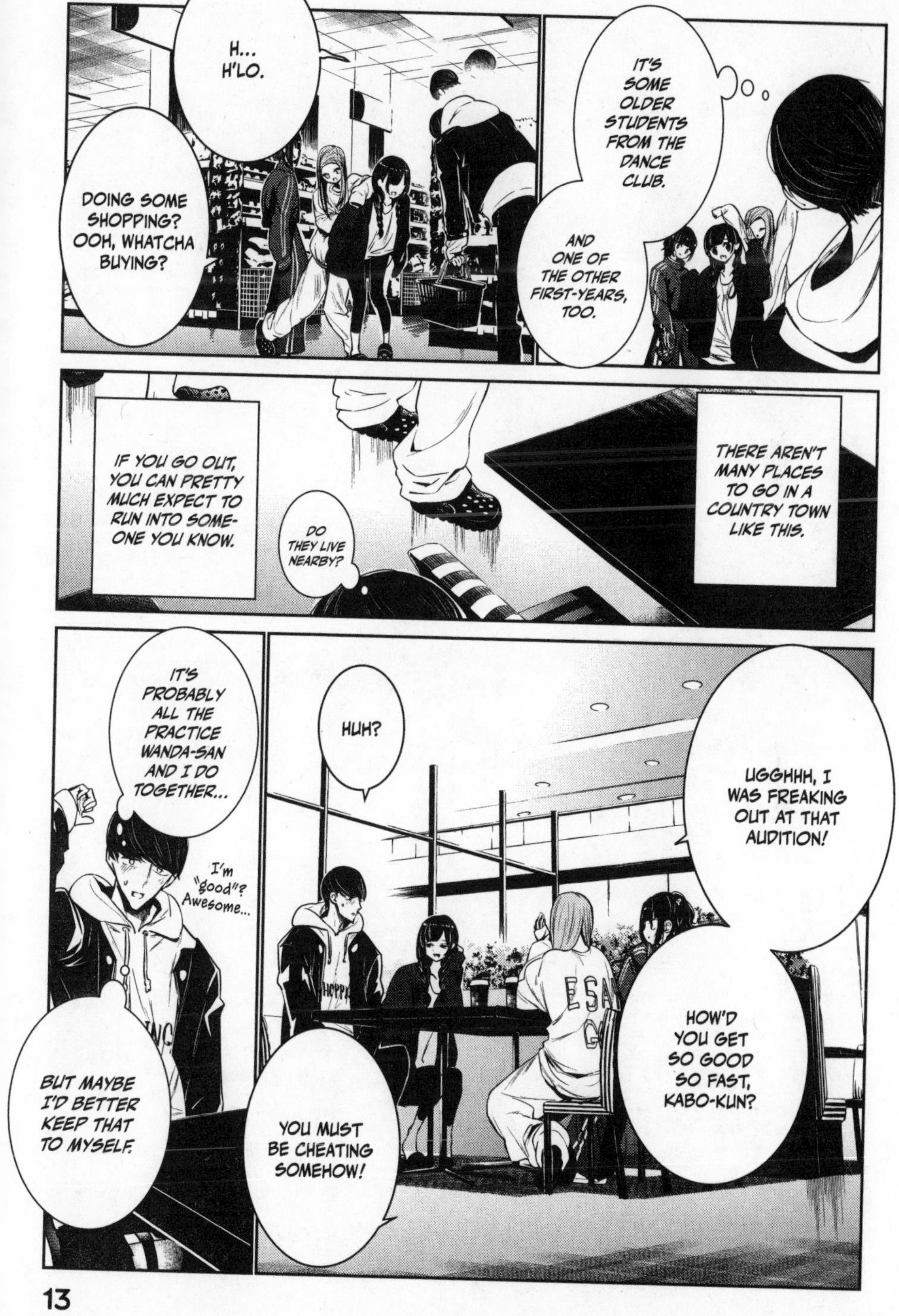
IT'S SOME OLDER STUDENTS FROM THE DANCE CLUB.
AND ONE OF THE OTHER FIRST-YEARS, TOO.
H... H'LO.
DOING SOME SHOPPING? OOH, WHATCHA BUYING?
THERE AREN'T MANY PLACES TO GO IN A COUNTRY TOWN LIKE THIS.
DO THEY LIVE NEARBY?
IF YOU GO OUT, YOU CAN PRETTY MUCH EXPECT TO RUN INTO SOME-ONE YOU KNOW.
UGGHHH, I WAS FREAKING OUT AT THAT AUDITION!
HUH?
HOW'D YOU GET SO GOOD SO FAST, KABO-KUN?
YOU MUST BE CHEATING SOMEHOW!
IT'S PROBABLY ALL THE PRACTICE WANDA-SAN AND I DO TOGETHER...
I'm "good"? Awesome...
BUT MAYBE I'D BETTER KEEP THAT TO MYSELF.

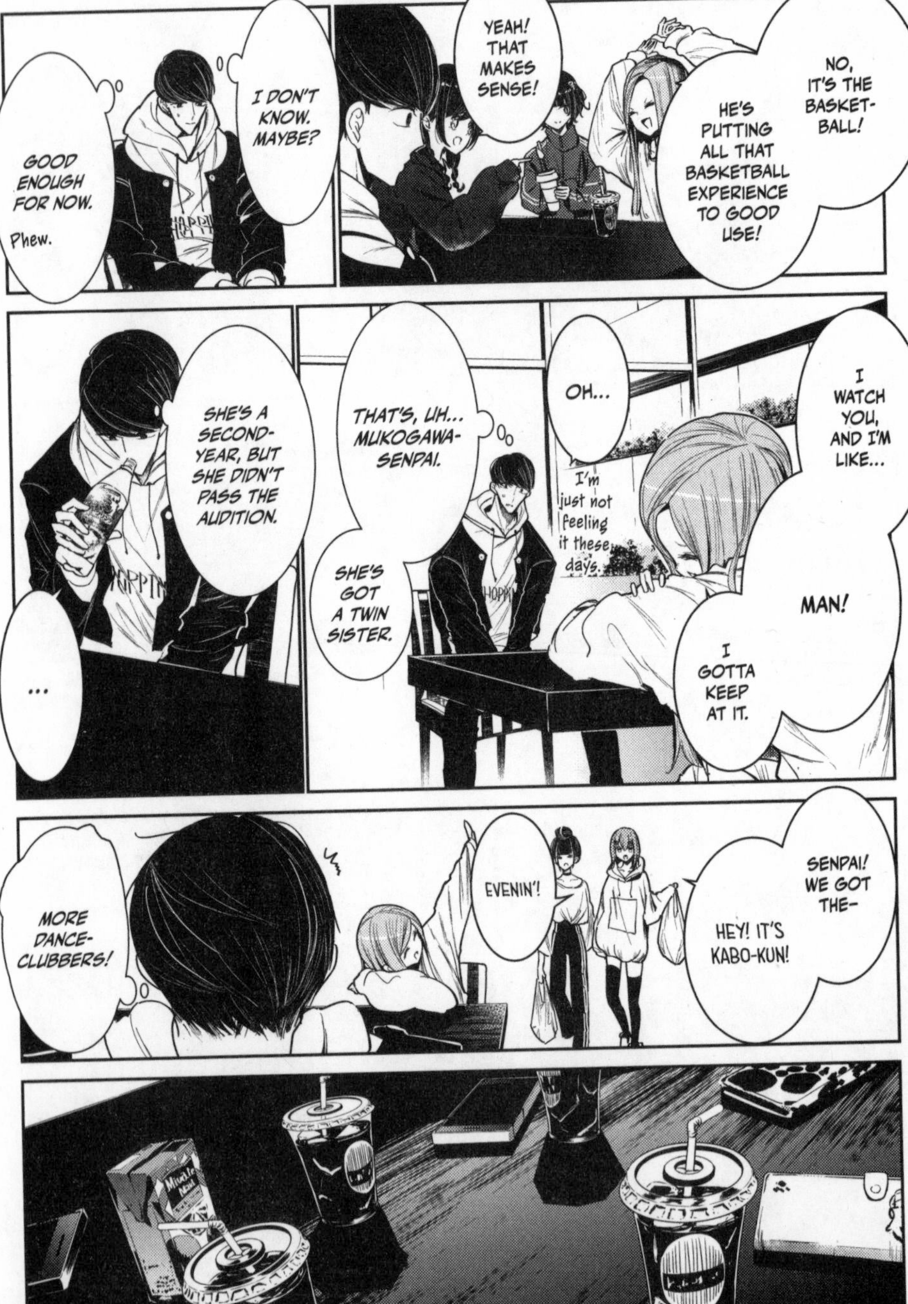
NO, IT'S THE BASKET-BALL!
HE'S PUTTING ALL THAT BASKETBALL EXPERIENCE TO GOOD USE!
YEAH! THAT MAKES SENSE!
I DON'T KNOW. MAYBE?
GOOD ENOUGH FOR NOW.
Phew.
I WATCH YOU, AND I'M LIKE...
MAN!
I GOTTA KEEP AT IT.
OH...
I'm just not feeling it these days.
THAT'S, UH... MUKOGAWA-SENPAI.
SHE'S GOT A TWIN SISTER.
SHE'S A SECOND-YEAR, BUT SHE DIDN'T PASS THE AUDITION.
...
SENPAI! WE GOT THE-
HEY! IT'S KABO-KUN!
EVENIN'!
MORE DANCE-CLUBBERS!

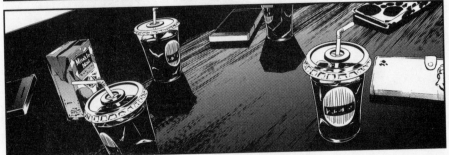

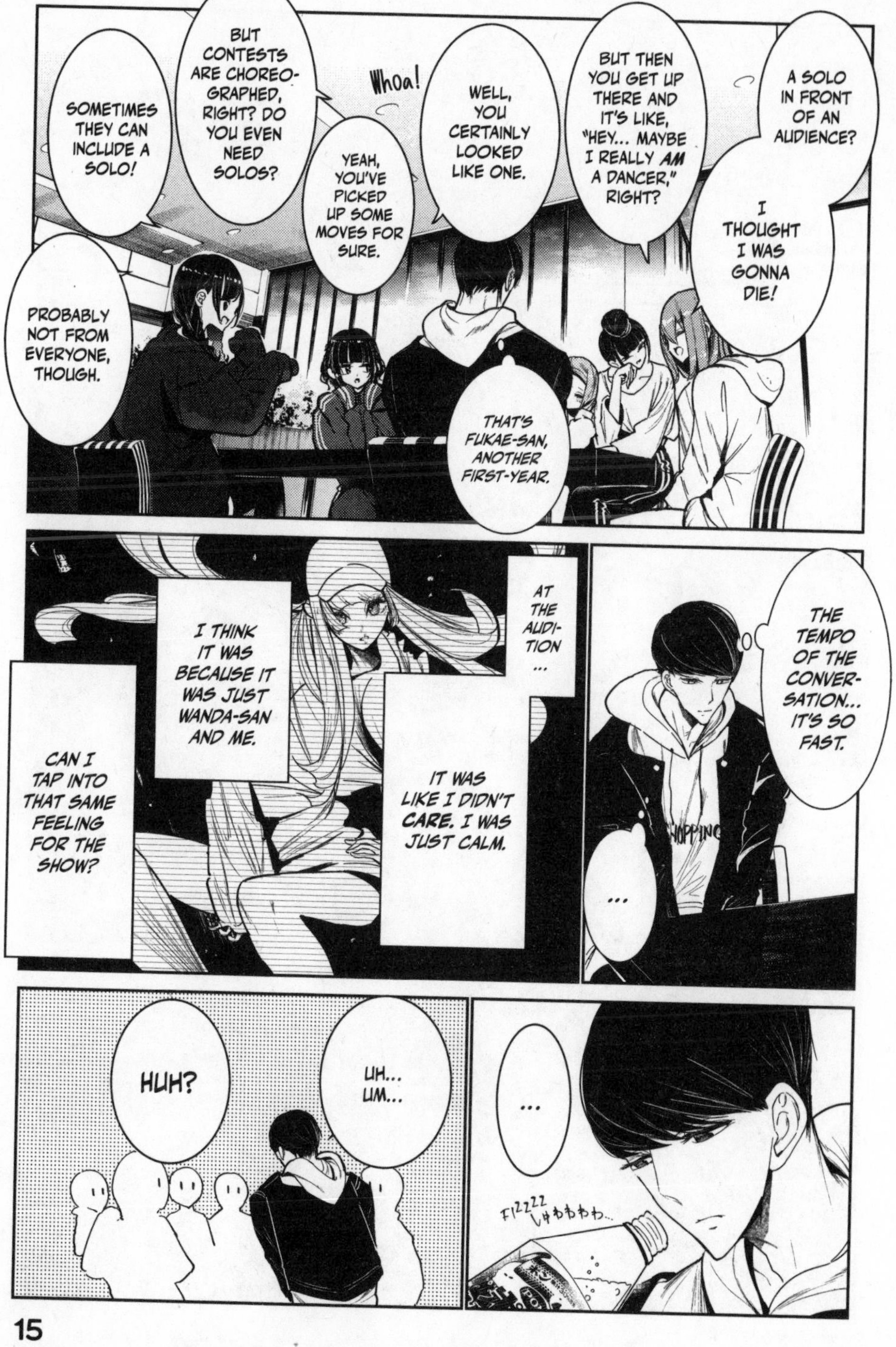
A SOLO IN FRONT OF AN AUDIENCE?
I THOUGHT I WAS GONNA DIE!
BUT THEN YOU GET UP THERE AND IT'S LIKE, "HEY... MAYBE I REALLY AM A DANCER," RIGHT?
WELL, YOU CERTAINLY LOOKED LIKE ONE.
Whoa!
YEAH, YOU'VE PICKED UP SOME MOVES FOR SURE.
THAT'S FUKAE-SAN, ANOTHER FIRST-YEAR.
BUT CONTESTS ARE CHOREOGRAPHED, RIGHT? DO YOU EVEN NEED SOLOS?
SOMETIMES THEY CAN INCLUDE A SOLO!
PROBABLY NOT FROM EVERYONE, THOUGH.
THE TEMPO OF THE CONVERSATION... IT'S SO FAST.
...
AT THE AUDITION...
I THINK IT WAS BECAUSE IT WAS JUST WANDA-SAN AND ME.
IT WAS LIKE I DIDN'T CARE. I WAS JUST CALM.
CAN I TAP INTO THAT SAME FEELING FOR THE SHOW?
...
FIZZZZ
UH... UM...
HUH?

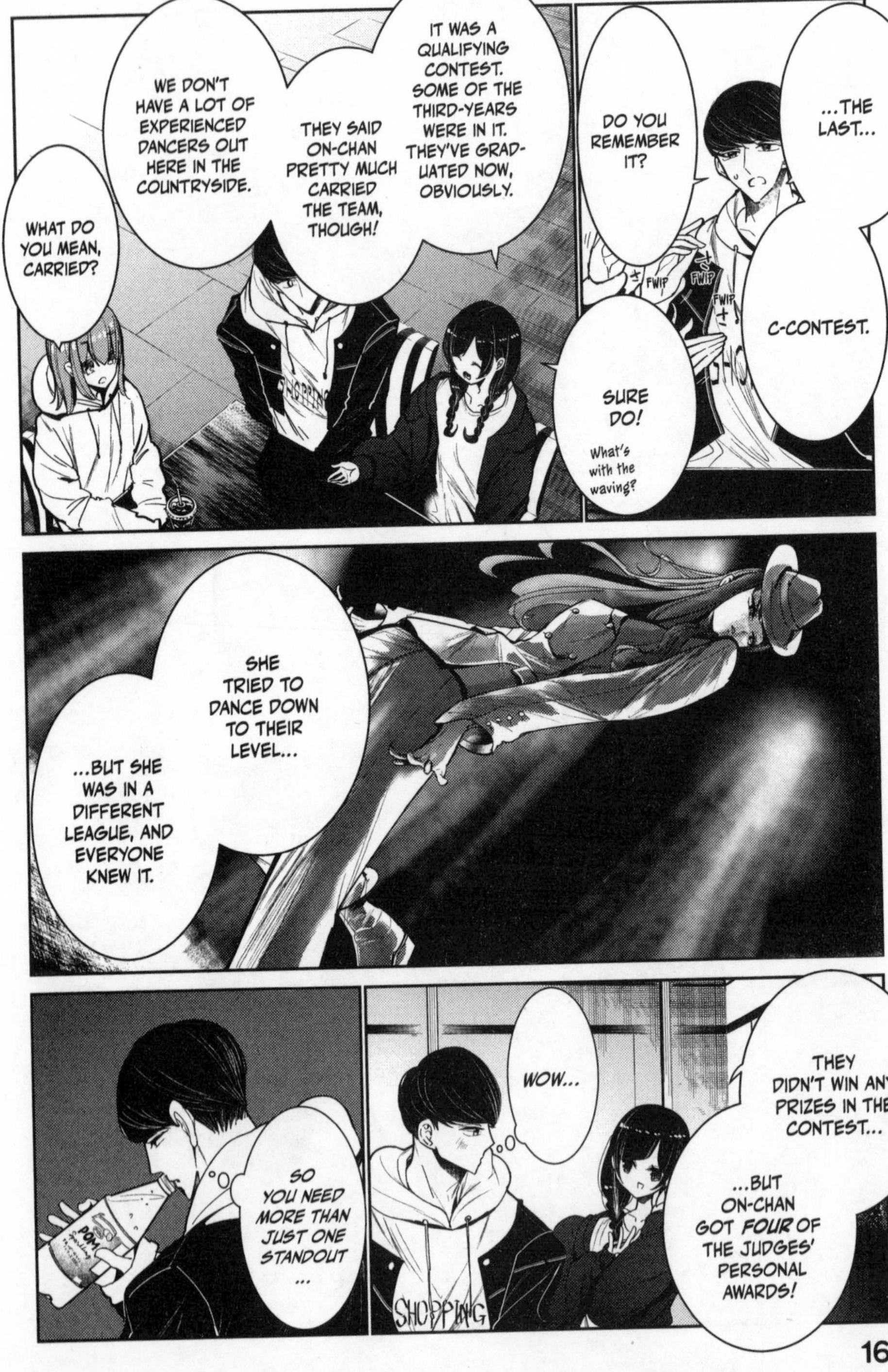
...THE LAST...
DO YOU REMEMBER IT?
C-CONTEST.
FWIP FWIP FWIP
SURE DO!
What's with the waving?
IT WAS A QUALIFYING CONTEST. SOME OF THE THIRD-YEARS WERE IN IT. THEY'VE GRADUATED NOW, OBVIOUSLY.
THEY SAID ON-CHAN PRETTY MUCH CARRIED THE TEAM, THOUGH!
WE DON'T HAVE A LOT OF EXPERIENCED DANCERS OUT HERE IN THE COUNTRYSIDE.
WHAT DO YOU MEAN, CARRIED?
SHE TRIED TO DANCE DOWN TO THEIR LEVEL...
...BUT SHE WAS IN A DIFFERENT LEAGUE, AND EVERYONE KNEW IT.
THEY DIDN'T WIN ANY PRIZES IN THE CONTEST...
...BUT ON-CHAN GOT *FOUR* OF THE JUDGES' PERSONAL AWARDS!
WOW...
SO YOU NEED MORE THAN JUST ONE STANDOUT...

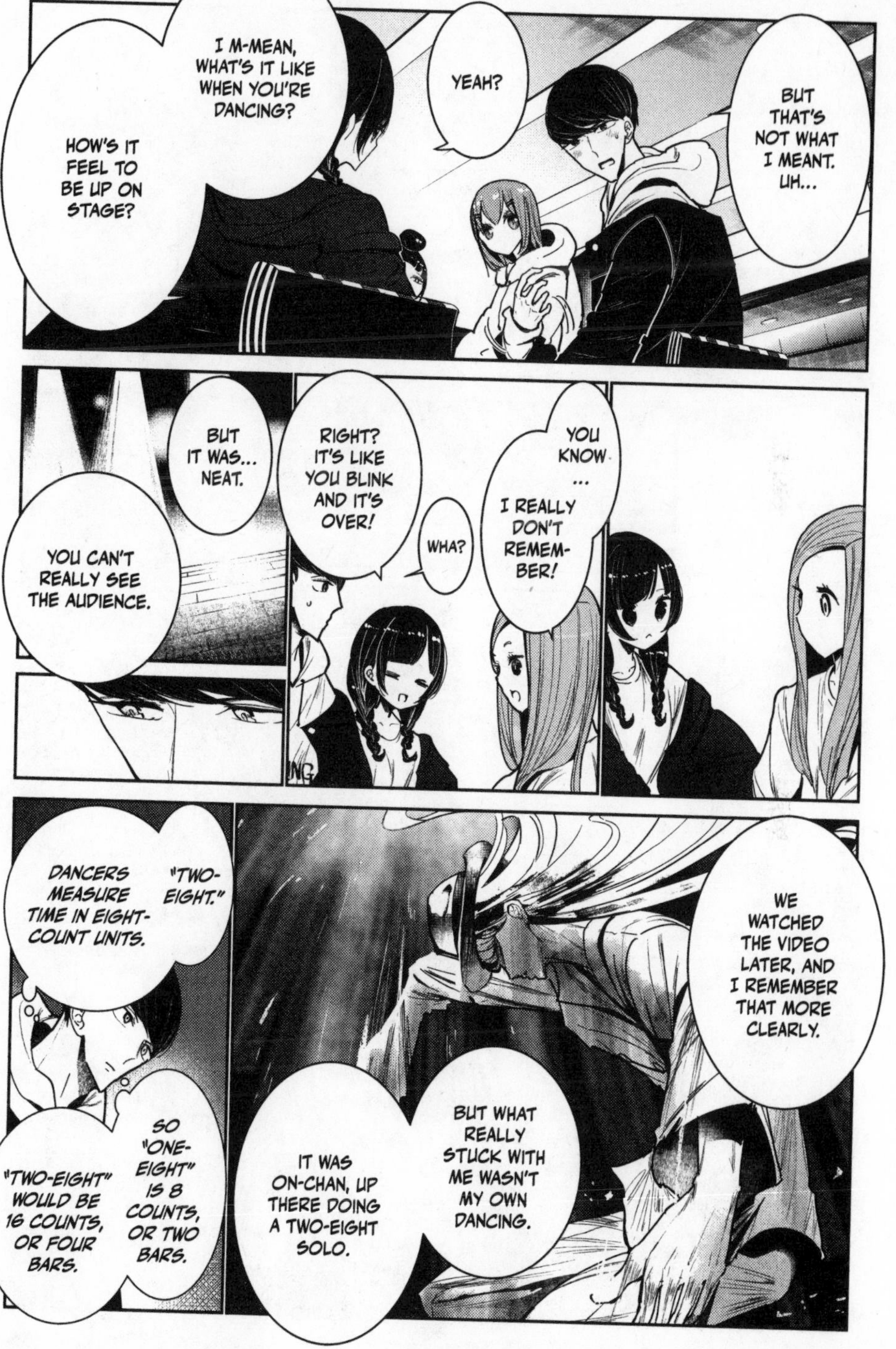
BUT THAT'S NOT WHAT I MEANT. UH...
YEAH?
I M-MEAN, WHAT'S IT LIKE WHEN YOU'RE DANCING?
HOW'S IT FEEL TO BE UP ON STAGE?
YOU KNOW ...
I REALLY DON'T REMEMBER!
WHA?
RIGHT? IT'S LIKE YOU BLINK AND IT'S OVER!
BUT IT WAS... NEAT.
YOU CAN'T REALLY SEE THE AUDIENCE.
WE WATCHED THE VIDEO LATER, AND I REMEMBER THAT MORE CLEARLY.
BUT WHAT REALLY STUCK WITH ME WASN'T MY OWN DANCING.
IT WAS ON-CHAN, UP THERE DOING A TWO-EIGHT SOLO.
"TWO-EIGHT."
DANCERS MEASURE TIME IN EIGHT-COUNT UNITS.
SO "ONE-EIGHT" IS 8 COUNTS, OR TWO BARS.
"TWO-EIGHT" WOULD BE 16 COUNTS, OR FOUR BARS.

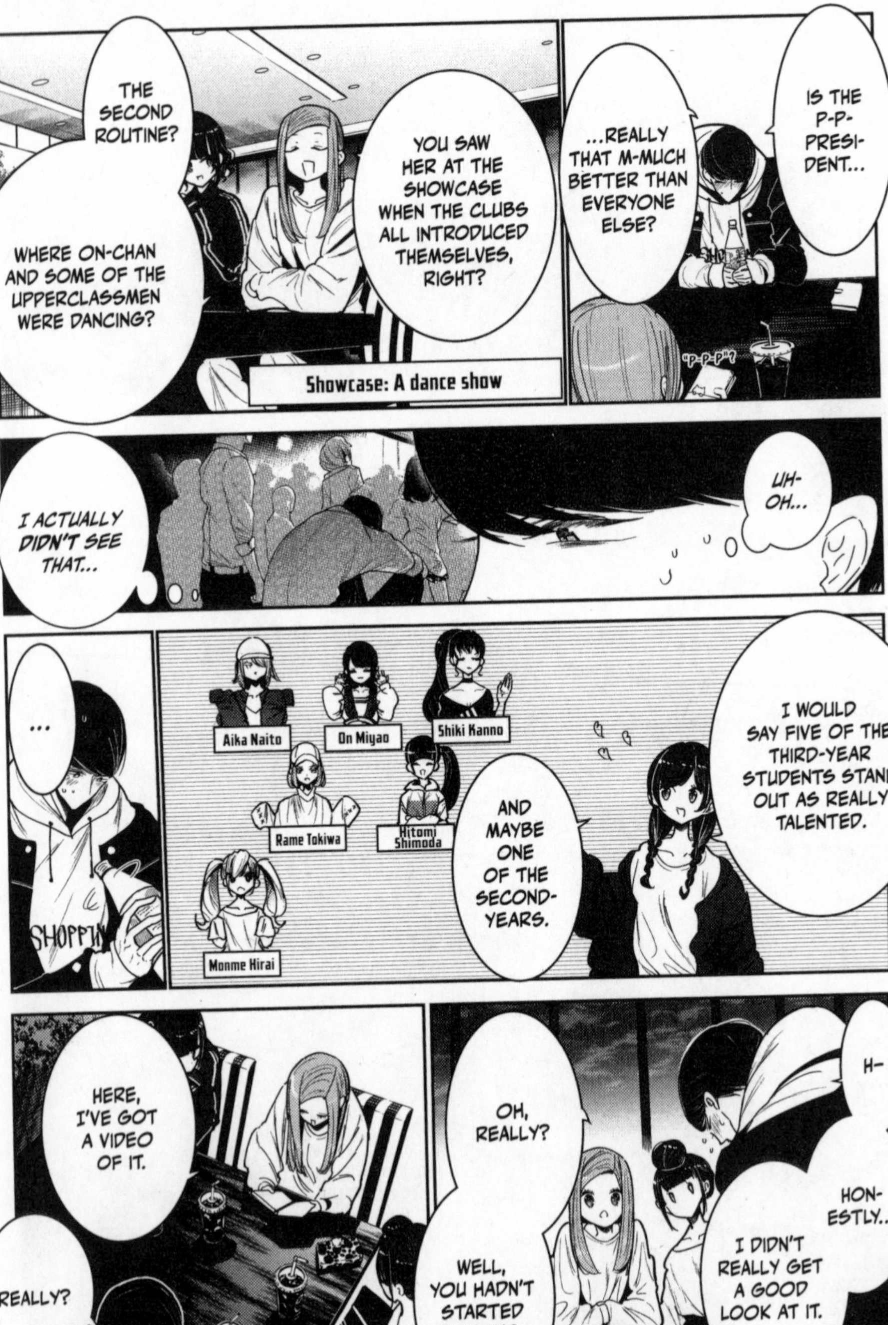
IS THE P-P-PRESI-DENT...
...REALLY THAT M-MUCH BETTER THAN EVERYONE ELSE?
"P-P-P"?
YOU SAW HER AT THE SHOWCASE WHEN THE CLUBS ALL INTRODUCED THEMSELVES, RIGHT?
THE SECOND ROUTINE?
WHERE ON-CHAN AND SOME OF THE UPPERCLASSMEN WERE DANCING?
Showcase: A dance show
UH-OH...
I ACTUALLY DIDN'T SEE THAT...
I WOULD SAY FIVE OF THE THIRD-YEAR STUDENTS STAND OUT AS REALLY TALENTED.
AND MAYBE ONE OF THE SECOND-YEARS.
Shiki Kanno
On Miyao
Aika Naito
Hitomi Shimoda
Rame Tokiwa
Monme Hirai
...
SHOPPIN
H-
HON-ESTLY...
I DIDN'T REALLY GET A GOOD LOOK AT IT.
OH, REALLY?
WELL, YOU HADN'T STARTED DANCING YET.
HERE, I'VE GOT A VIDEO OF IT.
REALLY?

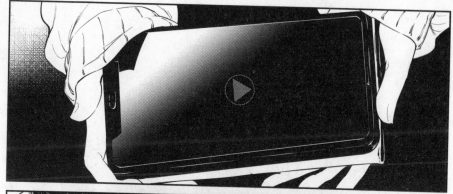

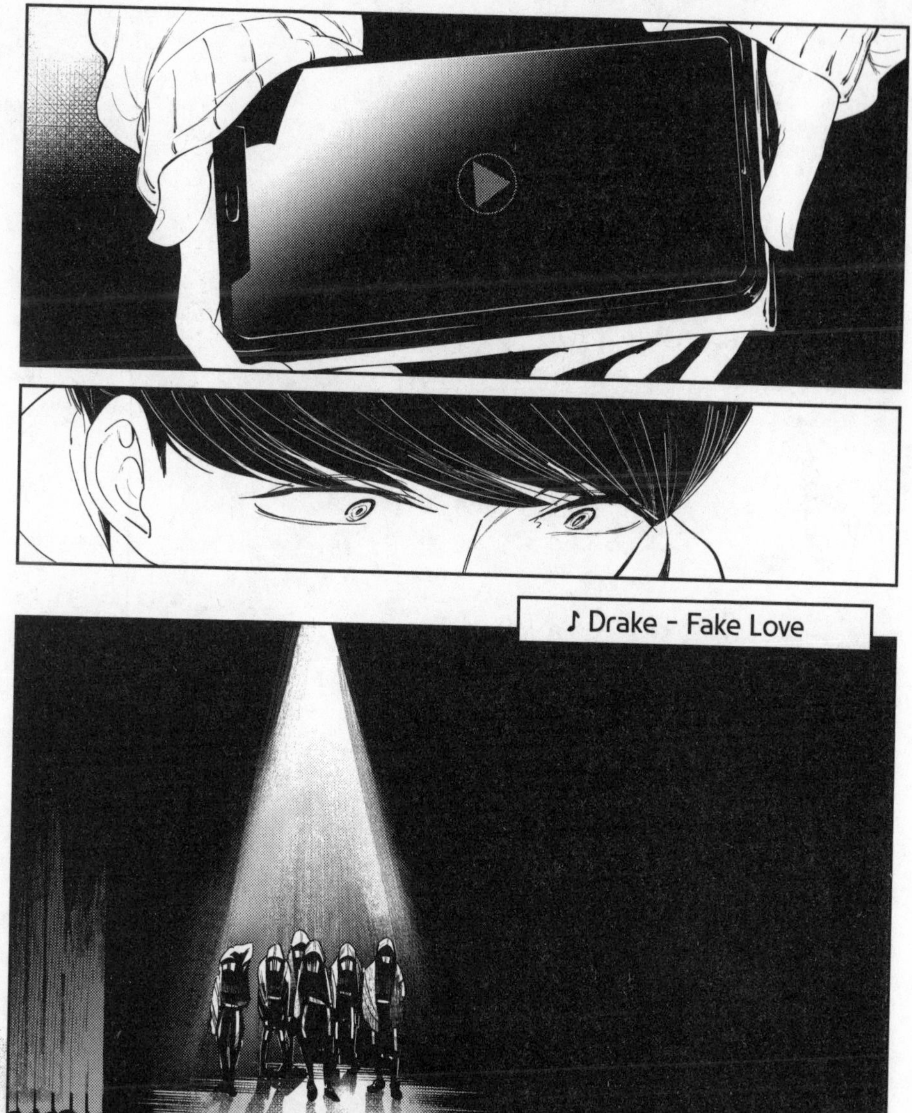

♪ Drake - Fake Love

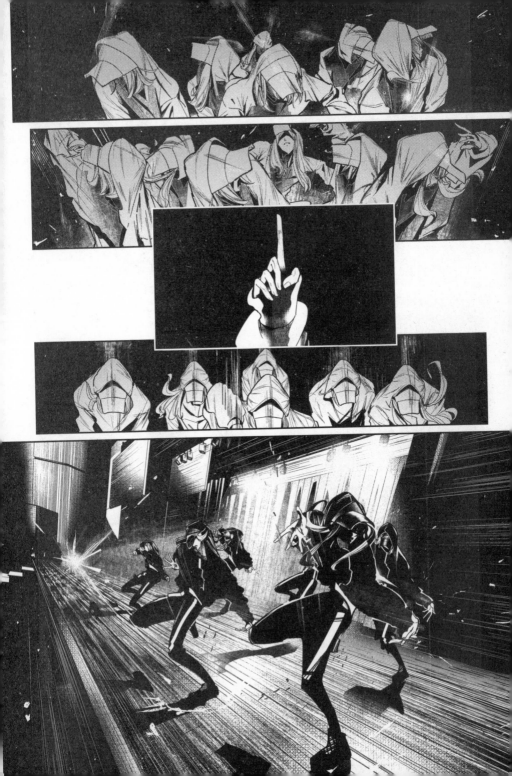

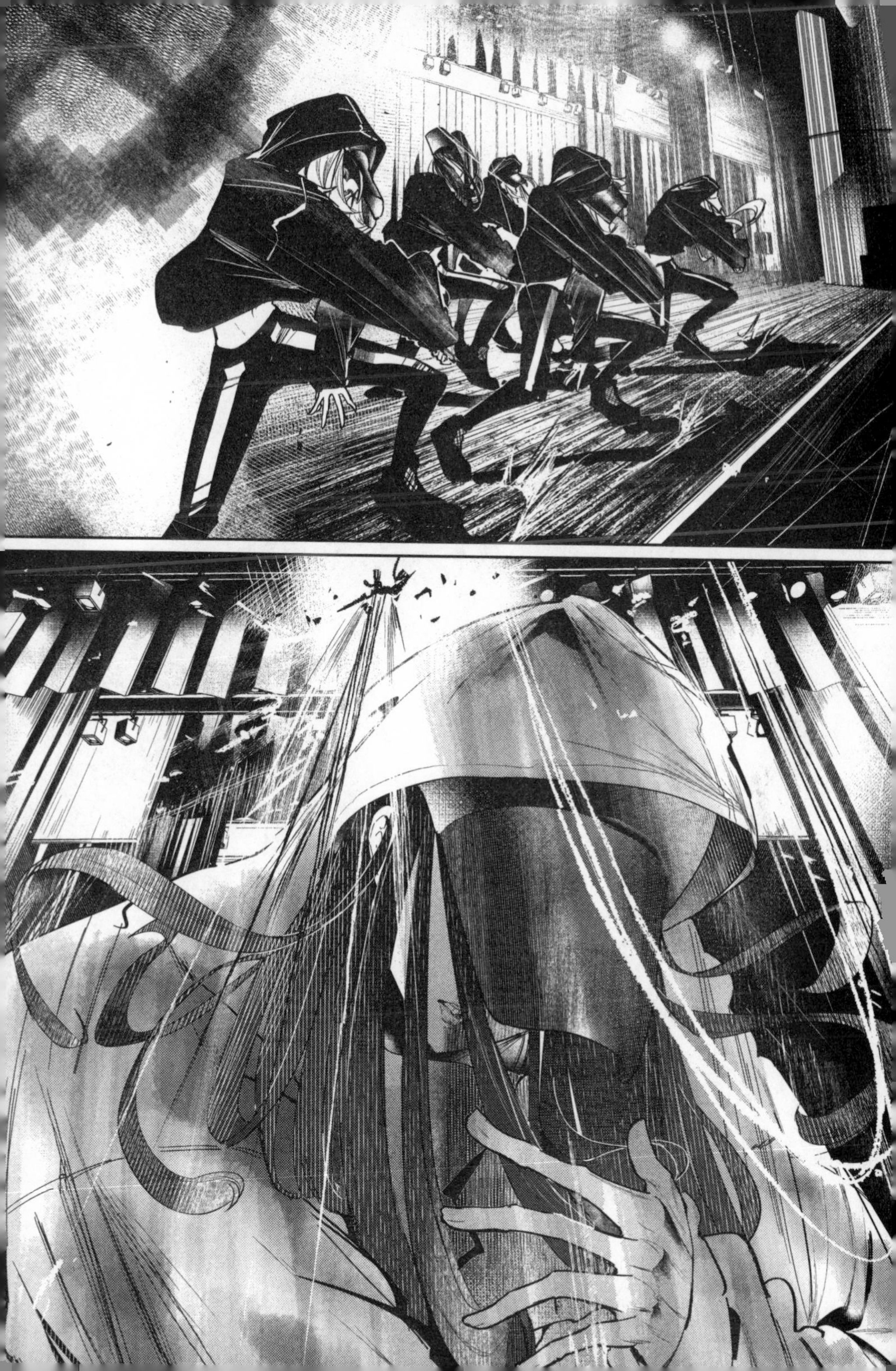

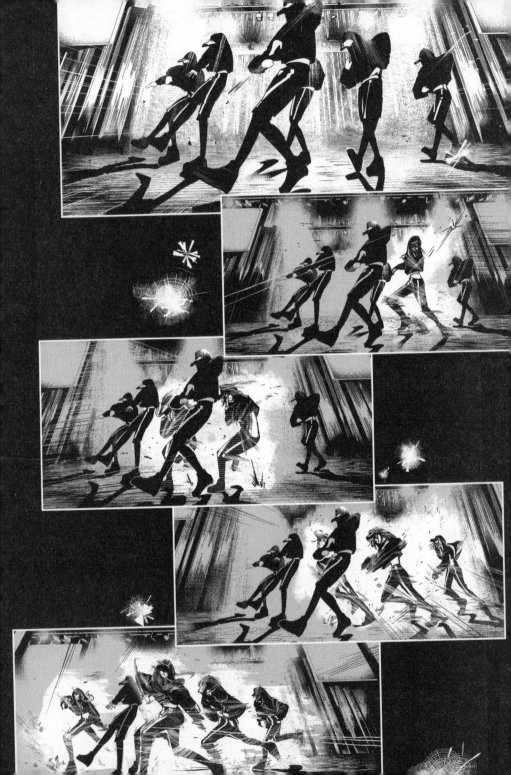

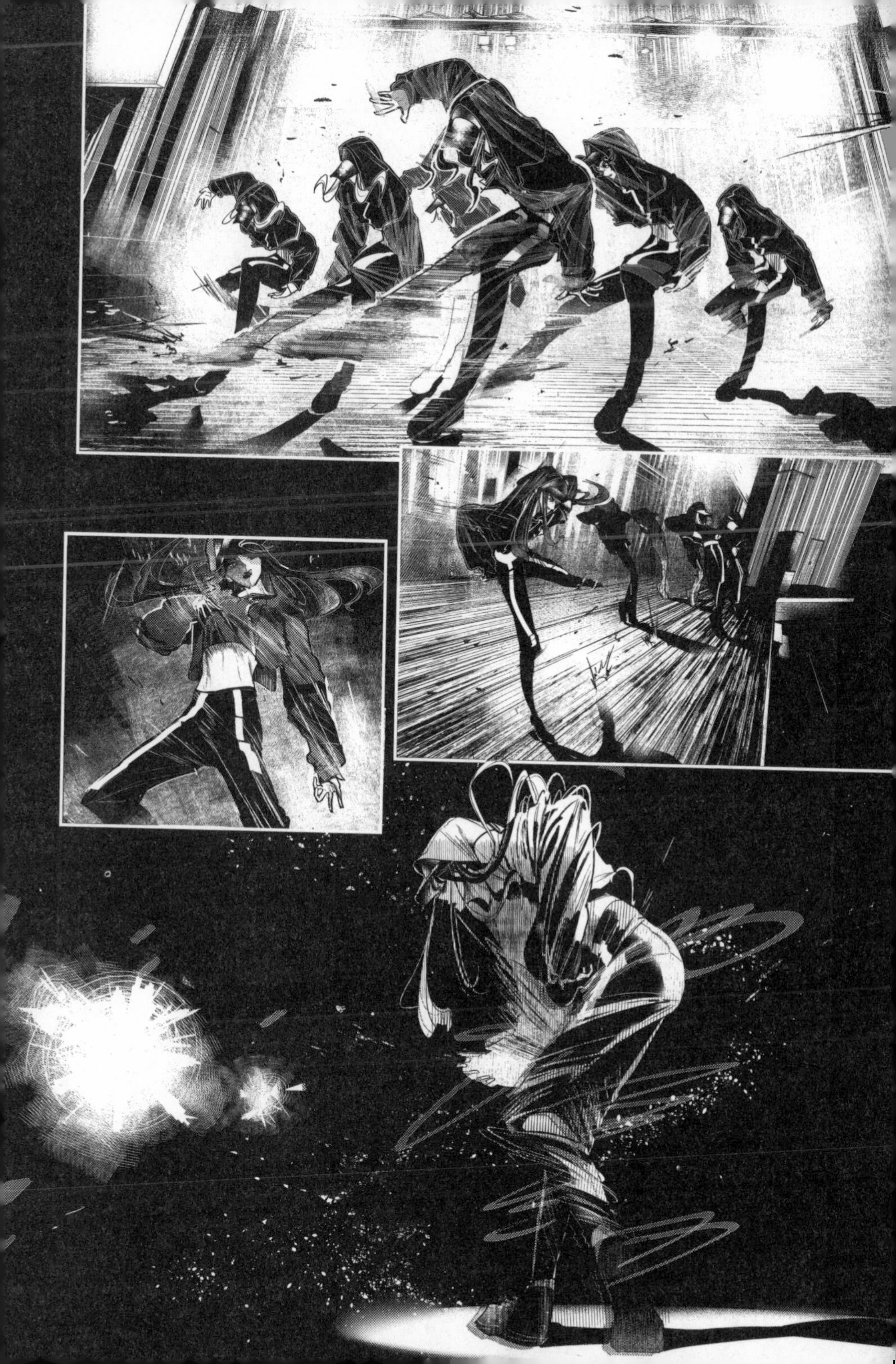

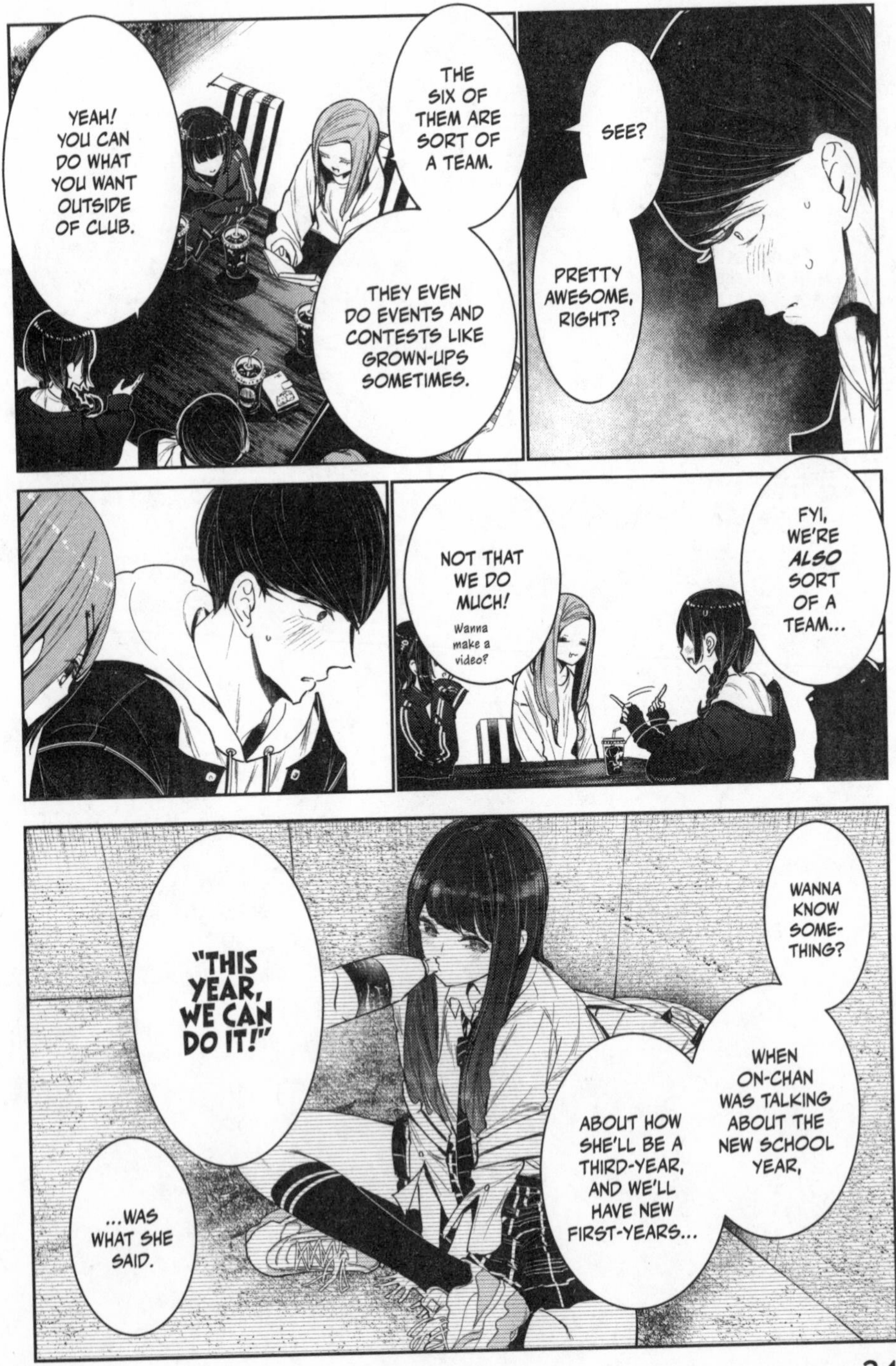
SEE?
PRETTY AWESOME, RIGHT?
THE SIX OF THEM ARE SORT OF A TEAM.
THEY EVEN DO EVENTS AND CONTESTS LIKE GROWN-UPS SOMETIMES.
YEAH! YOU CAN DO WHAT YOU WANT OUTSIDE OF CLUB.
FYI, WE'RE *ALSO* SORT OF A TEAM...
NOT THAT WE DO MUCH!
Wanna make a video?
WANNA KNOW SOMETHING?
WHEN ON-CHAN WAS TALKING ABOUT THE NEW SCHOOL YEAR,
ABOUT HOW SHE'LL BE A THIRD-YEAR, AND WE'LL HAVE NEW FIRST-YEARS...
"THIS YEAR, WE CAN DO IT!"
...WAS WHAT SHE SAID.

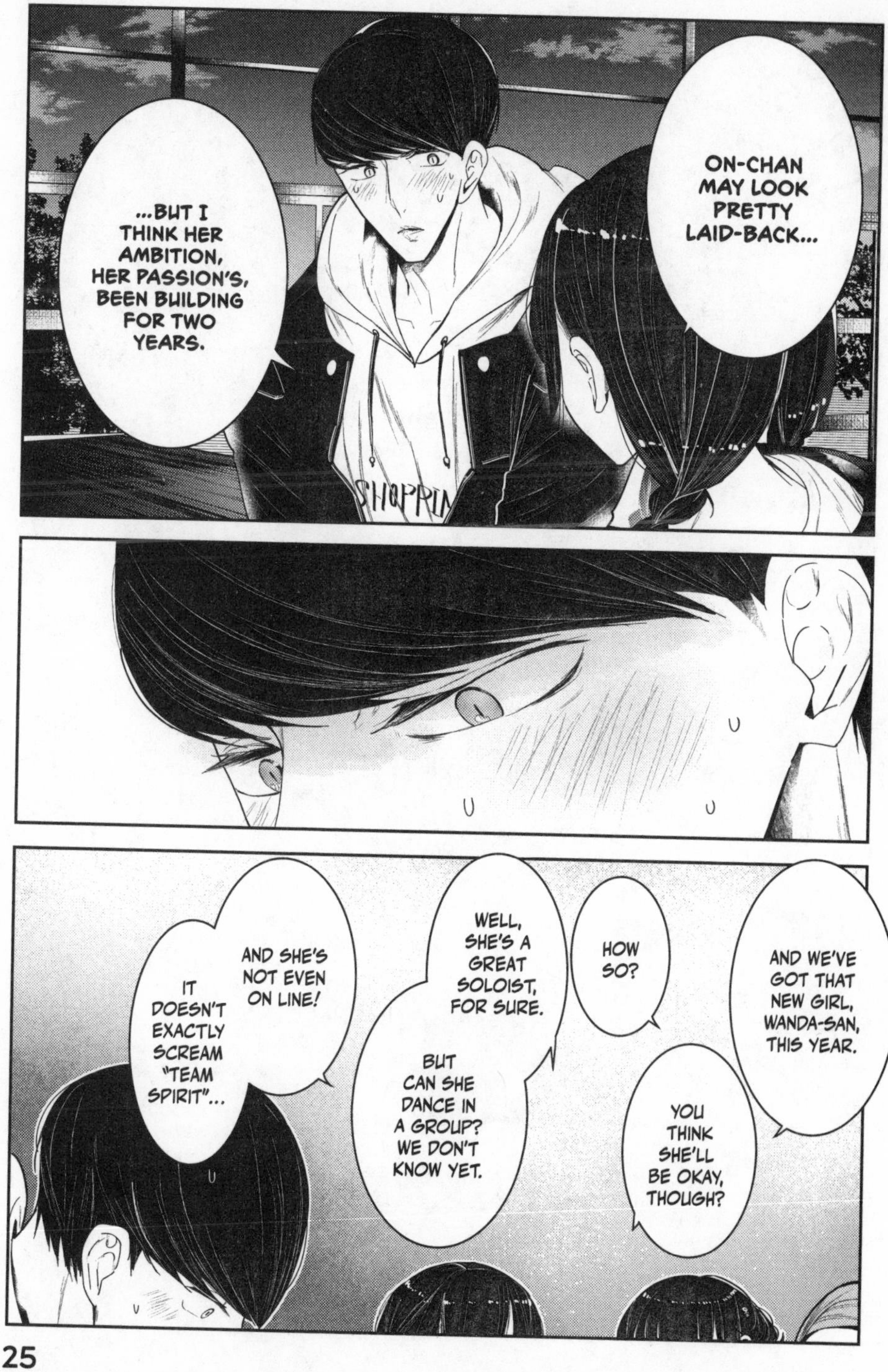
ON-CHAN MAY LOOK PRETTY LAID-BACK...
...BUT I THINK HER AMBITION, HER PASSION'S, BEEN BUILDING FOR TWO YEARS.
SHOPPIN
AND WE'VE GOT THAT NEW GIRL, WANDA-SAN, THIS YEAR.
YOU THINK SHE'LL BE OKAY, THOUGH?
HOW SO?
WELL, SHE'S A GREAT SOLOIST, FOR SURE.
BUT CAN SHE DANCE IN A GROUP? WE DON'T KNOW YET.
AND SHE'S NOT EVEN ON LINE!
IT DOESN'T EXACTLY SCREAM "TEAM SPIRIT"...

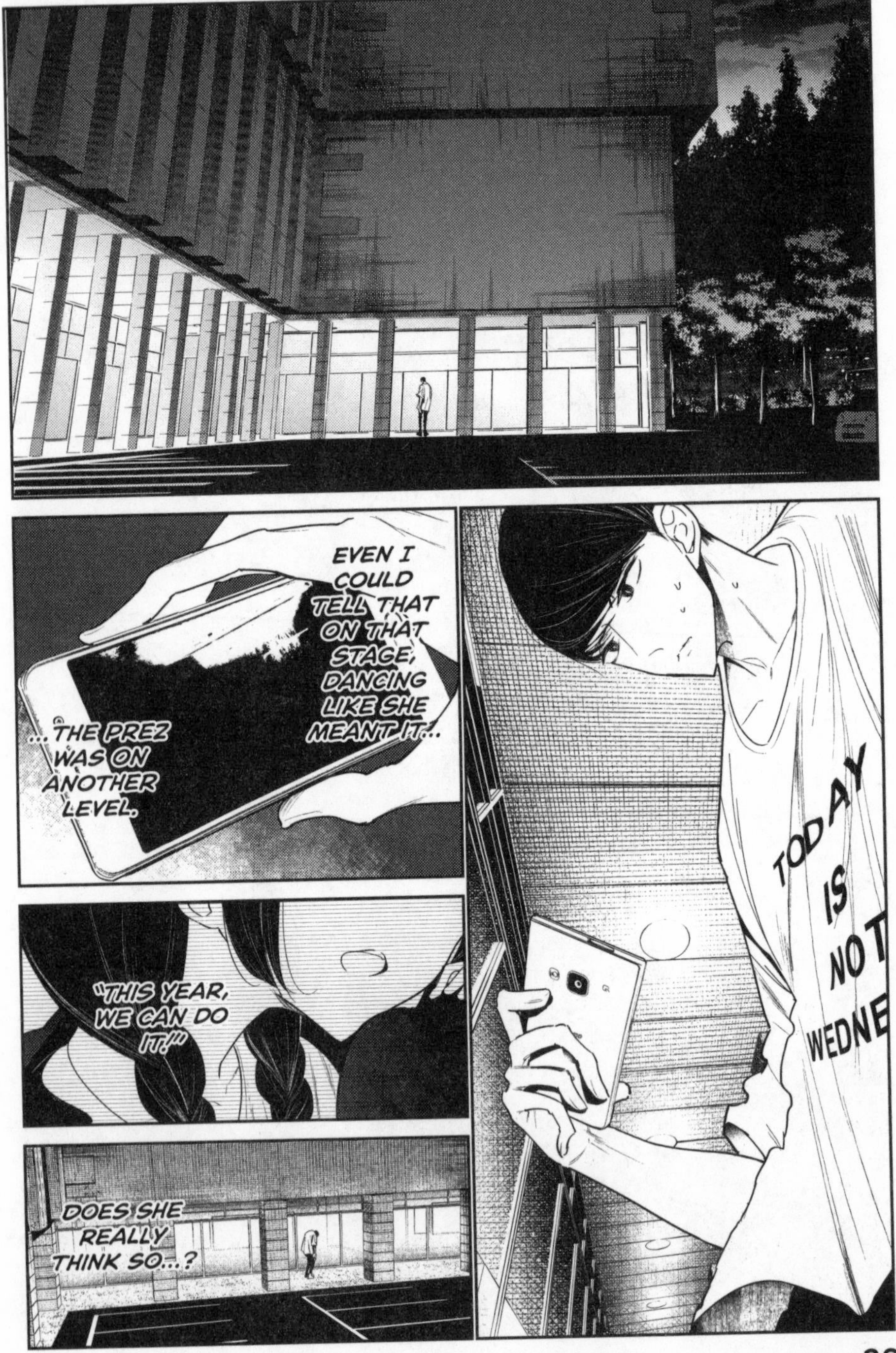
TODAY IS NOT WEDNE
EVEN I COULD TELL THAT ON THAT STAGE, DANCING LIKE SHE MEANT IT...
...THE PREZ WAS ON ANOTHER LEVEL.
"THIS YEAR, WE CAN DO IT!"
DOES SHE REALLY THINK SO...?

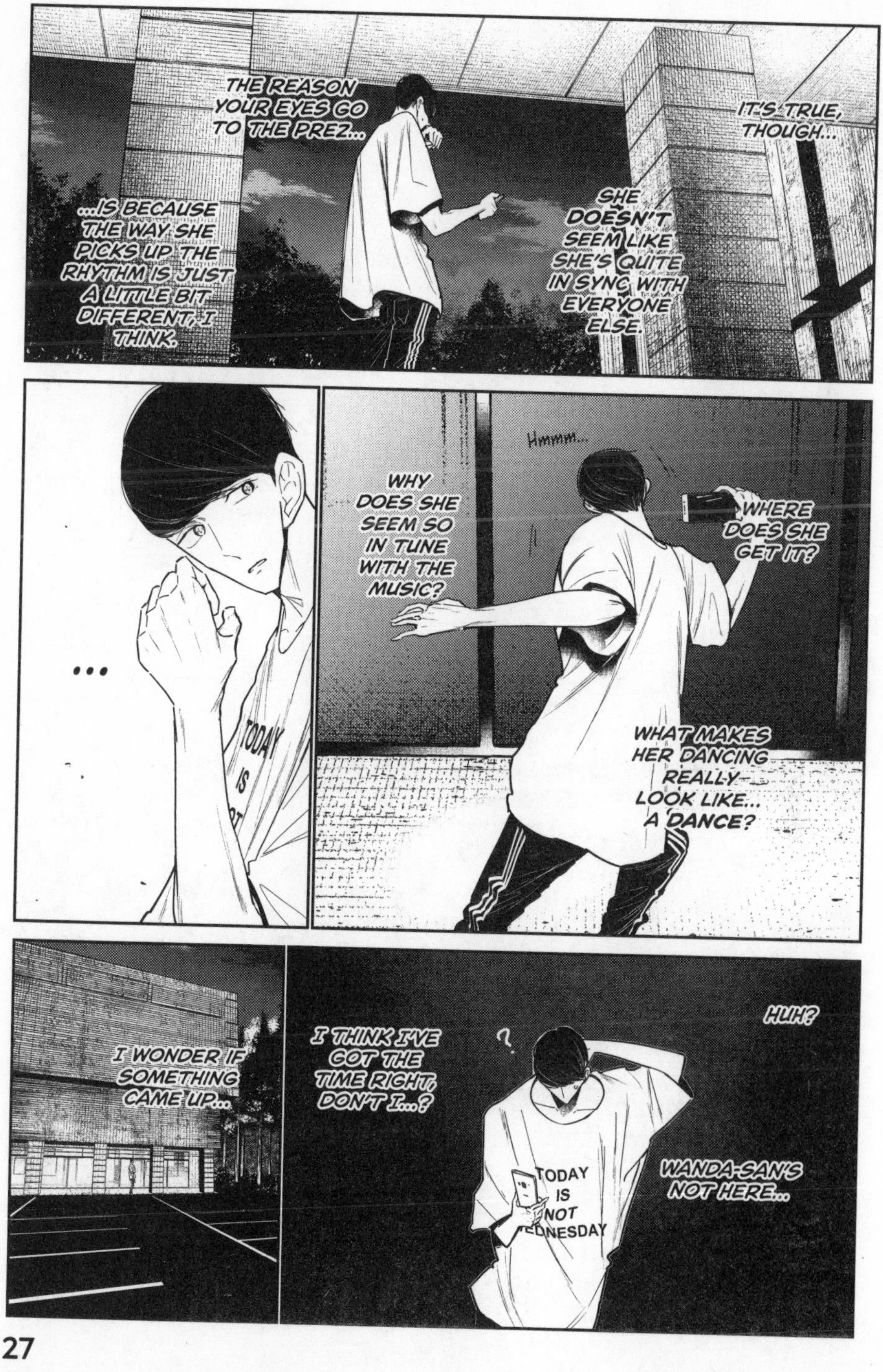
IT'S TRUE, THOUGH...
THE REASON YOUR EYES GO TO THE PREZ...
SHE DOESN'T SEEM LIKE SHE'S QUITE IN SYNC WITH EVERYONE ELSE.
...IS BECAUSE THE WAY SHE PICKS UP THE RHYTHM IS JUST A LITTLE BIT DIFFERENT, I THINK.
Hmmm...
WHERE DOES SHE GET IT?
WHY DOES SHE SEEM SO IN TUNE WITH THE MUSIC?
WHAT MAKES HER DANCING REALLY LOOK LIKE... A DANCE?
...
HUH?
I THINK I'VE GOT THE TIME RIGHT, DON'T I...?
WANDA-SAN'S NOT HERE...
I WONDER IF SOMETHING CAME UP...

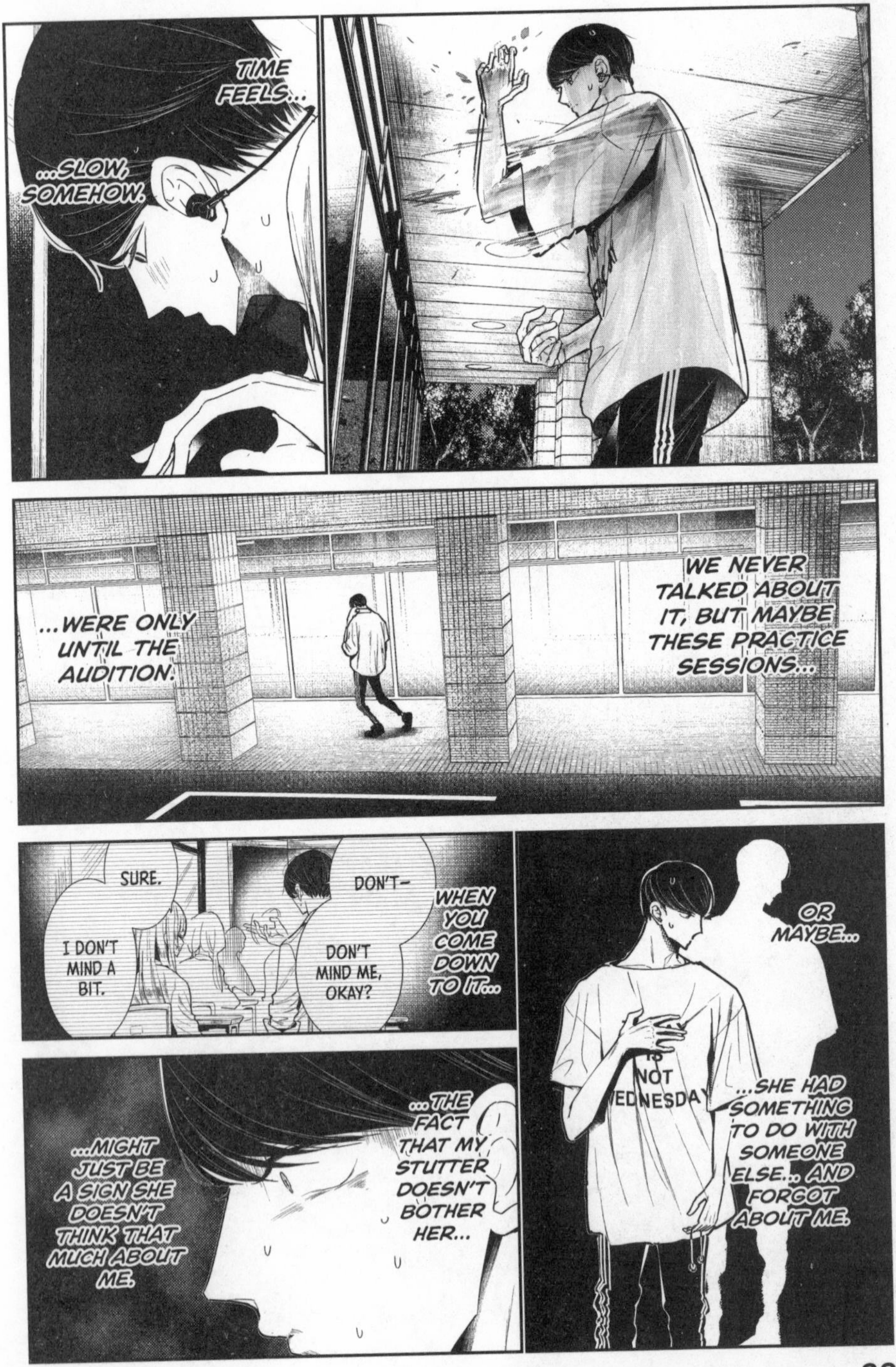
TIME FEELS...
...SLOW, SOMEHOW.
WE NEVER TALKED ABOUT IT, BUT MAYBE THESE PRACTICE SESSIONS...
...WERE ONLY UNTIL THE AUDITION.
OR MAYBE...
...SHE HAD SOMETHING TO DO WITH SOMEONE ELSE... AND FORGOT ABOUT ME.
WHEN YOU COME DOWN TO IT...
DON'T-
DON'T MIND ME, OKAY?
SURE.
I DON'T MIND A BIT.
...THE FACT THAT MY STUTTER DOESN'T BOTHER HER...
...MIGHT JUST BE A SIGN SHE DOESN'T THINK THAT MUCH ABOUT ME.
IS NOT WEDNESDAY

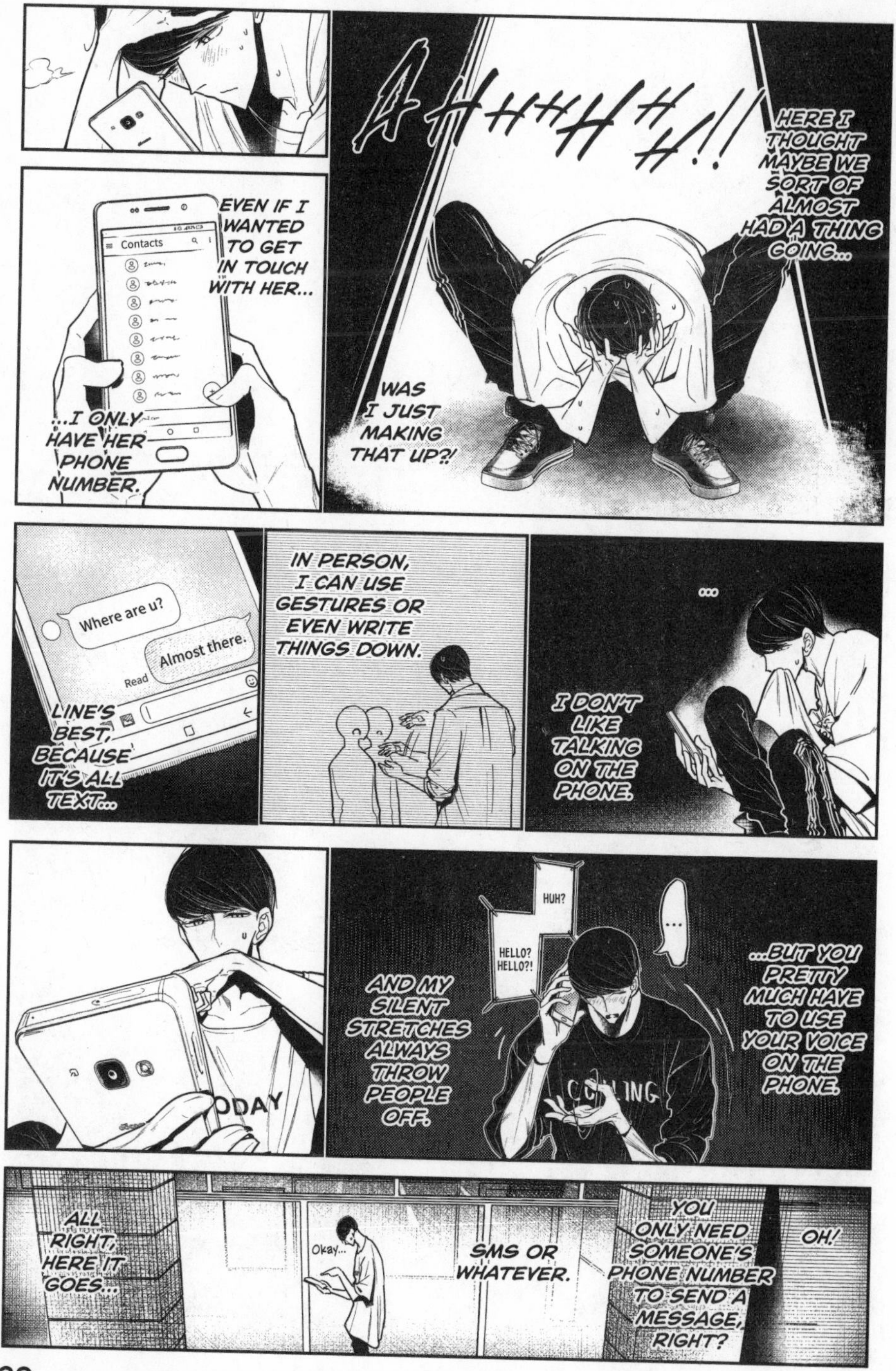
AHHHHHHH!!
HERE I THOUGHT MAYBE WE SORT OF ALMOST HAD A THING GOING...
WAS I JUST MAKING THAT UP?!
Contacts
EVEN IF I WANTED TO GET IN TOUCH WITH HER...
...I ONLY HAVE HER PHONE NUMBER.
...
I DON'T LIKE TALKING ON THE PHONE.
IN PERSON, I CAN USE GESTURES OR EVEN WRITE THINGS DOWN.
Where are u?
Almost there.
Read
LINE'S BEST, BECAUSE IT'S ALL TEXT...
HUH?
HELLO? HELLO?!
...
...BUT YOU PRETTY MUCH HAVE TO USE YOUR VOICE ON THE PHONE.
AND MY SILENT STRETCHES ALWAYS THROW PEOPLE OFF.
OH!
YOU ONLY NEED SOMEONE'S PHONE NUMBER TO SEND A MESSAGE, RIGHT?
SMS OR WHATEVER.
Okay...
ALL RIGHT, HERE IT GOES...

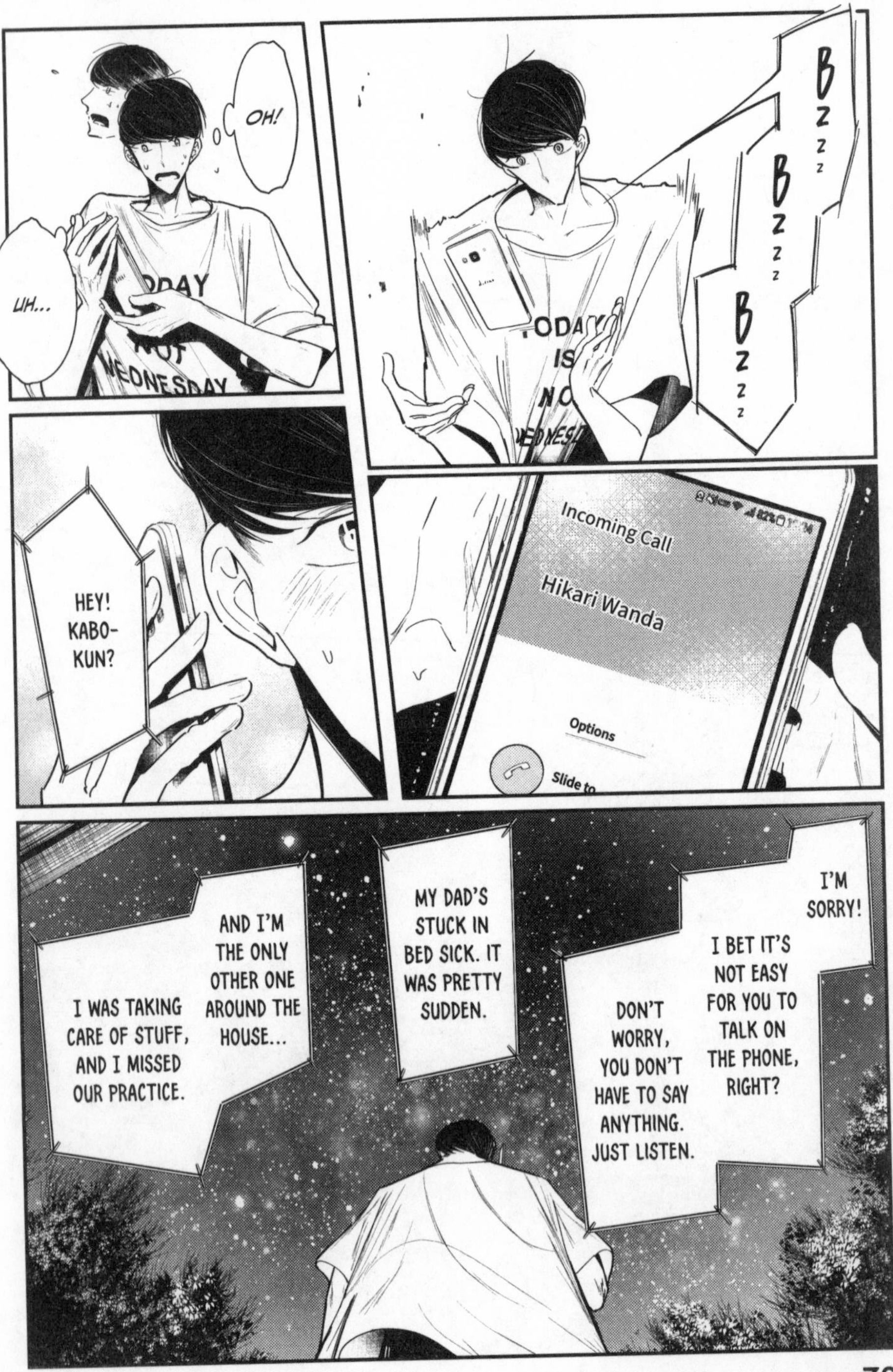
BZzz BZzz BZzz
OH!
UH...
Incoming Call
Hikari Wanda
Options
Slide to
HEY! KABO-KUN?
I'M SORRY!
I BET IT'S NOT EASY FOR YOU TO TALK ON THE PHONE, RIGHT?
DON'T WORRY, YOU DON'T HAVE TO SAY ANYTHING. JUST LISTEN.
MY DAD'S STUCK IN BED SICK. IT WAS PRETTY SUDDEN.
AND I'M THE ONLY OTHER ONE AROUND THE HOUSE...
I WAS TAKING CARE OF STUFF, AND I MISSED OUR PRACTICE.

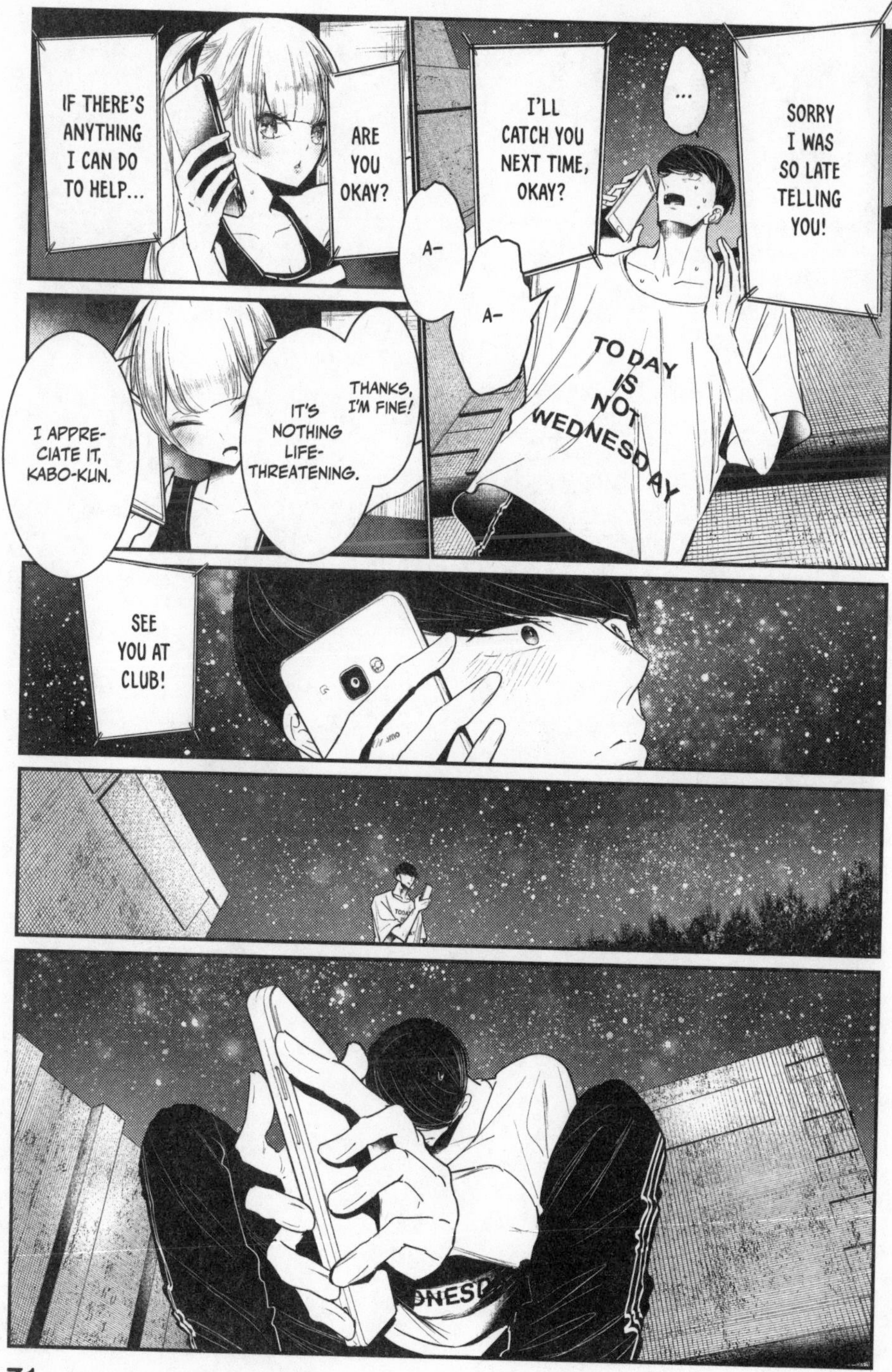
SORRY I WAS SO LATE TELLING YOU!
...
I'LL CATCH YOU NEXT TIME, OKAY?
ARE YOU OKAY?
IF THERE'S ANYTHING I CAN DO TO HELP...
A–
A–
TO DAY IS NOT WEDNESDAY
THANKS, I'M FINE!
IT'S NOTHING LIFE-THREATENING.
I APPRECIATE IT, KABO-KUN.
SEE YOU AT CLUB!

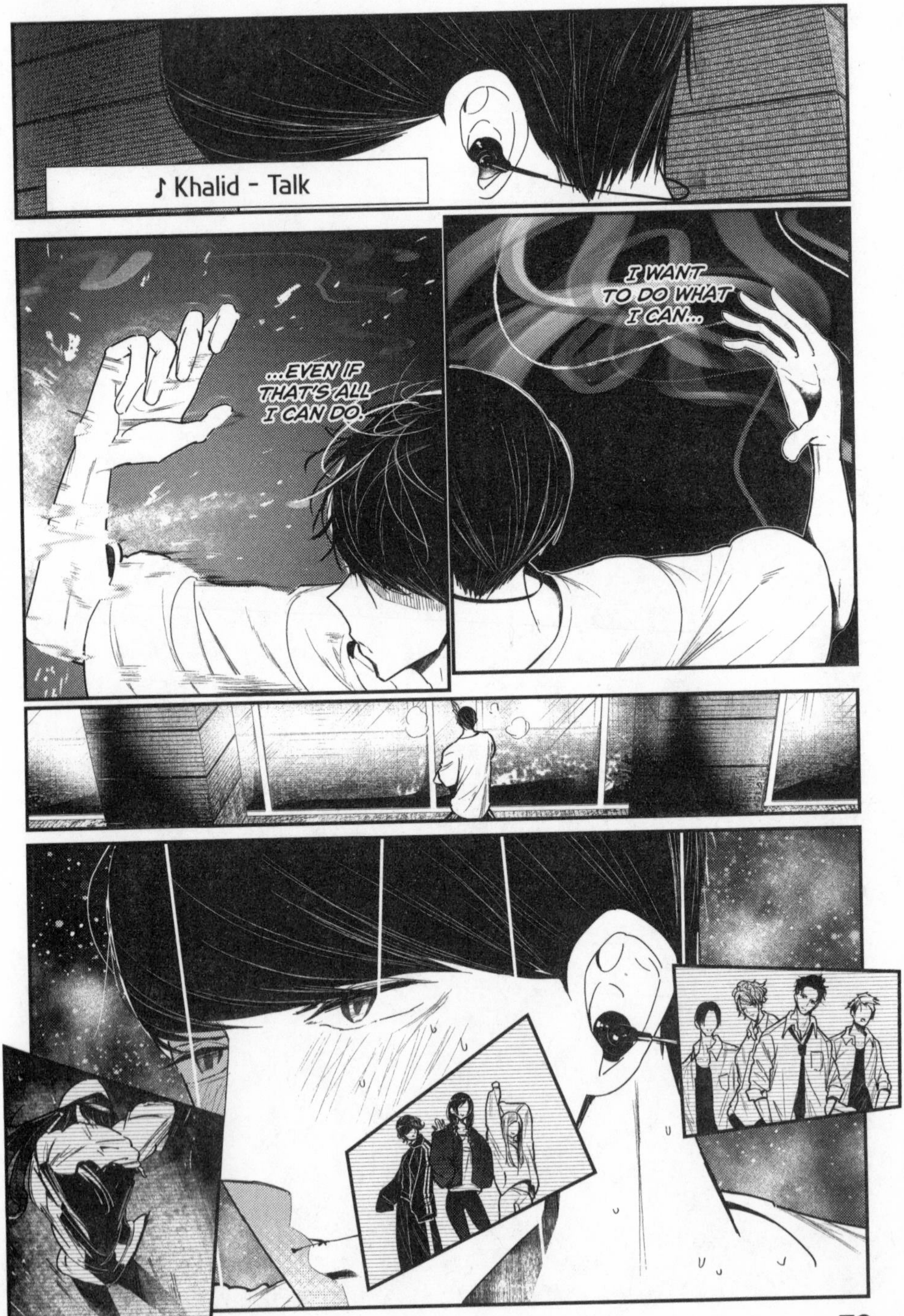
♪ Khalid - Talk
I WANT TO DO WHAT I CAN...
...EVEN IF THAT'S ALL I CAN DO.

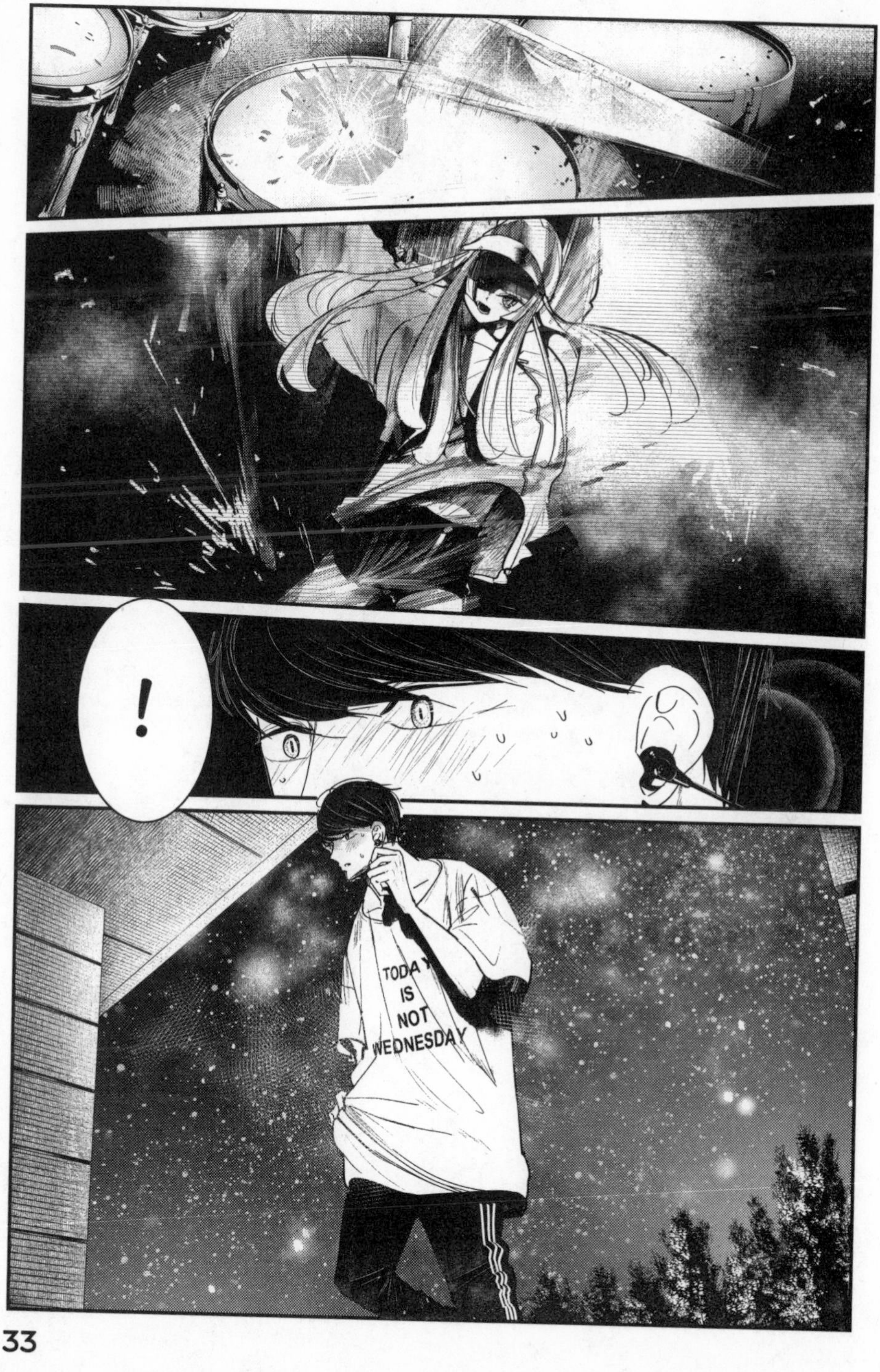
!
TODAY IS NOT WEDNESDAY

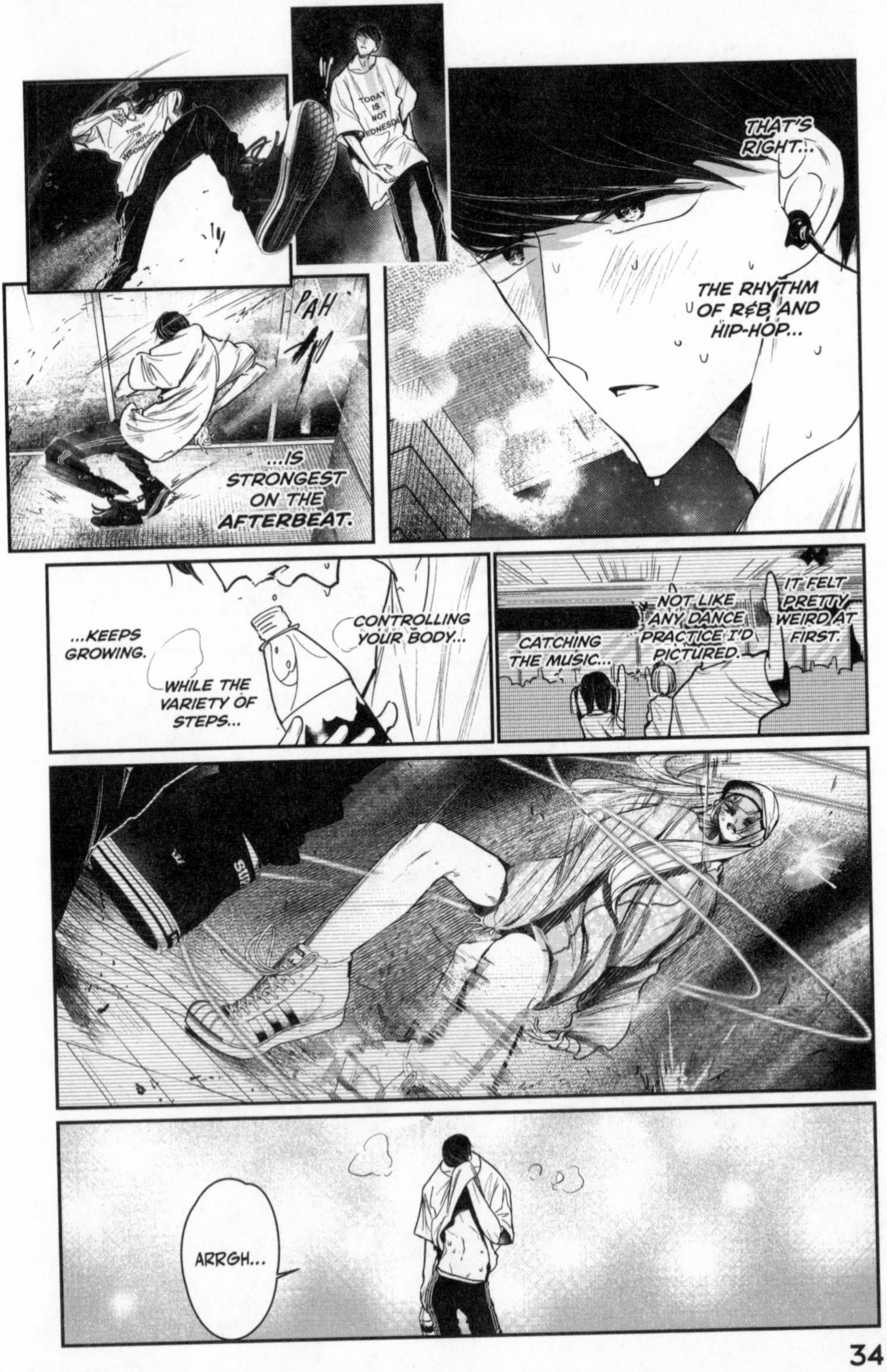
THAT'S RIGHT...
THE RHYTHM OF R&B AND HIP-HOP...
PAH
...IS STRONGEST ON THE AFTERBEAT.
IT FELT PRETTY WEIRD AT FIRST.
NOT LIKE ANY DANCE PRACTICE I'D PICTURED.
CATCHING THE MUSIC...
CONTROLLING YOUR BODY...
WHILE THE VARIETY OF STEPS...
...KEEPS GROWING.
ARRGH...

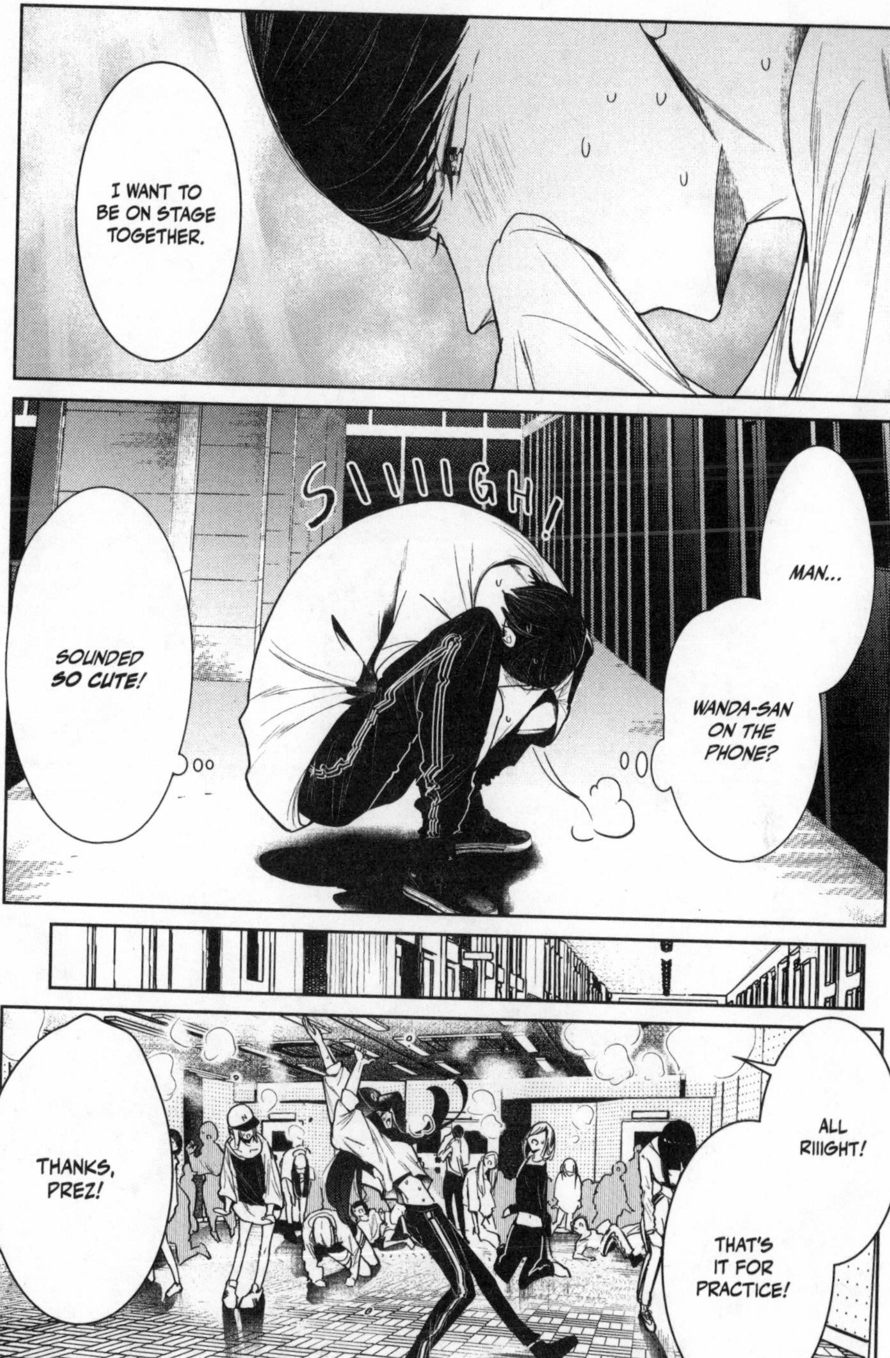
I WANT TO BE ON STAGE TOGETHER.
MAN...
WANDA-SAN ON THE PHONE?
SIIIGH!
SOUNDED SO CUTE!
ALL RIIIGHT!
THAT'S IT FOR PRACTICE!
THANKS, PREZ!

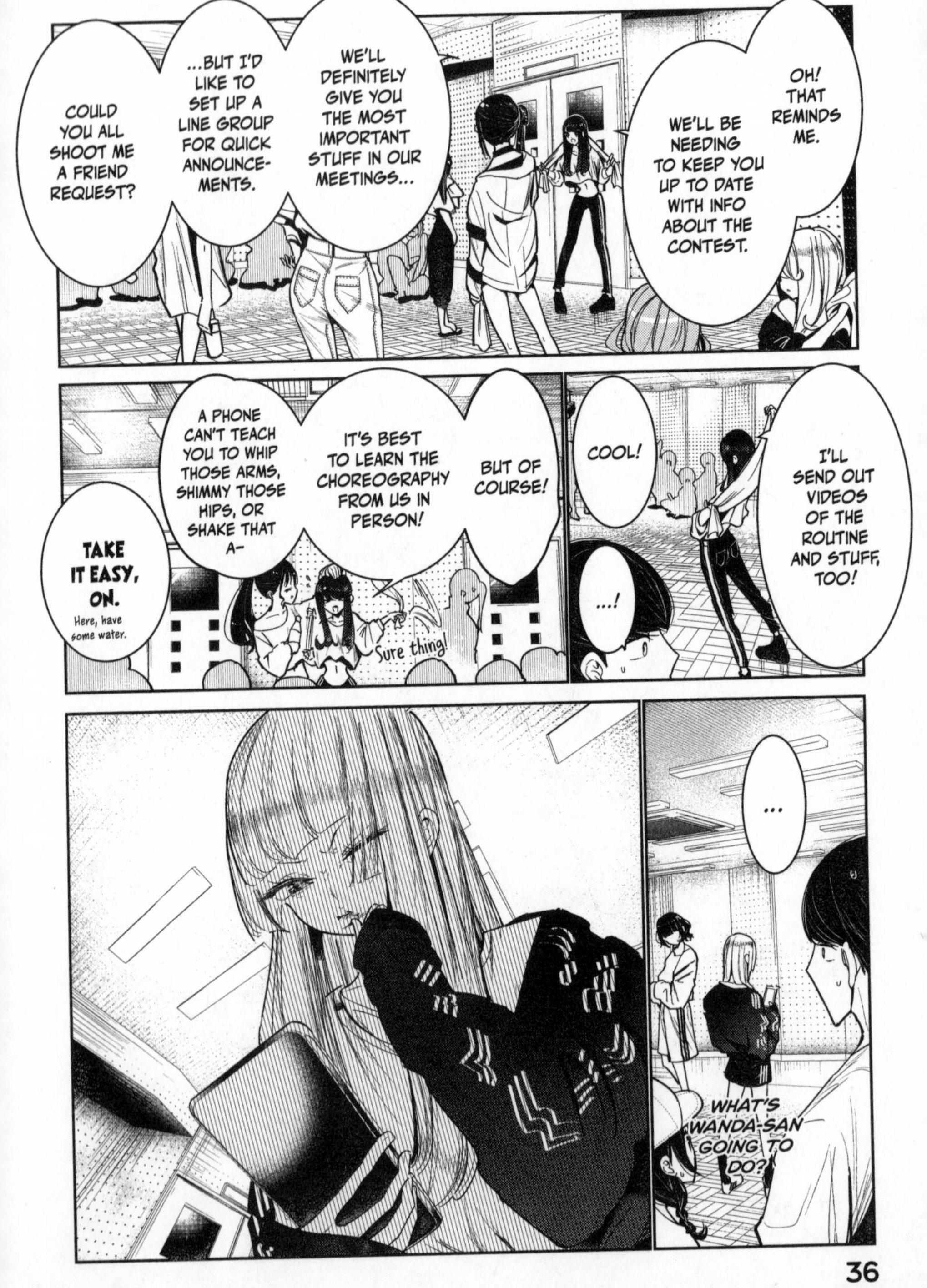
OH! THAT REMINDS ME.
WE'LL BE NEEDING TO KEEP YOU UP TO DATE WITH INFO ABOUT THE CONTEST.
WE'LL DEFINITELY GIVE YOU THE MOST IMPORTANT STUFF IN OUR MEETINGS...
...BUT I'D LIKE TO SET UP A LINE GROUP FOR QUICK ANNOUNCEMENTS.
COULD YOU ALL SHOOT ME A FRIEND REQUEST?
I'LL SEND OUT VIDEOS OF THE ROUTINE AND STUFF, TOO!
COOL!
...!
BUT OF COURSE!
IT'S BEST TO LEARN THE CHOREOGRAPHY FROM US IN PERSON!
A PHONE CAN'T TEACH YOU TO WHIP THOSE ARMS, SHIMMY THOSE HIPS, OR SHAKE THAT A-
Sure thing!
TAKE IT EASY, ON.
Here, have some water.
...
WHAT'S WANDA-SAN GOING TO DO?

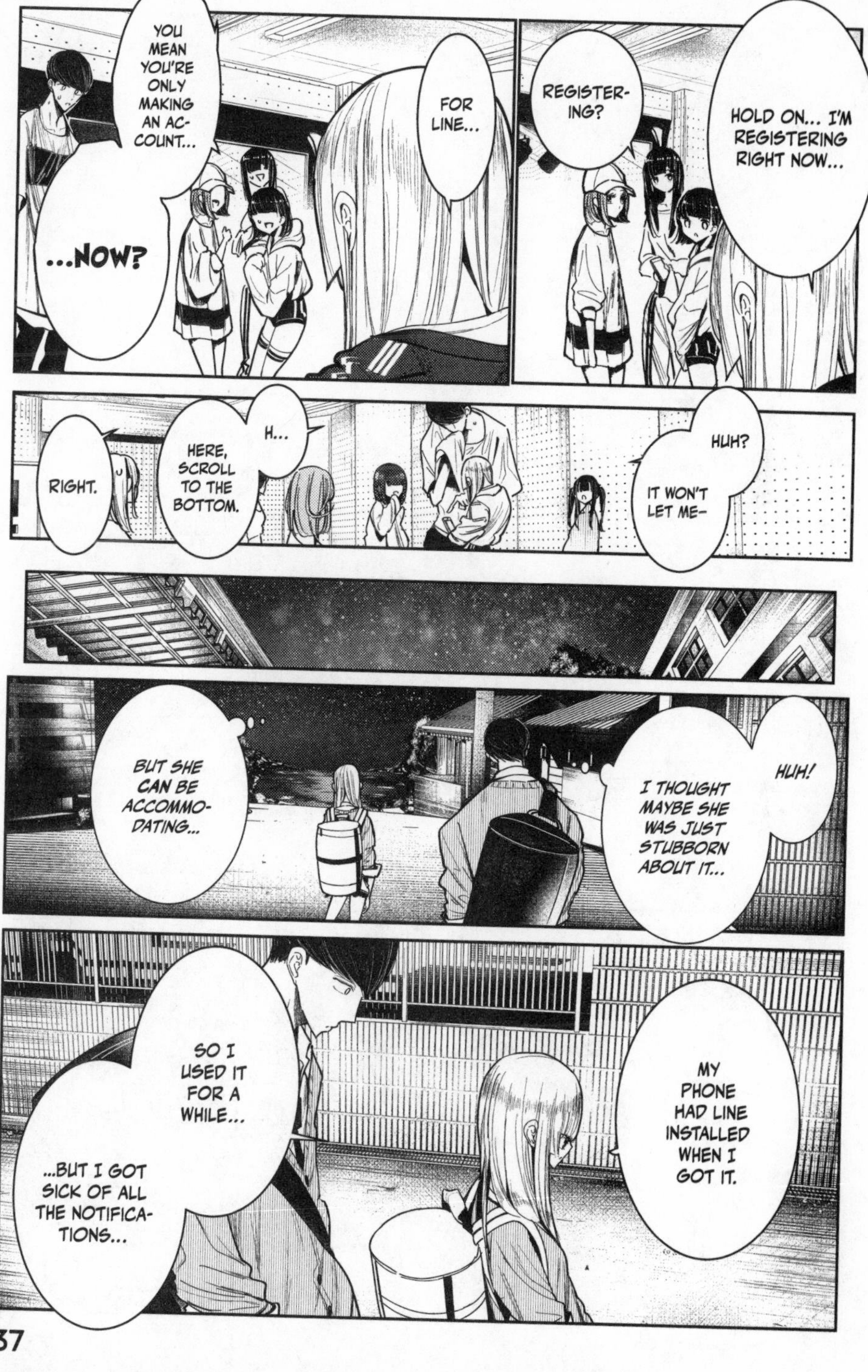
HOLD ON... I'M REGISTERING RIGHT NOW...
REGISTER-ING?
FOR LINE...
YOU MEAN YOU'RE ONLY MAKING AN AC-COUNT...
...NOW?
HUH?
IT WON'T LET ME-
H...
HERE, SCROLL TO THE BOTTOM.
RIGHT.
HUH!
I THOUGHT MAYBE SHE WAS JUST STUBBORN ABOUT IT...
BUT SHE CAN BE ACCOMMO-DATING...
MY PHONE HAD LINE INSTALLED WHEN I GOT IT.
SO I USED IT FOR A WHILE...
...BUT I GOT SICK OF ALL THE NOTIFICA-TIONS...

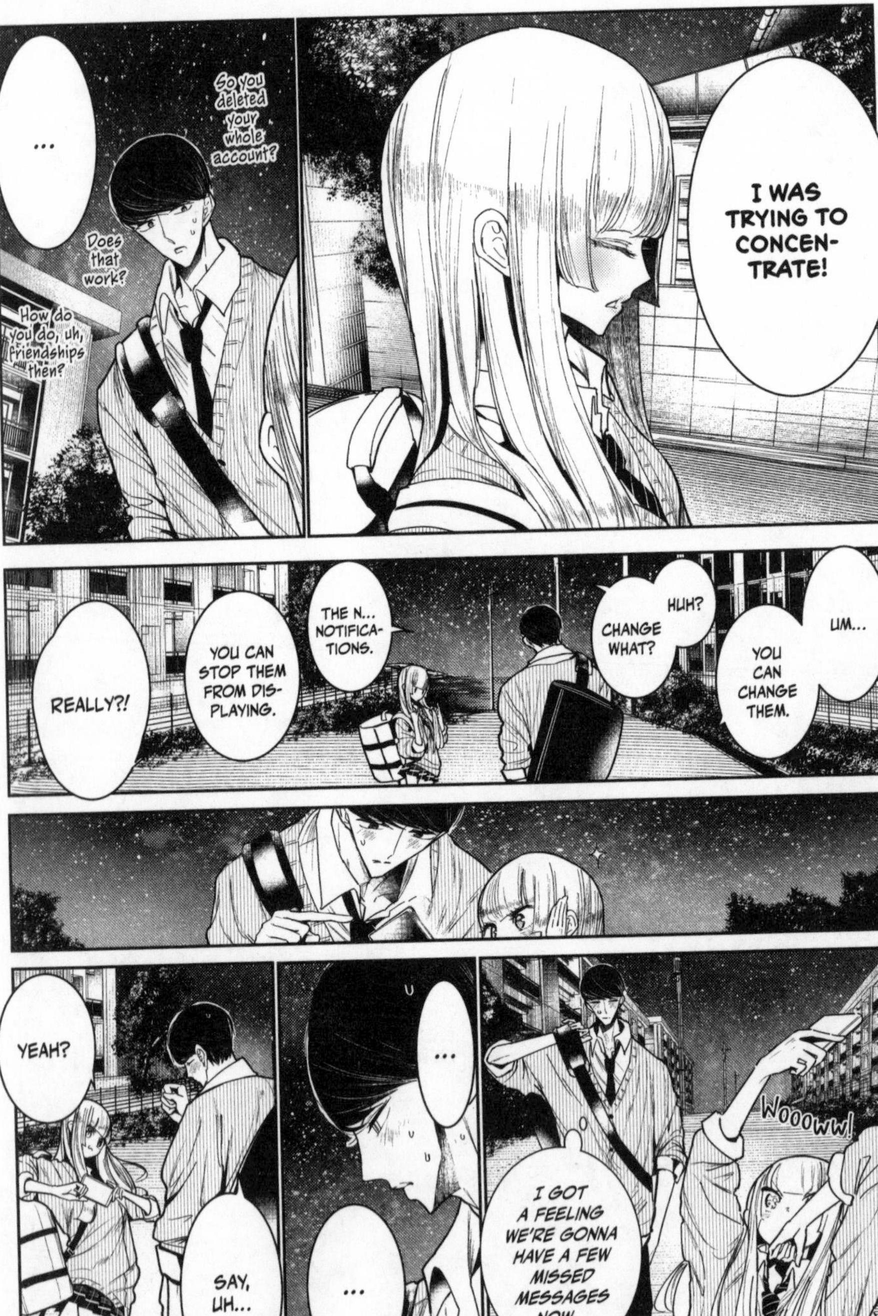
I WAS TRYING TO CONCENTRATE!
So you deleted your whole account?
Does that work?
How do you do, uh, friendships then?
...
UM...
YOU CAN CHANGE THEM.
HUH?
CHANGE WHAT?
THE N... NOTIFICATIONS.
YOU CAN STOP THEM FROM DISPLAYING.
REALLY?!
WOOOWW!
I GOT A FEELING WE'RE GONNA HAVE A FEW MISSED MESSAGES NOW...
...
...
SAY, UH...
YEAH?

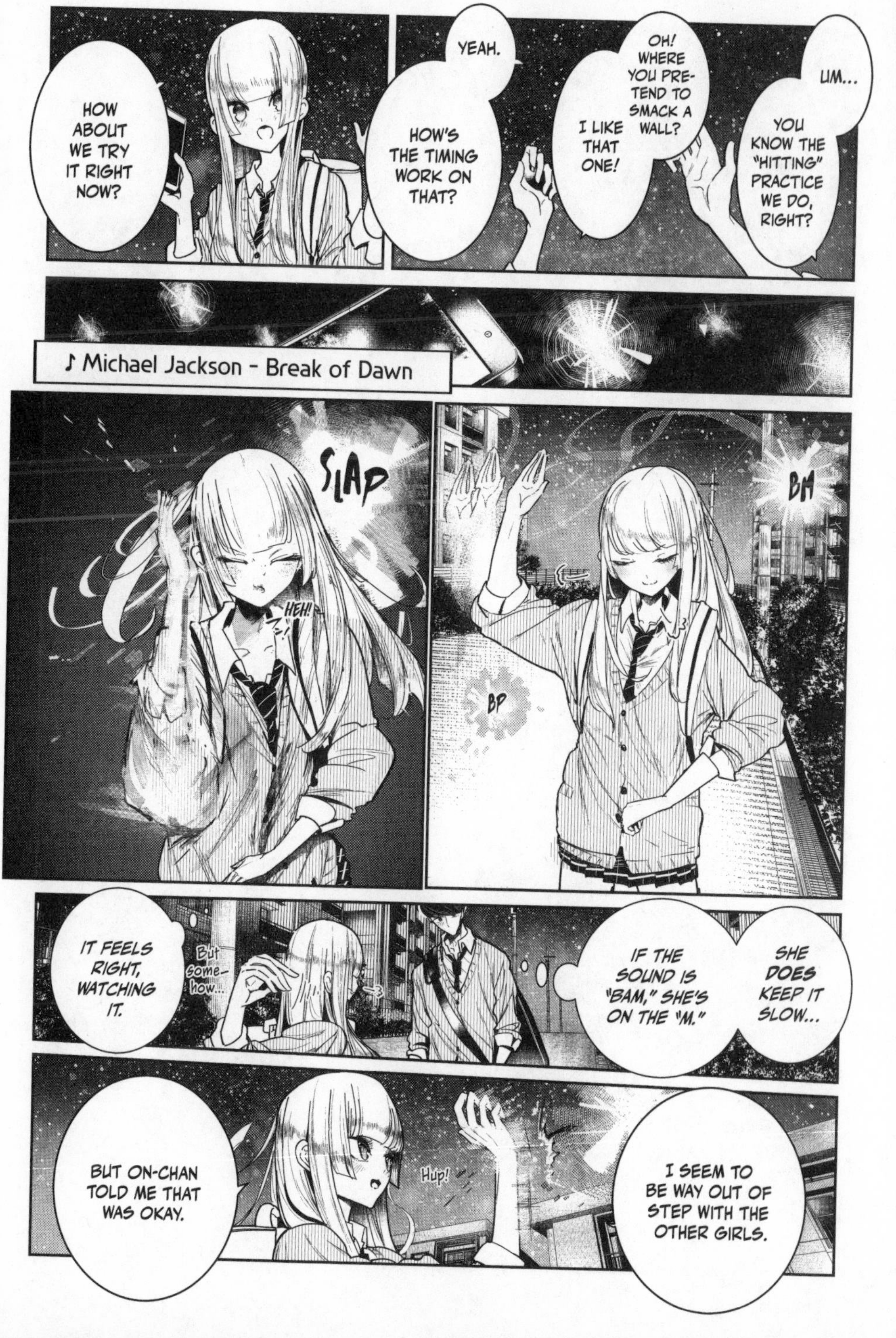
UM...
YOU KNOW THE "HITTING" PRACTICE WE DO, RIGHT?
OH! WHERE YOU PRETEND TO SMACK A WALL?
I LIKE THAT ONE!
YEAH.
HOW'S THE TIMING WORK ON THAT?
HOW ABOUT WE TRY IT RIGHT NOW?
♪ Michael Jackson - Break of Dawn
BM
BP
SLAP
HEH!
SHE DOES KEEP IT SLOW...
IF THE SOUND IS "BAM," SHE'S ON THE "M."
But some-how...
IT FEELS RIGHT, WATCHING IT.
I SEEM TO BE WAY OUT OF STEP WITH THE OTHER GIRLS.
Hup!
BUT ON-CHAN TOLD ME THAT WAS OKAY.

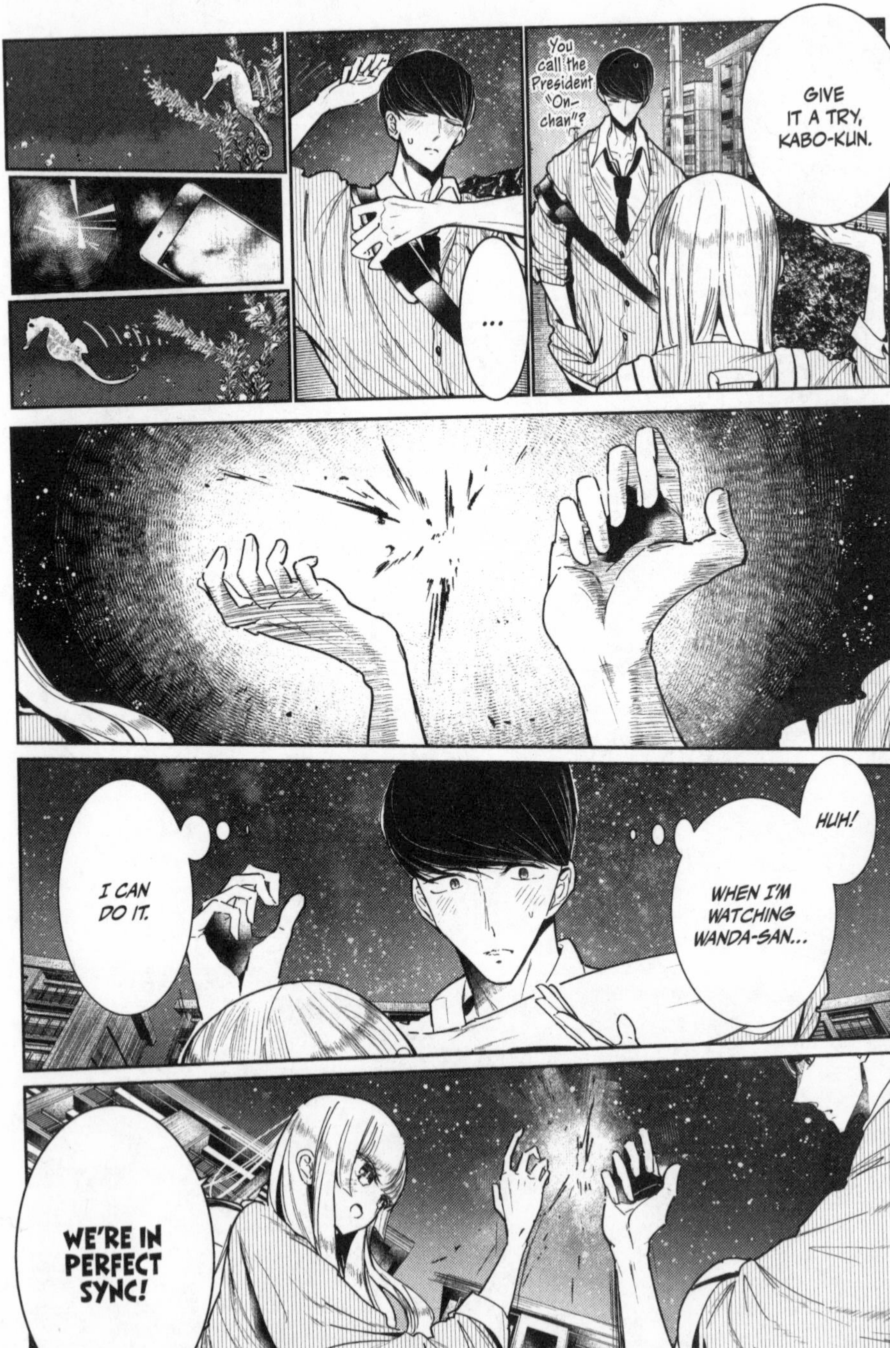
GIVE IT A TRY, KABO-KUN.
You call the President "On-chan"?
...
HUH!
WHEN I'M WATCHING WANDA-SAN...
I CAN DO IT.
WE'RE IN PERFECT SYNC!

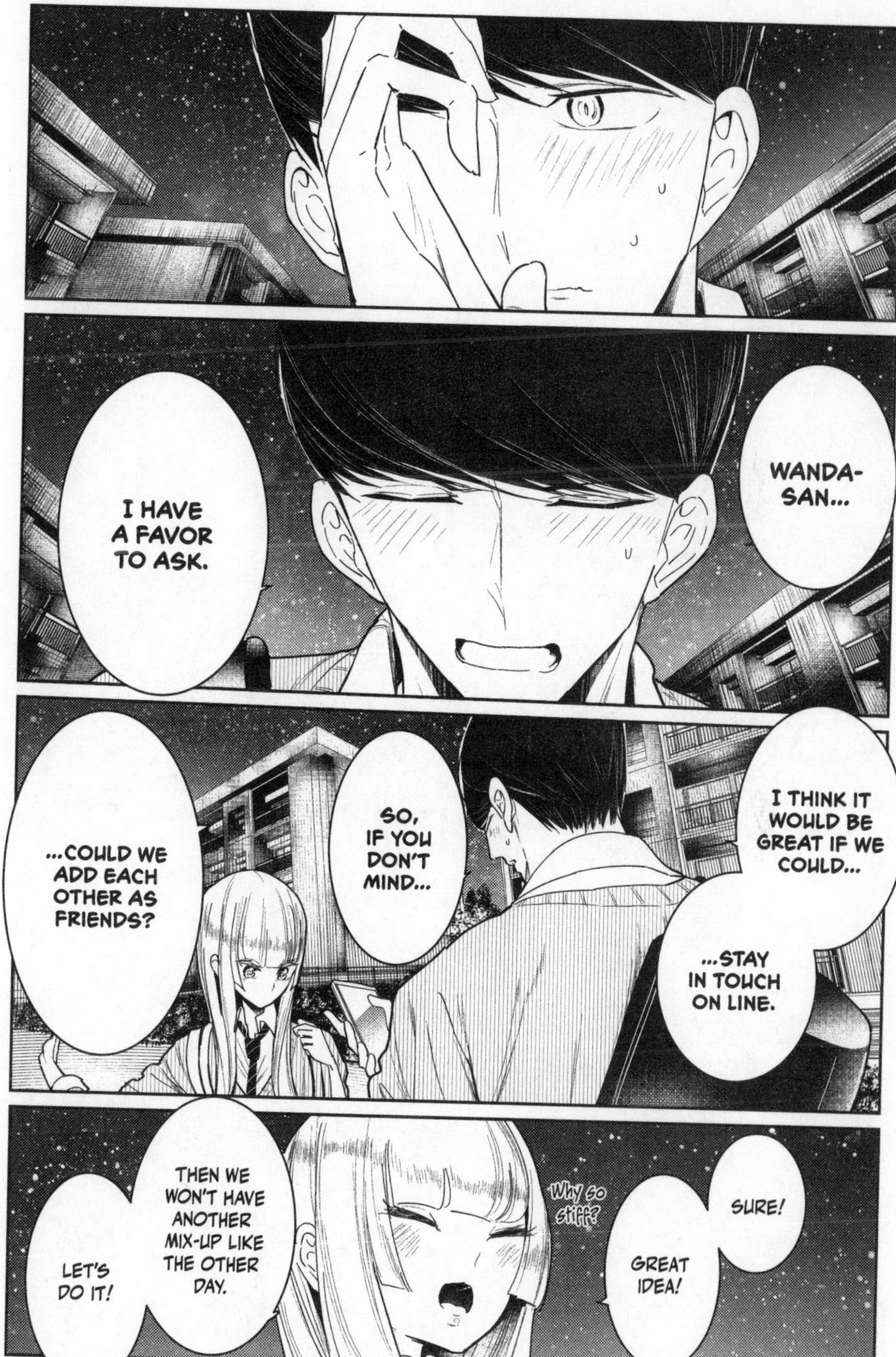
WANDA-SAN...
I HAVE A FAVOR TO ASK.
I THINK IT WOULD BE GREAT IF WE COULD...
...STAY IN TOUCH ON LINE.
SO, IF YOU DON'T MIND...
...COULD WE ADD EACH OTHER AS FRIENDS?
SURE!
GREAT IDEA!
Why so stiff?
THEN WE WON'T HAVE ANOTHER MIX-UP LIKE THE OTHER DAY.
LET'S DO IT!

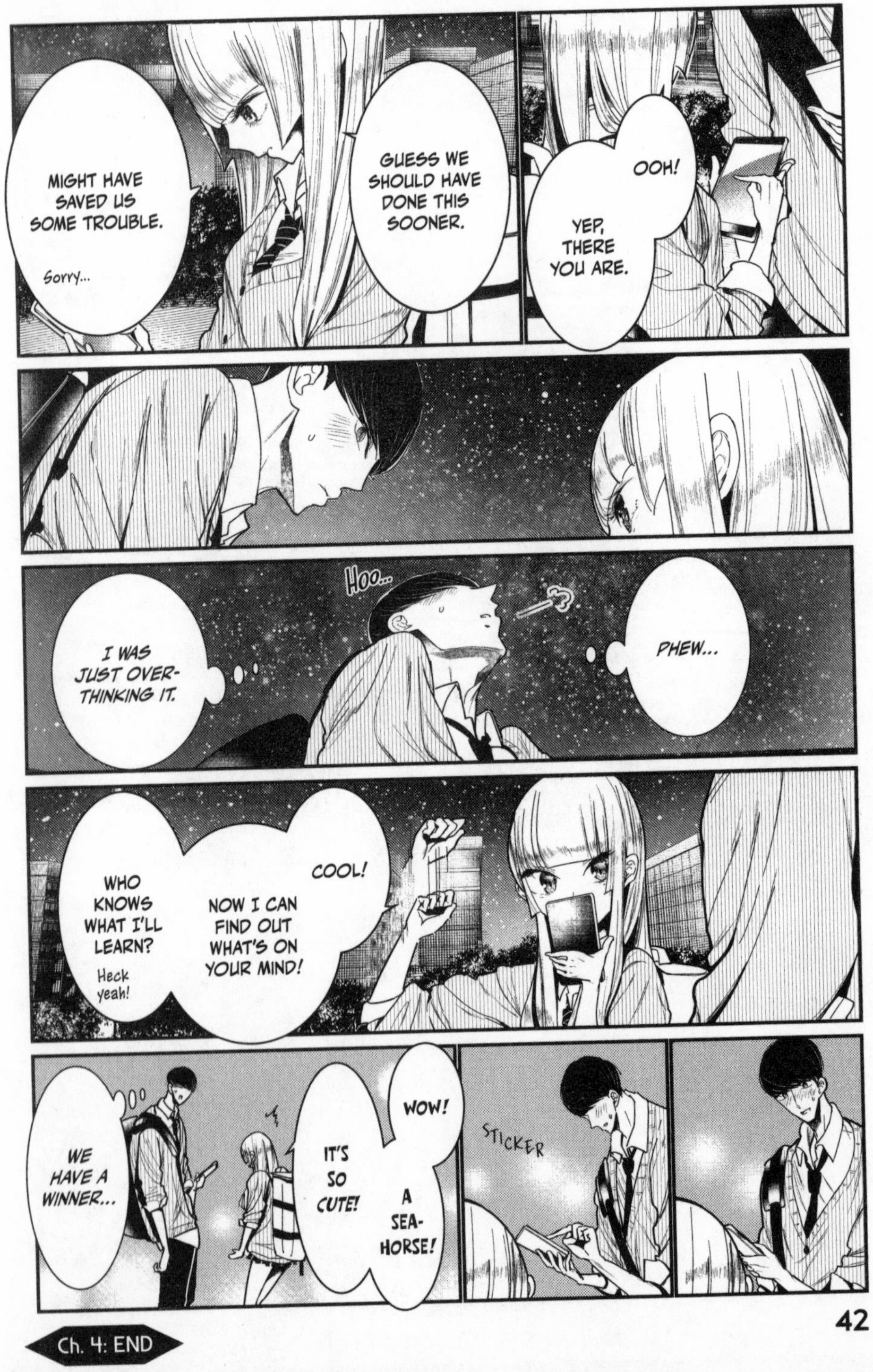
OOH!
YEP, THERE YOU ARE.
GUESS WE SHOULD HAVE DONE THIS SOONER.
MIGHT HAVE SAVED US SOME TROUBLE.
Sorry...
Hoo...
PHEW...
I WAS JUST OVER-THINKING IT.
COOL!
NOW I CAN FIND OUT WHAT'S ON YOUR MIND!
WHO KNOWS WHAT I'LL LEARN?
Heck yeah!
STICKER
WOW!
A SEA-HORSE!
IT'S SO CUTE!
WE HAVE A WINNER...

Ch. 4: END

Ch. 5: The Routine

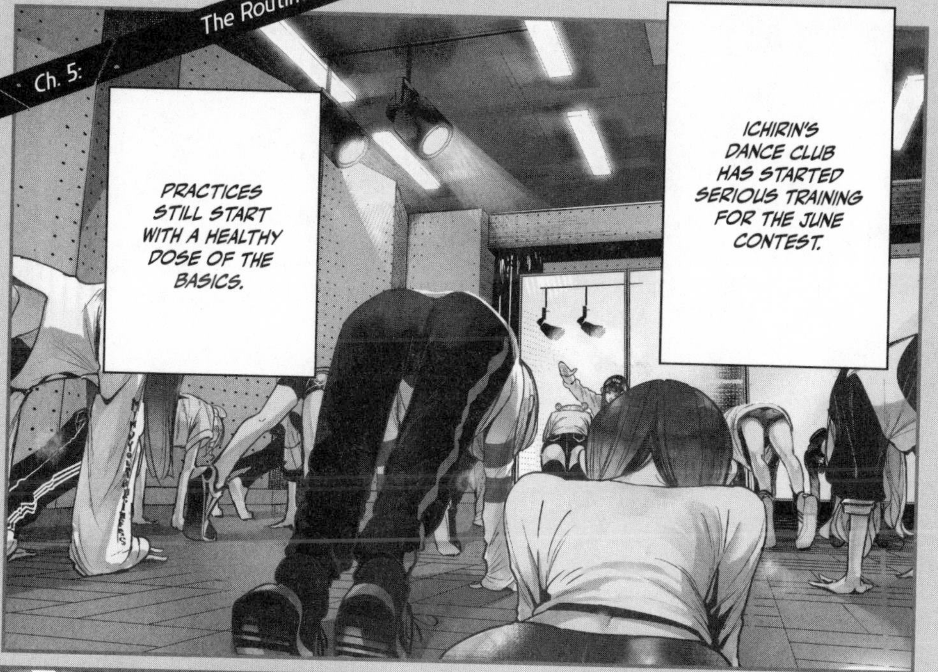
ICHIRIN'S DANCE CLUB HAS STARTED SERIOUS TRAINING FOR THE JUNE CONTEST.
PRACTICES STILL START WITH A HEALTHY DOSE OF THE BASICS.

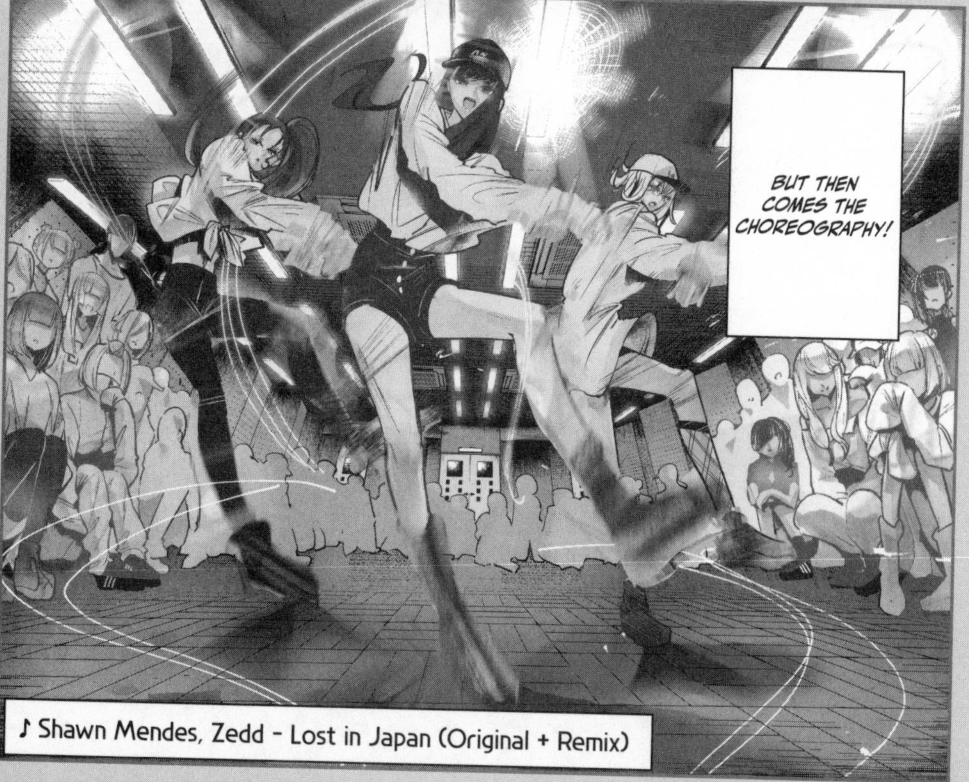
BUT THEN COMES THE CHOREOGRAPHY!
♪ Shawn Mendes, Zedd - Lost in Japan (Original + Remix)

Research
YUSUKE-SAMA (Arpeggio, SOUL TRIBE OSAKA, PLAYERS DANCE WORKS)
BEZI-SAMA (BUSTA JAKK BOOGIE)
YUKITOSHI SHIRASAKA-SAMA (The Dancing Math Teacher)
Uenomiya Senior High School Street Dance Club

Bun'ya Kawaguchi-sama
Ayukan.-sama
Art Assistants

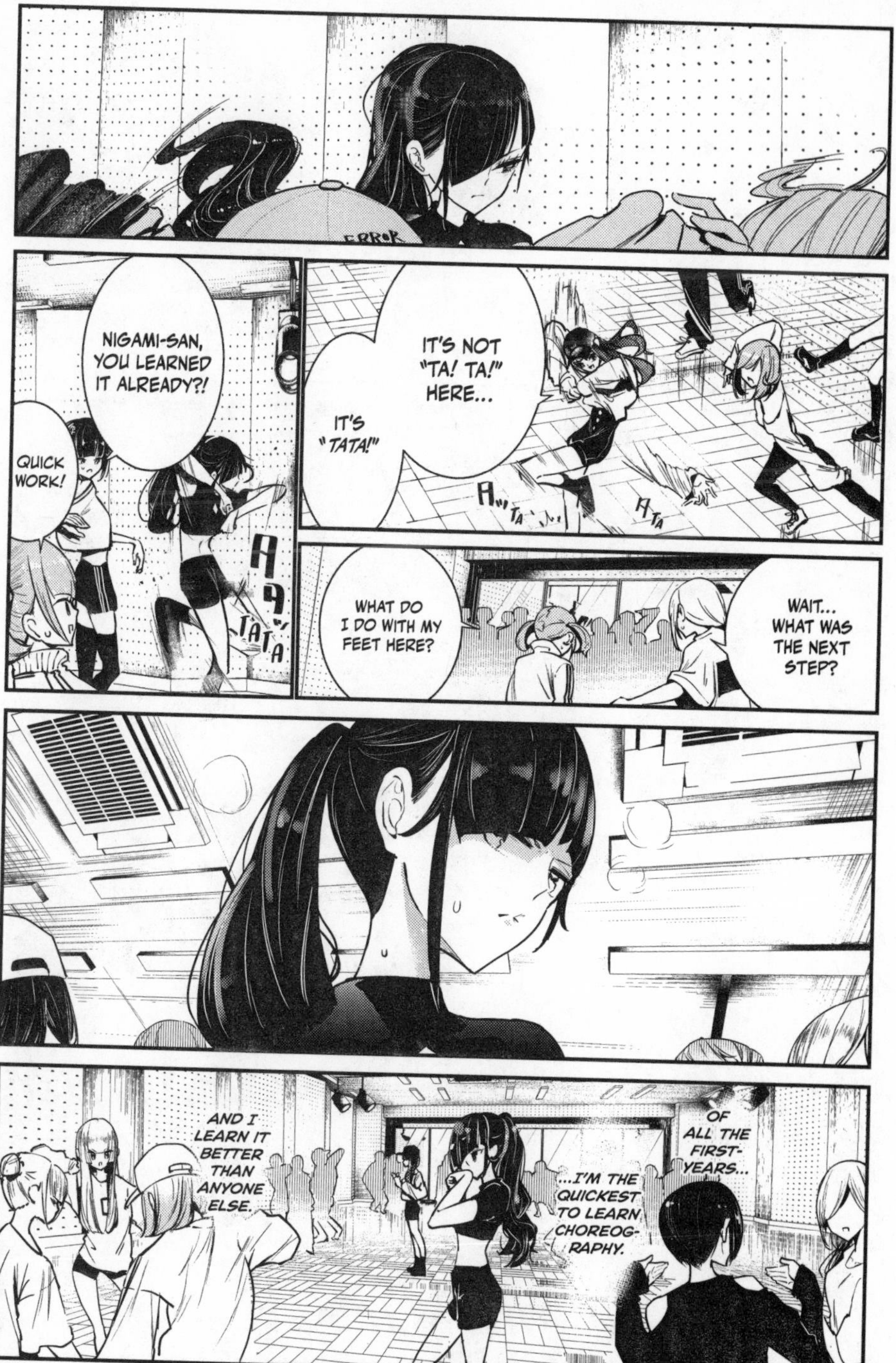
IT'S NOT "TA! TA!" HERE...
IT'S "TATA!"
WAIT... WHAT WAS THE NEXT STEP?
WHAT DO I DO WITH MY FEET HERE?
NIGAMI-SAN, YOU LEARNED IT ALREADY?!
QUICK WORK!
TATA
OF ALL THE FIRST-YEARS...
...I'M THE QUICKEST TO LEARN CHOREOGRAPHY.
AND I LEARN IT BETTER THAN ANYONE ELSE.

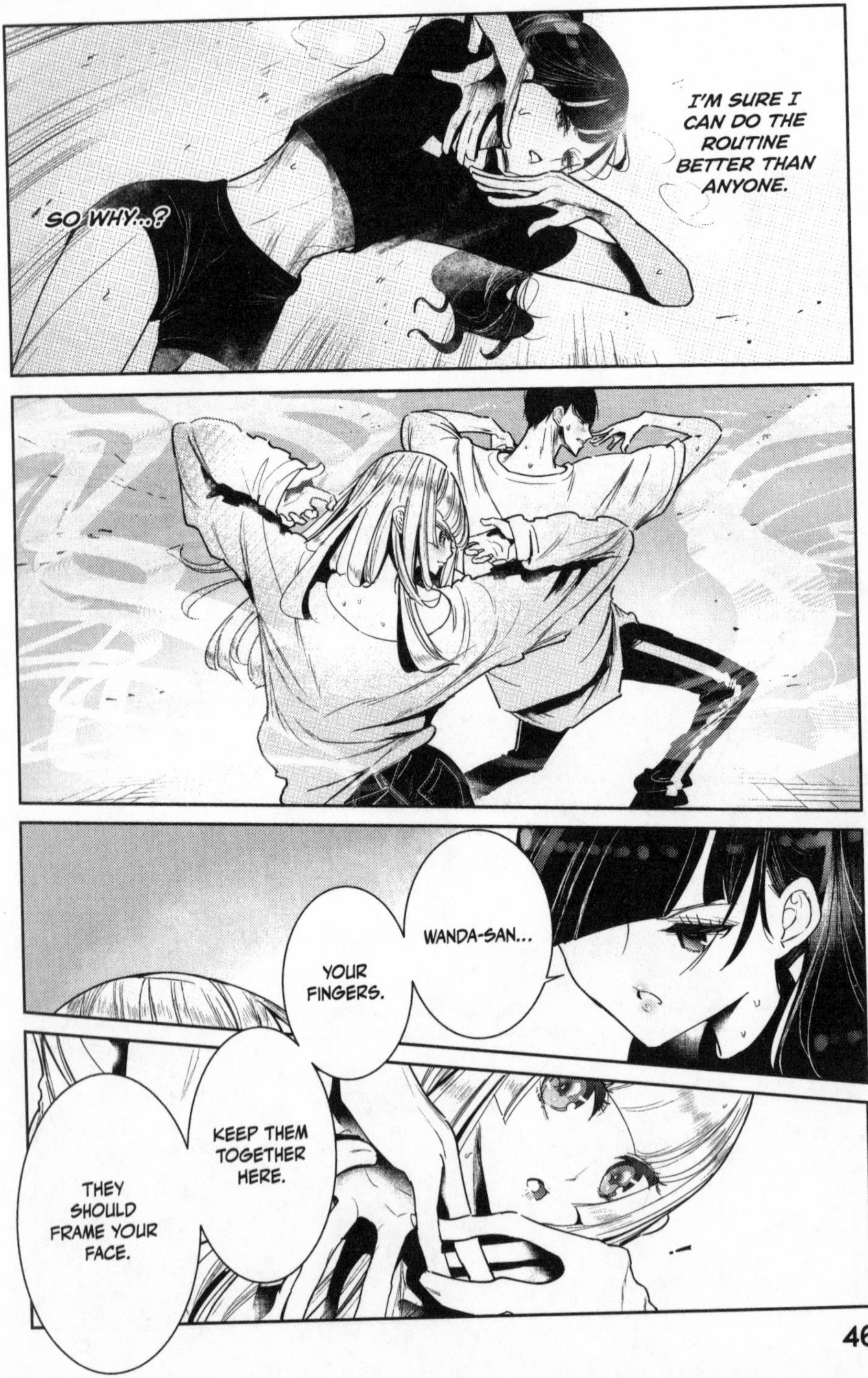
I'M SURE I CAN DO THE ROUTINE BETTER THAN ANYONE.
SO WHY...?
WANDA-SAN...
YOUR FINGERS.
KEEP THEM TOGETHER HERE.
THEY SHOULD FRAME YOUR FACE.

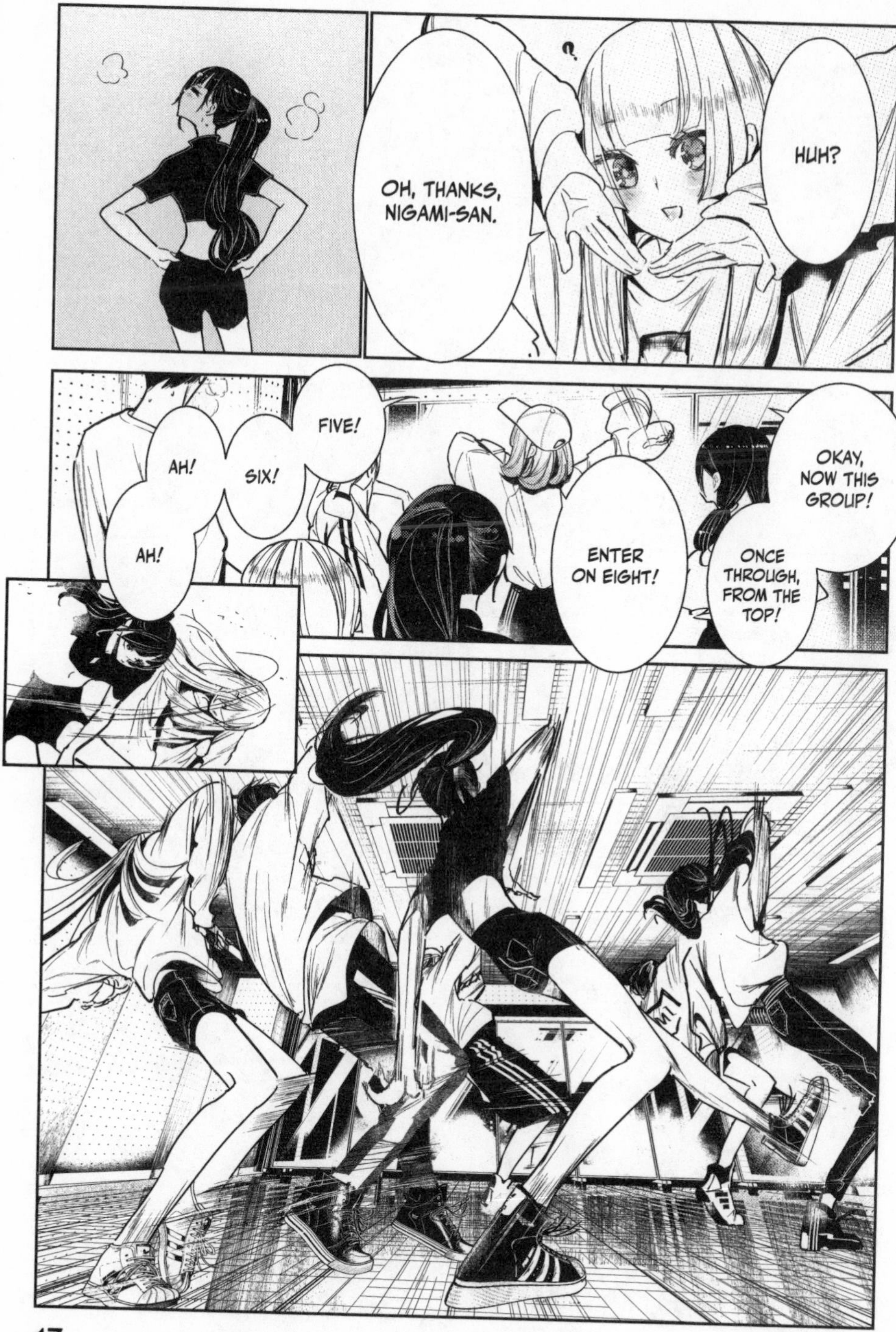
HUH?
OH, THANKS, NIGAMI-SAN.
OKAY, NOW THIS GROUP!
ONCE THROUGH, FROM THE TOP!
ENTER ON EIGHT!
FIVE!
SIX!
AH!
AH!

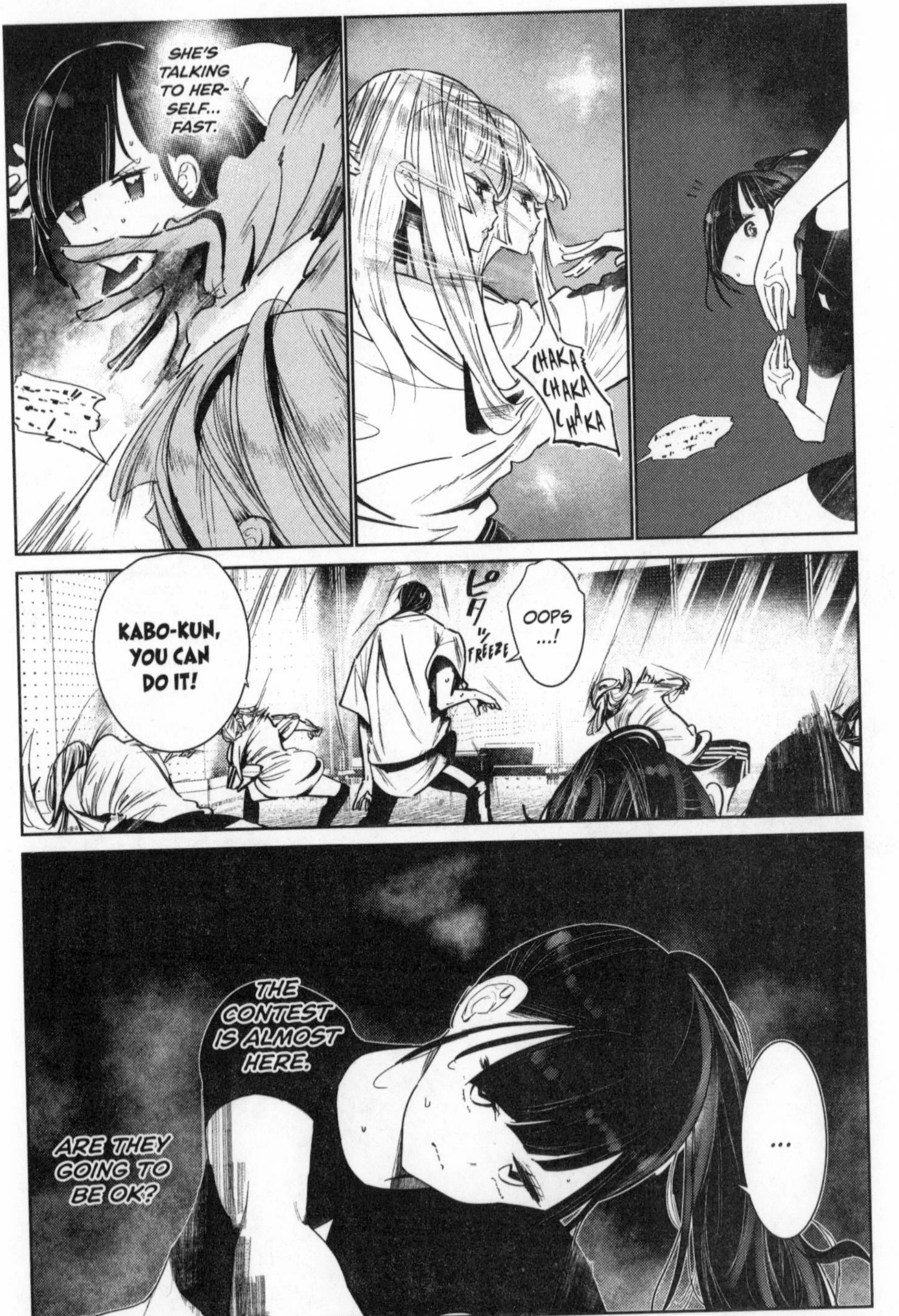
CHAKA CHAKA CHAKA
SHE'S TALKING TO HER-SELF... FAST.
OOPS ...!
ピタッ
FREEZE
KABO-KUN, YOU CAN DO IT!
...
THE CONTEST IS ALMOST HERE.
ARE THEY GOING TO BE OK?

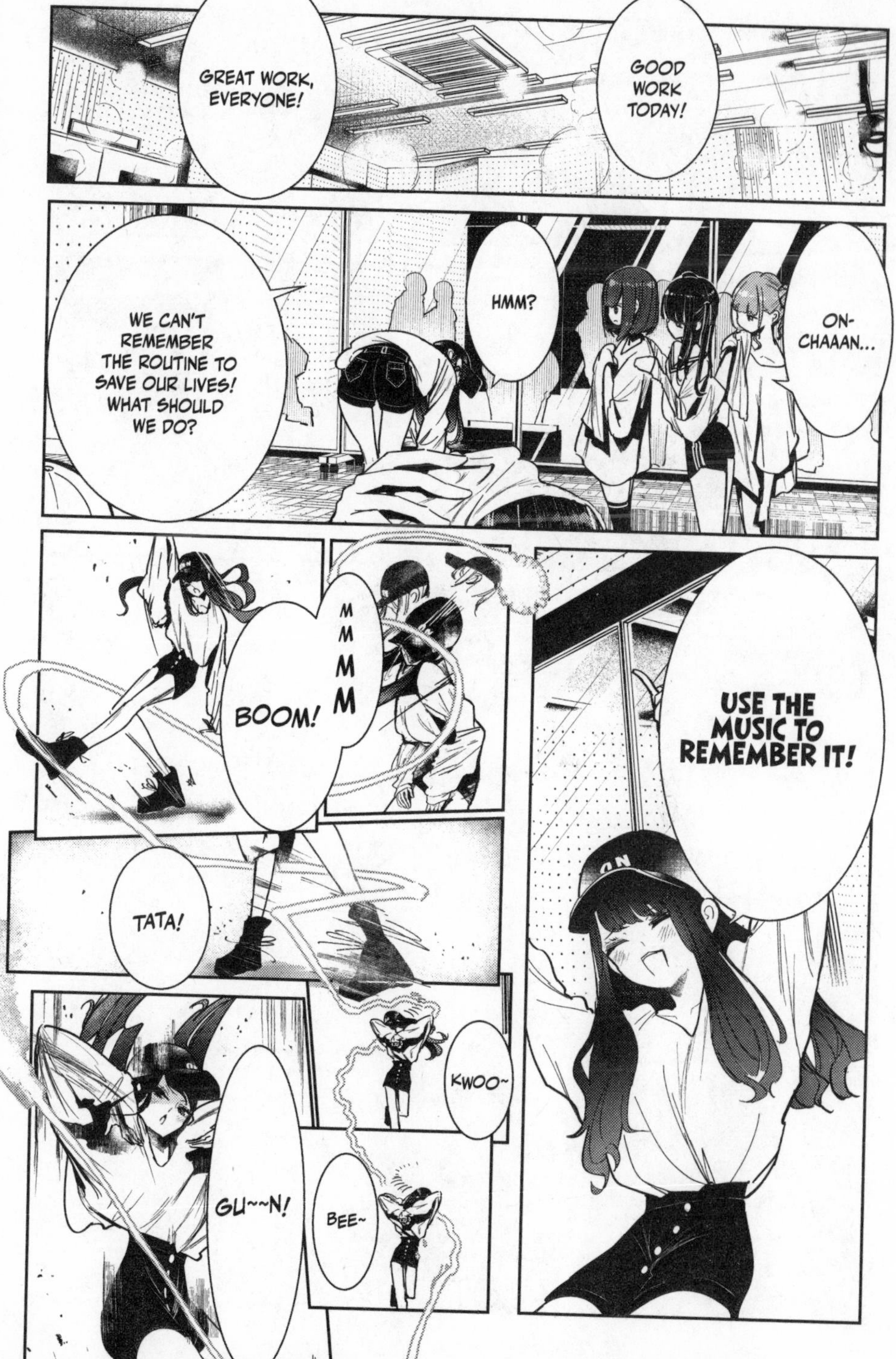
GOOD WORK TODAY!
GREAT WORK, EVERYONE!
ON-CHAAAN...
HMM?
WE CAN'T REMEMBER THE ROUTINE TO SAVE OUR LIVES! WHAT SHOULD WE DO?
USE THE MUSIC TO REMEMBER IT!
MMMM
BOOM!
TATA!
KWOO~
BEE~
GU~~N!

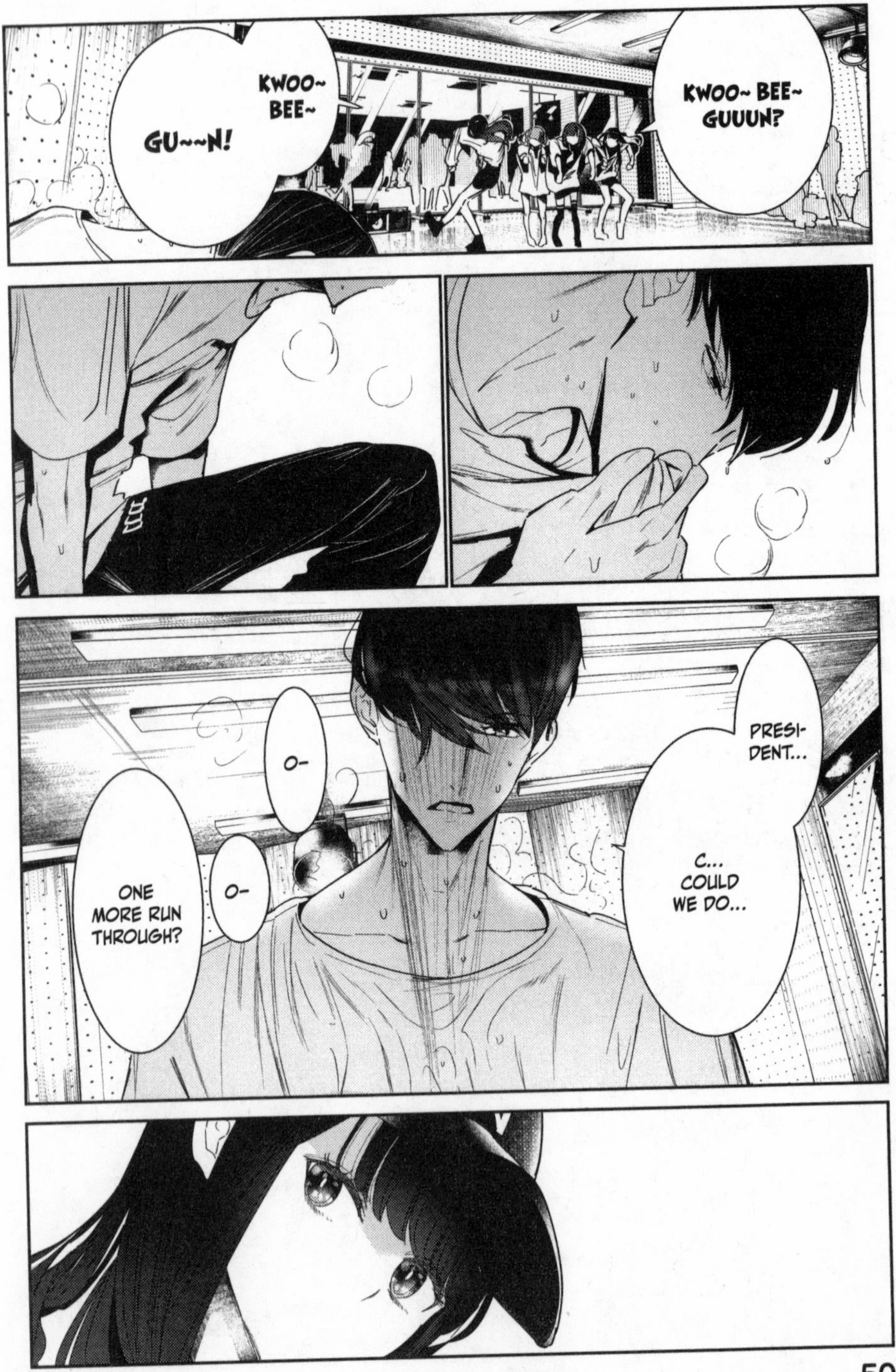
KWOO~ BEE~ GUUUN?
KWOO~ BEE~ GU~~N!
PRESI-DENT... C... COULD WE DO...
O-
O-
ONE MORE RUN THROUGH?

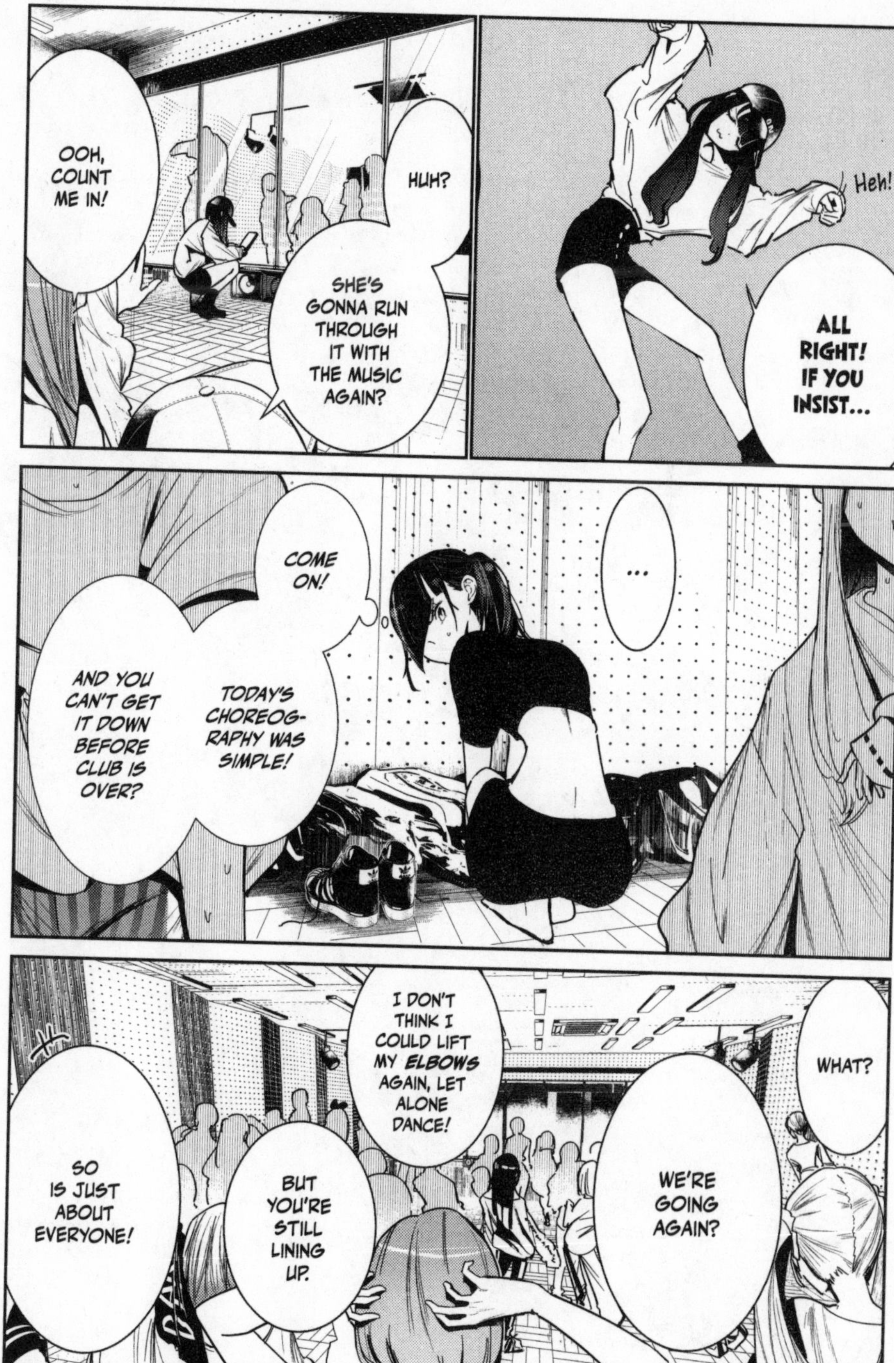
Heh!
ALL RIGHT! IF YOU INSIST...
HUH?
SHE'S GONNA RUN THROUGH IT WITH THE MUSIC AGAIN?
OOH, COUNT ME IN!
...
COME ON!
TODAY'S CHOREOG-RAPHY WAS SIMPLE!
AND YOU CAN'T GET IT DOWN BEFORE CLUB IS OVER?
WHAT?
WE'RE GOING AGAIN?
I DON'T THINK I COULD LIFT MY ELBOWS AGAIN, LET ALONE DANCE!
BUT YOU'RE STILL LINING UP.
SO IS JUST ABOUT EVERYONE!

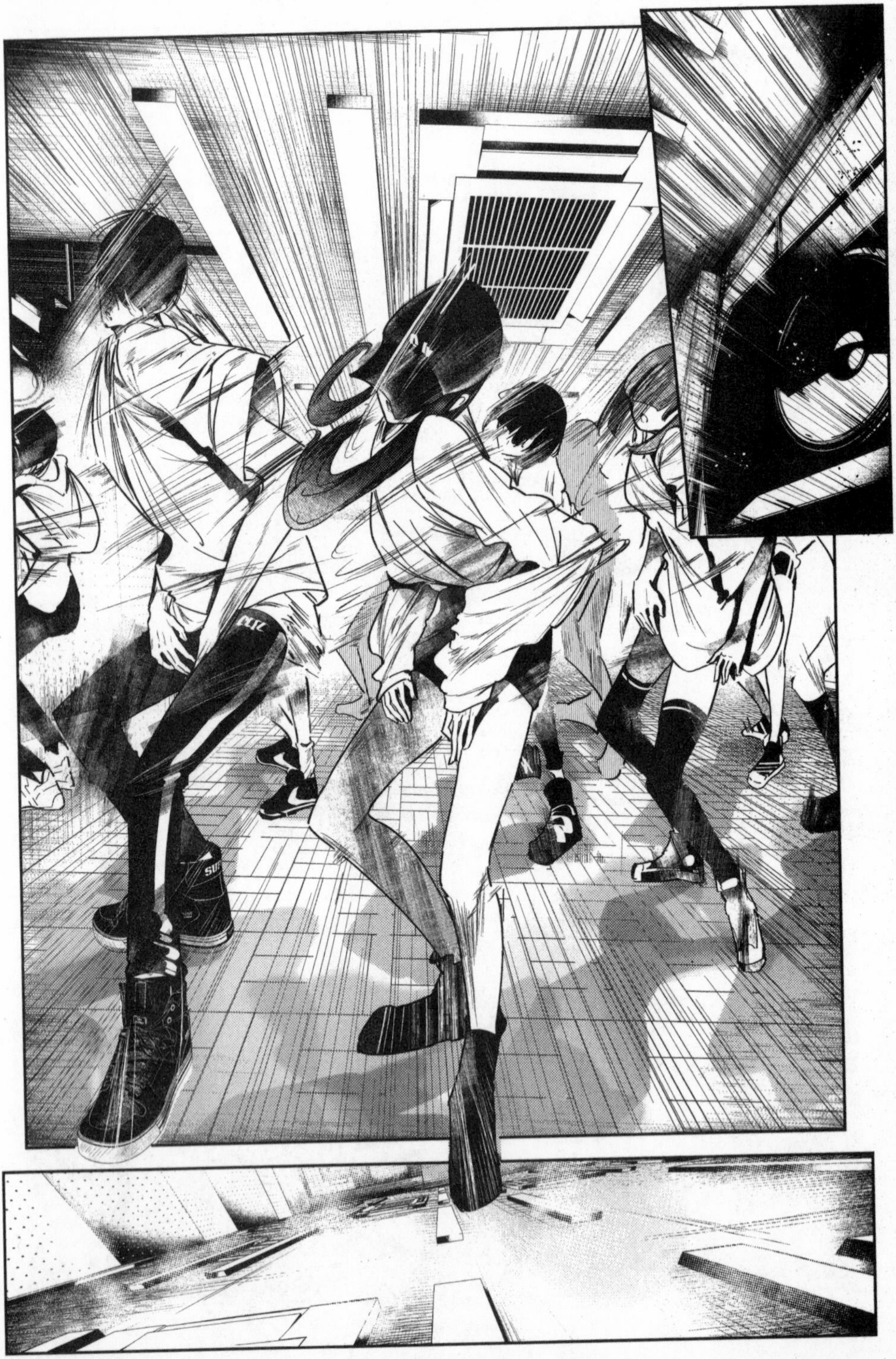

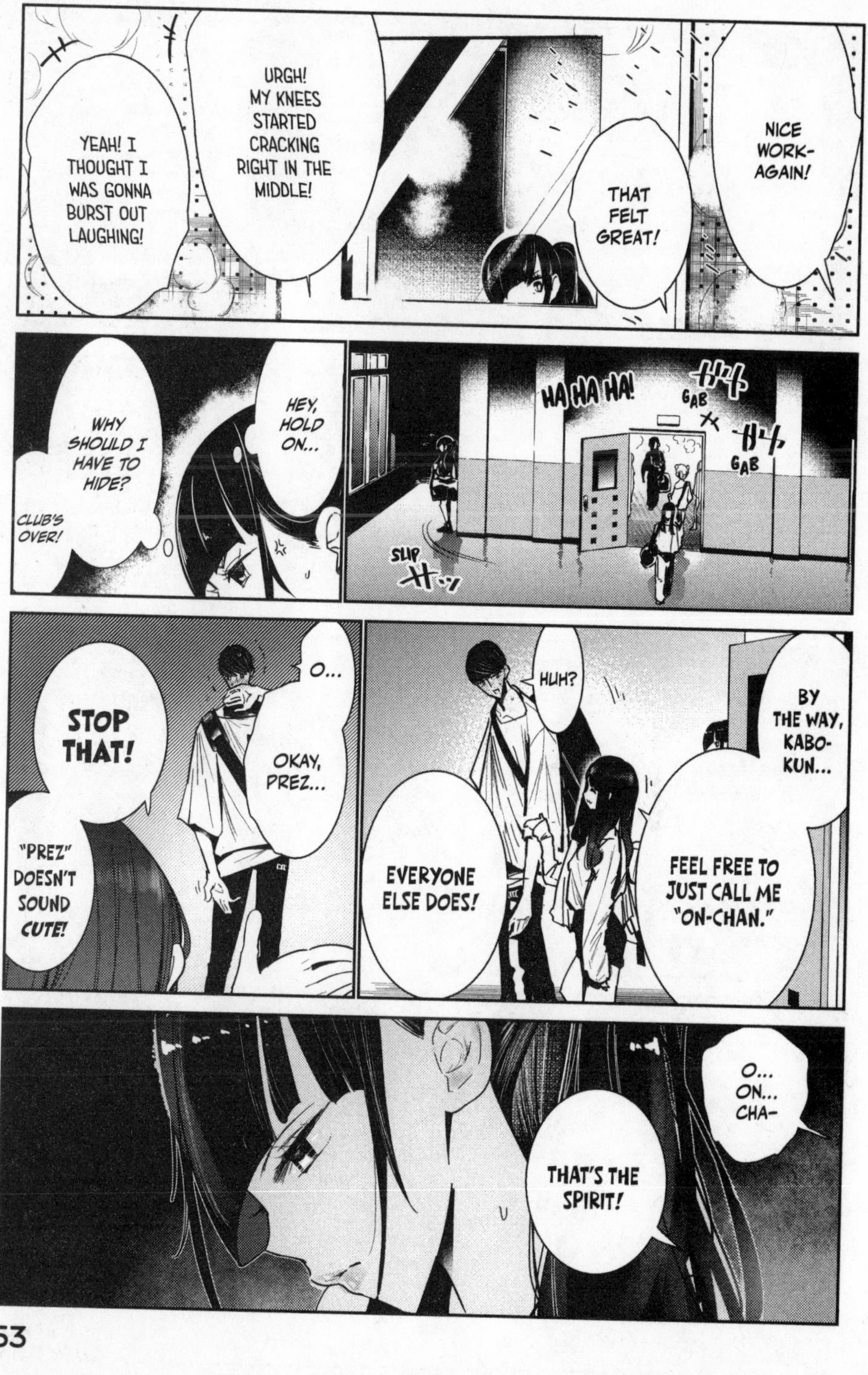
NICE WORK- AGAIN!
THAT FELT GREAT!
URGH! MY KNEES STARTED CRACKING RIGHT IN THE MIDDLE!
YEAH! I THOUGHT I WAS GONNA BURST OUT LAUGHING!
HA HA HA!
GAB
GAB
SLIP
HEY, HOLD ON...
WHY SHOULD I HAVE TO HIDE?
CLUB'S OVER!
BY THE WAY, KABO-KUN...
FEEL FREE TO JUST CALL ME "ON-CHAN."
HUH?
EVERYONE ELSE DOES!
O...
OKAY, PREZ...
STOP THAT!
"PREZ" DOESN'T SOUND CUTE!
O... ON... CHA-
THAT'S THE SPIRIT!

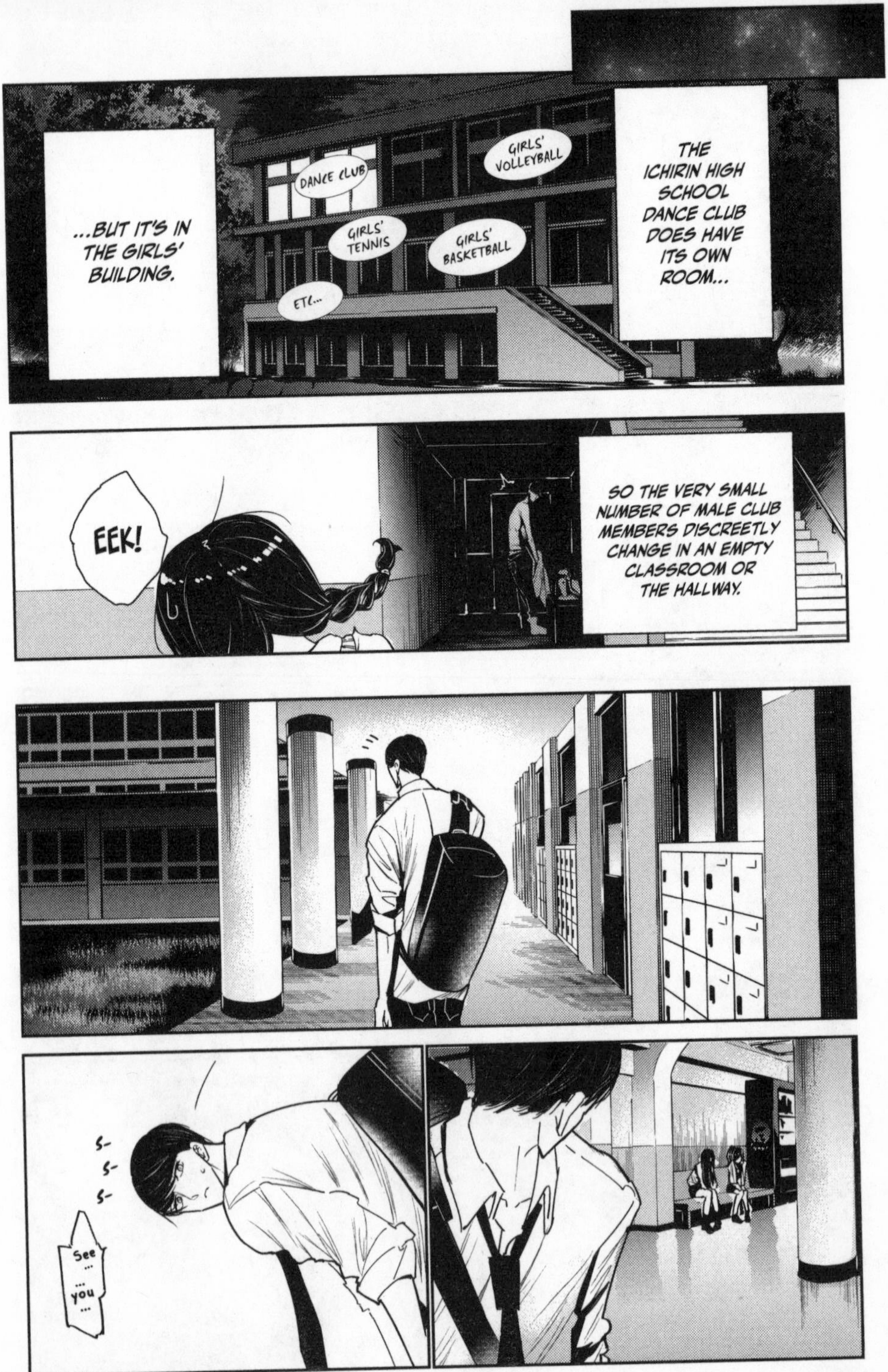
THE ICHIRIN HIGH SCHOOL DANCE CLUB DOES HAVE ITS OWN ROOM...
GIRLS' VOLLEYBALL
DANCE CLUB
GIRLS' BASKETBALL
GIRLS' TENNIS
ETC...
...BUT IT'S IN THE GIRLS' BUILDING.
SO THE VERY SMALL NUMBER OF MALE CLUB MEMBERS DISCREETLY CHANGE IN AN EMPTY CLASSROOM OR THE HALLWAY.
EEK!
S-
S-
S-
See... ...you...

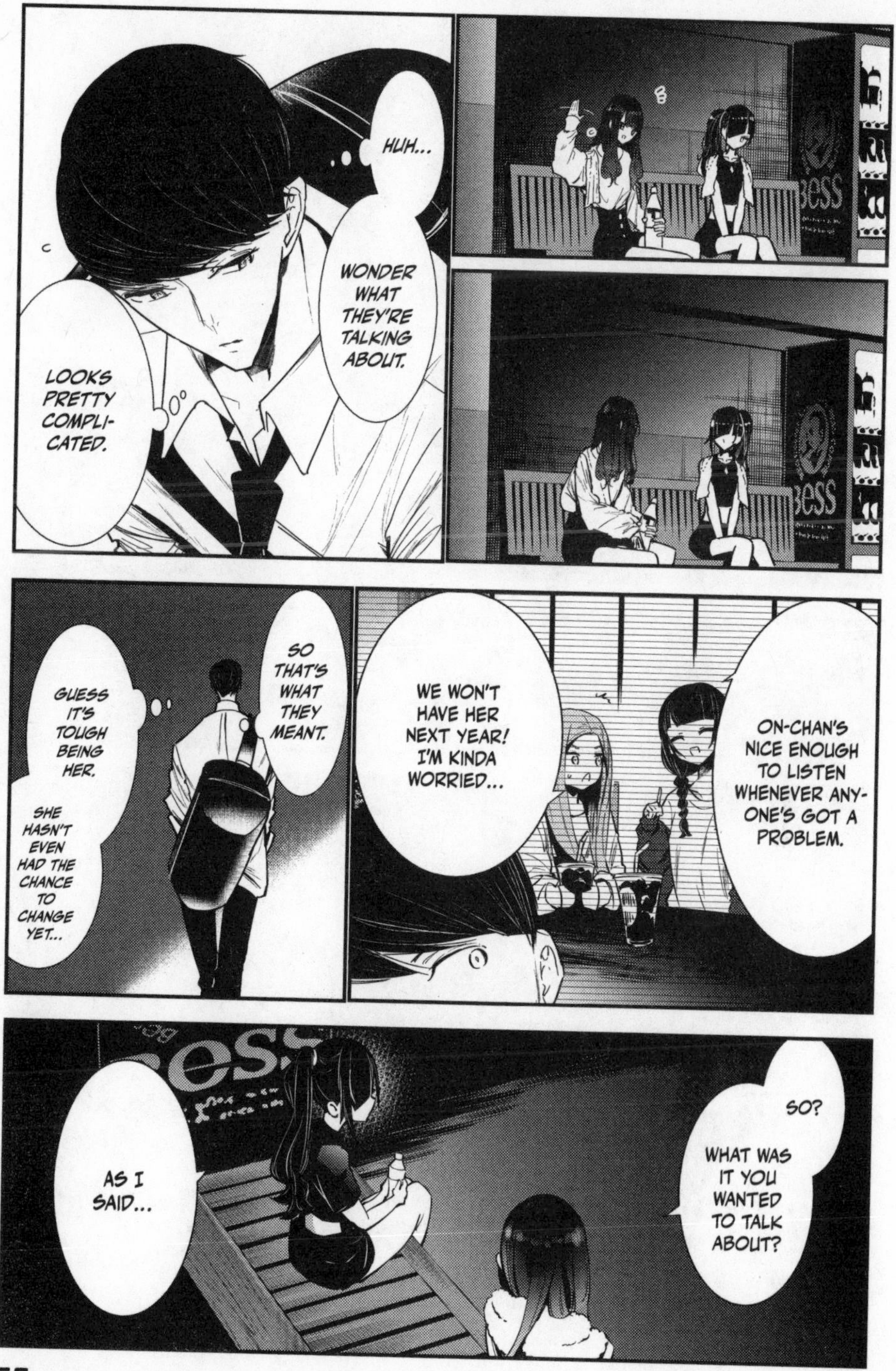
HUH...
WONDER WHAT THEY'RE TALKING ABOUT.
LOOKS PRETTY COMPLICATED.
ON-CHAN'S NICE ENOUGH TO LISTEN WHENEVER ANYONE'S GOT A PROBLEM.
WE WON'T HAVE HER NEXT YEAR! I'M KINDA WORRIED...
SO THAT'S WHAT THEY MEANT.
GUESS IT'S TOUGH BEING HER.
SHE HASN'T EVEN HAD THE CHANCE TO CHANGE YET...
SO?
WHAT WAS IT YOU WANTED TO TALK ABOUT?
AS I SAID...

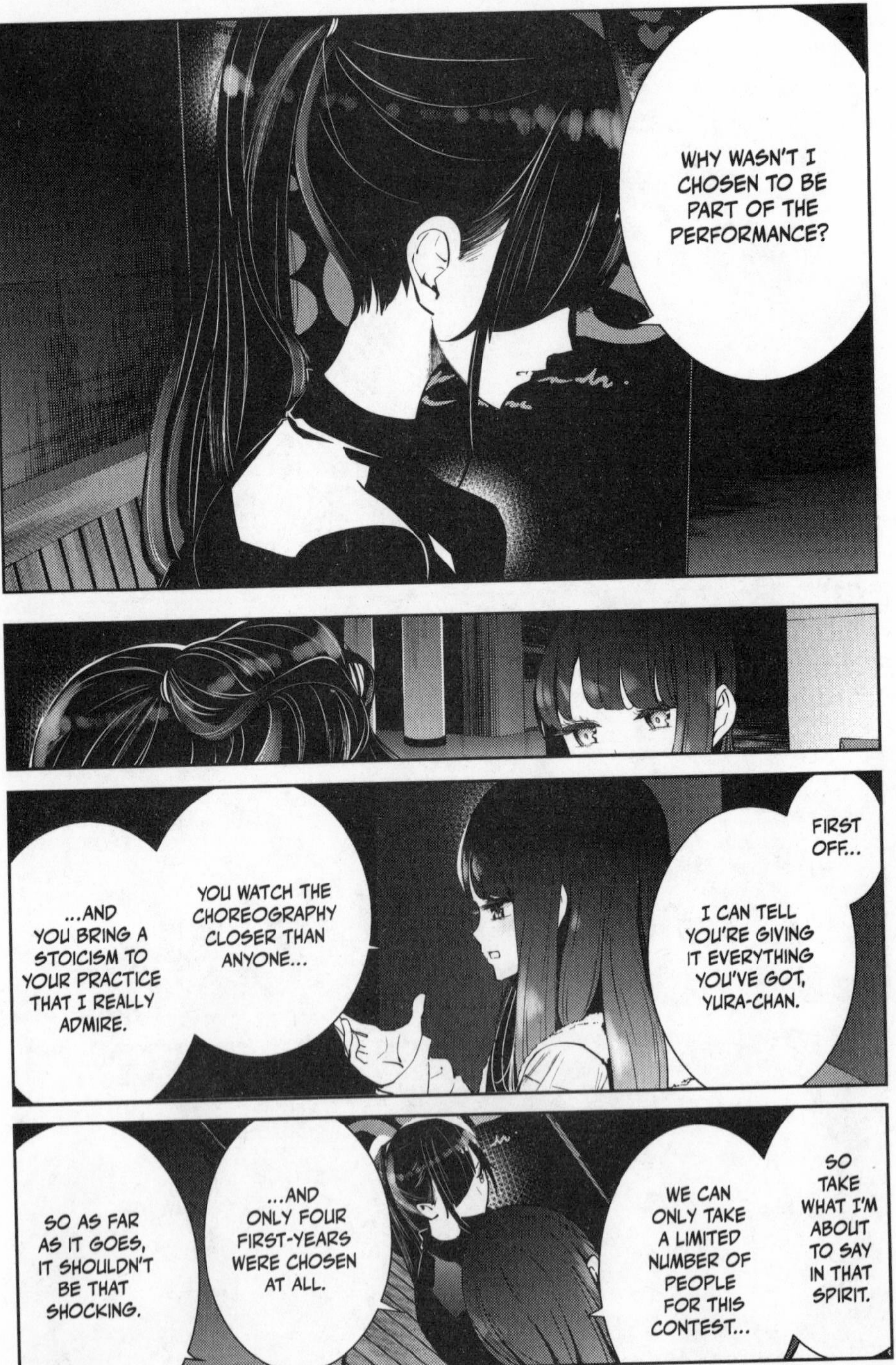
WHY WASN'T I CHOSEN TO BE PART OF THE PERFORMANCE?
FIRST OFF...
I CAN TELL YOU'RE GIVING IT EVERYTHING YOU'VE GOT, YURA-CHAN.
YOU WATCH THE CHOREOGRAPHY CLOSER THAN ANYONE...
...AND YOU BRING A STOICISM TO YOUR PRACTICE THAT I REALLY ADMIRE.
SO TAKE WHAT I'M ABOUT TO SAY IN THAT SPIRIT.
WE CAN ONLY TAKE A LIMITED NUMBER OF PEOPLE FOR THIS CONTEST...
...AND ONLY FOUR FIRST-YEARS WERE CHOSEN AT ALL.
SO AS FAR AS IT GOES, IT SHOULDN'T BE THAT SHOCKING.

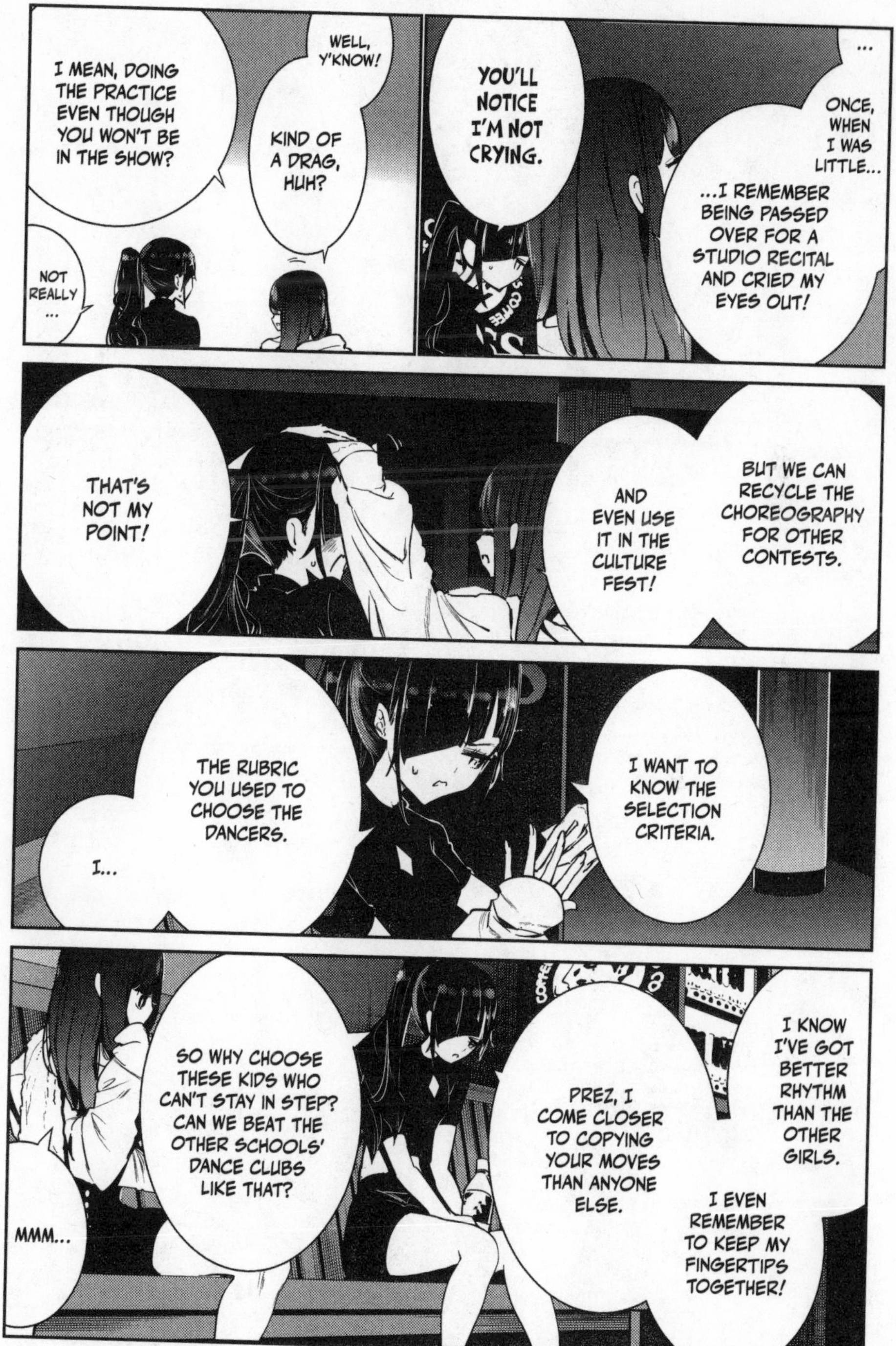
...
ONCE, WHEN I WAS LITTLE...
...I REMEMBER BEING PASSED OVER FOR A STUDIO RECITAL AND CRIED MY EYES OUT!
YOU'LL NOTICE I'M NOT CRYING.
WELL, Y'KNOW!
KIND OF A DRAG, HUH?
I MEAN, DOING THE PRACTICE EVEN THOUGH YOU WON'T BE IN THE SHOW?
NOT REALLY ...
BUT WE CAN RECYCLE THE CHOREOGRAPHY FOR OTHER CONTESTS.
AND EVEN USE IT IN THE CULTURE FEST!
THAT'S NOT MY POINT!
I WANT TO KNOW THE SELECTION CRITERIA.
THE RUBRIC YOU USED TO CHOOSE THE DANCERS.
I...
I KNOW I'VE GOT BETTER RHYTHM THAN THE OTHER GIRLS.
I EVEN REMEMBER TO KEEP MY FINGERTIPS TOGETHER!
PREZ, I COME CLOSER TO COPYING YOUR MOVES THAN ANYONE ELSE.
SO WHY CHOOSE THESE KIDS WHO CAN'T STAY IN STEP? CAN WE BEAT THE OTHER SCHOOLS' DANCE CLUBS LIKE THAT?
MMM...

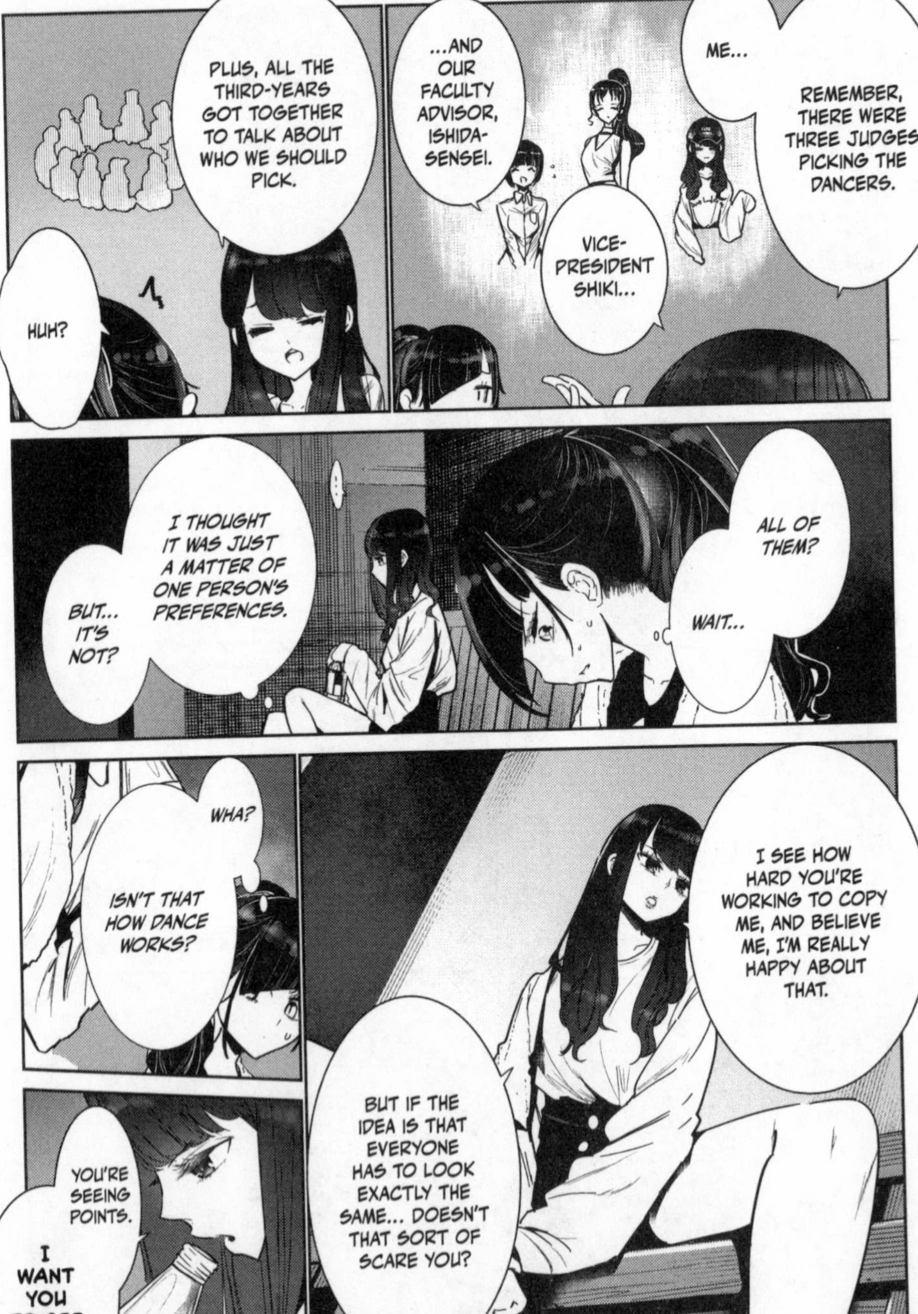
ME...
REMEMBER, THERE WERE THREE JUDGES PICKING THE DANCERS.
VICE-PRESIDENT SHIKI...
...AND OUR FACULTY ADVISOR, ISHIDA-SENSEI.
PLUS, ALL THE THIRD-YEARS GOT TOGETHER TO TALK ABOUT WHO WE SHOULD PICK.
HUH?
ALL OF THEM?
WAIT...
I THOUGHT IT WAS JUST A MATTER OF ONE PERSON'S PREFERENCES.
BUT... IT'S NOT?
I SEE HOW HARD YOU'RE WORKING TO COPY ME, AND BELIEVE ME, I'M REALLY HAPPY ABOUT THAT.
BUT IF THE IDEA IS THAT EVERYONE HAS TO LOOK EXACTLY THE SAME... DOESN'T THAT SORT OF SCARE YOU?
WHA?
ISN'T THAT HOW DANCE WORKS?
YOU'RE SEEING POINTS.
I WANT YOU TO SEE LINES.

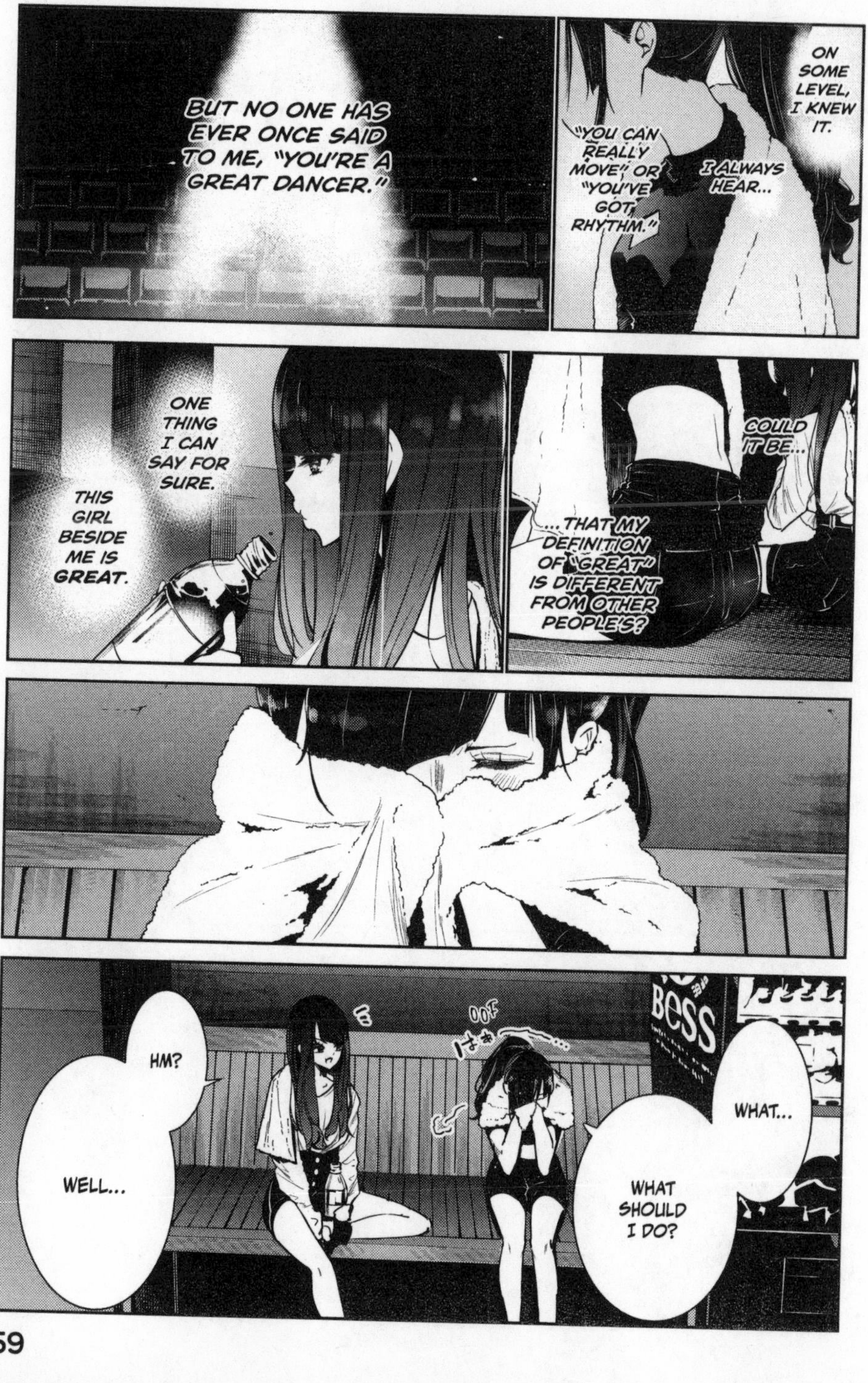
ON SOME LEVEL, I KNEW IT.
I ALWAYS HEAR...
"YOU CAN REALLY MOVE" OR "YOU'VE GOT RHYTHM."
BUT NO ONE HAS EVER ONCE SAID TO ME, "YOU'RE A GREAT DANCER."
COULD IT BE...
...THAT MY DEFINITION OF "GREAT" IS DIFFERENT FROM OTHER PEOPLE'S?
ONE THING I CAN SAY FOR SURE.
THIS GIRL BESIDE ME IS GREAT.
WHAT...
WHAT SHOULD I DO?
HM?
WELL...

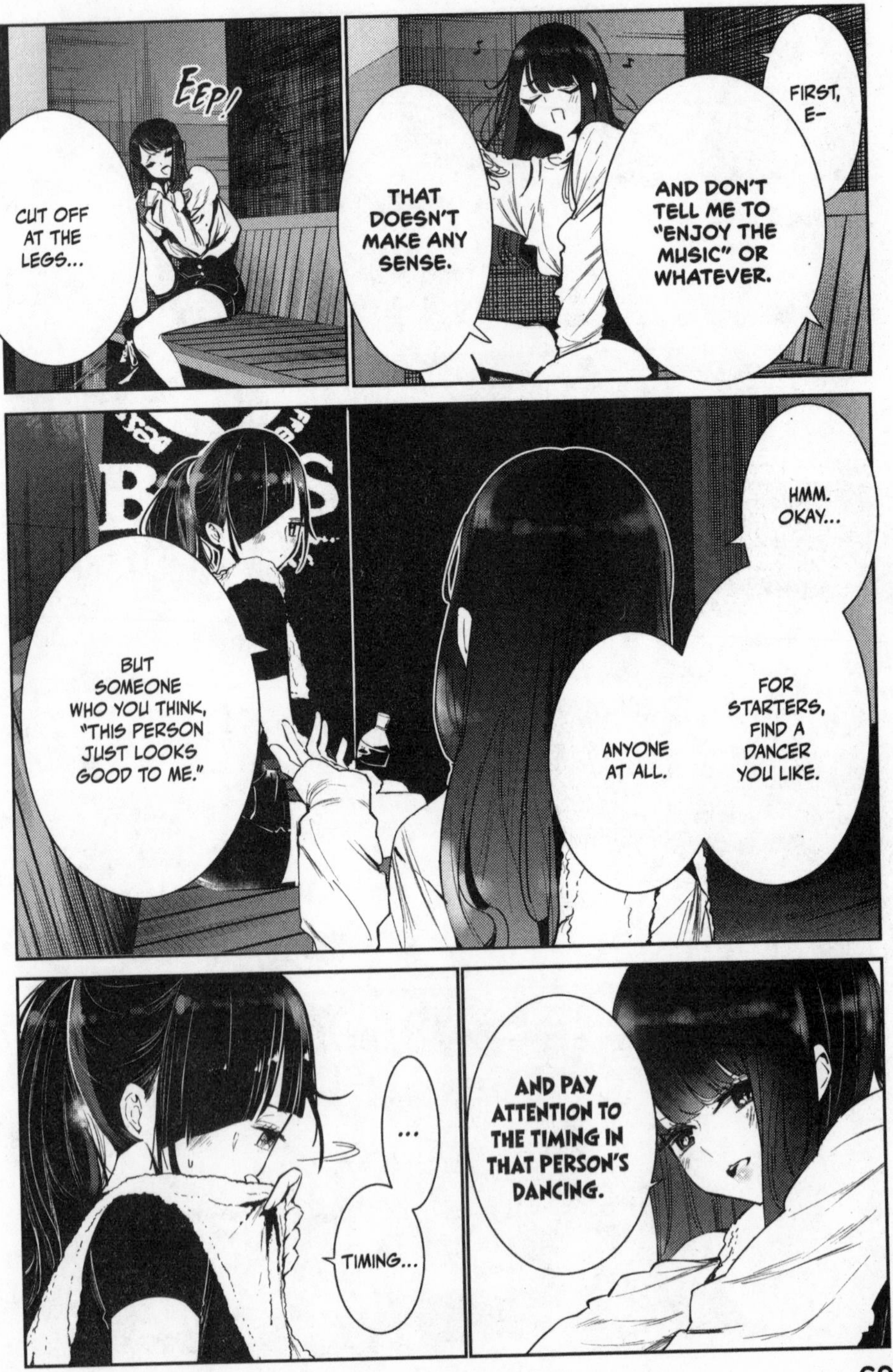
FIRST, E–
AND DON'T TELL ME TO "ENJOY THE MUSIC" OR WHATEVER.
THAT DOESN'T MAKE ANY SENSE.
EEP!
CUT OFF AT THE LEGS...
HMM. OKAY...
FOR STARTERS, FIND A DANCER YOU LIKE.
ANYONE AT ALL.
BUT SOMEONE WHO YOU THINK, "THIS PERSON JUST LOOKS GOOD TO ME."
AND PAY ATTENTION TO THE TIMING IN THAT PERSON'S DANCING.
...
TIMING...

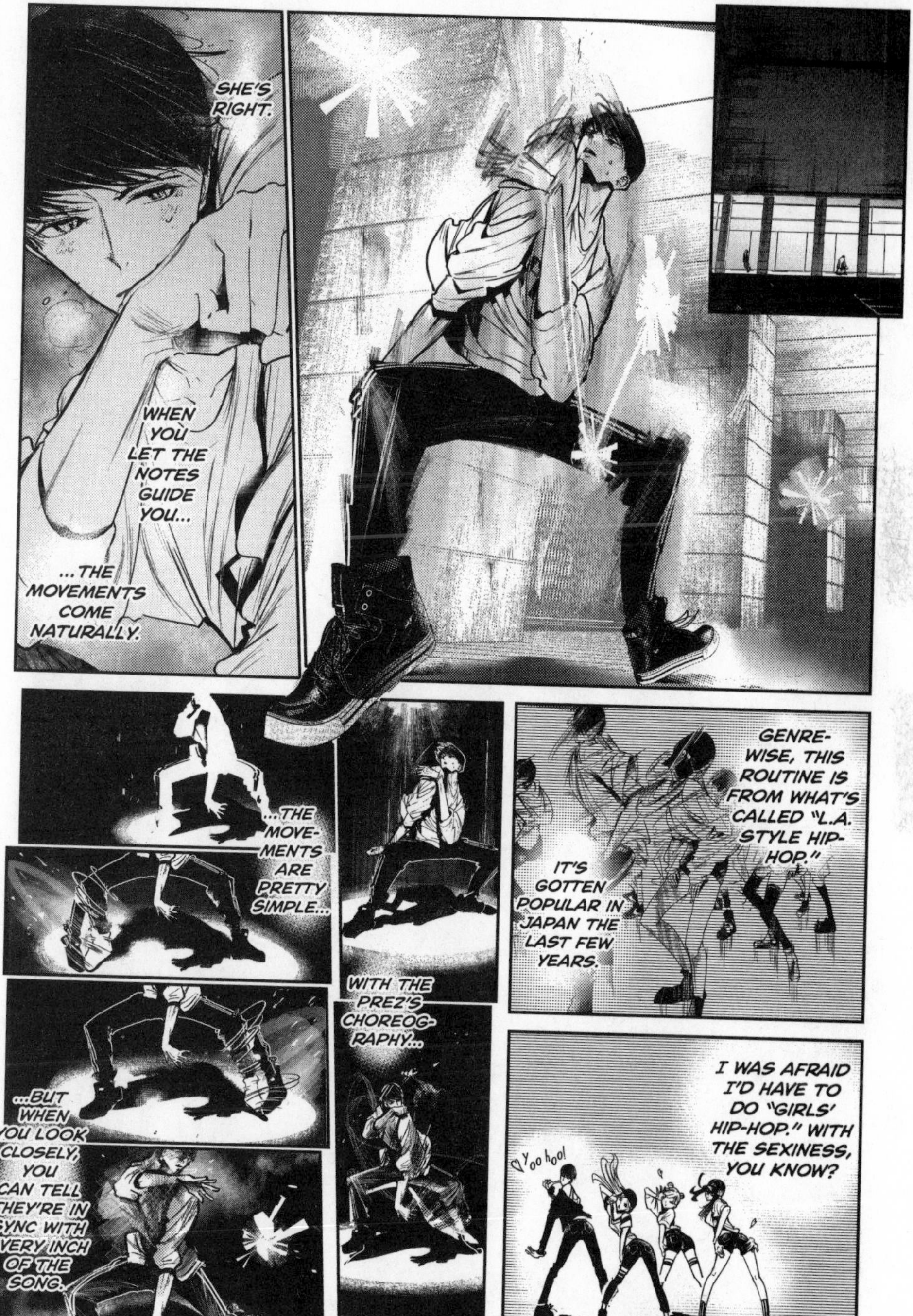
SHE'S RIGHT.
WHEN YOU LET THE NOTES GUIDE YOU...
...THE MOVEMENTS COME NATURALLY.
GENRE-WISE, THIS ROUTINE IS FROM WHAT'S CALLED "L.A. STYLE HIP-HOP."
IT'S GOTTEN POPULAR IN JAPAN THE LAST FEW YEARS.
I WAS AFRAID I'D HAVE TO DO "GIRLS' HIP-HOP." WITH THE SEXINESS, YOU KNOW?
Yoo hoo!
...THE MOVEMENTS ARE PRETTY SIMPLE...
WITH THE PREZ'S CHOREOGRAPHY...
...BUT WHEN YOU LOOK CLOSELY, YOU CAN TELL THEY'RE IN SYNC WITH EVERY INCH OF THE SONG.

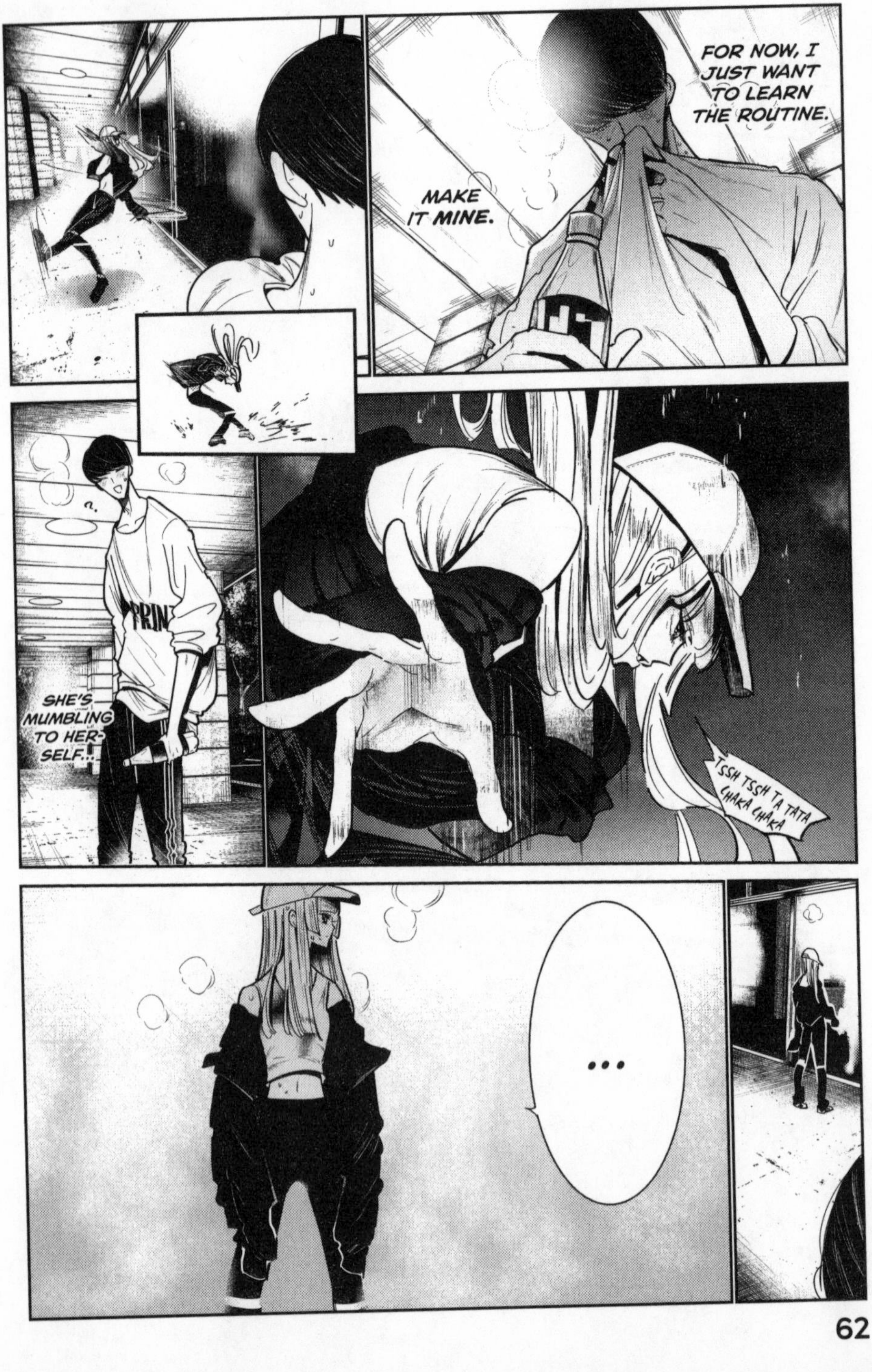
FOR NOW, I JUST WANT TO LEARN THE ROUTINE.
MAKE IT MINE.
TSSH TSSH TA TATA CHAKA CHAKA
SHE'S MUMBLING TO HER-SELF...
...

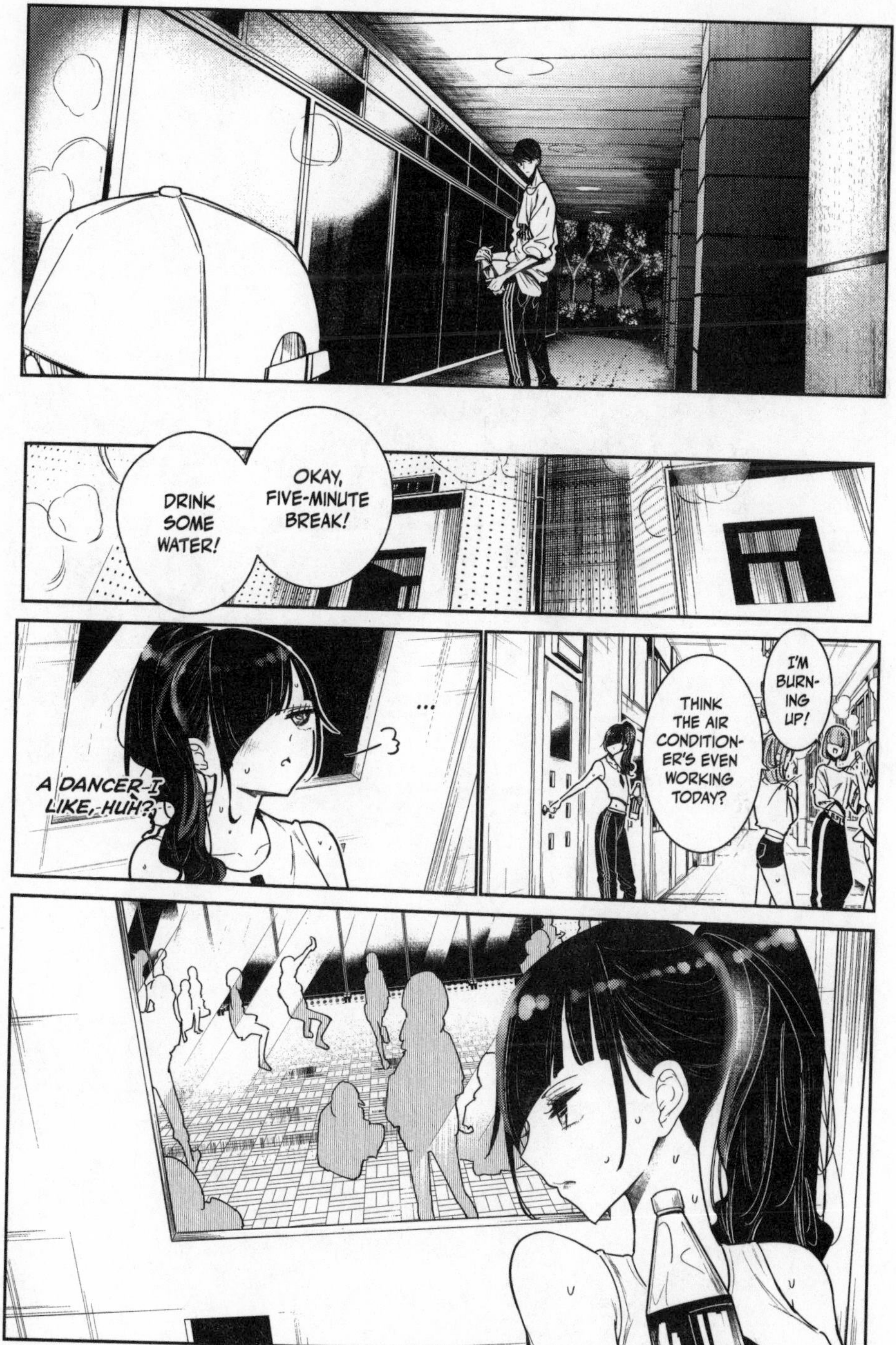
OKAY, FIVE-MINUTE BREAK!
DRINK SOME WATER!
I'M BURNING-UP!
THINK THE AIR CONDITIONER'S EVEN WORKING TODAY?
...
A DANCER I LIKE, HUH?

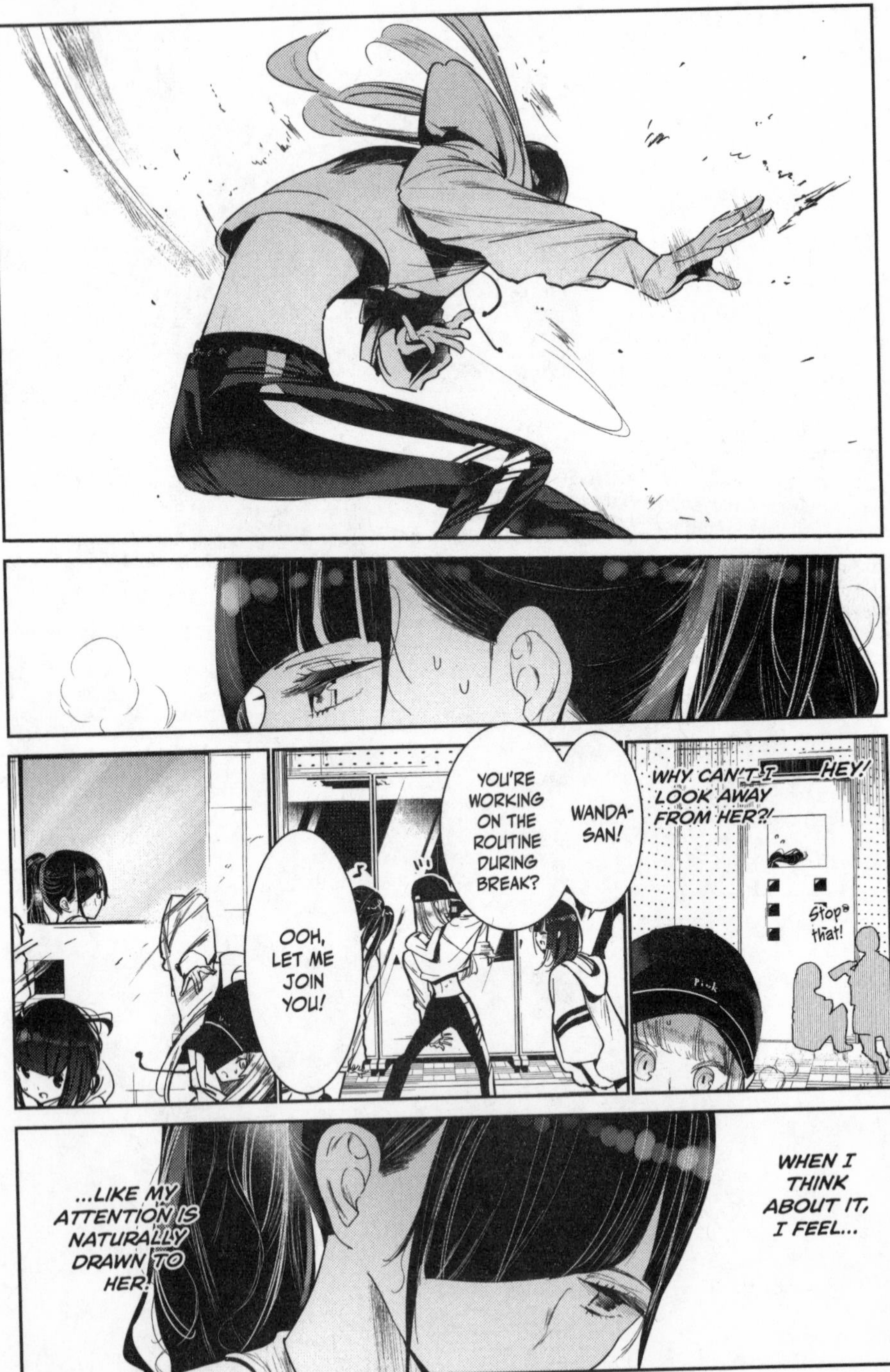
HEY!
WHY CAN'T I LOOK AWAY FROM HER?!
Stop that!
WANDA-SAN!
YOU'RE WORKING ON THE ROUTINE DURING BREAK?
OOH, LET ME JOIN YOU!
WHEN I THINK ABOUT IT, I FEEL...
...LIKE MY ATTENTION IS NATURALLY DRAWN TO HER!

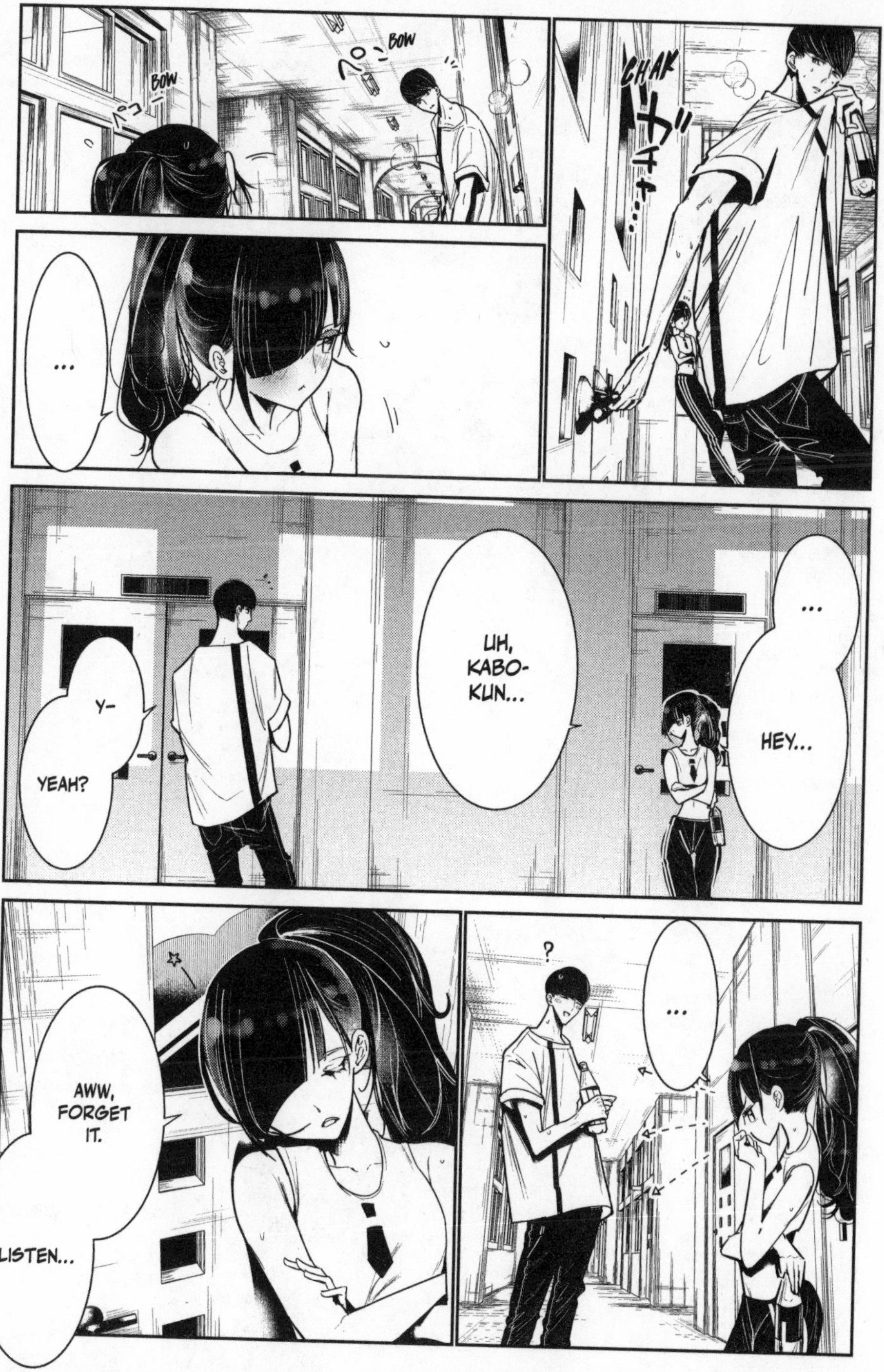
CHAK
ガチャ…
BOW
ぺこ
BOW
ぺこ
...
...
HEY...
UH, KABO-KUN...
Y- YEAH?
?
...
AWW, FORGET IT.
LISTEN...

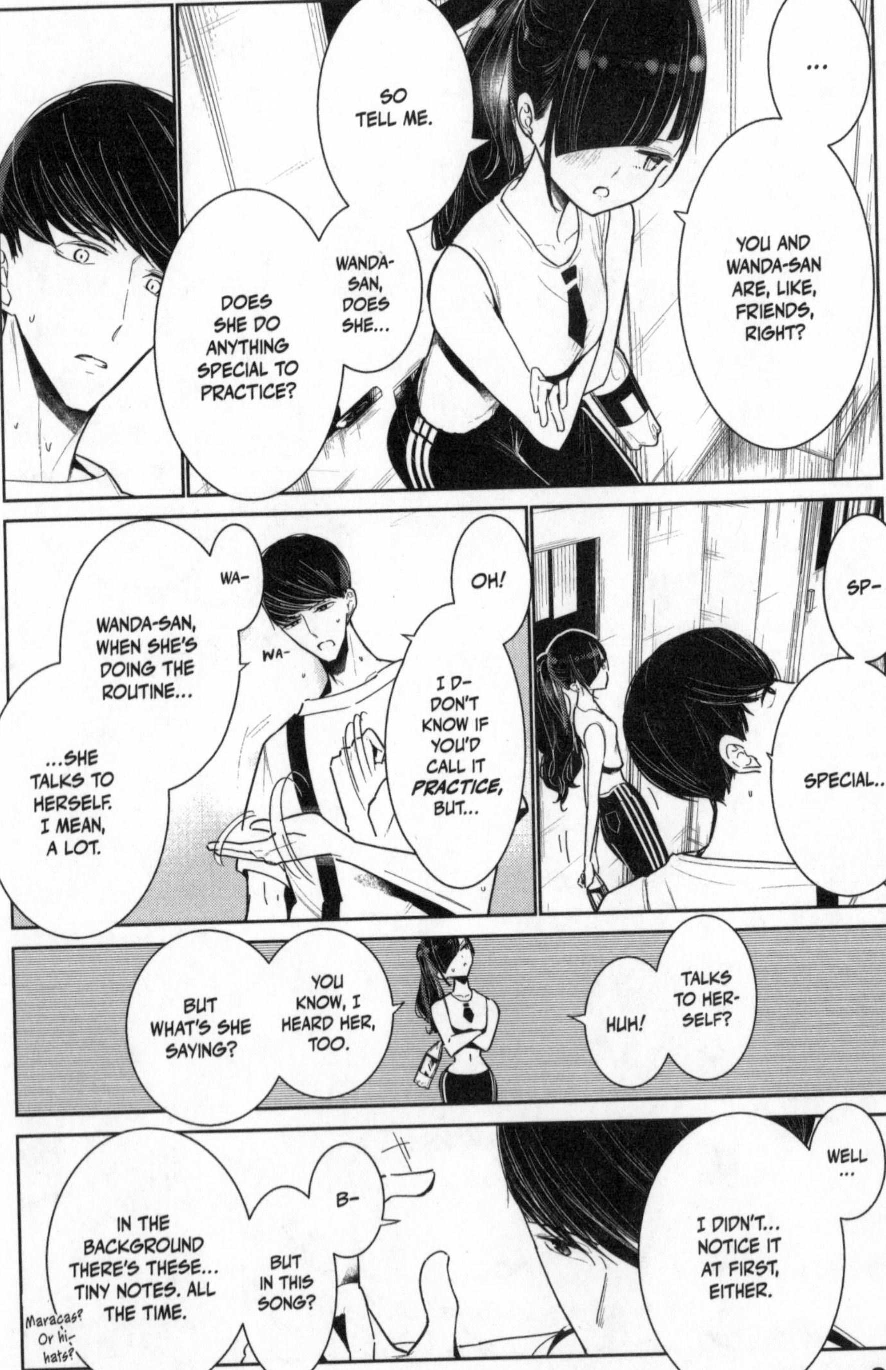
...
YOU AND WANDA-SAN ARE, LIKE, FRIENDS, RIGHT?
SO TELL ME.
WANDA-SAN, DOES SHE...
DOES SHE DO ANYTHING SPECIAL TO PRACTICE?
SP-
SPECIAL...
OH!
I D-DON'T KNOW IF YOU'D CALL IT *PRACTICE*, BUT...
WA-
WA-
WANDA-SAN, WHEN SHE'S DOING THE ROUTINE...
...SHE TALKS TO HERSELF. I MEAN, A LOT.
TALKS TO HER-SELF?
HUH!
YOU KNOW, I HEARD HER, TOO.
BUT WHAT'S SHE SAYING?
WELL ...
I DIDN'T... NOTICE IT AT FIRST, EITHER.
B-
BUT IN THIS SONG?
IN THE BACKGROUND THERE'S THESE... TINY NOTES. ALL THE TIME.
Maracas? Or hi-hats?

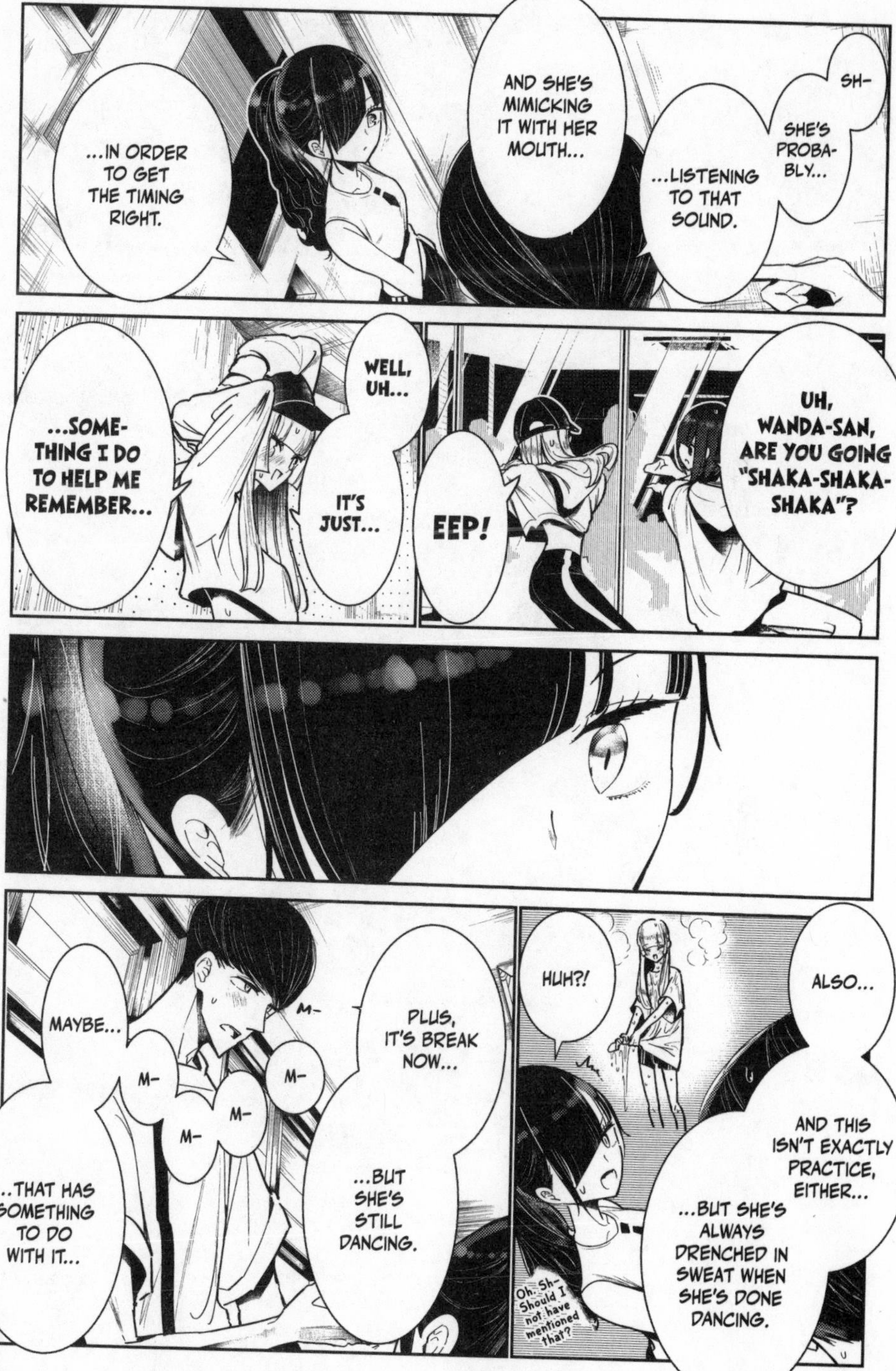
SH-
SHE'S PROBABLY...
...LISTENING TO THAT SOUND.
AND SHE'S MIMICKING IT WITH HER MOUTH...
...IN ORDER TO GET THE TIMING RIGHT.
UH, WANDA-SAN, ARE YOU GOING "SHAKA-SHAKA-SHAKA"?
EEP!
WELL, UH...
IT'S JUST...
...SOMETHING I DO TO HELP ME REMEMBER...
ALSO...
AND THIS ISN'T EXACTLY PRACTICE, EITHER...
HUH?!
...BUT SHE'S ALWAYS DRENCHED IN SWEAT WHEN SHE'S DONE DANCING.
Oh. Sh- Should I not have mentioned that?
PLUS, IT'S BREAK NOW...
M-
...BUT SHE'S STILL DANCING.
M-
MAYBE...
M-
M-
M-
...THAT HAS SOMETHING TO DO WITH IT...

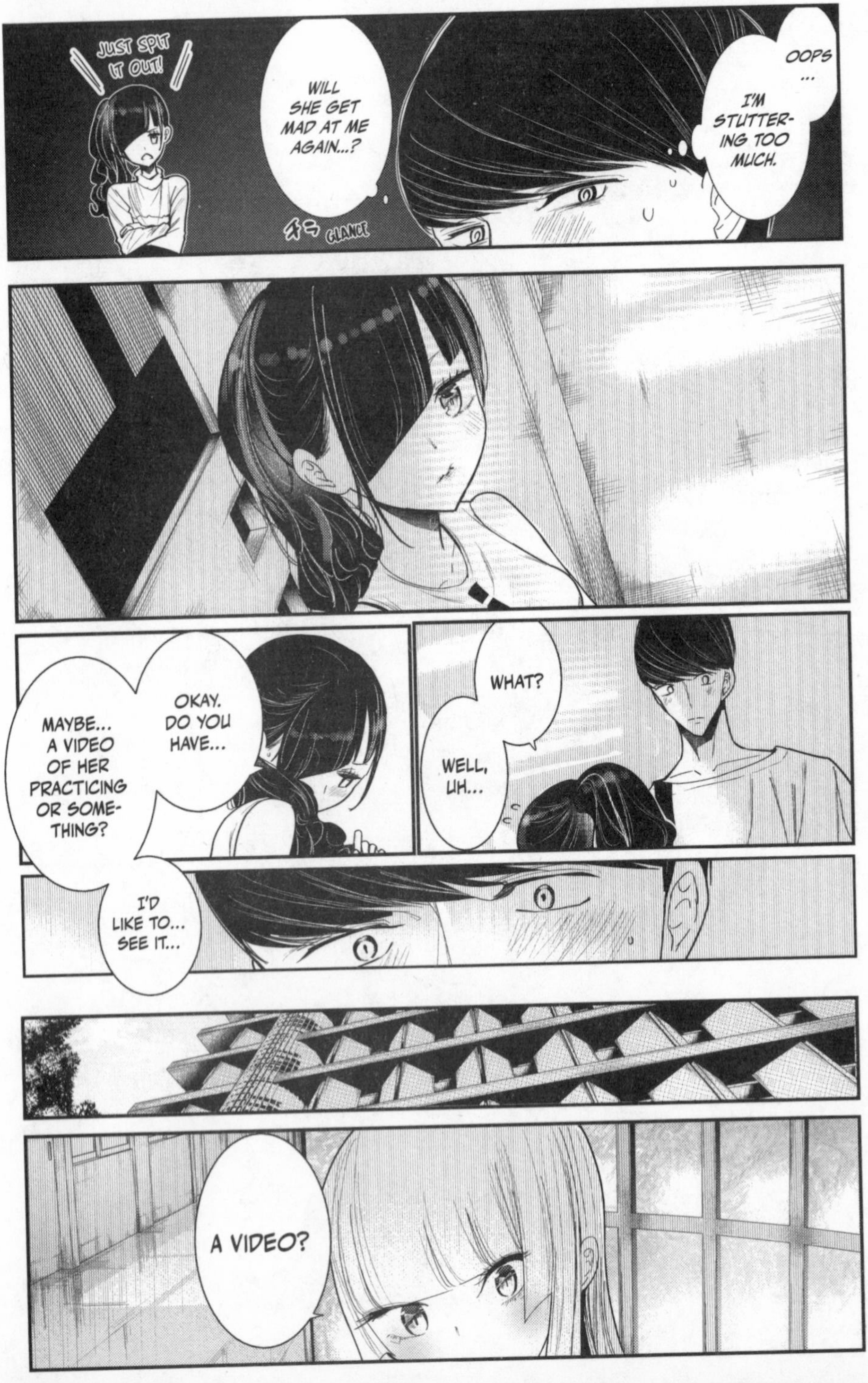
OOPS...
I'M STUTTERING TOO MUCH.
WILL SHE GET MAD AT ME AGAIN...?
GLANCE
JUST SPIT IT OUT!
WHAT?
WELL, UH...
OKAY. DO YOU HAVE...
MAYBE... A VIDEO OF HER PRACTICING OR SOMETHING?
I'D LIKE TO... SEE IT...
A VIDEO?

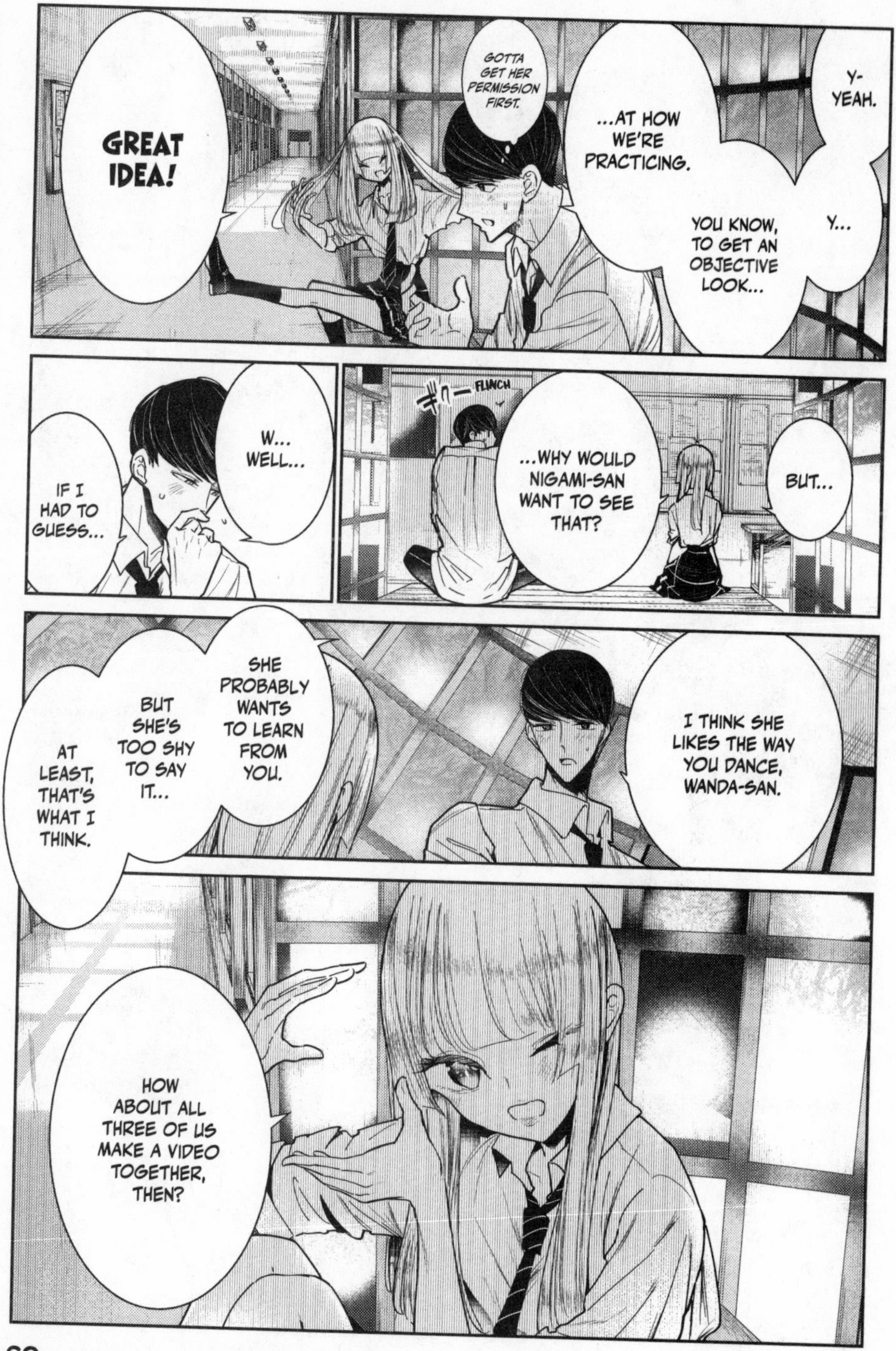
Y- YEAH.
Y...
...AT HOW WE'RE PRACTICING.
YOU KNOW, TO GET AN OBJECTIVE LOOK...
GOTTA GET HER PERMISSION FIRST.
GREAT IDEA!
BUT...
ギクー
FLINCH
...WHY WOULD NIGAMI-SAN WANT TO SEE THAT?
W... WELL...
IF I HAD TO GUESS...
I THINK SHE LIKES THE WAY YOU DANCE, WANDA-SAN.
SHE PROBABLY WANTS TO LEARN FROM YOU.
BUT SHE'S TOO SHY TO SAY IT...
AT LEAST, THAT'S WHAT I THINK.
HOW ABOUT ALL THREE OF US MAKE A VIDEO TOGETHER, THEN?

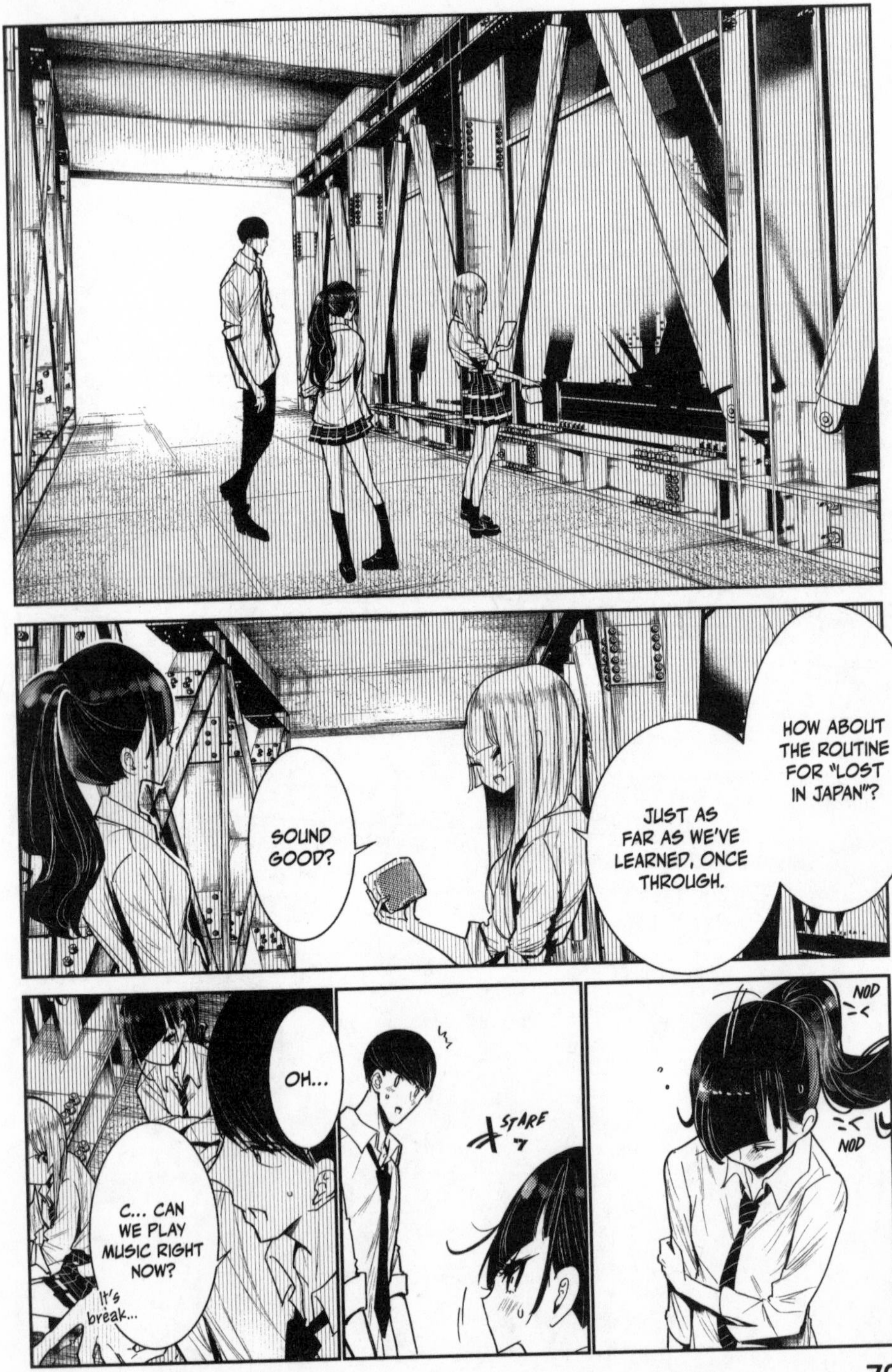
HOW ABOUT THE ROUTINE FOR "LOST IN JAPAN"?
JUST AS FAR AS WE'VE LEARNED, ONCE THROUGH.
SOUND GOOD?
NOD
NOD
STARE
OH...
C... CAN WE PLAY MUSIC RIGHT NOW?
It's break...

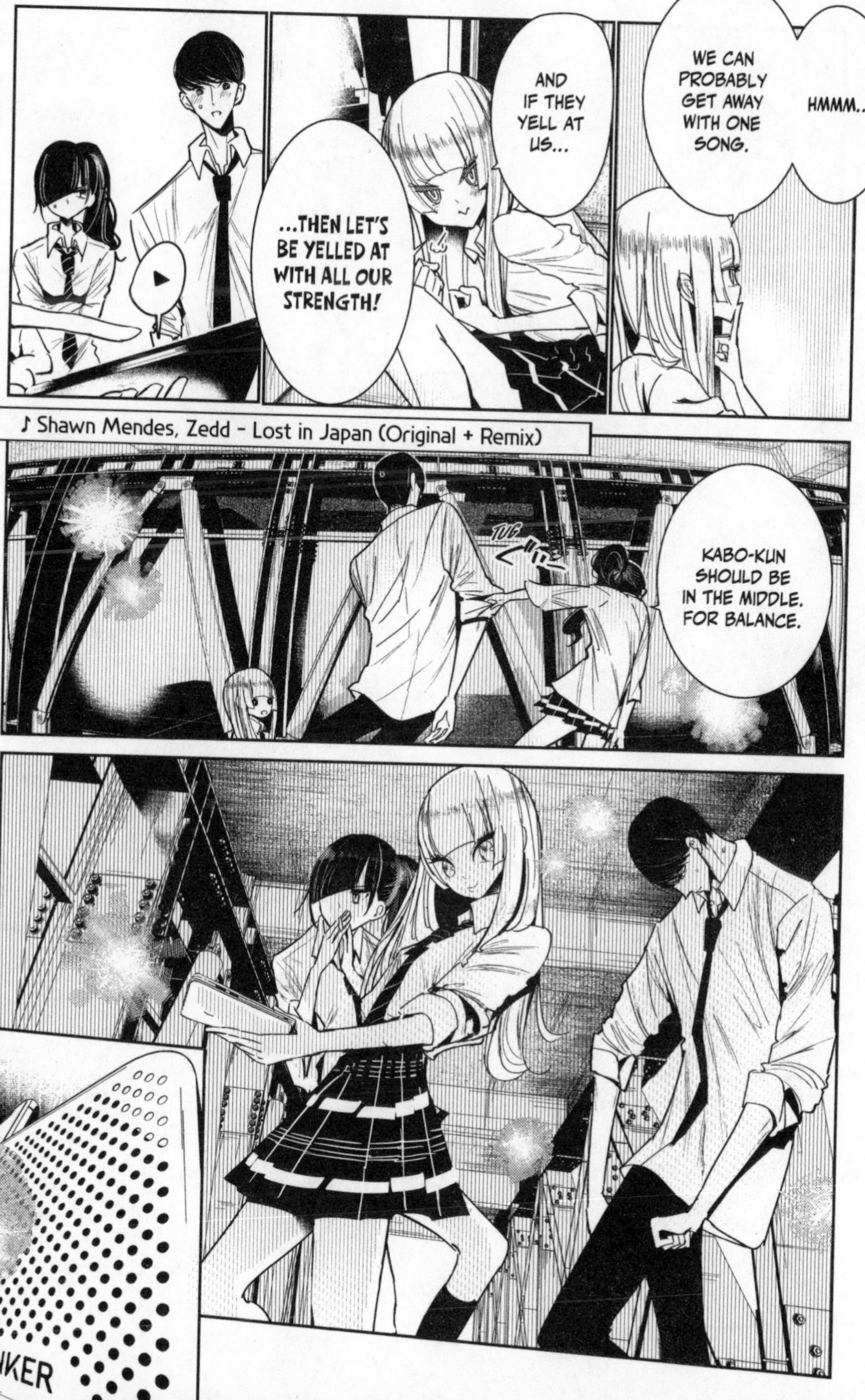
HMMM...
WE CAN PROBABLY GET AWAY WITH ONE SONG.
AND IF THEY YELL AT US...
...THEN LET'S BE YELLED AT WITH ALL OUR STRENGTH!
♪ Shawn Mendes, Zedd - Lost in Japan (Original + Remix)
KABO-KUN SHOULD BE IN THE MIDDLE. FOR BALANCE.
TUG
ANKER

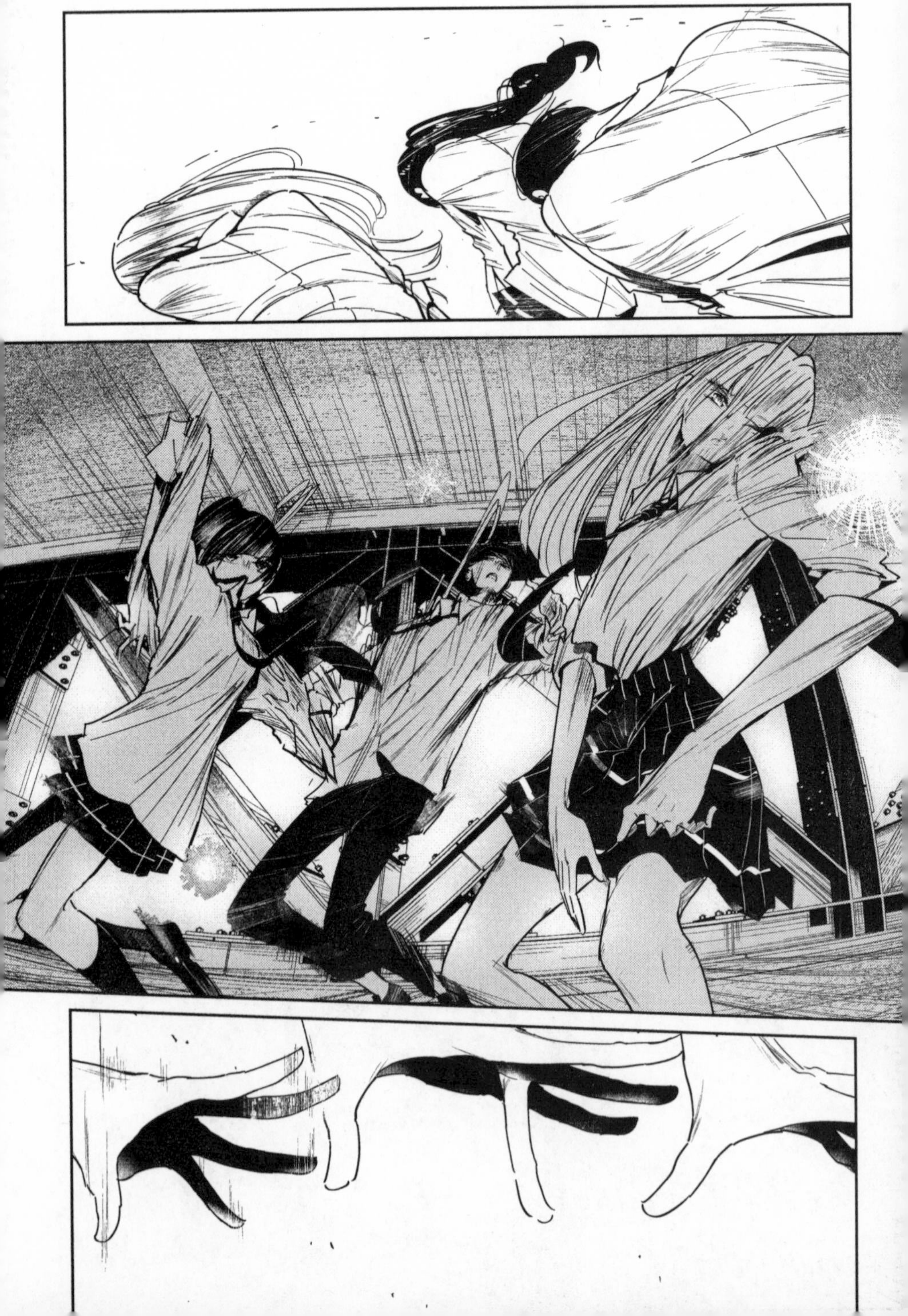

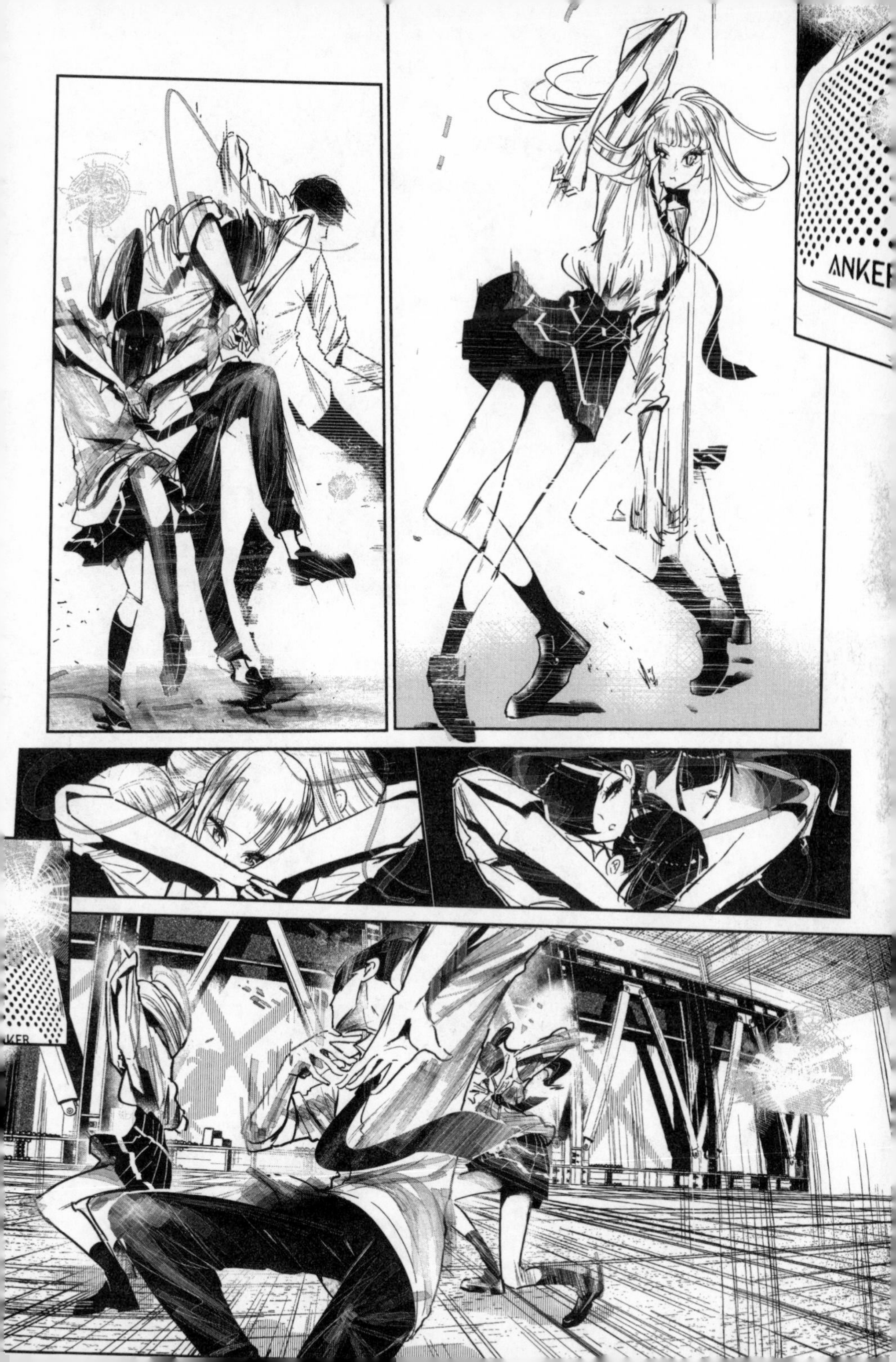

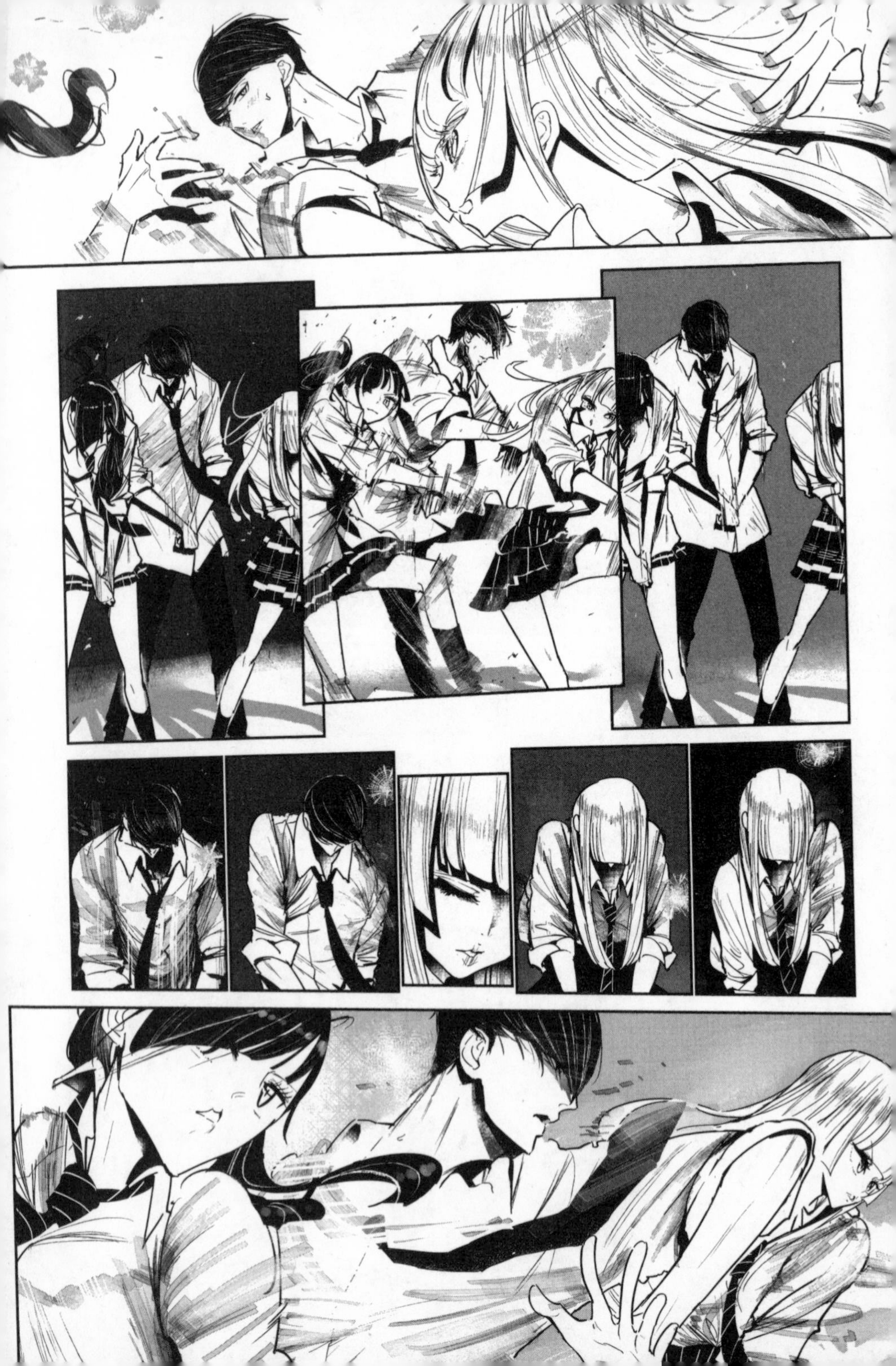

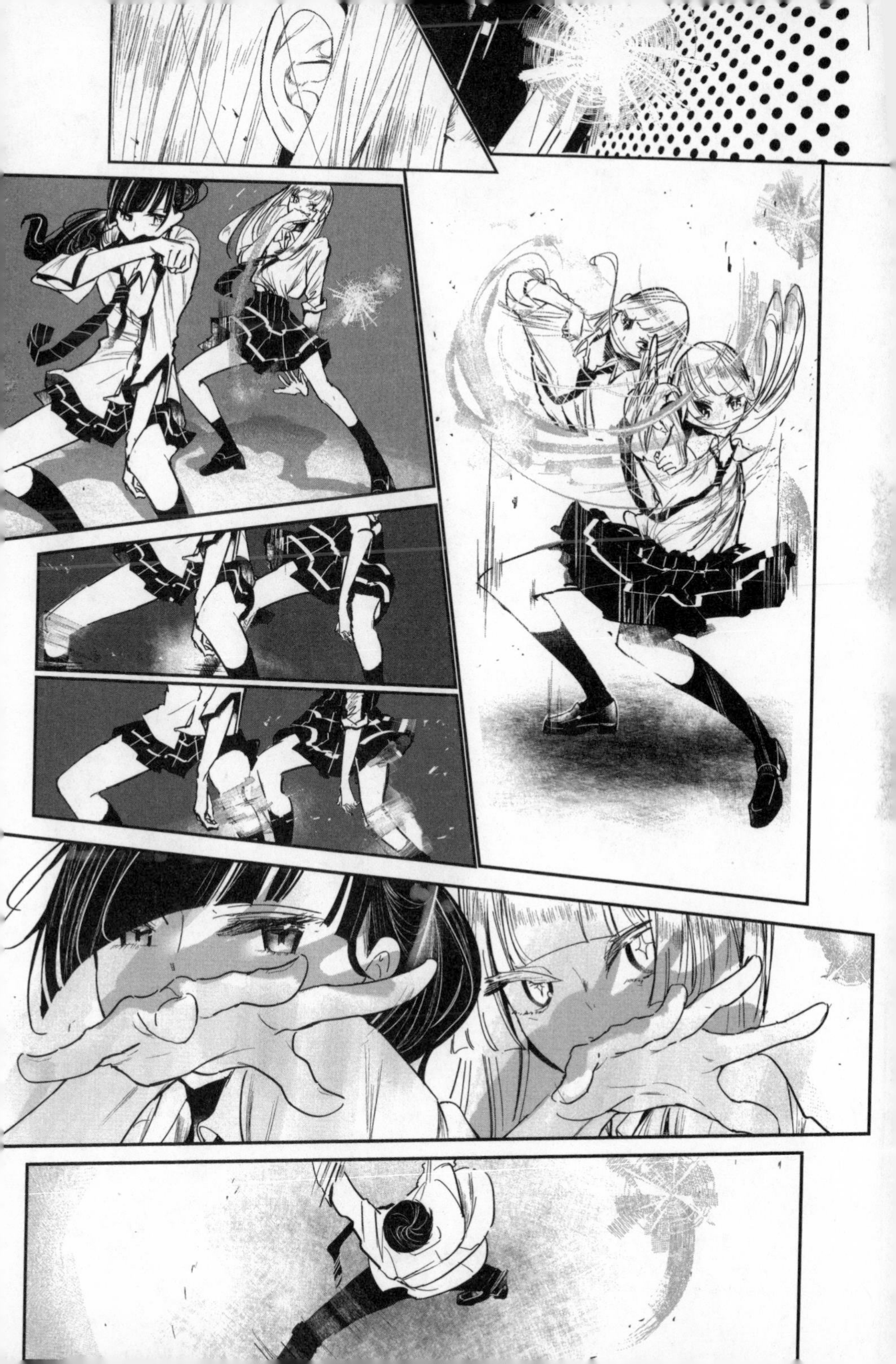

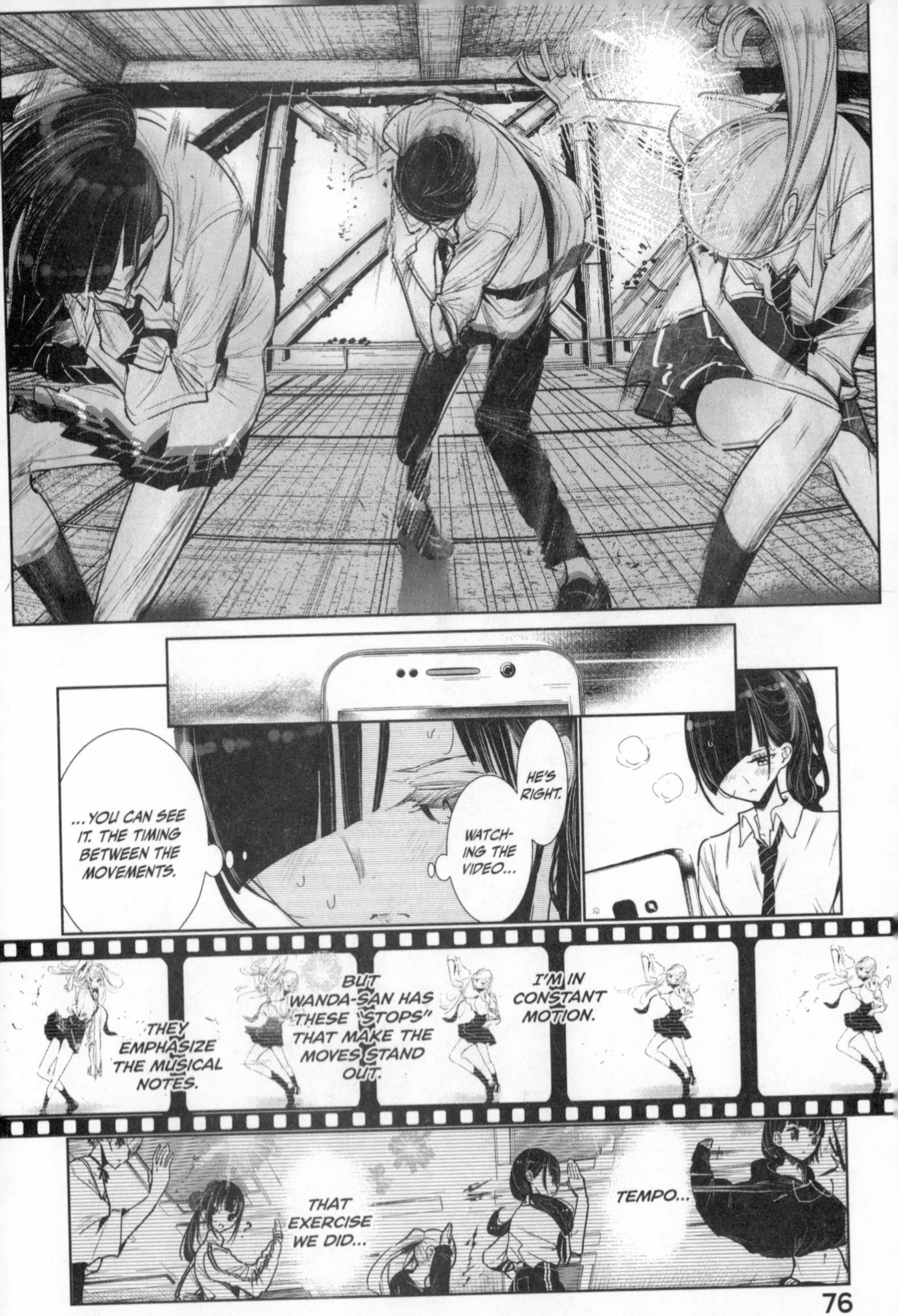
HE'S RIGHT.
WATCHING THE VIDEO...
...YOU CAN SEE IT. THE TIMING BETWEEN THE MOVEMENTS.
I'M IN CONSTANT MOTION.
BUT WANDA-SAN HAS THESE "STOPS" THAT MAKE THE MOVES STAND OUT.
THEY EMPHASIZE THE MUSICAL NOTES.
TEMPO...
THAT EXERCISE WE DID...

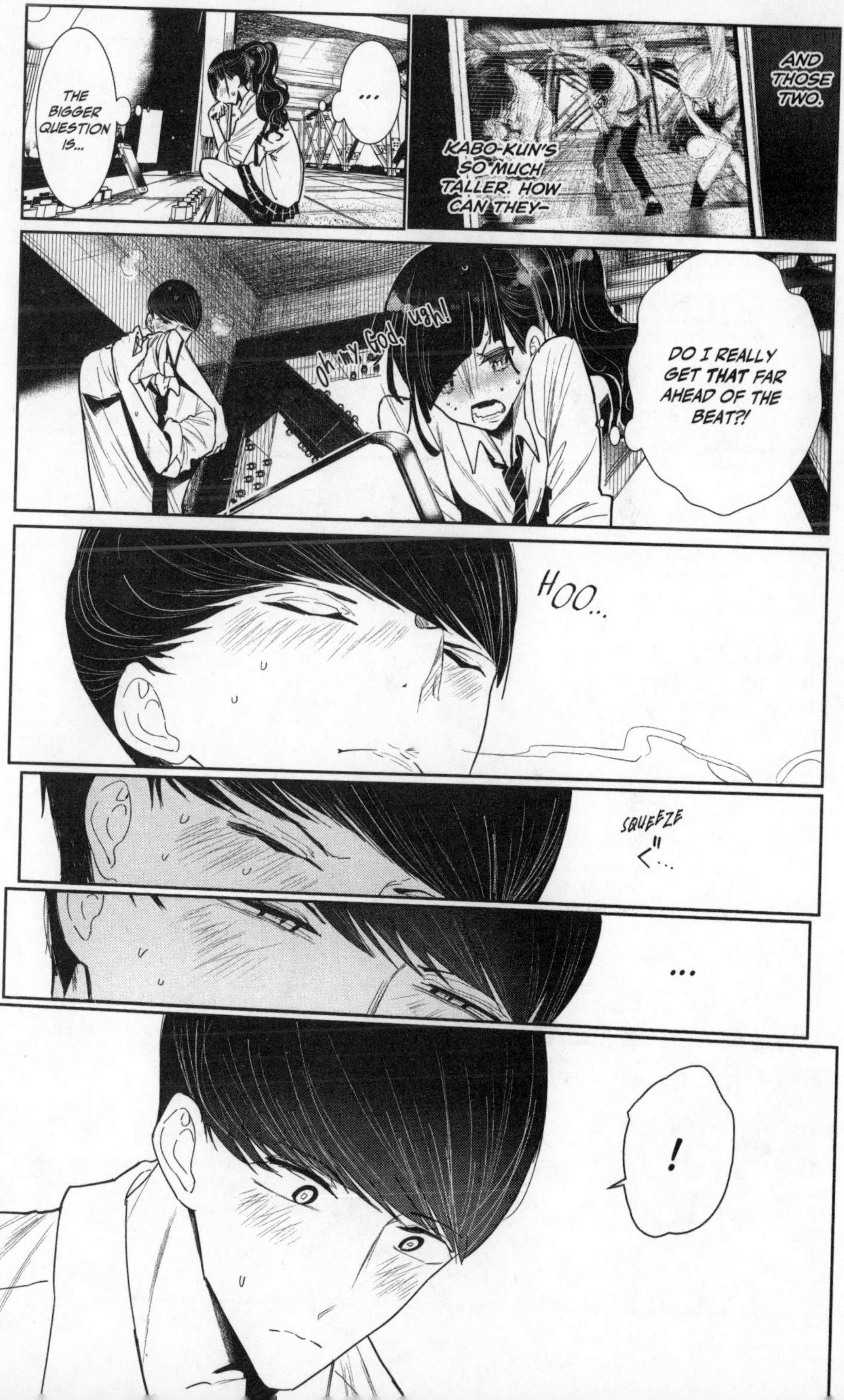
AND THOSE TWO.
KABO-KUN'S SO MUCH TALLER. HOW CAN THEY-
...
THE BIGGER QUESTION IS...
DO I REALLY GET THAT FAR AHEAD OF THE BEAT?!
oh my God, ugh!
HOO...
SQUEEZE
...
!

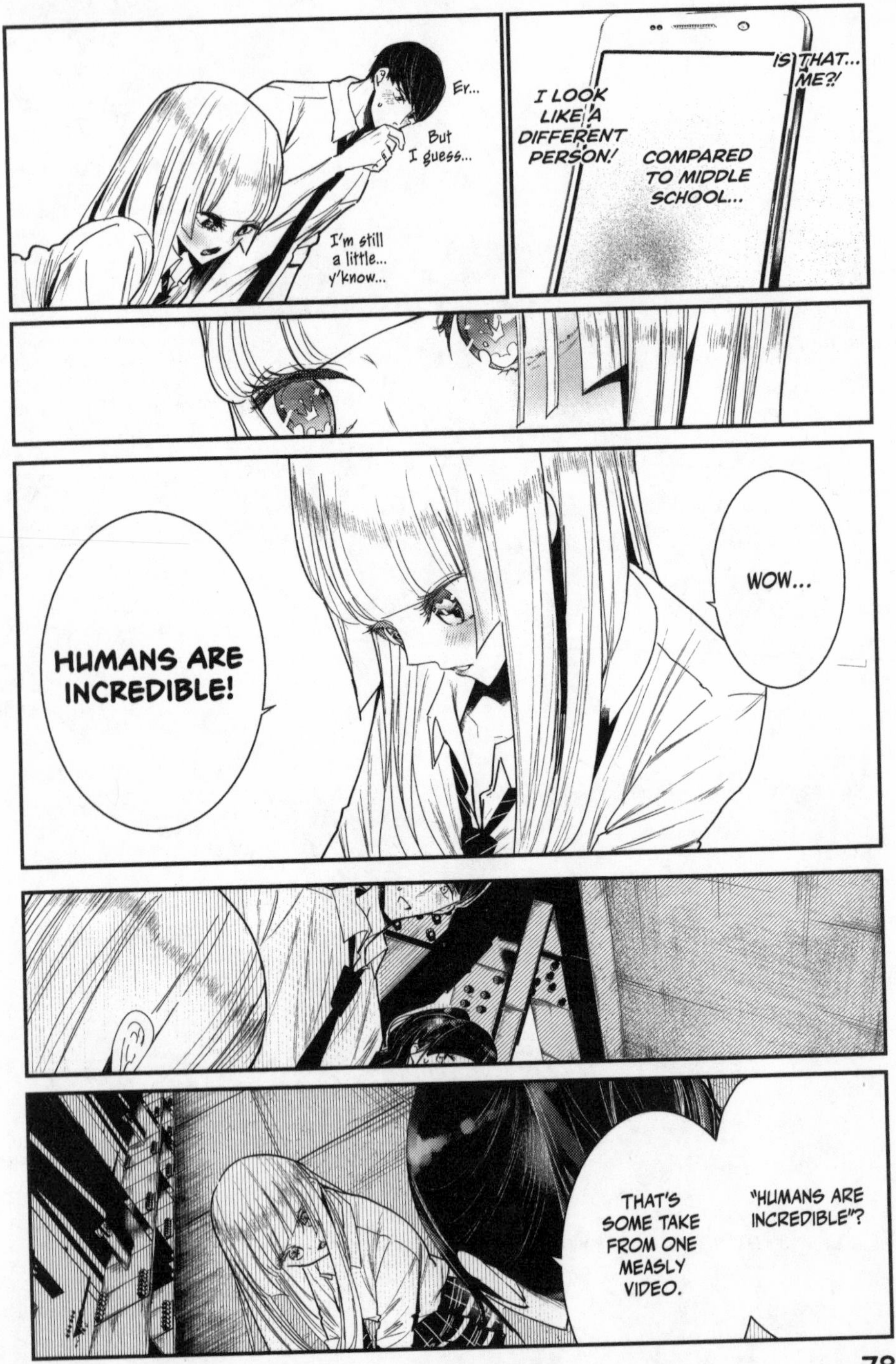
IS THAT... ME?!
I LOOK LIKE A DIFFERENT PERSON!
COMPARED TO MIDDLE SCHOOL...
Er...
But I guess...
I'm still a little... y'know...
WOW...
HUMANS ARE INCREDIBLE!
"HUMANS ARE INCREDIBLE"?
THAT'S SOME TAKE FROM ONE MEASLY VIDEO.

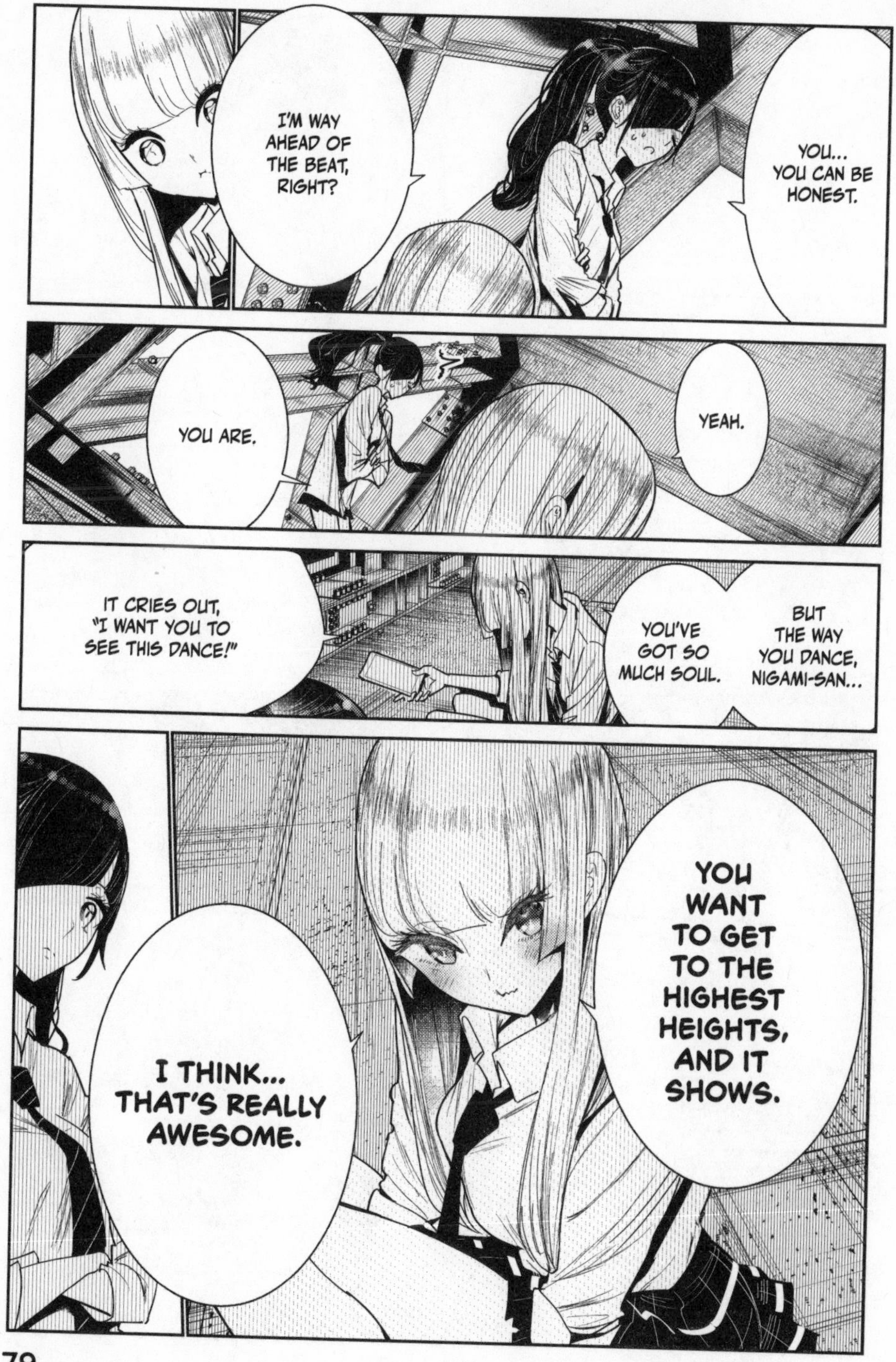
YOU... YOU CAN BE HONEST.
I'M WAY AHEAD OF THE BEAT, RIGHT?
YEAH.
YOU ARE.
BUT THE WAY YOU DANCE, NIGAMI-SAN...
YOU'VE GOT SO MUCH SOUL.
IT CRIES OUT, "I WANT YOU TO SEE THIS DANCE!"
YOU WANT TO GET TO THE HIGHEST HEIGHTS, AND IT SHOWS.
I THINK... THAT'S REALLY AWESOME.

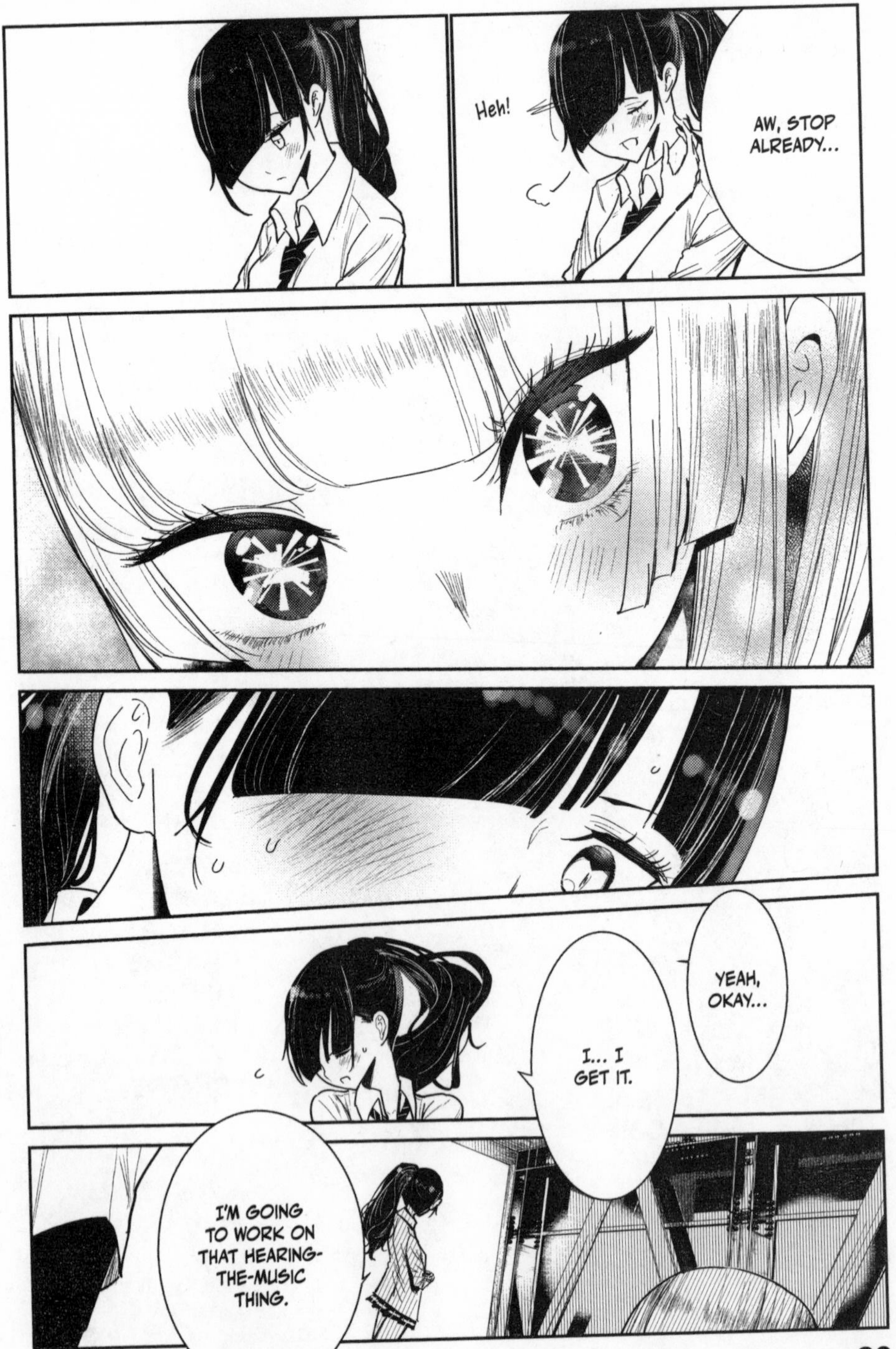
AW, STOP ALREADY...
Heh!
YEAH, OKAY...
I... I GET IT.
I'M GOING TO WORK ON THAT HEARING-THE-MUSIC THING.

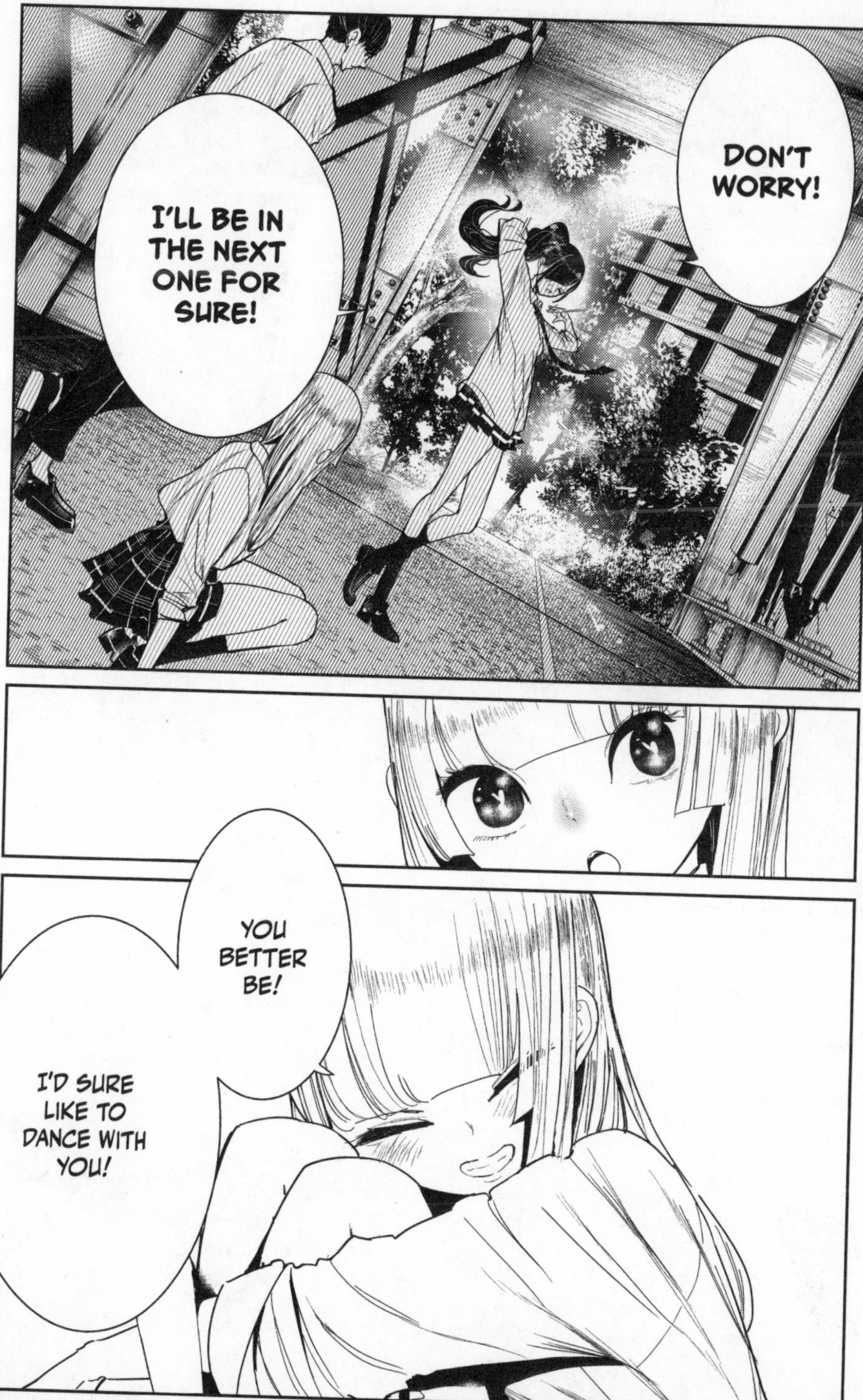
DON'T WORRY!
I'LL BE IN THE NEXT ONE FOR SURE!
YOU BETTER BE!
I'D SURE LIKE TO DANCE WITH YOU!

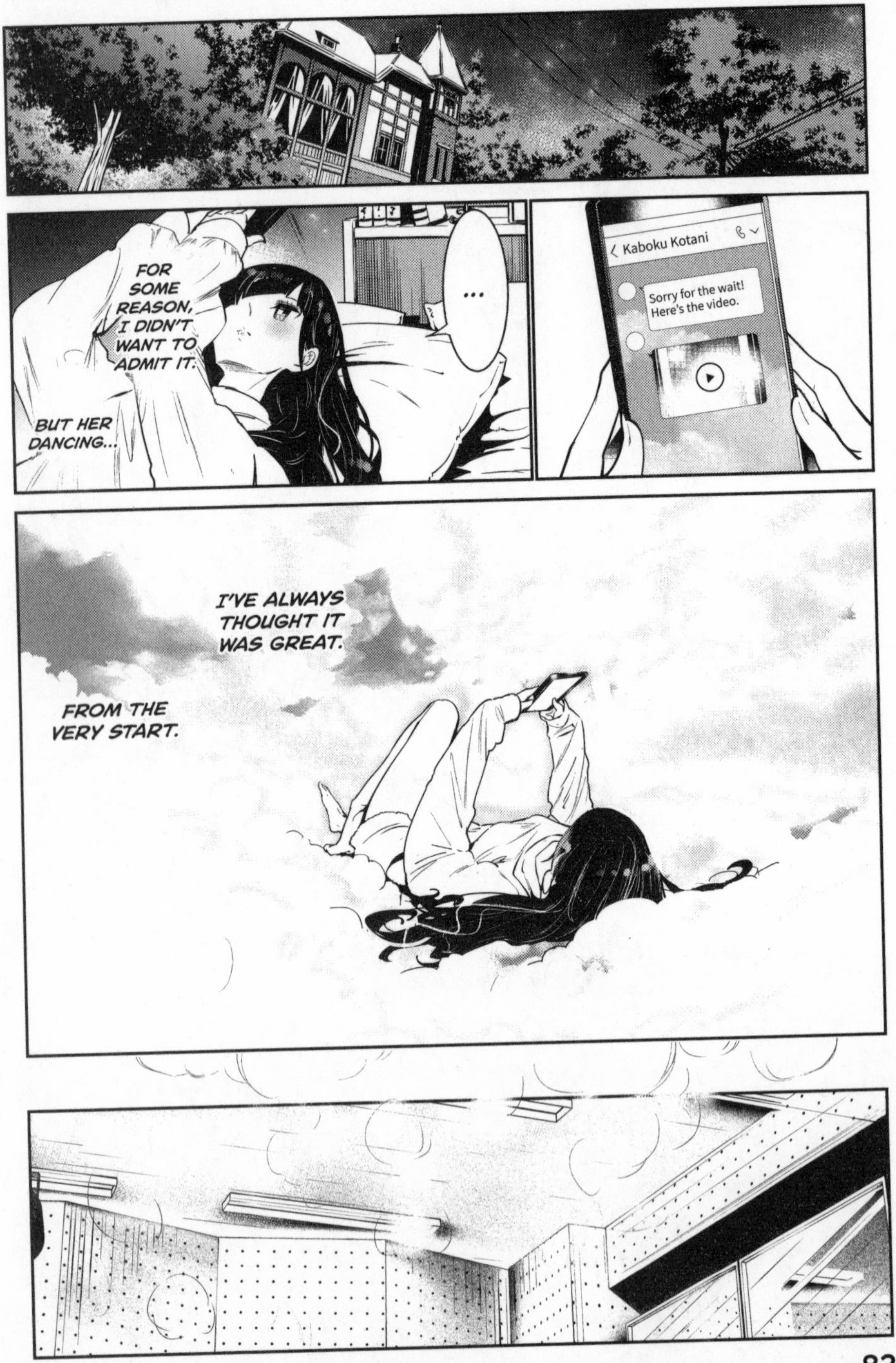
Kaboku Kotani
Sorry for the wait! Here's the video.
...
FOR SOME REASON, I DIDN'T WANT TO ADMIT IT.
BUT HER DANCING...
I'VE ALWAYS THOUGHT IT WAS GREAT.
FROM THE VERY START.

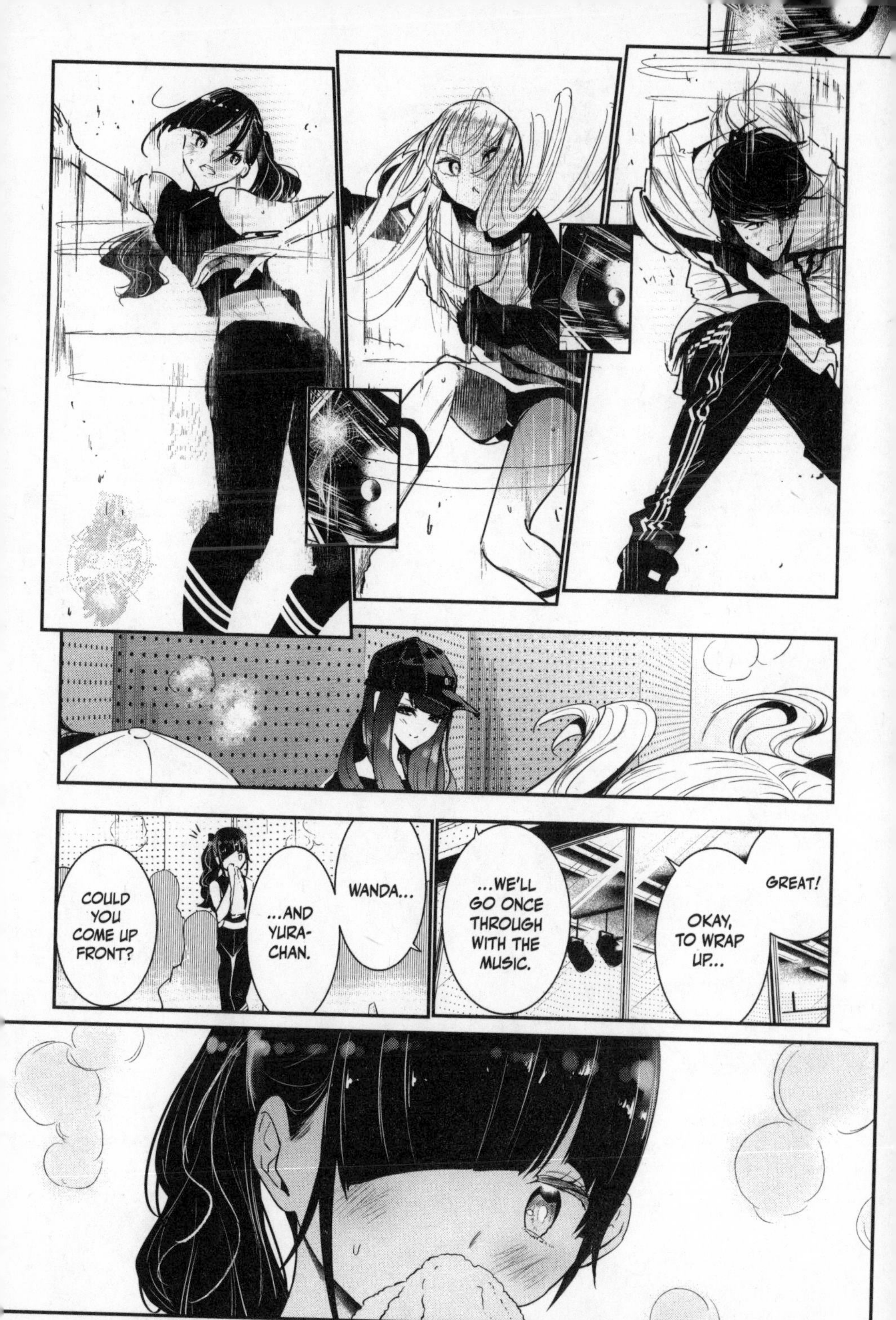
GREAT!
OKAY, TO WRAP UP...
...WE'LL GO ONCE THROUGH WITH THE MUSIC.
WANDA...
...AND YURA-CHAN.
COULD YOU COME UP FRONT?

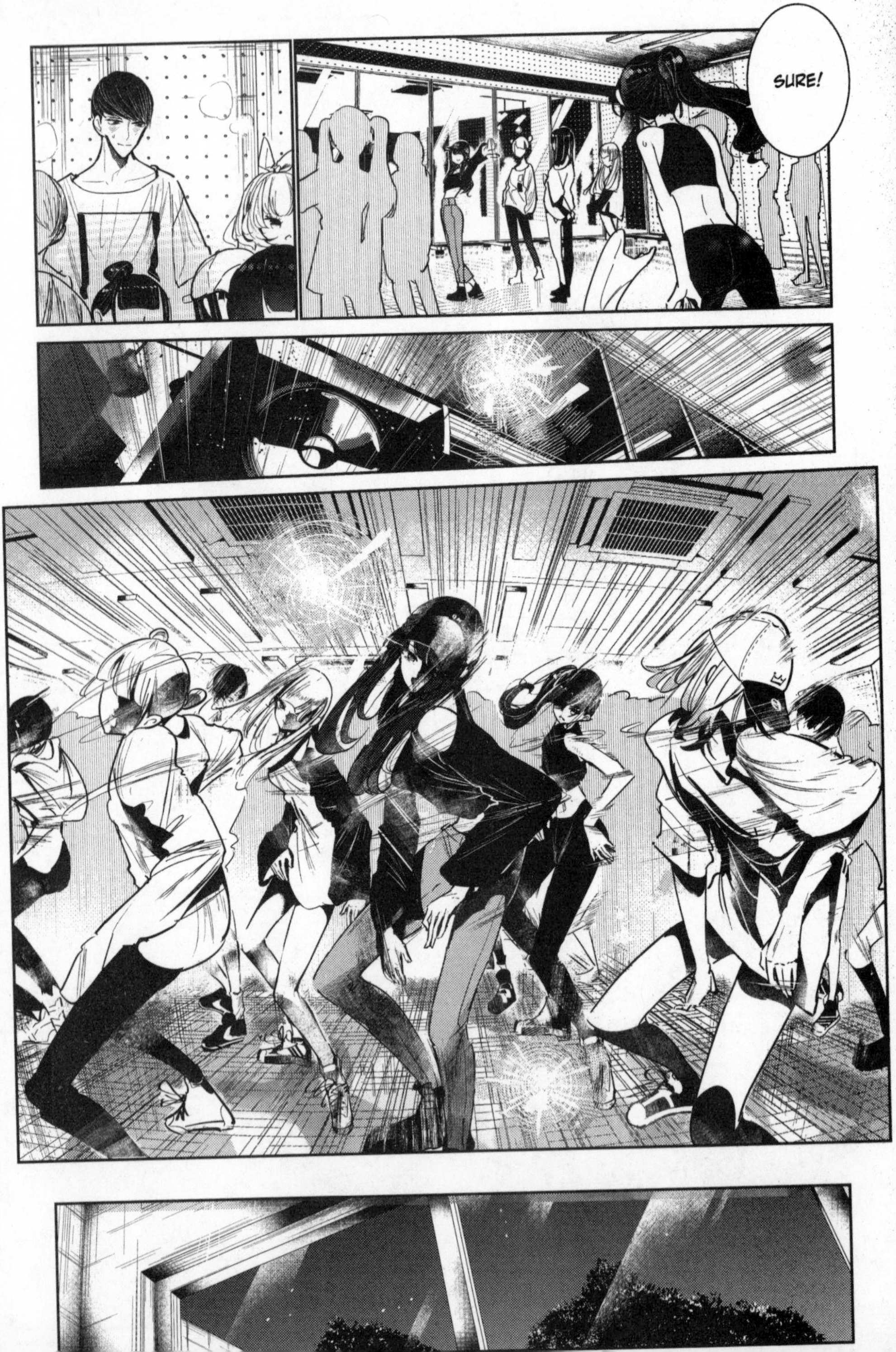
SURE!

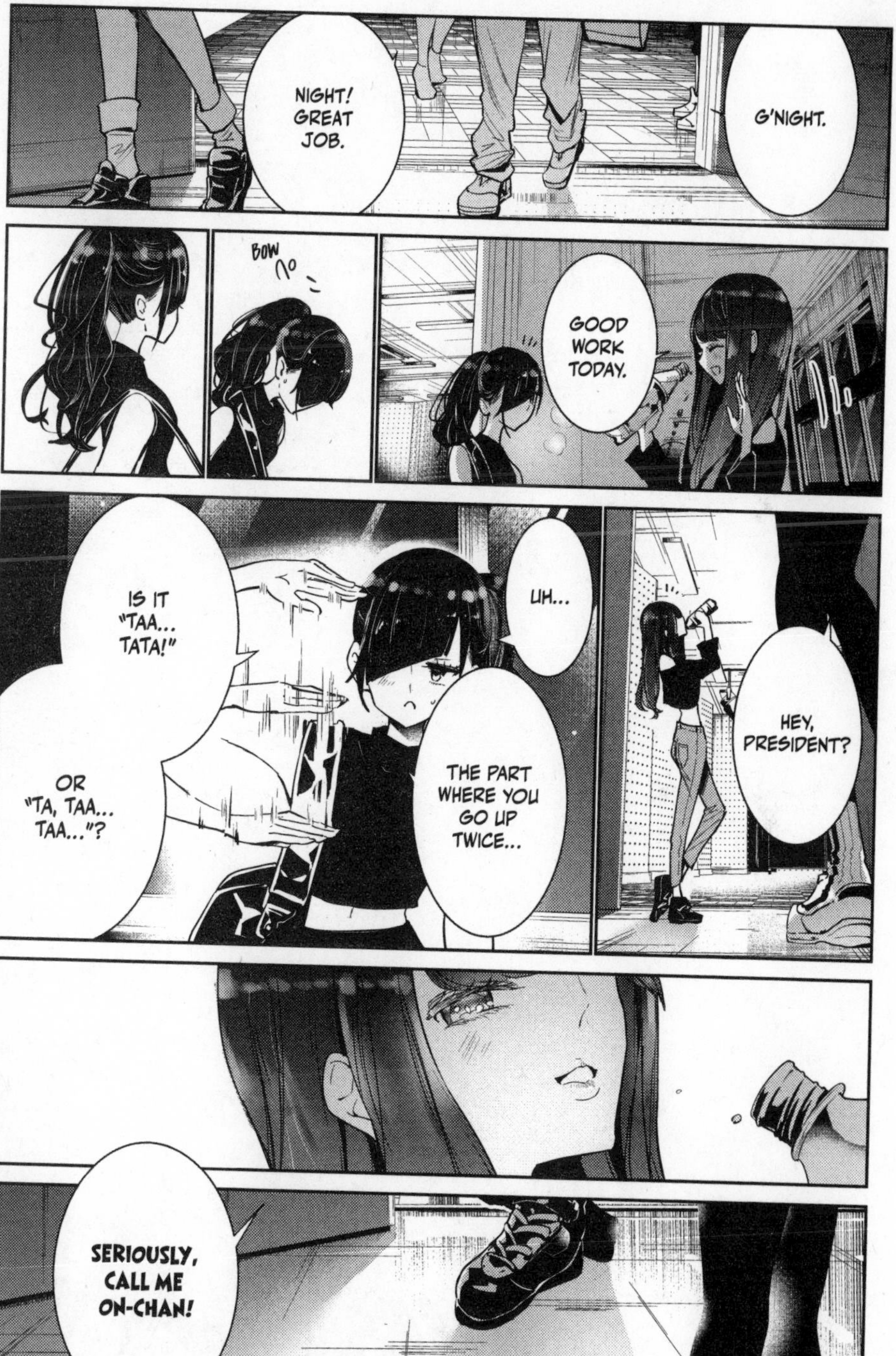
G'NIGHT.
NIGHT! GREAT JOB.
GOOD WORK TODAY.
BOW
HEY, PRESIDENT?
UH...
THE PART WHERE YOU GO UP TWICE...
IS IT "TAA... TATA!"
OR "TA, TAA... TAA..."?
SERIOUSLY, CALL ME ON-CHAN!

Ch. 5: END

WANDANCE

Ch. 6: Feeling (Pt. 1)

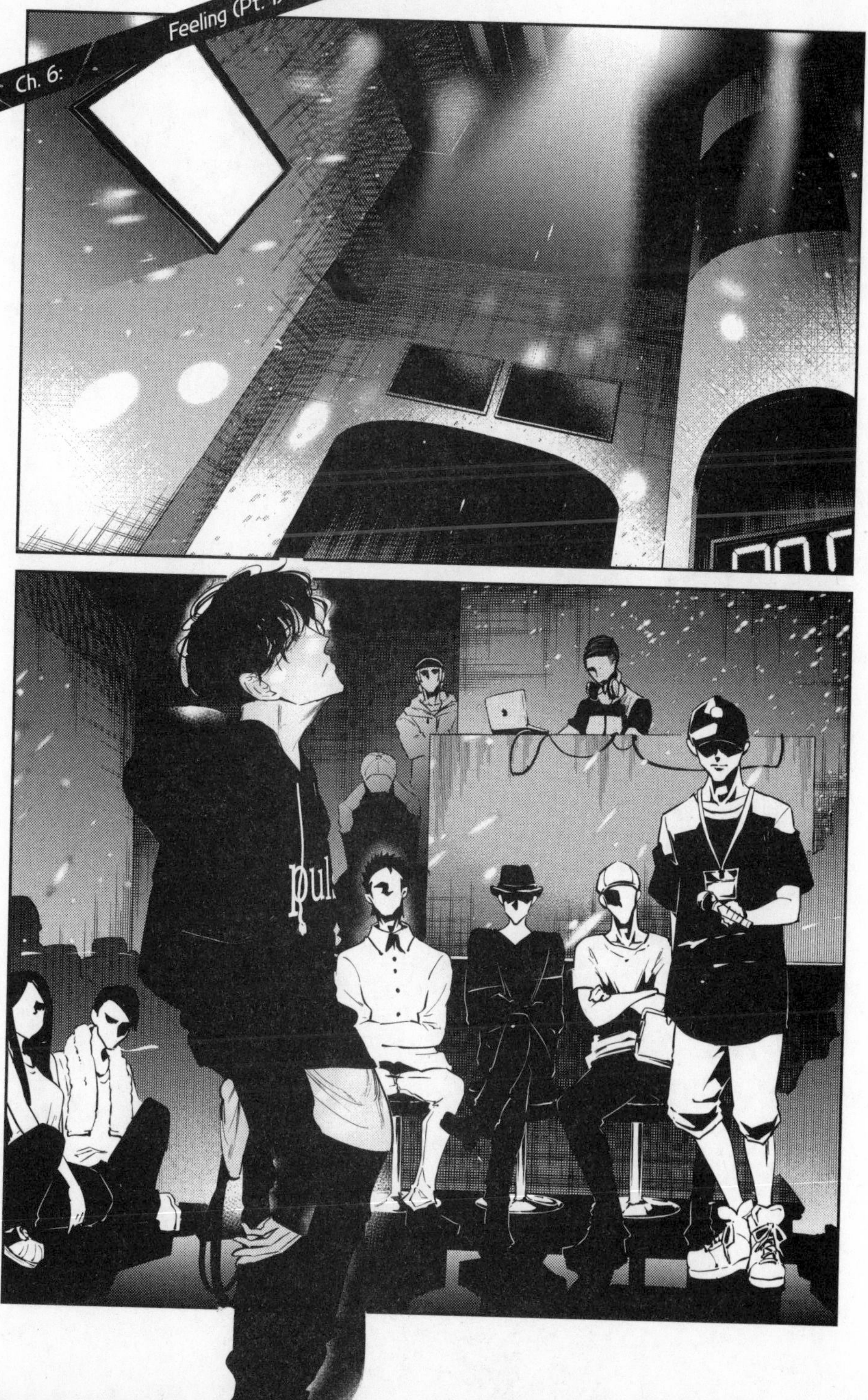

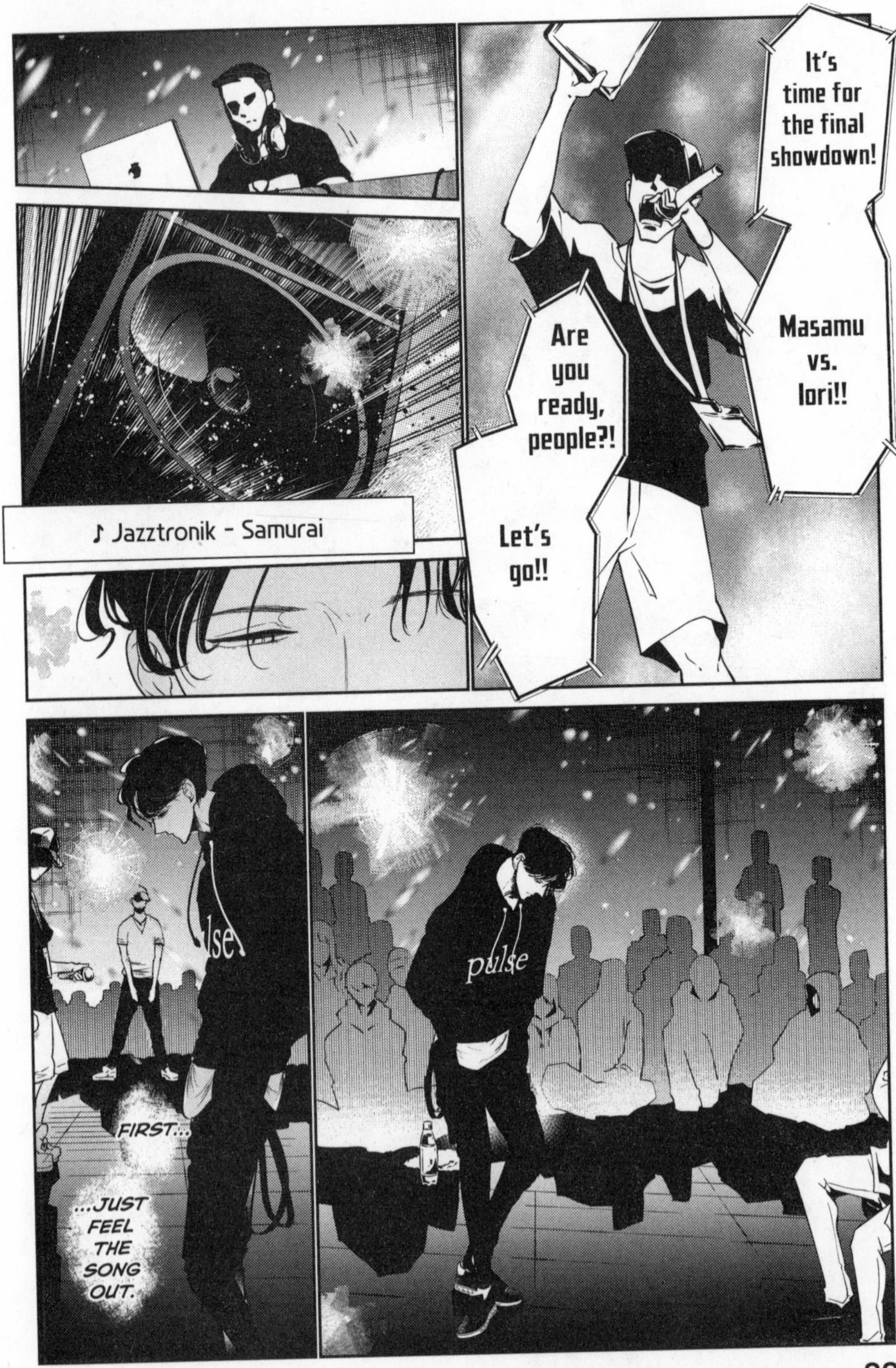
It's time for the final showdown!
Masamu vs. Iori!!
Are you ready, people?!
Let's go!!
♪ Jazztronik - Samurai
FIRST...
...JUST FEEL THE SONG OUT.

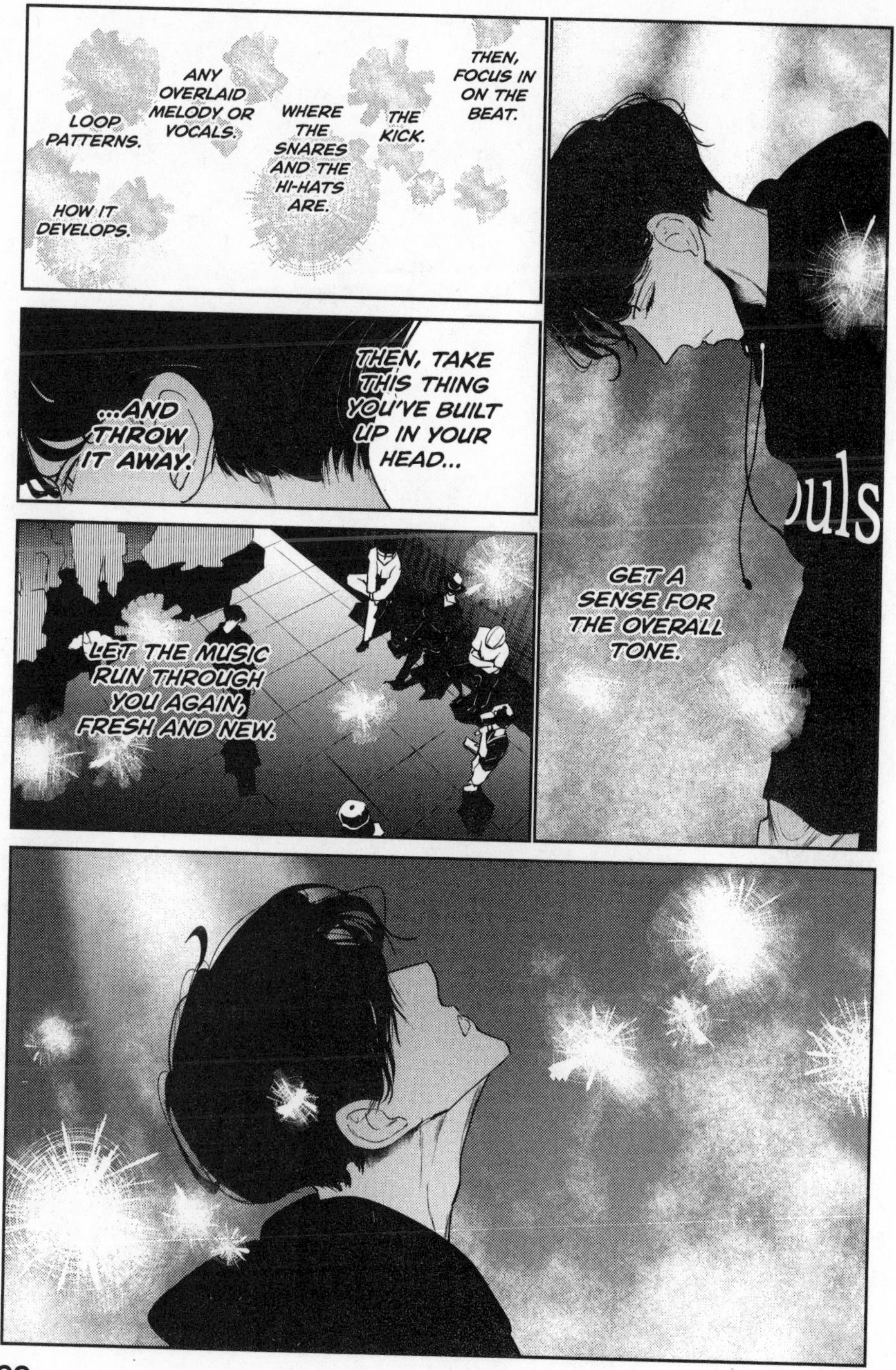

GET A SENSE FOR THE OVERALL TONE.
THEN, FOCUS IN ON THE BEAT.
THE KICK.
WHERE THE SNARES AND THE HI-HATS ARE.
ANY OVERLAID MELODY OR VOCALS.
LOOP PATTERNS.
HOW IT DEVELOPS.
THEN, TAKE THIS THING YOU'VE BUILT UP IN YOUR HEAD...
...AND THROW IT AWAY.
LET THE MUSIC RUN THROUGH YOU AGAIN, FRESH AND NEW.

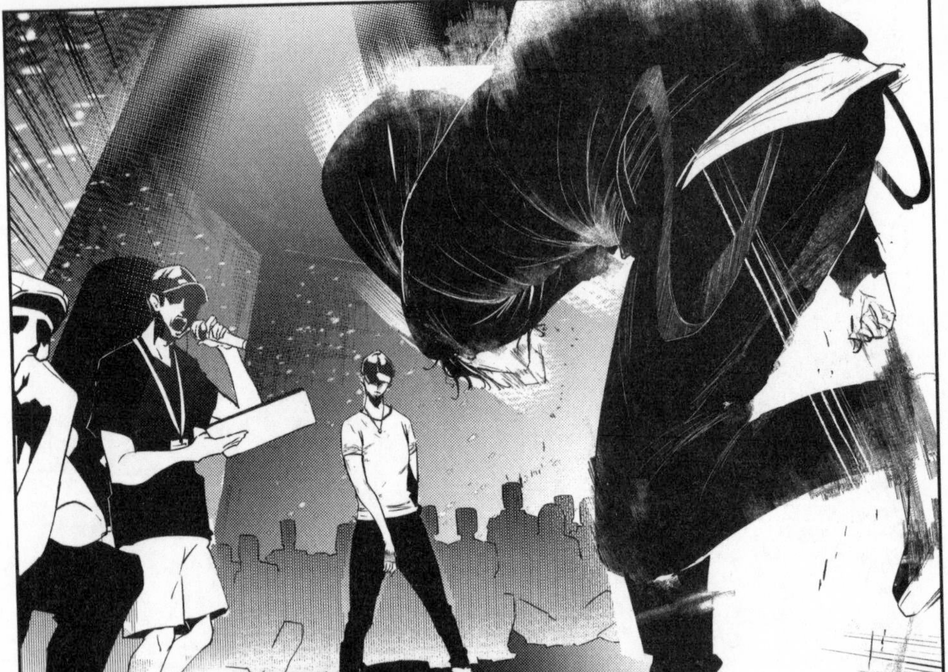

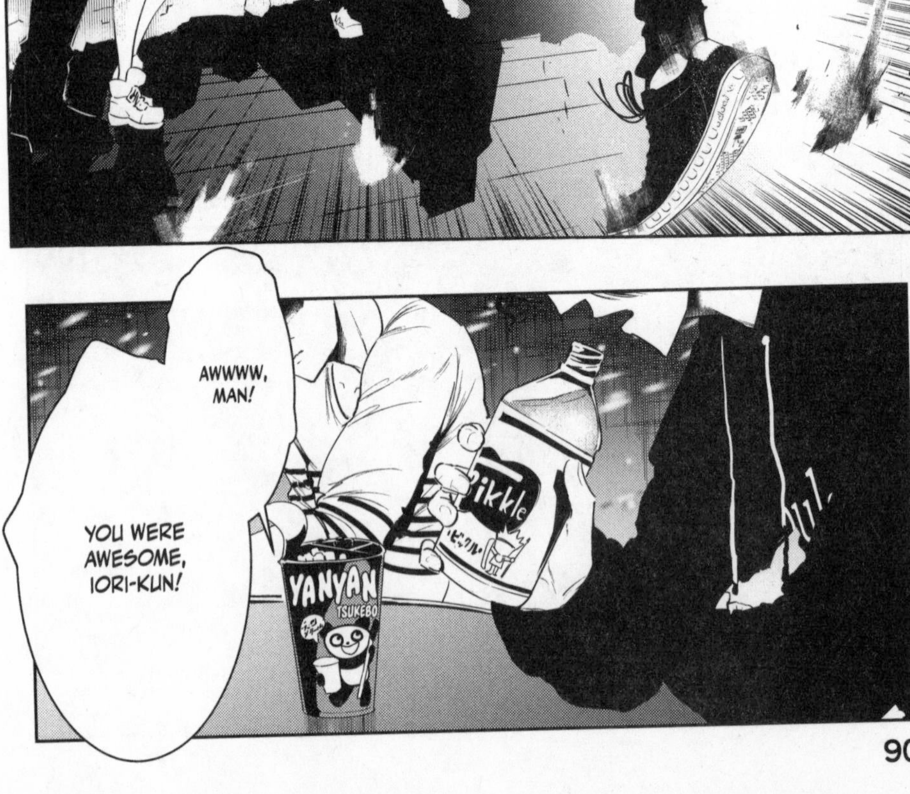
AWWWW, MAN!
YOU WERE AWESOME, IORI-KUN!
YANYAN
TSUKEBO

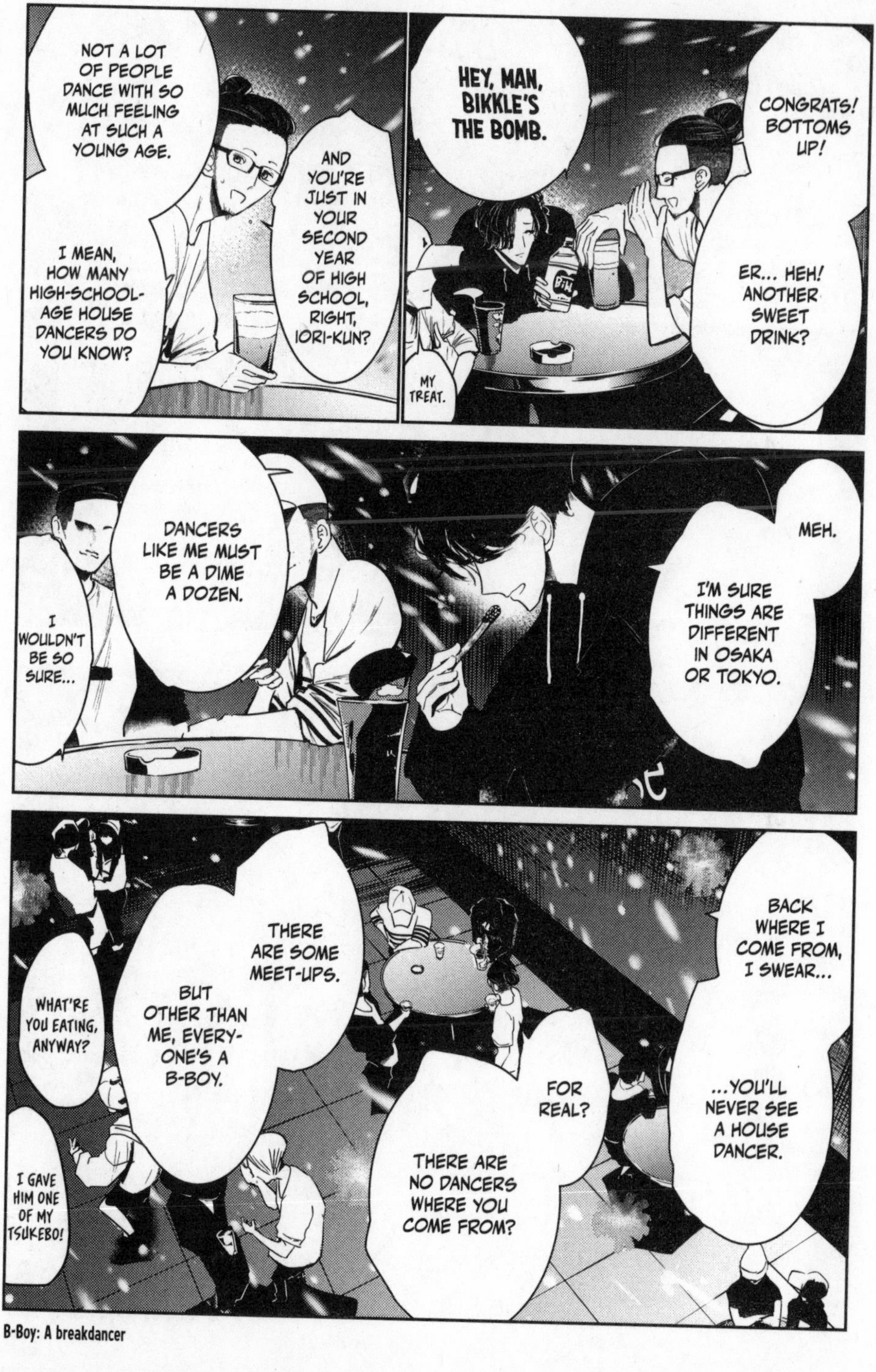
CONGRATS! BOTTOMS UP!
HEY, MAN, BIKKLE'S THE BOMB.
ER... HEH! ANOTHER SWEET DRINK?
MY TREAT.
NOT A LOT OF PEOPLE DANCE WITH SO MUCH FEELING AT SUCH A YOUNG AGE.
AND YOU'RE JUST IN YOUR SECOND YEAR OF HIGH SCHOOL, RIGHT, IORI-KUN?
I MEAN, HOW MANY HIGH-SCHOOL-AGE HOUSE DANCERS DO YOU KNOW?
MEH.
I'M SURE THINGS ARE DIFFERENT IN OSAKA OR TOKYO.
DANCERS LIKE ME MUST BE A DIME A DOZEN.
I WOULDN'T BE SO SURE...
BACK WHERE I COME FROM, I SWEAR...
...YOU'LL NEVER SEE A HOUSE DANCER.
FOR REAL?
THERE ARE NO DANCERS WHERE YOU COME FROM?
THERE ARE SOME MEET-UPS.
BUT OTHER THAN ME, EVERY-ONE'S A B-BOY.
WHAT'RE YOU EATING, ANYWAY?
I GAVE HIM ONE OF MY TSUKEBO!

B-Boy: A breakdancer

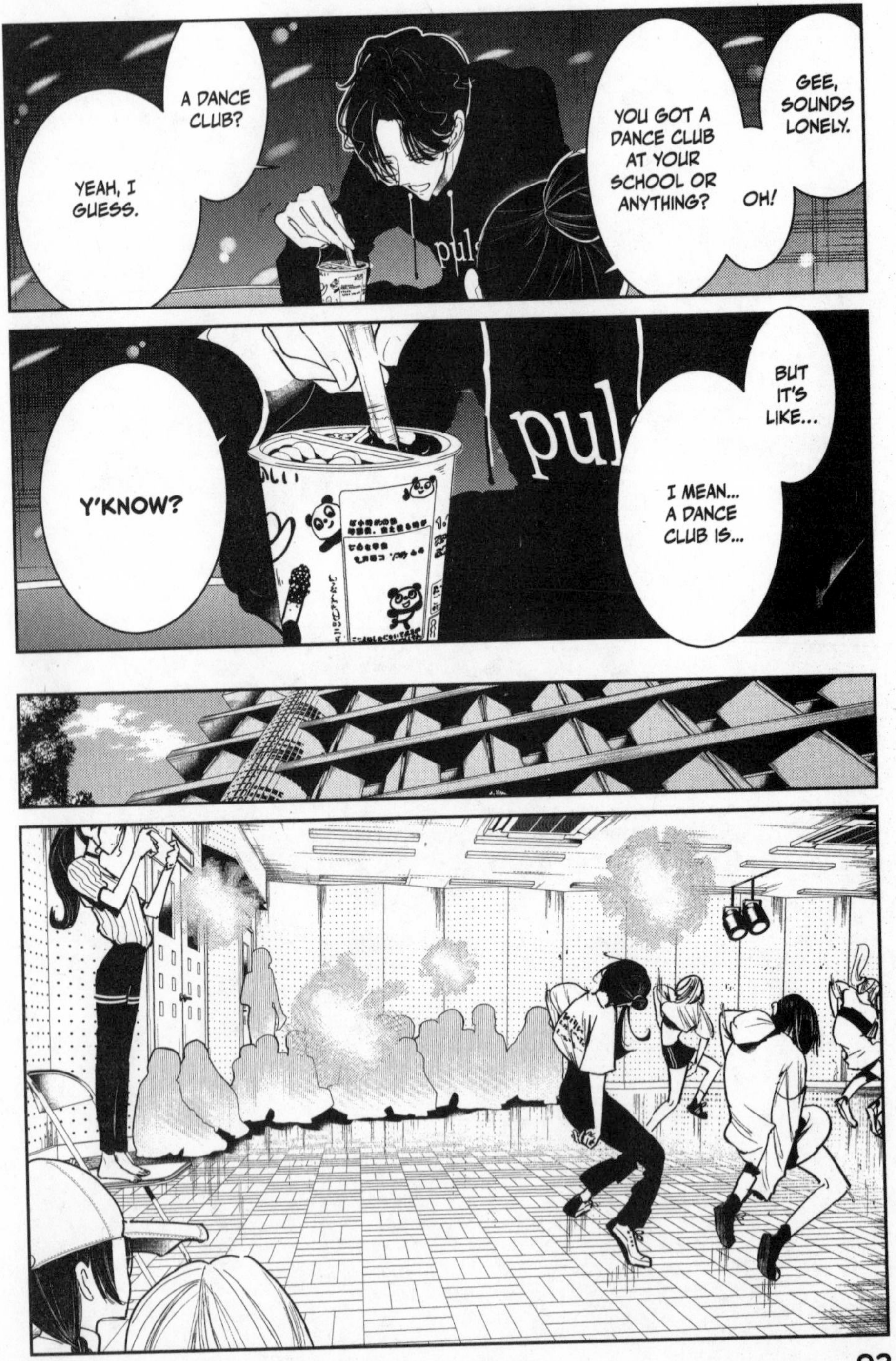
GEE, SOUNDS LONELY.
OH!
YOU GOT A DANCE CLUB AT YOUR SCHOOL OR ANYTHING?
A DANCE CLUB?
YEAH, I GUESS.
BUT IT'S LIKE...
I MEAN... A DANCE CLUB IS...
Y'KNOW?

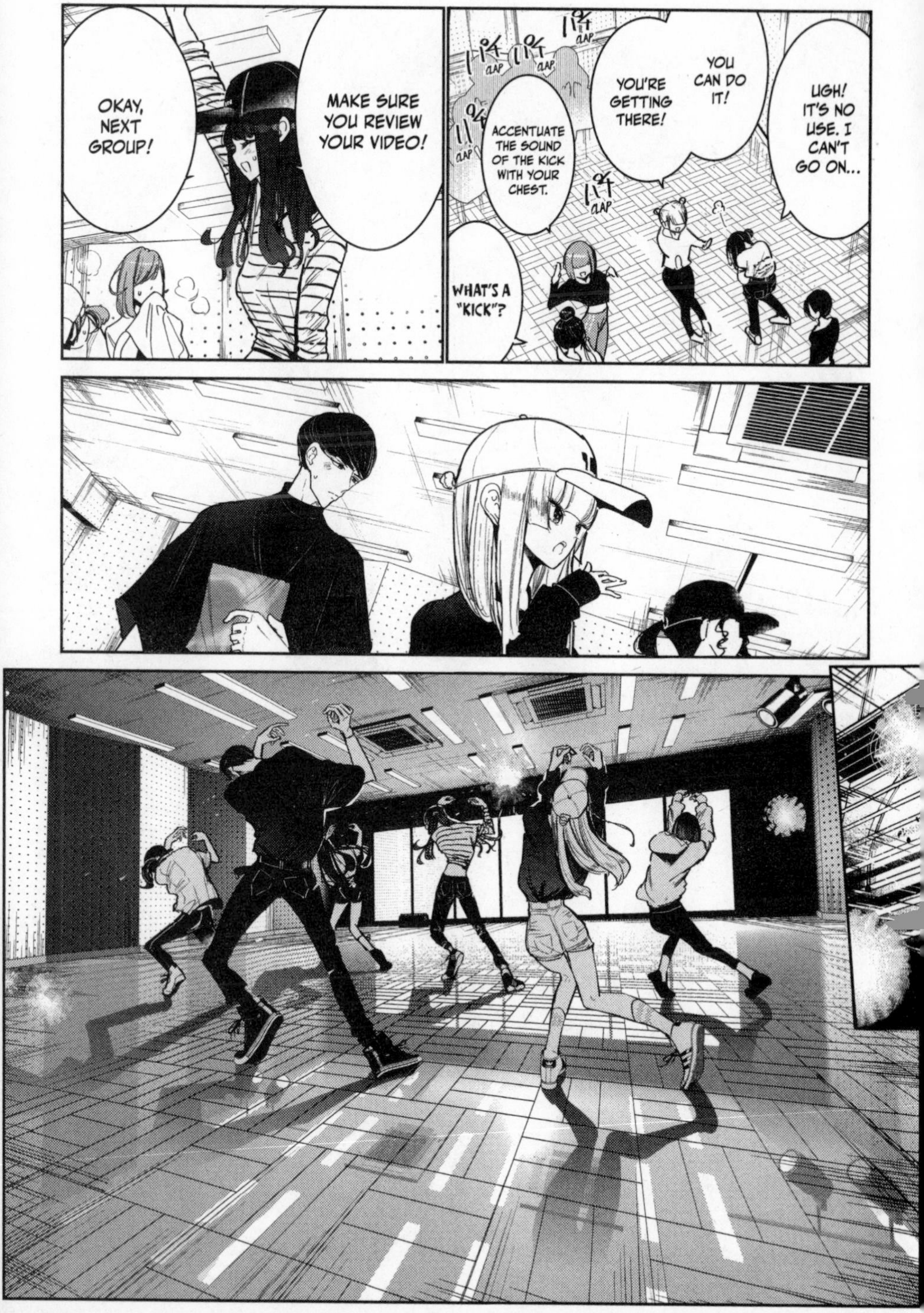
UGH! IT'S NO USE. I CAN'T GO ON...
YOU CAN DO IT!
YOU'RE GETTING THERE!
CLAP
CLAP
CLAP
ACCENTUATE THE SOUND OF THE KICK WITH YOUR CHEST.
CLAP
CLAP
WHAT'S A "KICK"?
MAKE SURE YOU REVIEW YOUR VIDEO!
OKAY, NEXT GROUP!

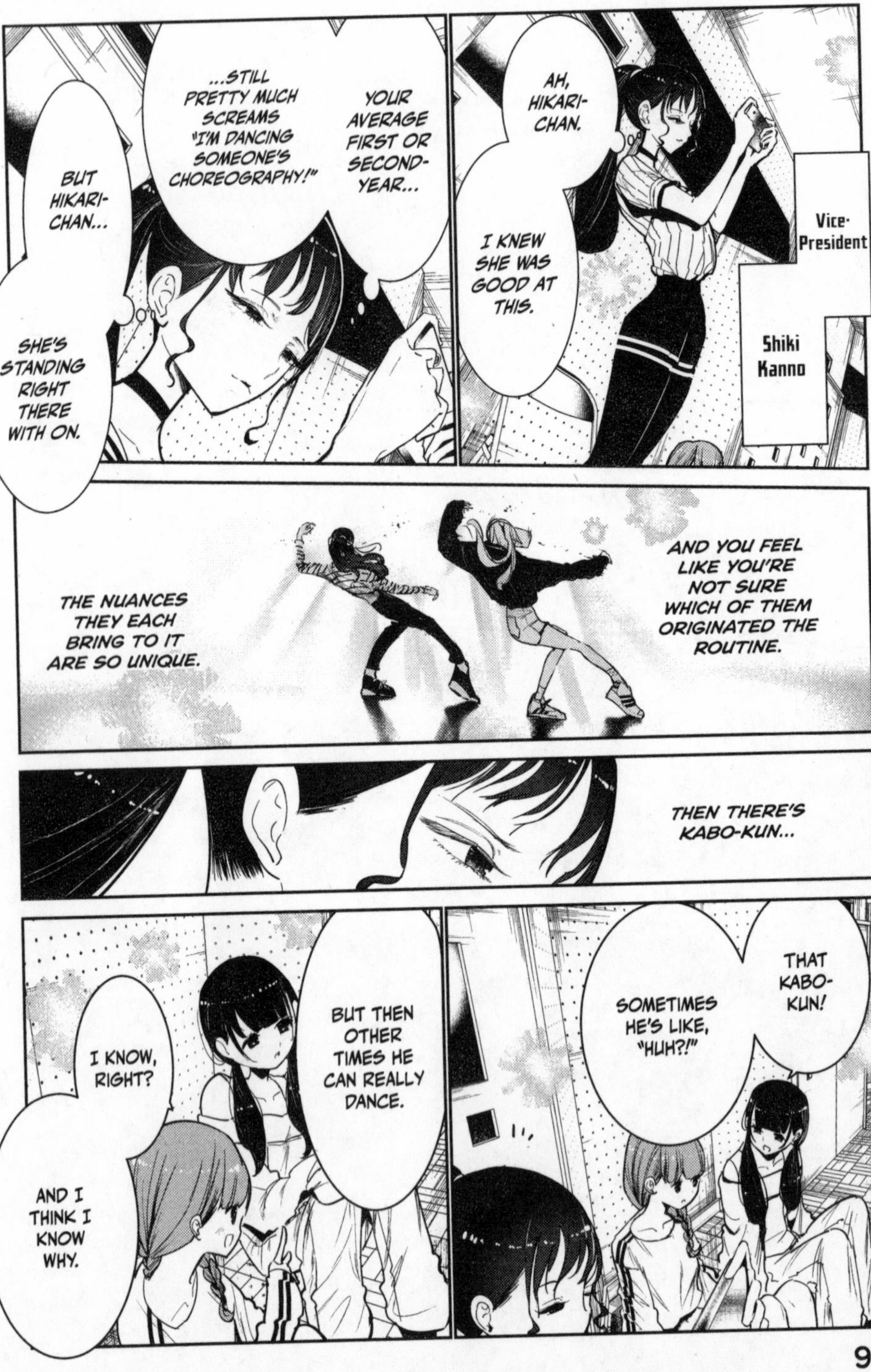
AH, HIKARI-CHAN.
I KNEW SHE WAS GOOD AT THIS.
Vice-President
Shiki Kanno
YOUR AVERAGE FIRST OR SECOND-YEAR...
...STILL PRETTY MUCH SCREAMS "I'M DANCING SOMEONE'S CHOREOGRAPHY!"
BUT HIKARI-CHAN...
SHE'S STANDING RIGHT THERE WITH ON.
THE NUANCES THEY EACH BRING TO IT ARE SO UNIQUE.
AND YOU FEEL LIKE YOU'RE NOT SURE WHICH OF THEM ORIGINATED THE ROUTINE.
THEN THERE'S KABO-KUN...
THAT KABO-KUN!
SOMETIMES HE'S LIKE, "HUH?!"
BUT THEN OTHER TIMES HE CAN REALLY DANCE.
I KNOW, RIGHT?
AND I THINK I KNOW WHY.

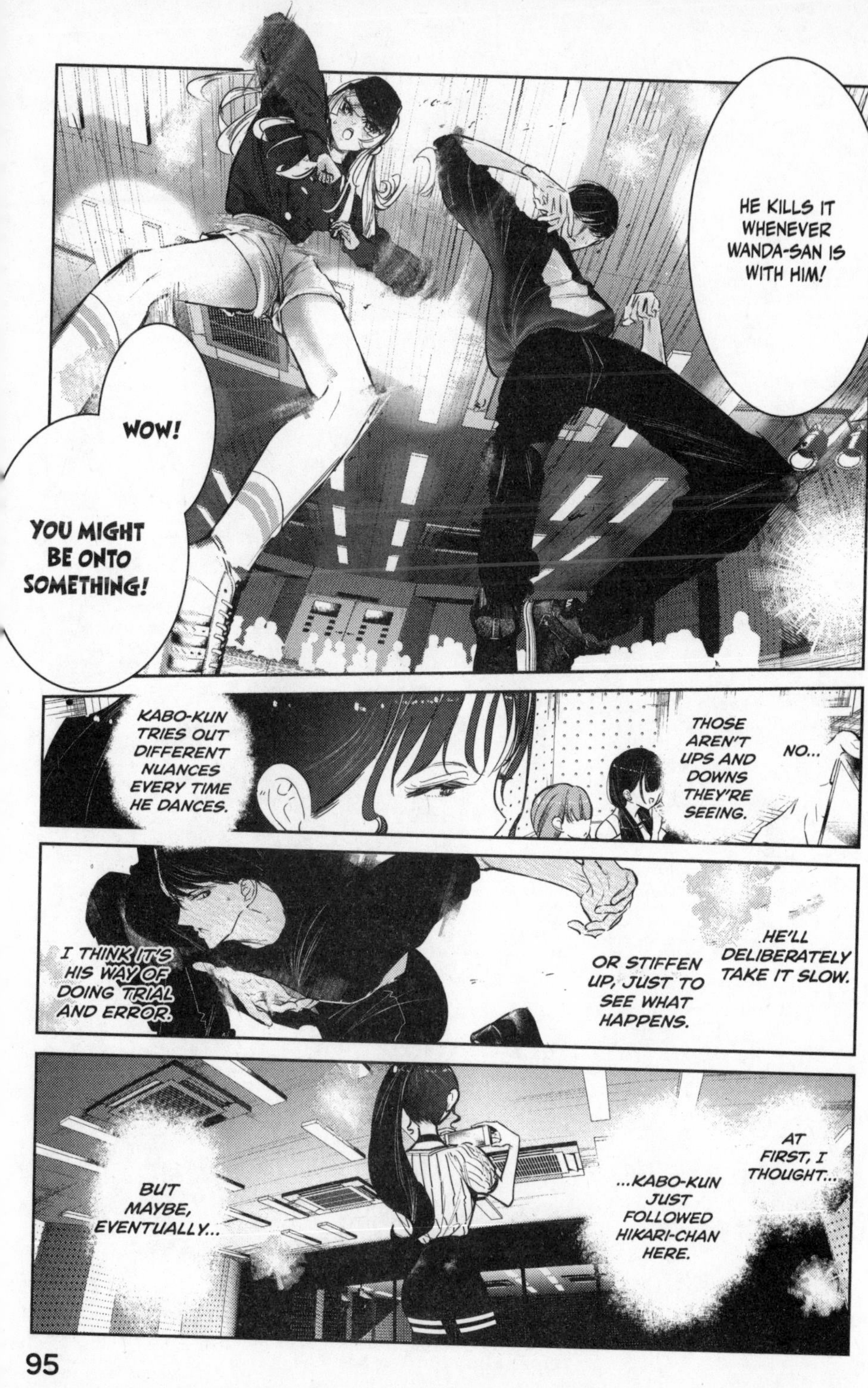
HE KILLS IT WHENEVER WANDA-SAN IS WITH HIM!
WOW!
YOU MIGHT BE ONTO SOMETHING!
NO...
THOSE AREN'T UPS AND DOWNS THEY'RE SEEING.
KABO-KUN TRIES OUT DIFFERENT NUANCES EVERY TIME HE DANCES.
.HE'LL DELIBERATELY TAKE IT SLOW.
OR STIFFEN UP, JUST TO SEE WHAT HAPPENS.
I THINK IT'S HIS WAY OF DOING TRIAL AND ERROR.
AT FIRST, I THOUGHT...
...KABO-KUN JUST FOLLOWED HIKARI-CHAN HERE.
BUT MAYBE, EVENTUALLY...

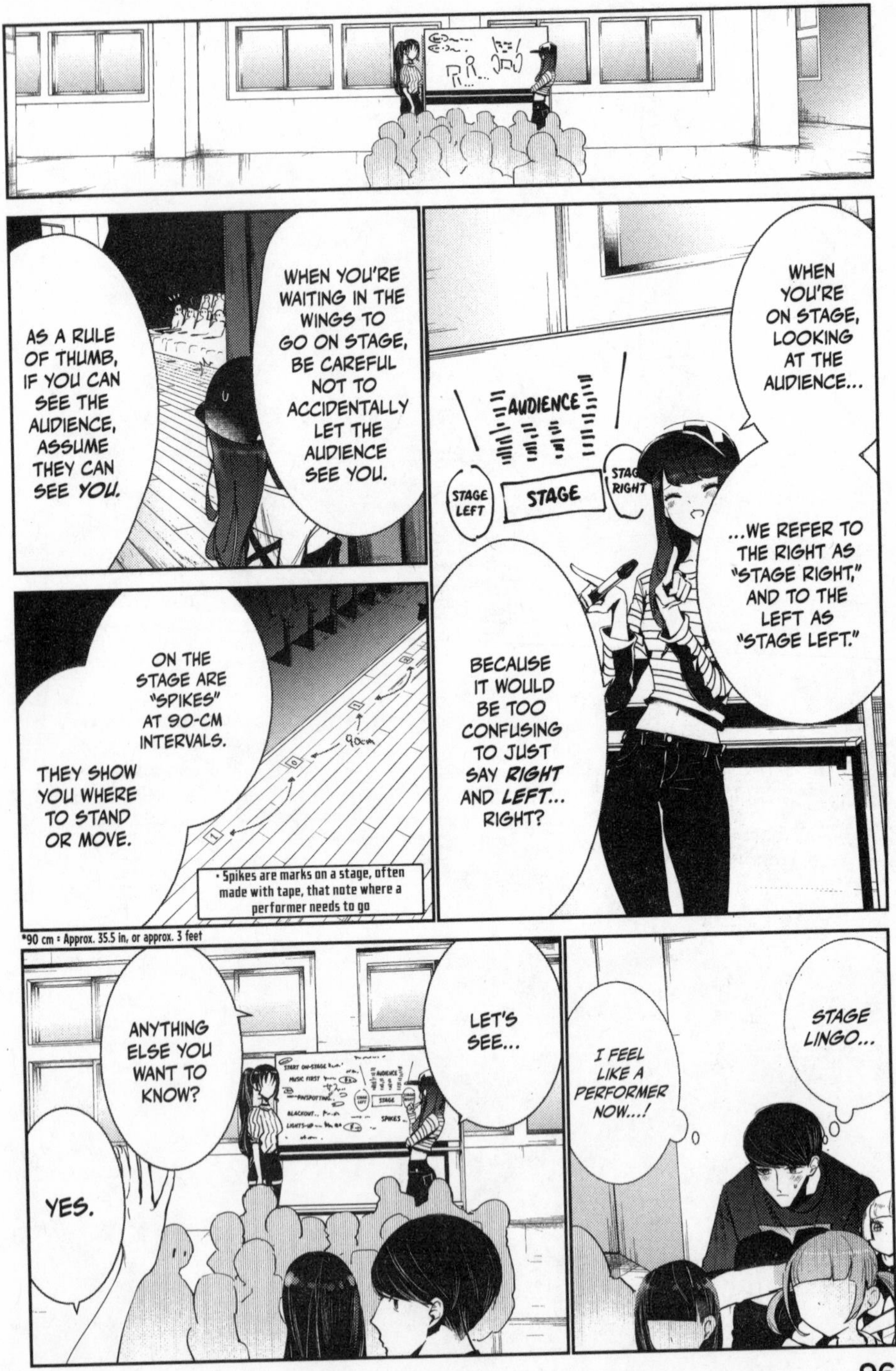
WHEN YOU'RE ON STAGE, LOOKING AT THE AUDIENCE...
AUDIENCE
STAGE RIGHT
STAGE
STAGE LEFT
...WE REFER TO THE RIGHT AS "STAGE RIGHT," AND TO THE LEFT AS "STAGE LEFT."
BECAUSE IT WOULD BE TOO CONFUSING TO JUST SAY *RIGHT* AND *LEFT*... RIGHT?
WHEN YOU'RE WAITING IN THE WINGS TO GO ON STAGE, BE CAREFUL NOT TO ACCIDENTALLY LET THE AUDIENCE SEE YOU.
AS A RULE OF THUMB, IF YOU CAN SEE THE AUDIENCE, ASSUME THEY CAN SEE *YOU*.
ON THE STAGE ARE "SPIKES" AT 90-CM INTERVALS.
90cm
THEY SHOW YOU WHERE TO STAND OR MOVE.
• Spikes are marks on a stage, often made with tape, that note where a performer needs to go
*90 cm = Approx. 35.5 in, or approx. 3 feet
STAGE LINGO...
I FEEL LIKE A PERFORMER NOW...!
LET'S SEE...
ANYTHING ELSE YOU WANT TO KNOW?
YES.

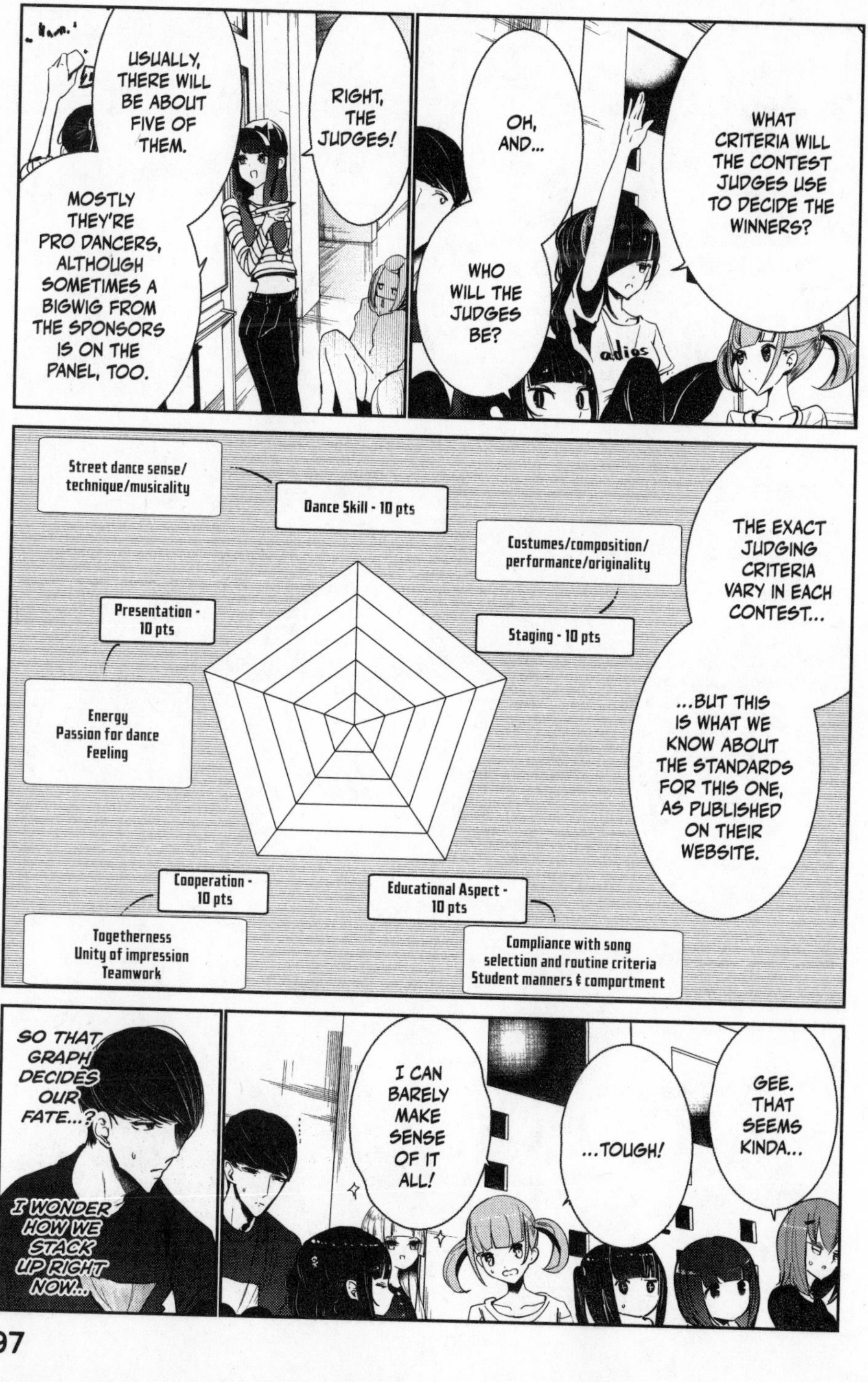
WHAT CRITERIA WILL THE CONTEST JUDGES USE TO DECIDE THE WINNERS?
OH, AND...
WHO WILL THE JUDGES BE?
RIGHT, THE JUDGES!
USUALLY, THERE WILL BE ABOUT FIVE OF THEM.
MOSTLY THEY'RE PRO DANCERS, ALTHOUGH SOMETIMES A BIGWIG FROM THE SPONSORS IS ON THE PANEL, TOO.
THE EXACT JUDGING CRITERIA VARY IN EACH CONTEST...
...BUT THIS IS WHAT WE KNOW ABOUT THE STANDARDS FOR THIS ONE, AS PUBLISHED ON THEIR WEBSITE.
Street dance sense/ technique/musicality
Dance Skill - 10 pts
Costumes/composition/ performance/originality
Staging - 10 pts
Presentation - 10 pts
Energy Passion for dance Feeling
Cooperation - 10 pts
Togetherness Unity of impression Teamwork
Educational Aspect - 10 pts
Compliance with song selection and routine criteria Student manners & comportment
GEE. THAT SEEMS KINDA...
...TOUGH!
I CAN BARELY MAKE SENSE OF IT ALL!
SO THAT GRAPH DECIDES OUR FATE...?
I WONDER HOW WE STACK UP RIGHT NOW...

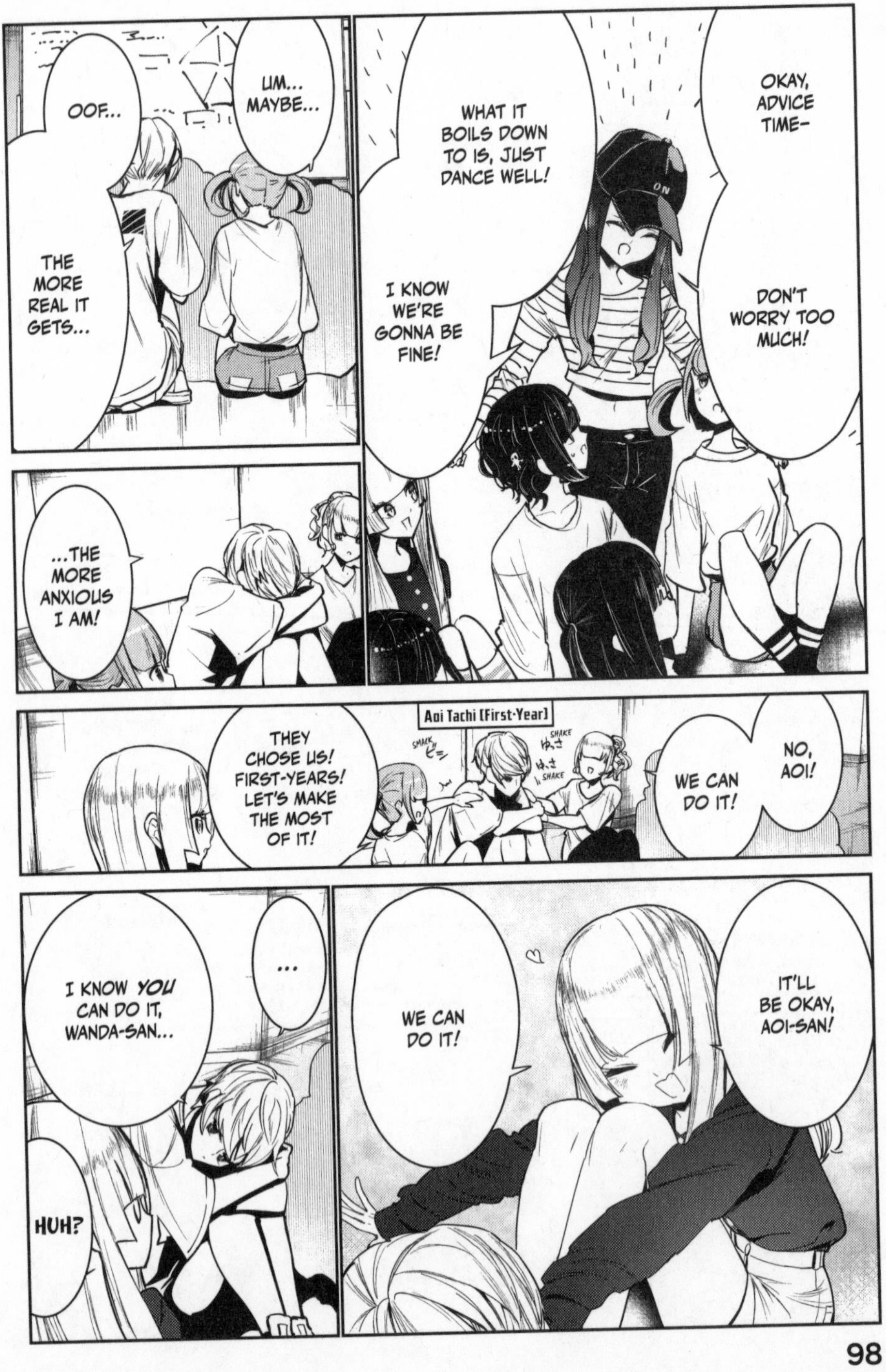
OKAY, ADVICE TIME–
WHAT IT BOILS DOWN TO IS, JUST DANCE WELL!
DON'T WORRY TOO MUCH!
I KNOW WE'RE GONNA BE FINE!
UM... MAYBE...
OOF...
THE MORE REAL IT GETS...
...THE MORE ANXIOUS I AM!
NO, AOI!
WE CAN DO IT!
Aoi Tachi [First·Year]
SHAKE ゆっさ
ゆっさ SHAKE
SMACK ビシ
THEY CHOSE US! FIRST-YEARS! LET'S MAKE THE MOST OF IT!
IT'LL BE OKAY, AOI-SAN!
WE CAN DO IT!
...
I KNOW *YOU* CAN DO IT, WANDA-SAN...
HUH?

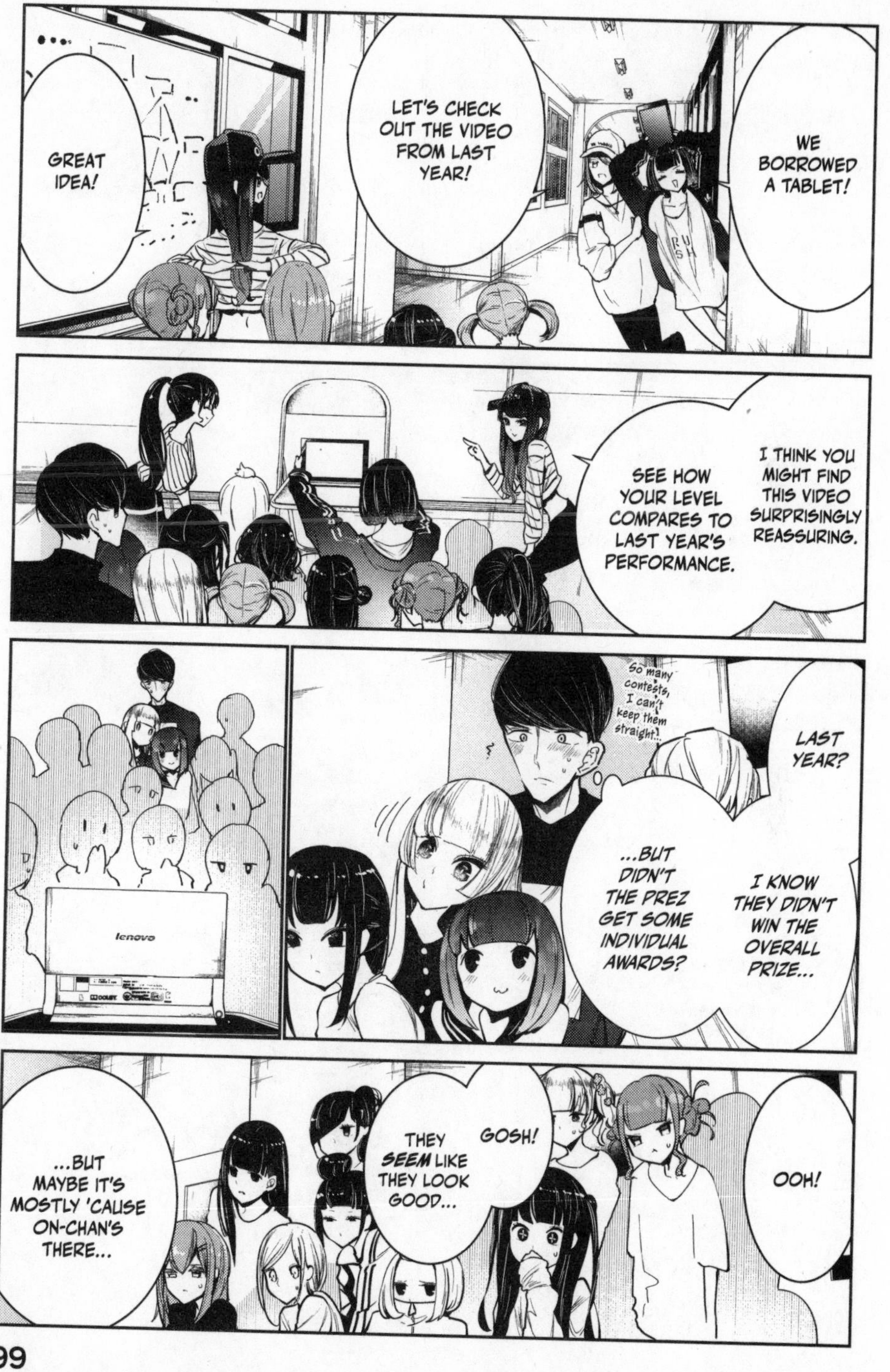
WE BORROWED A TABLET!
LET'S CHECK OUT THE VIDEO FROM LAST YEAR!
GREAT IDEA!
I THINK YOU MIGHT FIND THIS VIDEO SURPRISINGLY REASSURING.
SEE HOW YOUR LEVEL COMPARES TO LAST YEAR'S PERFORMANCE.
LAST YEAR?
So many contests, I can't keep them straight!
I KNOW THEY DIDN'T WIN THE OVERALL PRIZE...
...BUT DIDN'T THE PREZ GET SOME INDIVIDUAL AWARDS?
lenovo
OOH!
GOSH!
THEY *SEEM* LIKE THEY LOOK GOOD...
...BUT MAYBE IT'S MOSTLY 'CAUSE ON-CHAN'S THERE...

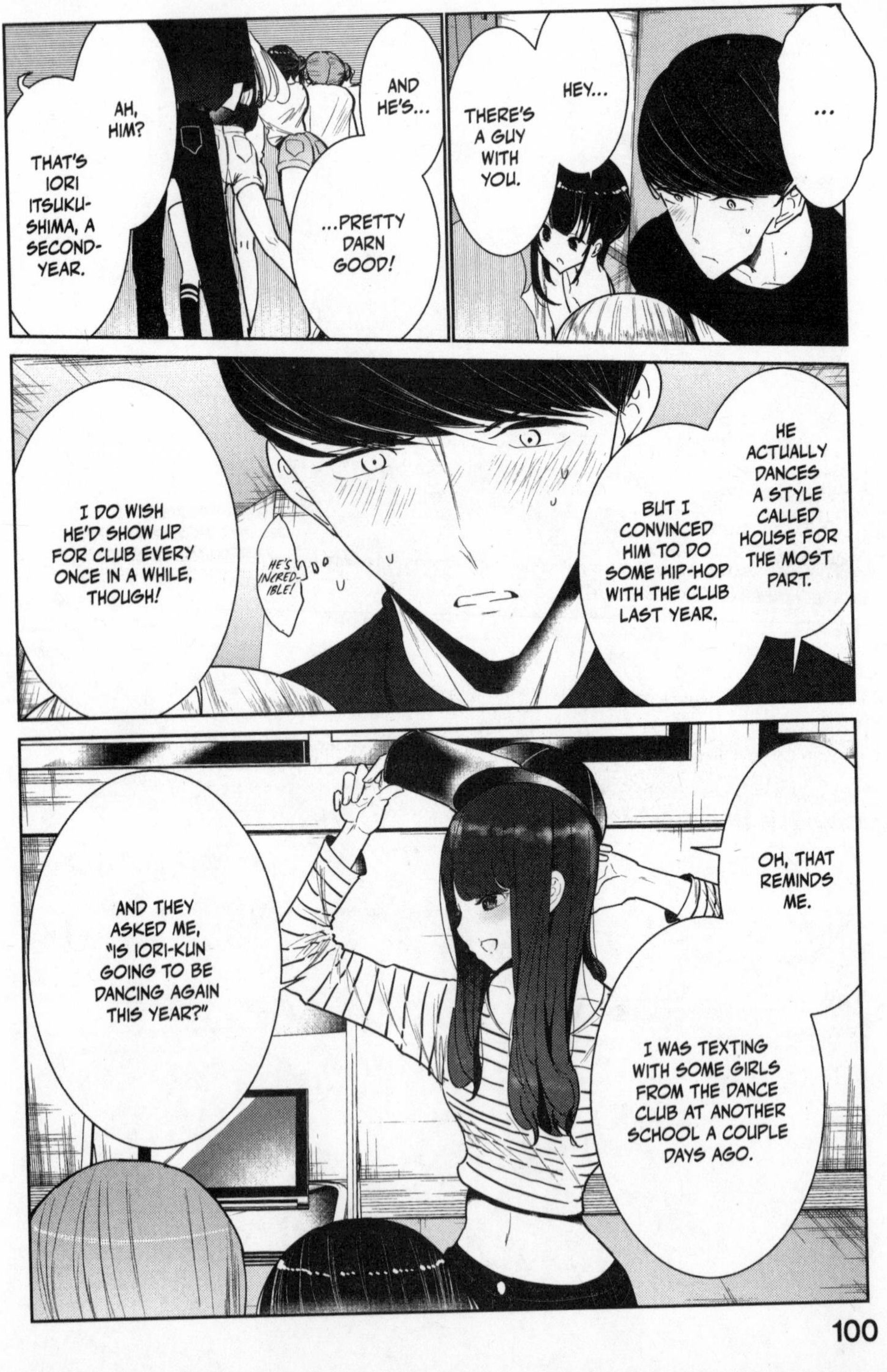
...
HEY... THERE'S A GUY WITH YOU.
AND HE'S...
...PRETTY DARN GOOD!
AH, HIM? THAT'S IORI ITSUKUSHIMA, A SECOND-YEAR.
HE ACTUALLY DANCES A STYLE CALLED HOUSE FOR THE MOST PART.
BUT I CONVINCED HIM TO DO SOME HIP-HOP WITH THE CLUB LAST YEAR.
HE'S INCREDIBLE!
I DO WISH HE'D SHOW UP FOR CLUB EVERY ONCE IN A WHILE, THOUGH!
OH, THAT REMINDS ME.
I WAS TEXTING WITH SOME GIRLS FROM THE DANCE CLUB AT ANOTHER SCHOOL A COUPLE DAYS AGO.
AND THEY ASKED ME, "IS IORI-KUN GOING TO BE DANCING AGAIN THIS YEAR?"

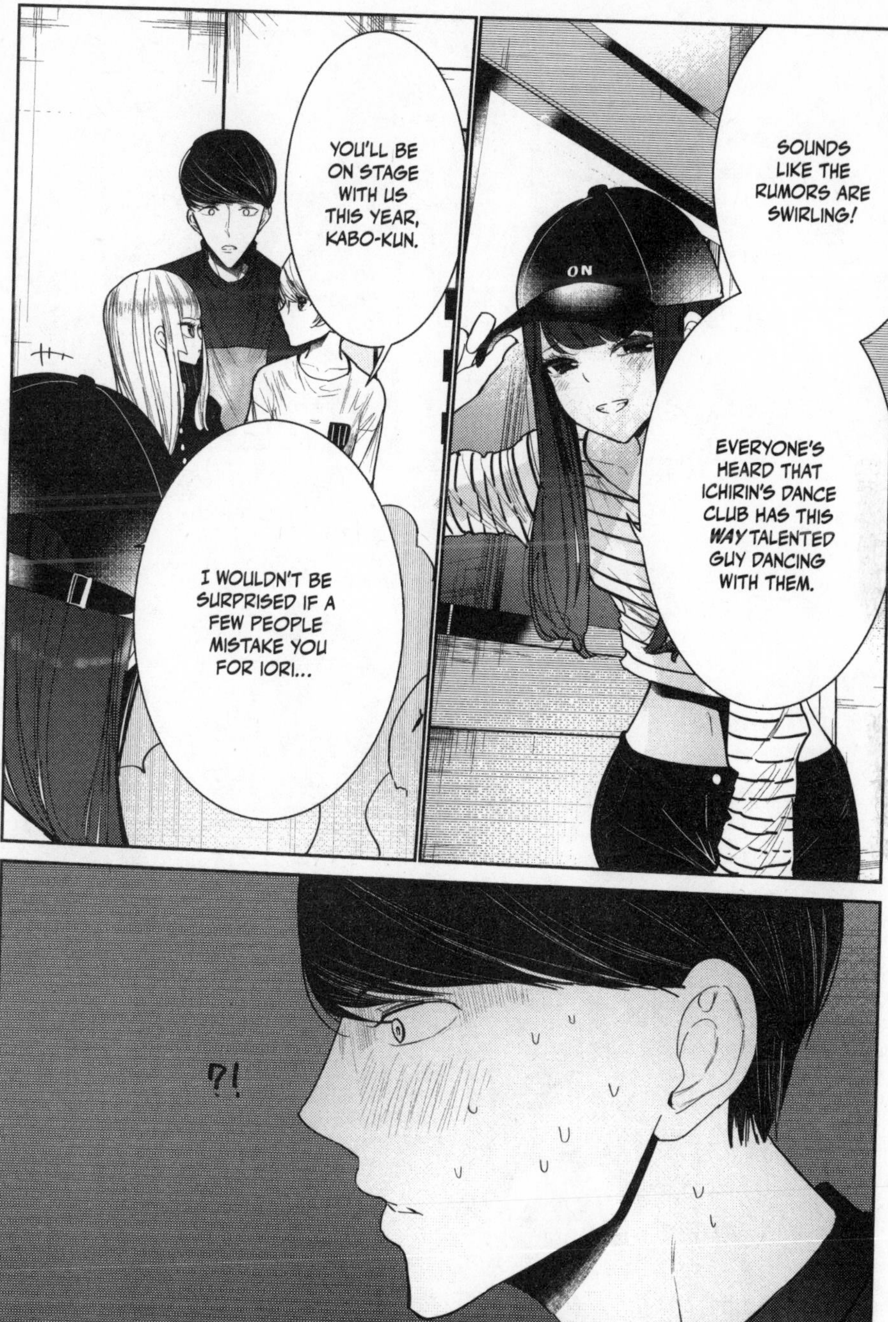
SOUNDS LIKE THE RUMORS ARE SWIRLING!
ON
EVERYONE'S HEARD THAT ICHIRIN'S DANCE CLUB HAS THIS *WAY* TALENTED GUY DANCING WITH THEM.
YOU'LL BE ON STAGE WITH US THIS YEAR, KABO-KUN.
I WOULDN'T BE SURPRISED IF A FEW PEOPLE MISTAKE YOU FOR IORI...
?!

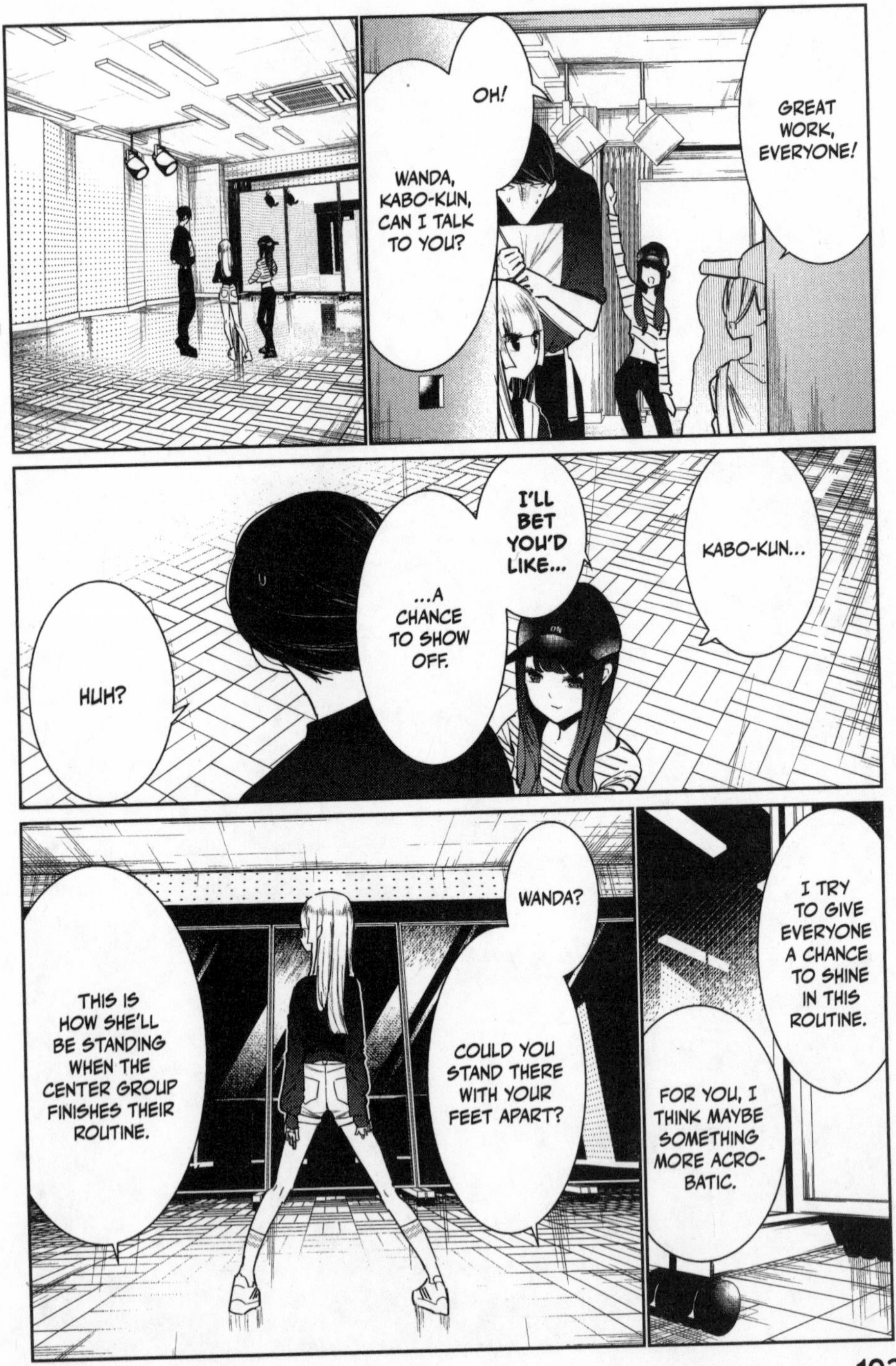
GREAT WORK, EVERYONE!
OH!
WANDA, KABO-KUN, CAN I TALK TO YOU?
KABO-KUN...
I'LL BET YOU'D LIKE...
...A CHANCE TO SHOW OFF.
HUH?
I TRY TO GIVE EVERYONE A CHANCE TO SHINE IN THIS ROUTINE.
FOR YOU, I THINK MAYBE SOMETHING MORE ACRO-BATIC.
WANDA?
COULD YOU STAND THERE WITH YOUR FEET APART?
THIS IS HOW SHE'LL BE STANDING WHEN THE CENTER GROUP FINISHES THEIR ROUTINE.

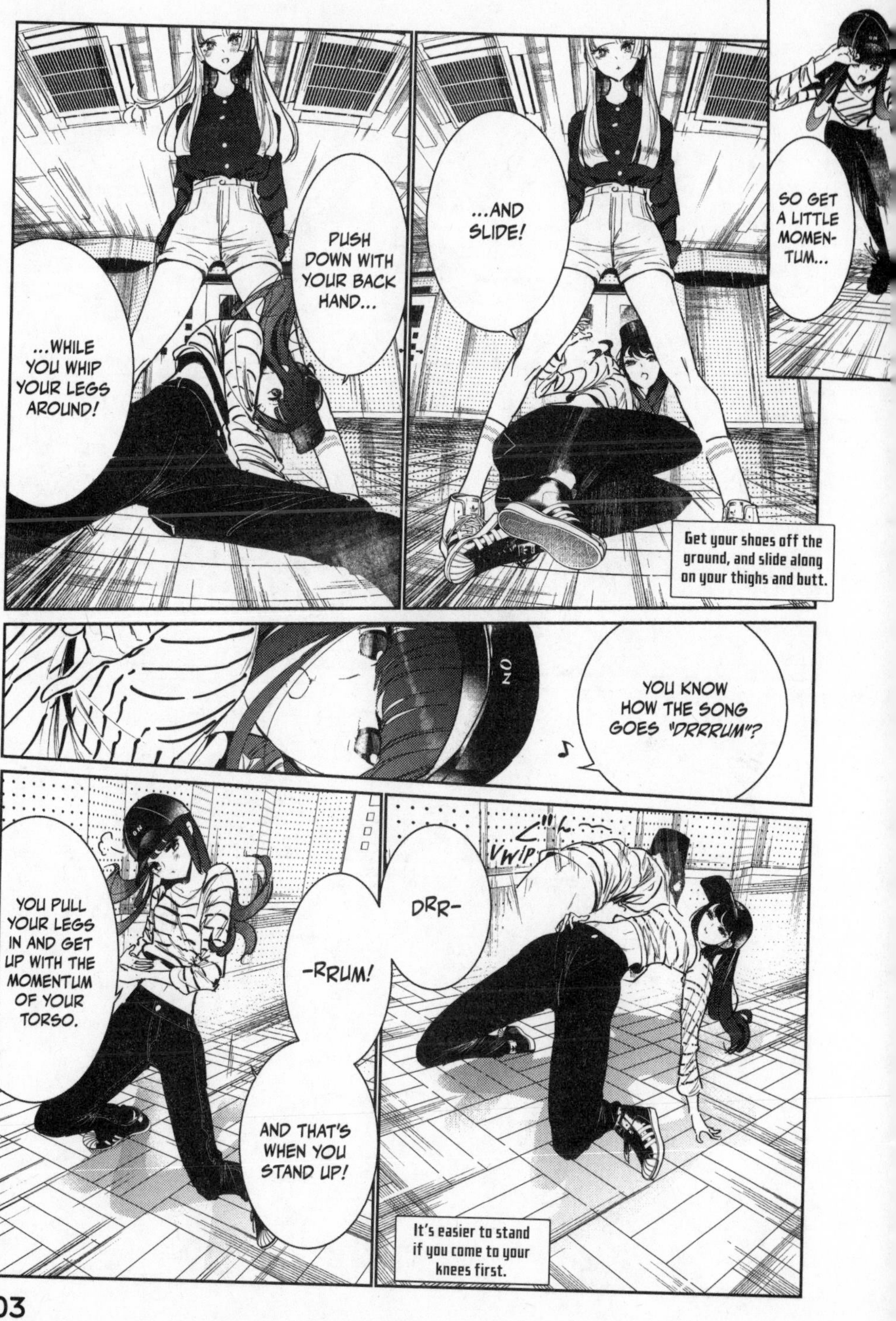
SO GET A LITTLE MOMENTUM...
...AND SLIDE!
Get your shoes off the ground, and slide along on your thighs and butt.
PUSH DOWN WITH YOUR BACK HAND...
...WHILE YOU WHIP YOUR LEGS AROUND!
YOU KNOW HOW THE SONG GOES "DRRRUM"?
VWIP
DRR-
-RRUM!
YOU PULL YOUR LEGS IN AND GET UP WITH THE MOMENTUM OF YOUR TORSO.
AND THAT'S WHEN YOU STAND UP!
It's easier to stand if you come to your knees first.

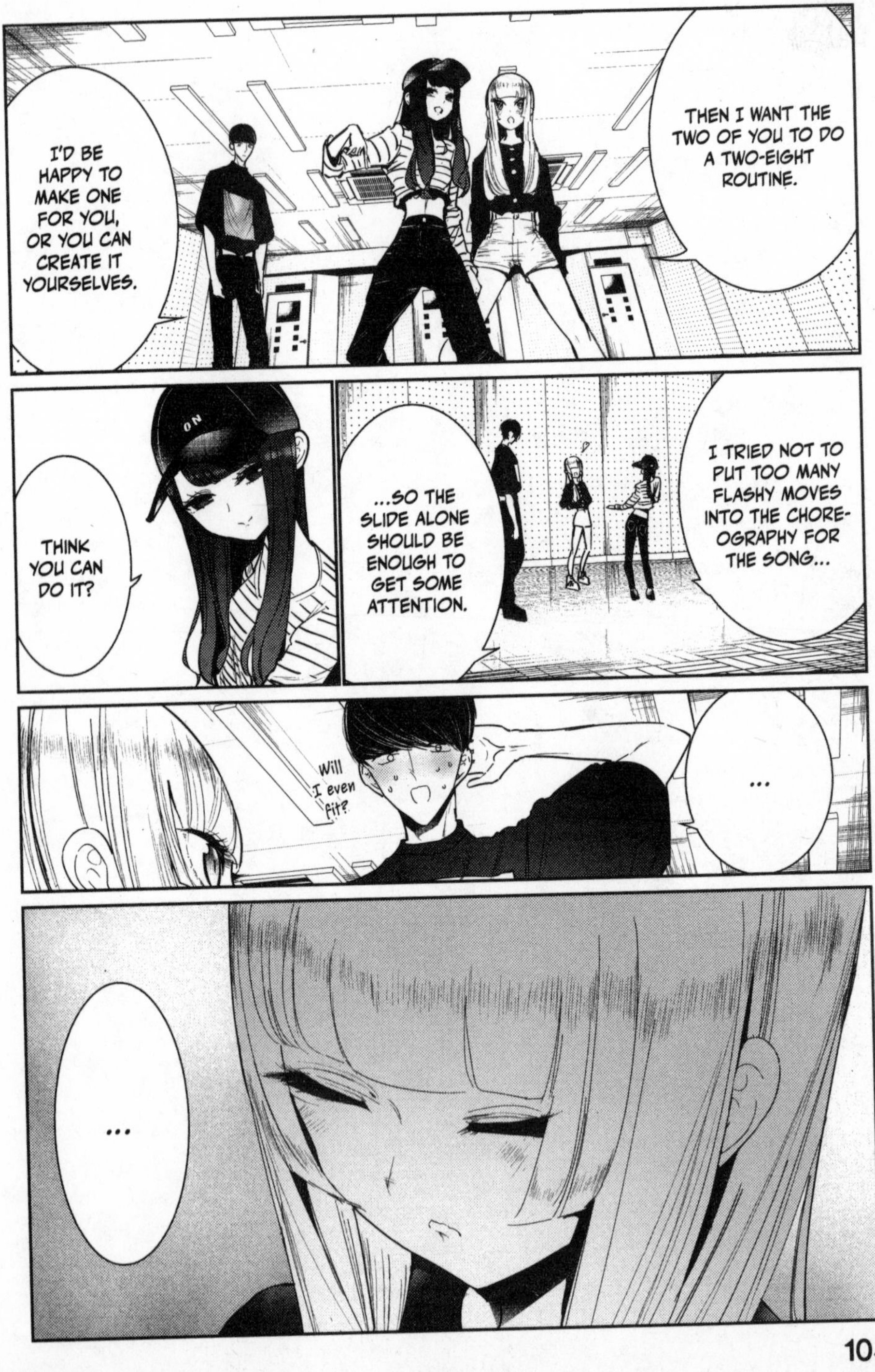
THEN I WANT THE TWO OF YOU TO DO A TWO-EIGHT ROUTINE.
I'D BE HAPPY TO MAKE ONE FOR YOU, OR YOU CAN CREATE IT YOURSELVES.
I TRIED NOT TO PUT TOO MANY FLASHY MOVES INTO THE CHORE-OGRAPHY FOR THE SONG...
...SO THE SLIDE ALONE SHOULD BE ENOUGH TO GET SOME ATTENTION.
THINK YOU CAN DO IT?
...
Will I even fit?
...

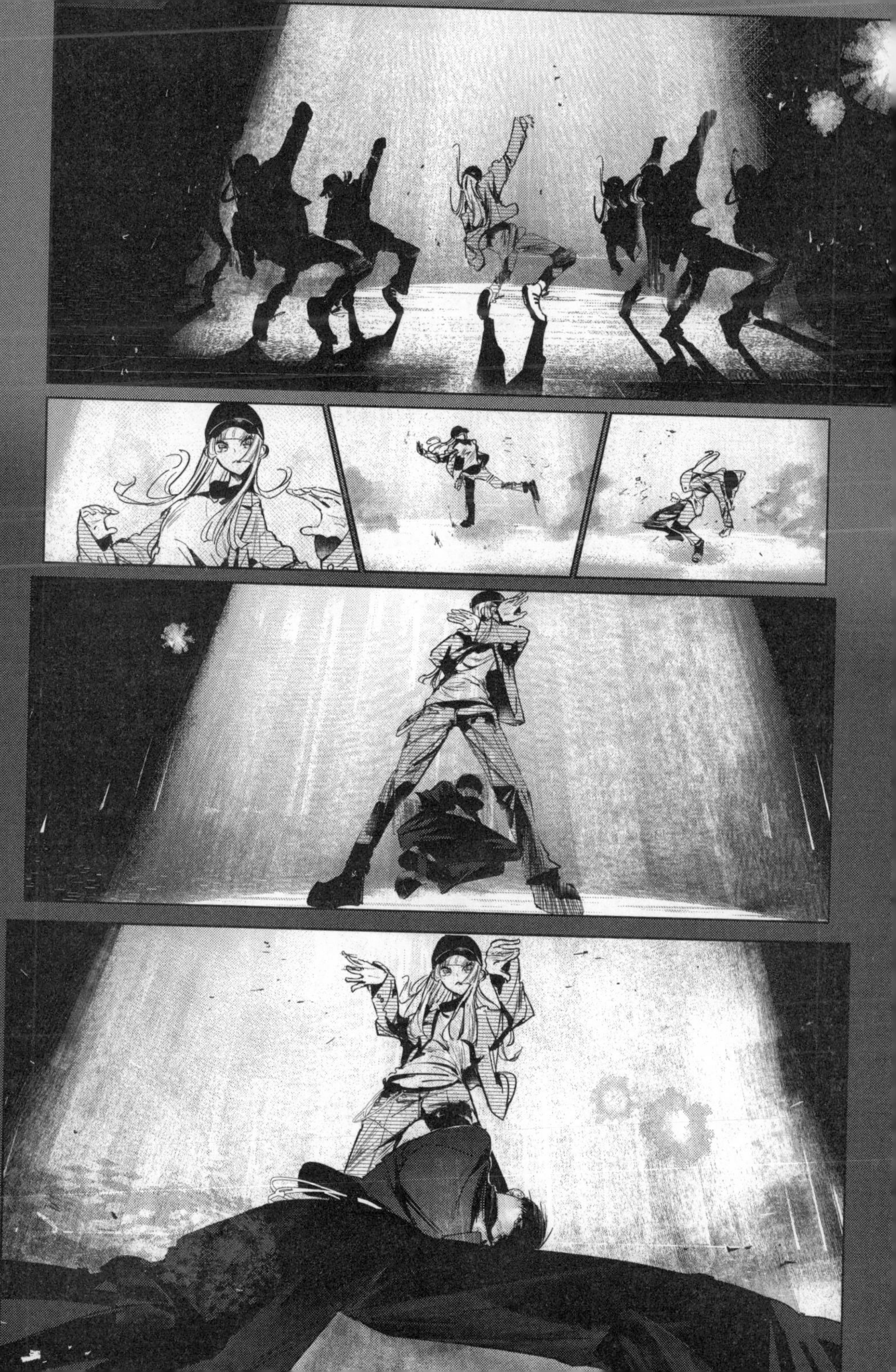

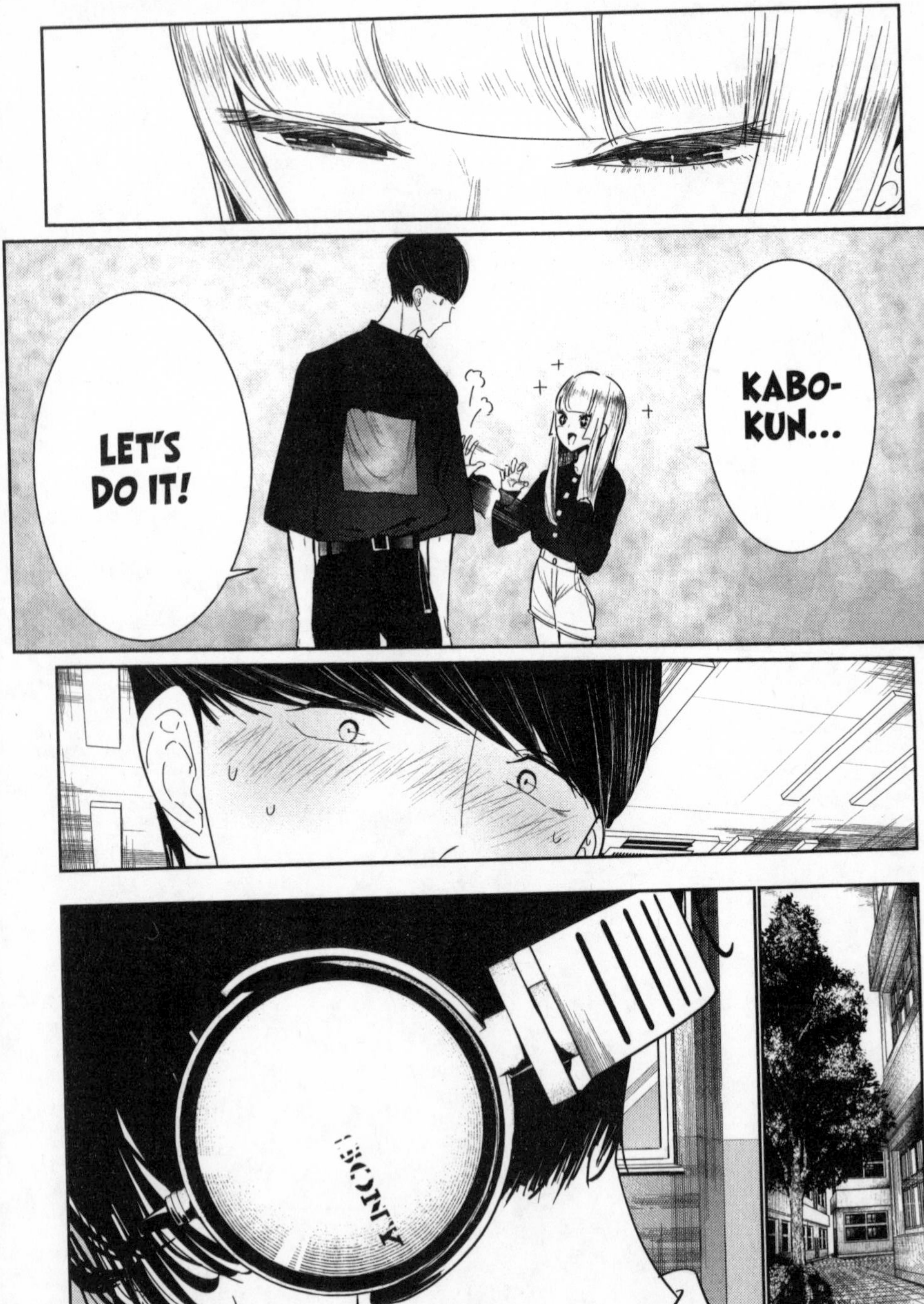
KABO-KUN...
LET'S DO IT!

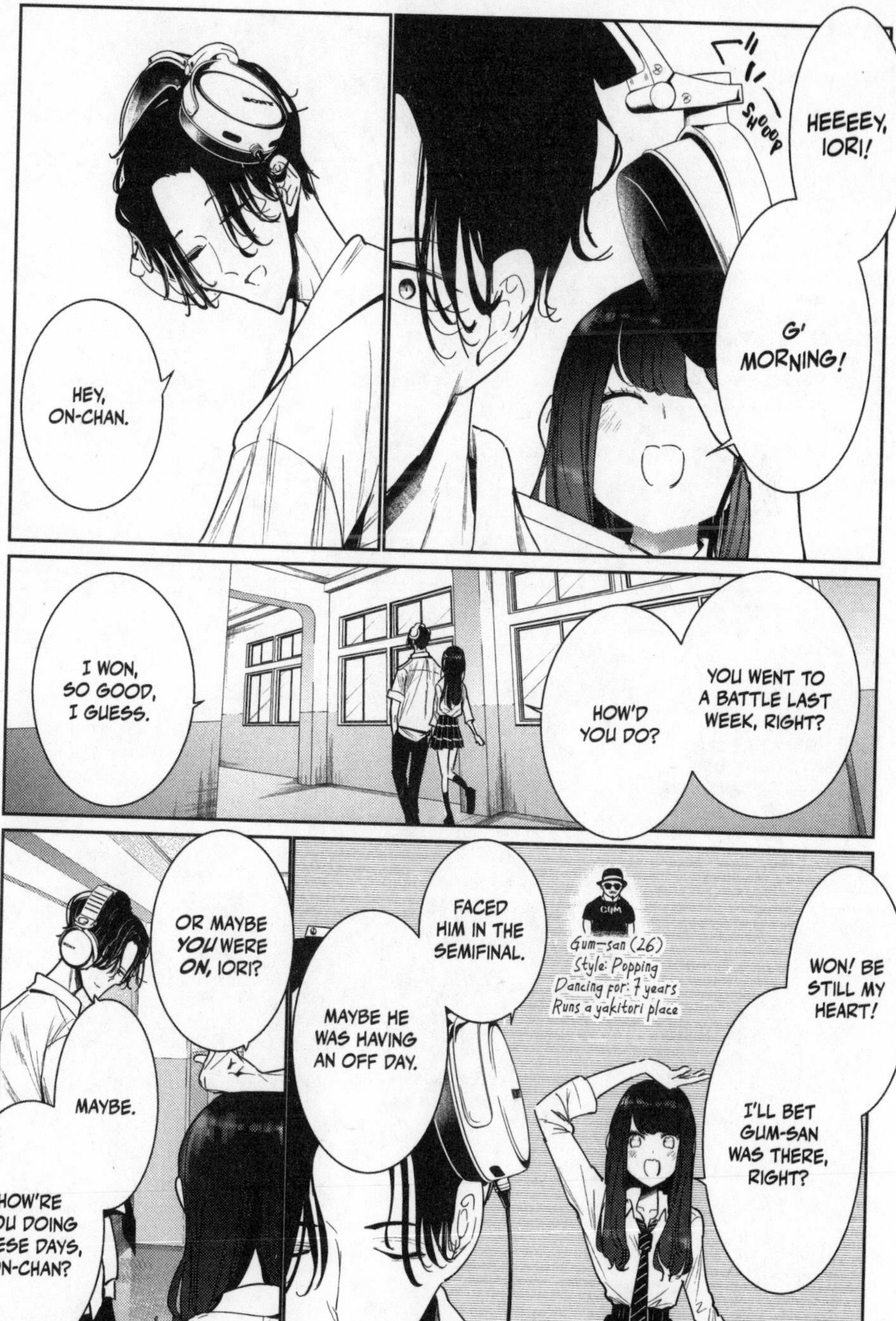
SHOOOP
HEEEEY, IORI!
G' MORNING!
HEY, ON-CHAN.
YOU WENT TO A BATTLE LAST WEEK, RIGHT?
HOW'D YOU DO?
I WON, SO GOOD, I GUESS.
WON! BE STILL MY HEART!
I'LL BET GUM-SAN WAS THERE, RIGHT?
Gum-san (26)
Style: Popping
Dancing for: 7 years
Runs a yakitori place
FACED HIM IN THE SEMIFINAL.
MAYBE HE WAS HAVING AN OFF DAY.
OR MAYBE *YOU* WERE ON, IORI?
MAYBE.
HOW'RE YOU DOING THESE DAYS, ON-CHAN?

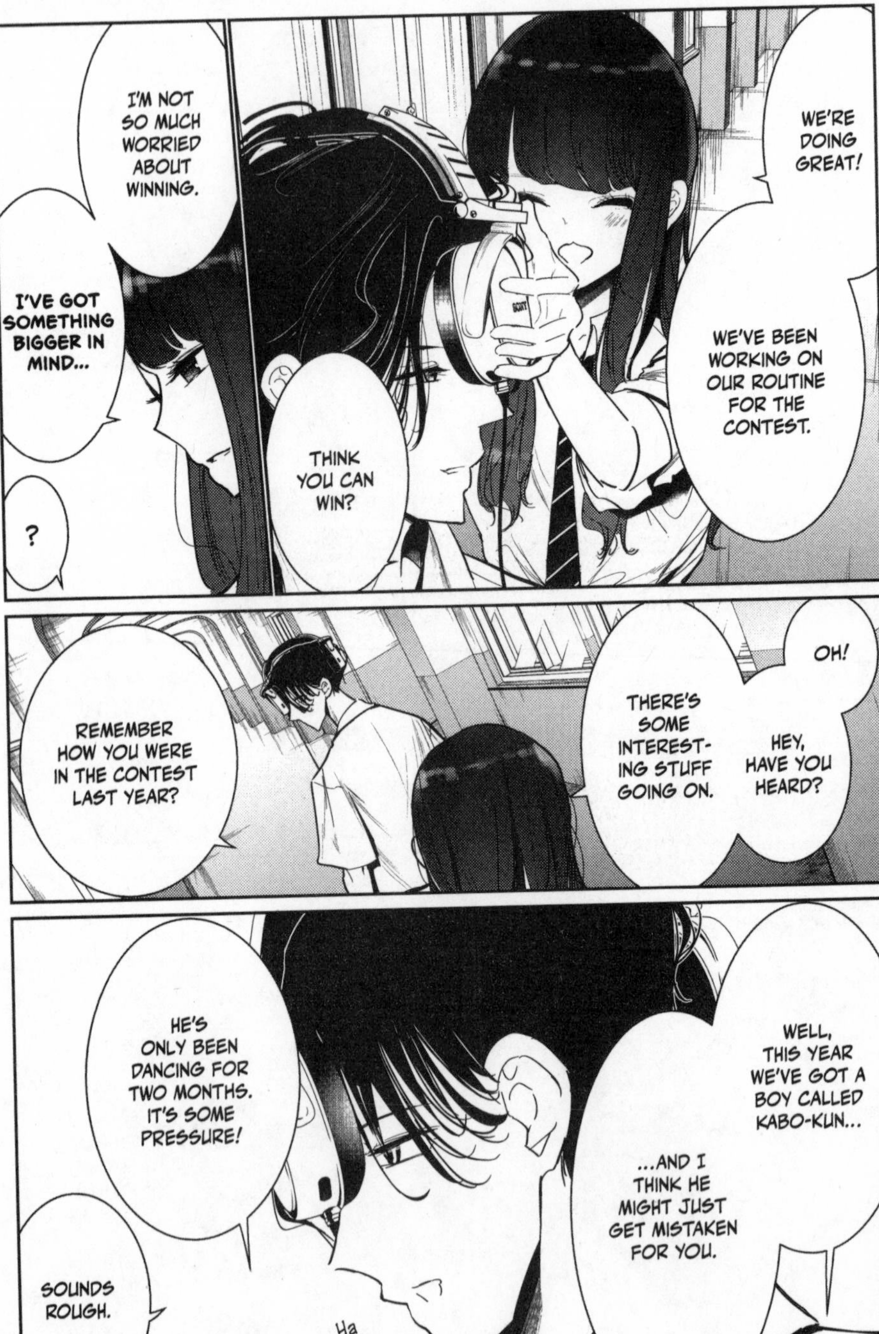
WE'RE DOING GREAT!
WE'VE BEEN WORKING ON OUR ROUTINE FOR THE CONTEST.
THINK YOU CAN WIN?
I'M NOT SO MUCH WORRIED ABOUT WINNING.
I'VE GOT SOMETHING BIGGER IN MIND...
?
OH!
HEY, HAVE YOU HEARD?
THERE'S SOME INTERESTING STUFF GOING ON.
REMEMBER HOW YOU WERE IN THE CONTEST LAST YEAR?
WELL, THIS YEAR WE'VE GOT A BOY CALLED KABO-KUN...
...AND I THINK HE MIGHT JUST GET MISTAKEN FOR YOU.
HE'S ONLY BEEN DANCING FOR TWO MONTHS. IT'S SOME PRESSURE!
Ha ha.
SOUNDS ROUGH.

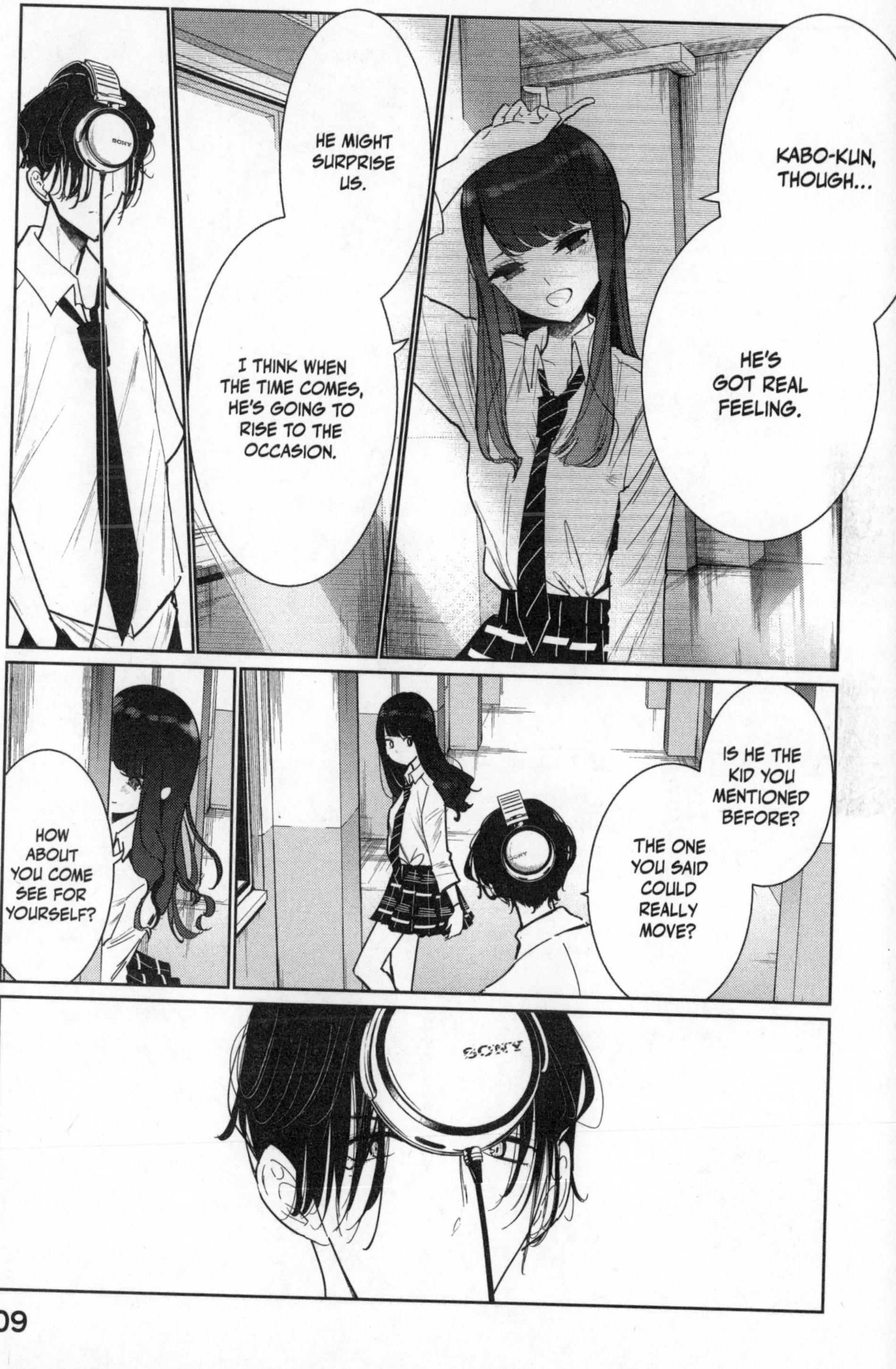
KABO-KUN, THOUGH...
HE'S GOT REAL FEELING.
HE MIGHT SURPRISE US.
I THINK WHEN THE TIME COMES, HE'S GOING TO RISE TO THE OCCASION.
SONY
IS HE THE KID YOU MENTIONED BEFORE?
THE ONE YOU SAID COULD REALLY MOVE?
SONY
HOW ABOUT YOU COME SEE FOR YOURSELF?
SONY

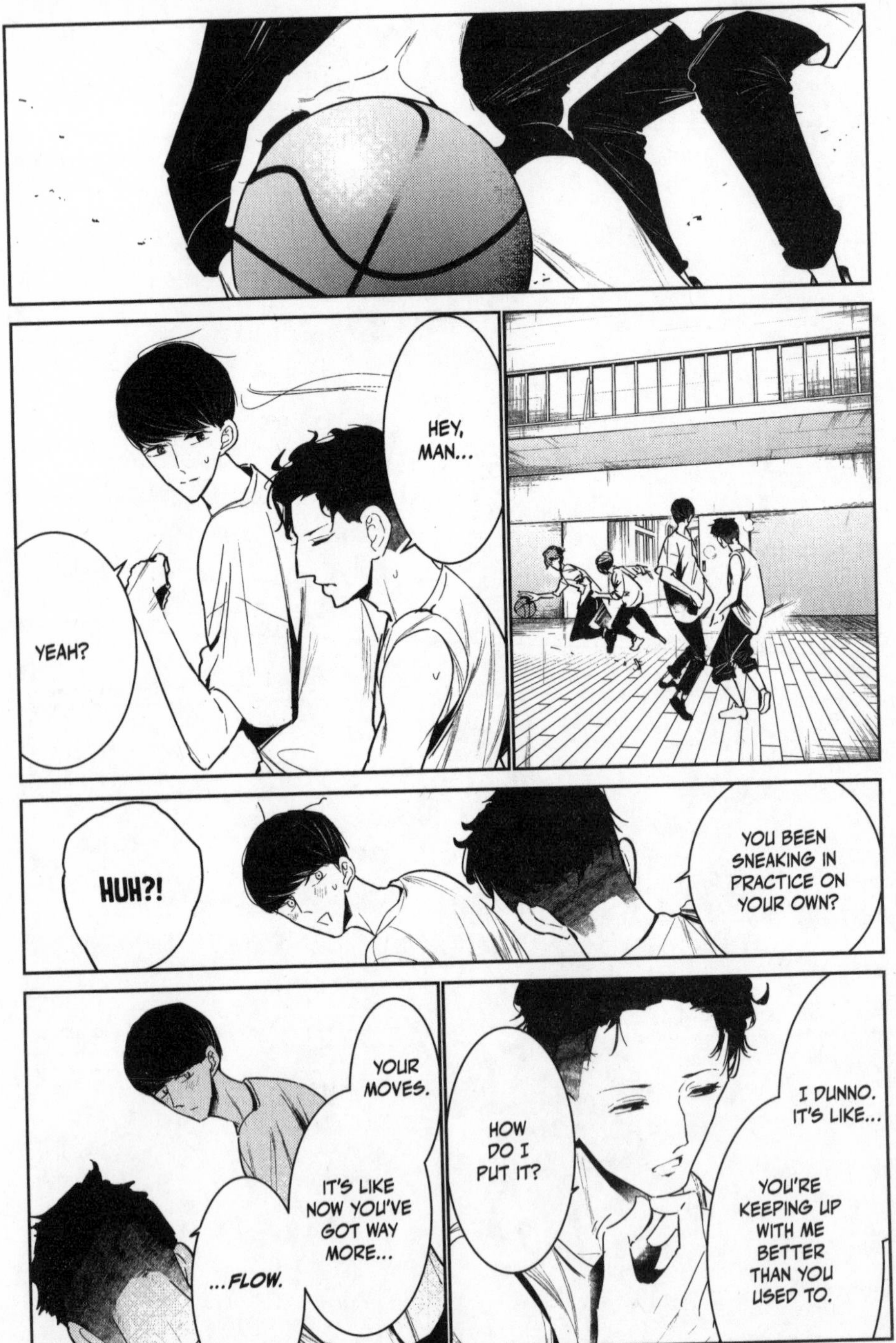
HEY, MAN...
YEAH?
YOU BEEN SNEAKING IN PRACTICE ON YOUR OWN?
HUH?!
I DUNNO. IT'S LIKE...
YOU'RE KEEPING UP WITH ME BETTER THAN YOU USED TO.
HOW DO I PUT IT?
YOUR MOVES.
IT'S LIKE NOW YOU'VE GOT WAY MORE...
...FLOW.

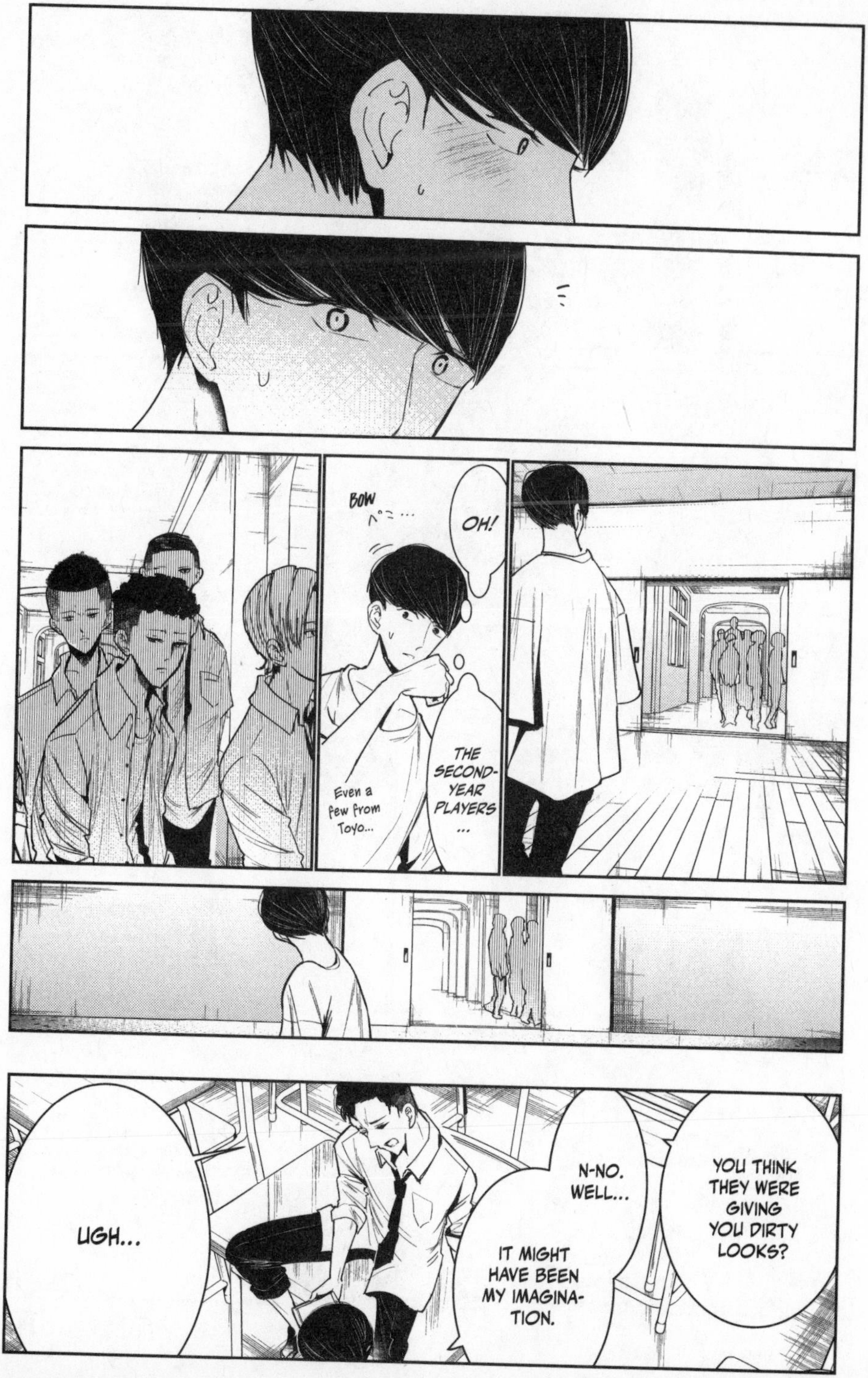
OH!
BOW
THE SECOND-YEAR PLAYERS ...
Even a few from Toyo...
YOU THINK THEY WERE GIVING YOU DIRTY LOOKS?
N-NO. WELL...
IT MIGHT HAVE BEEN MY IMAGINATION.
UGH...

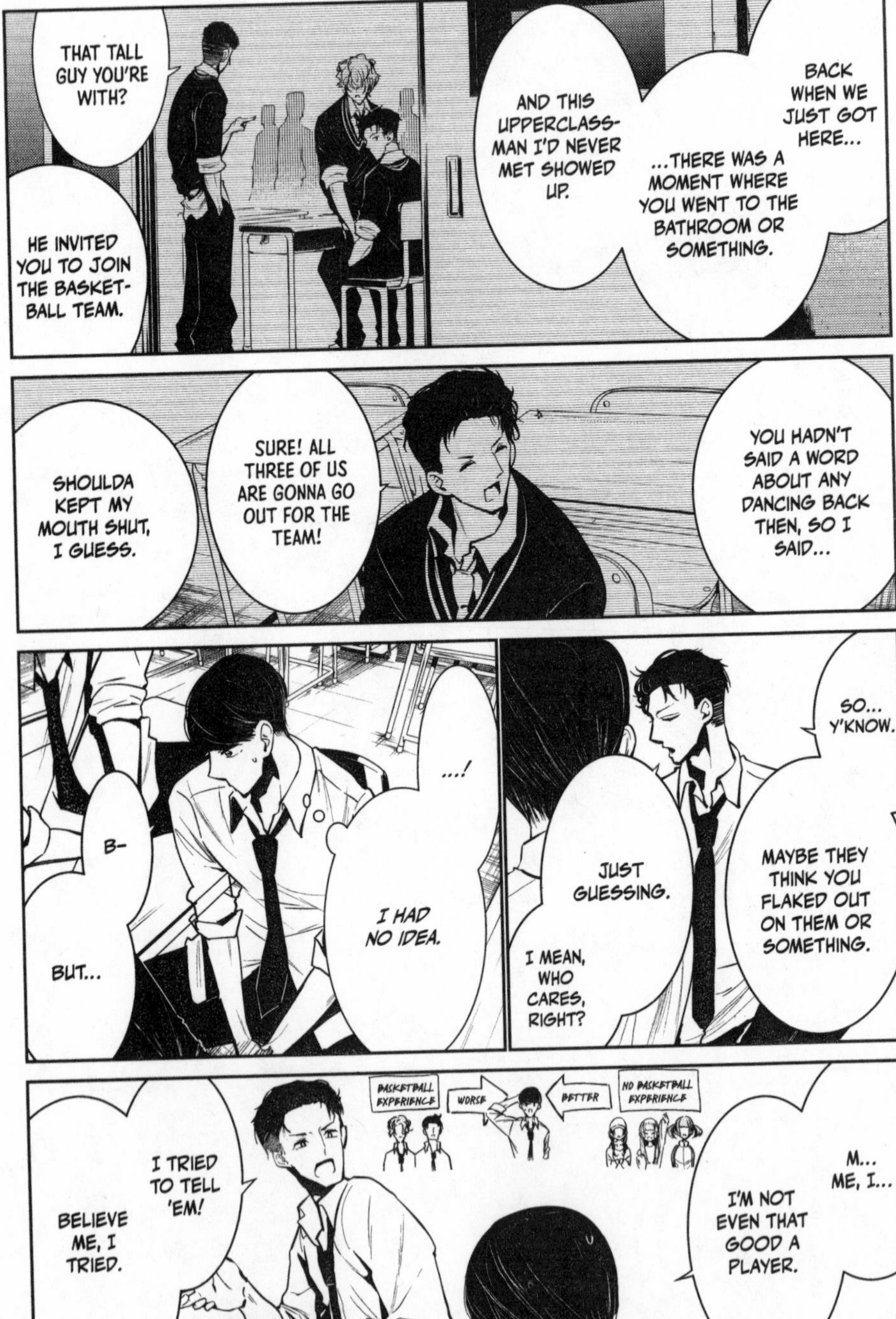
BACK WHEN WE JUST GOT HERE...
...THERE WAS A MOMENT WHERE YOU WENT TO THE BATHROOM OR SOMETHING.
AND THIS UPPERCLASSMAN I'D NEVER MET SHOWED UP.
THAT TALL GUY YOU'RE WITH?
HE INVITED YOU TO JOIN THE BASKETBALL TEAM.
YOU HADN'T SAID A WORD ABOUT ANY DANCING BACK THEN, SO I SAID...
SURE! ALL THREE OF US ARE GONNA GO OUT FOR THE TEAM!
SHOULDA KEPT MY MOUTH SHUT, I GUESS.
SO... Y'KNOW.
MAYBE THEY THINK YOU FLAKED OUT ON THEM OR SOMETHING.
JUST GUESSING.
I MEAN, WHO CARES, RIGHT?
...!
I HAD NO IDEA.
B-
BUT...
M... ME, I...
I'M NOT EVEN THAT GOOD A PLAYER.
BASKETBALL EXPERIENCE
WORSE
BETTER
NO BASKETBALL EXPERIENCE
I TRIED TO TELL 'EM!
BELIEVE ME, I TRIED.

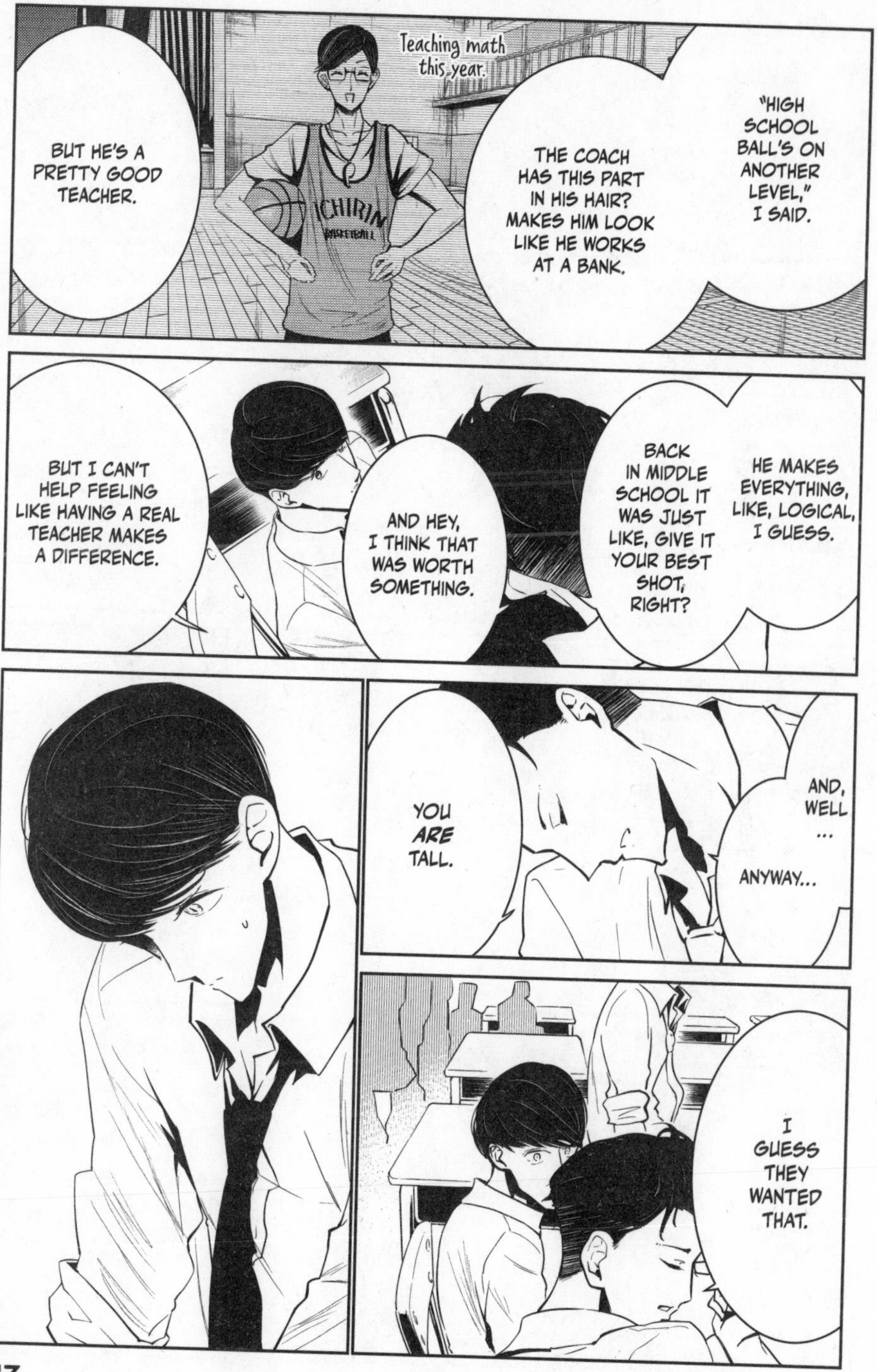
"HIGH SCHOOL BALL'S ON ANOTHER LEVEL," I SAID.
THE COACH HAS THIS PART IN HIS HAIR? MAKES HIM LOOK LIKE HE WORKS AT A BANK.
Teaching math this year.
BUT HE'S A PRETTY GOOD TEACHER.
HE MAKES EVERYTHING, LIKE, LOGICAL, I GUESS.
BACK IN MIDDLE SCHOOL IT WAS JUST LIKE, GIVE IT YOUR BEST SHOT, RIGHT?
AND HEY, I THINK THAT WAS WORTH SOMETHING.
BUT I CAN'T HELP FEELING LIKE HAVING A REAL TEACHER MAKES A DIFFERENCE.
AND, WELL ...
ANYWAY...
YOU *ARE* TALL.
I GUESS THEY WANTED THAT.

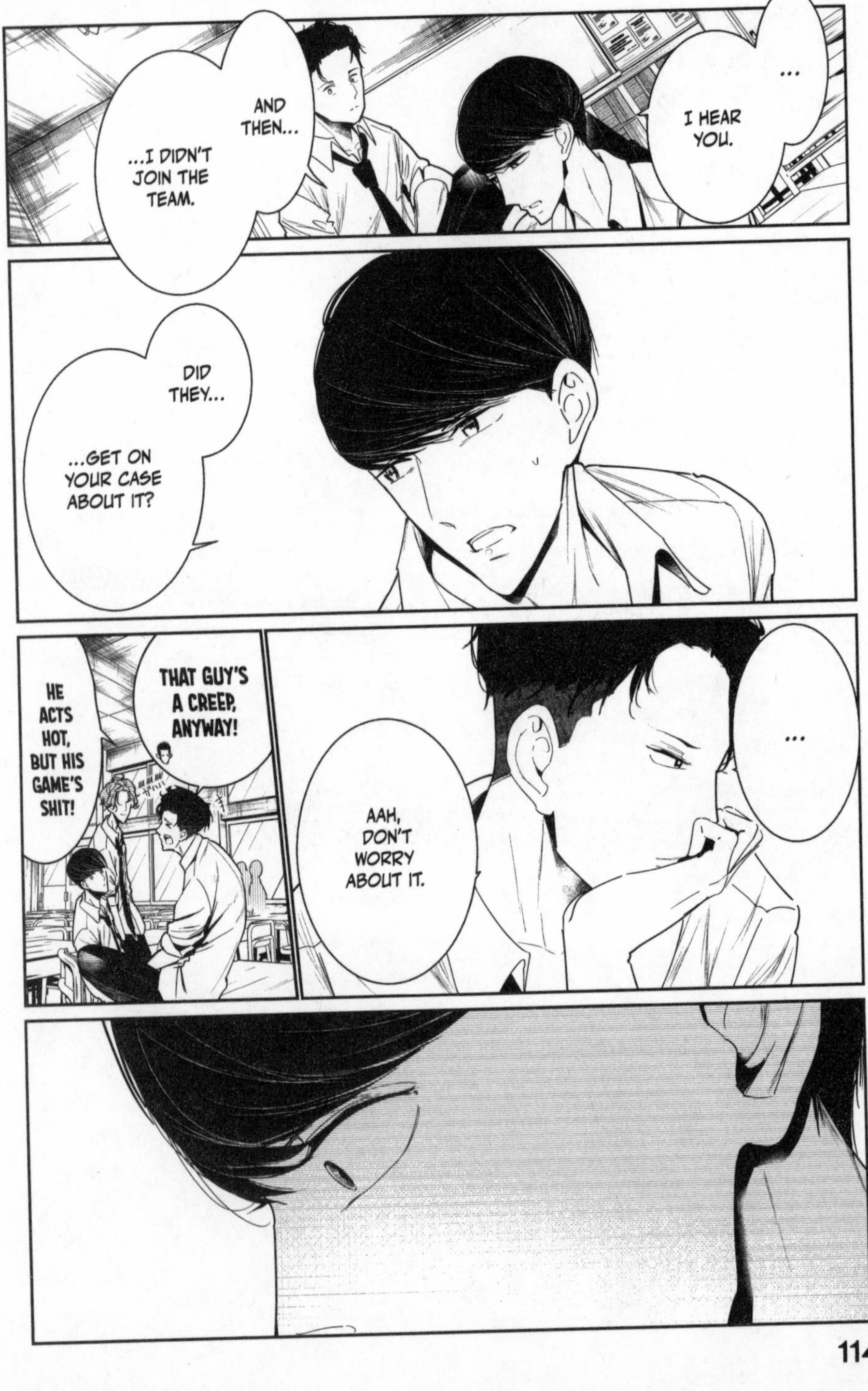
...
I HEAR YOU.
AND THEN...
...I DIDN'T JOIN THE TEAM.
DID THEY...
...GET ON YOUR CASE ABOUT IT?
...
AAH, DON'T WORRY ABOUT IT.
THAT GUY'S A CREEP, ANYWAY!
HE ACTS HOT, BUT HIS GAME'S SHIT!

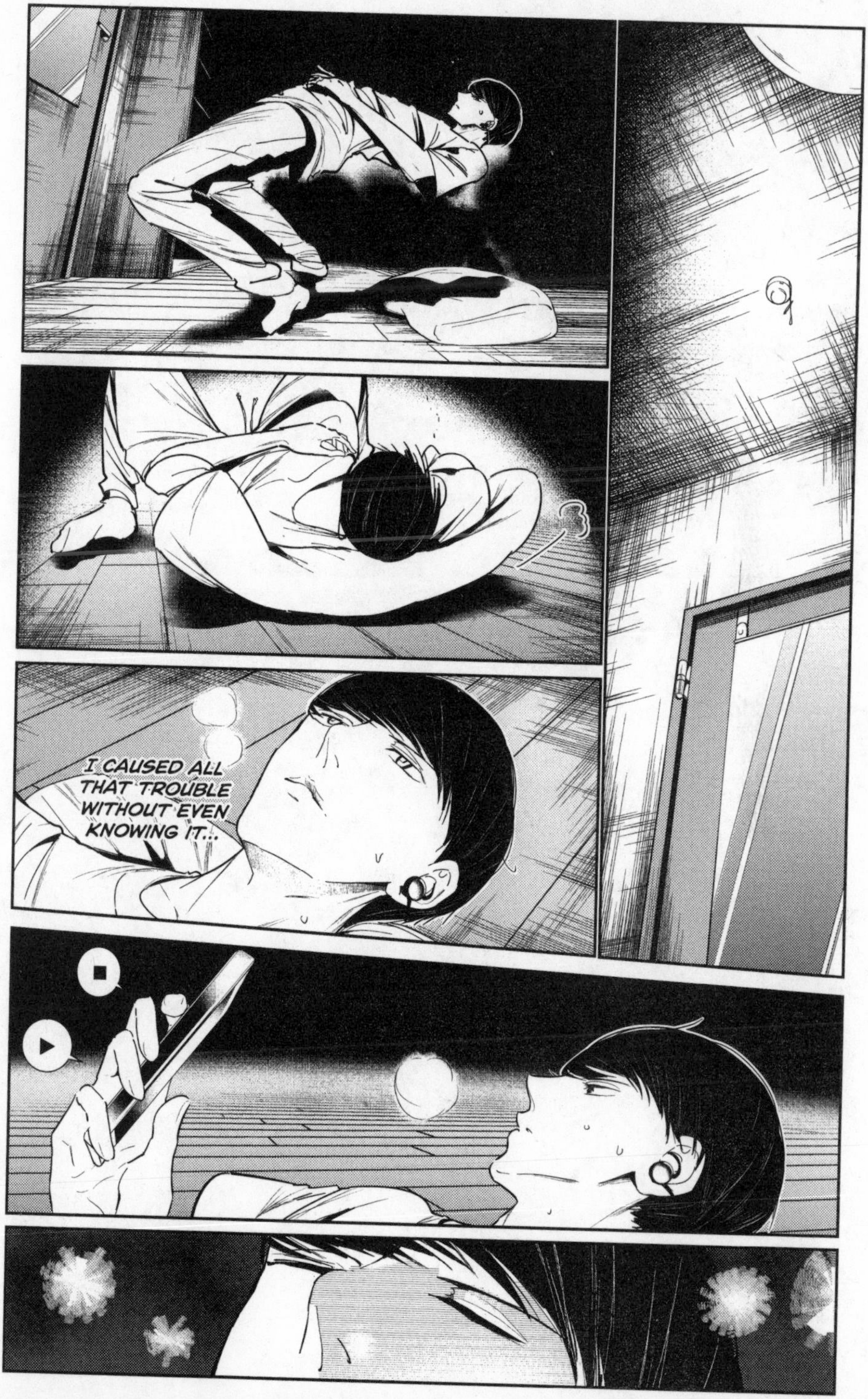
I CAUSED ALL THAT TROUBLE WITHOUT EVEN KNOWING IT...

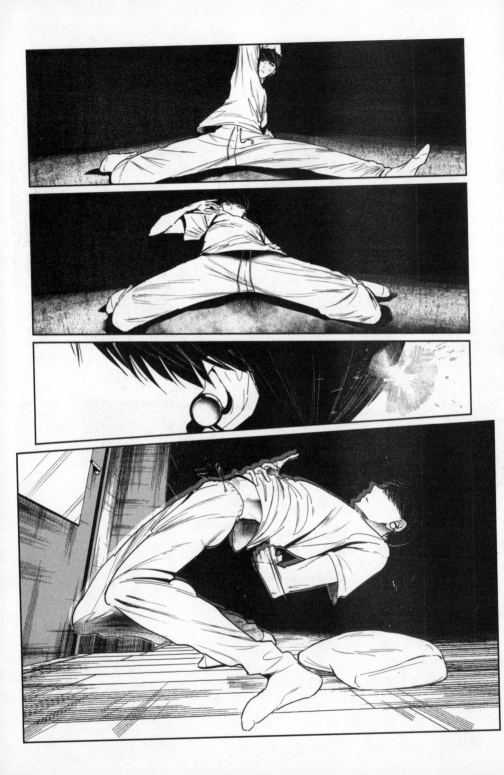

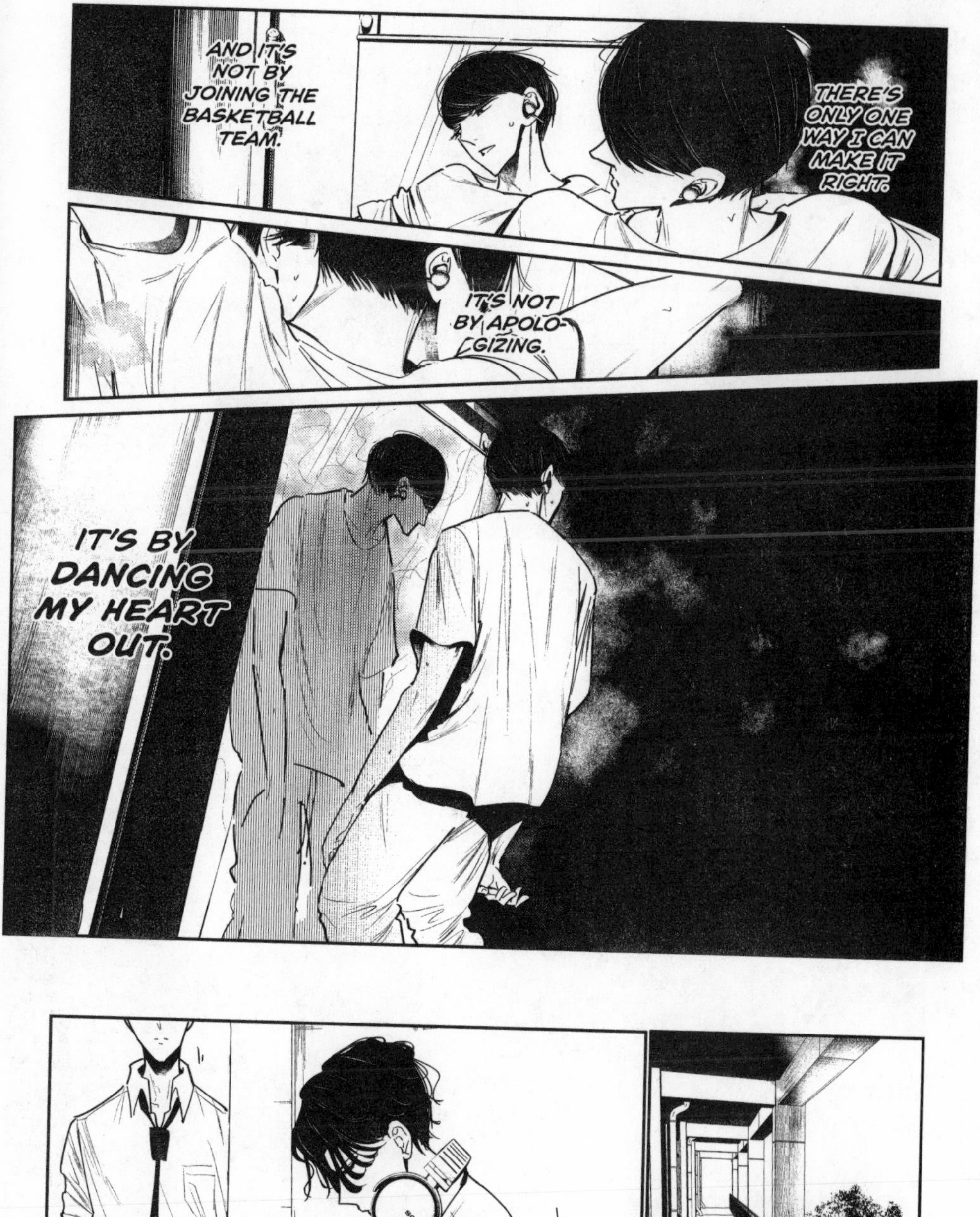
THERE'S ONLY ONE WAY I CAN MAKE IT RIGHT.
AND IT'S NOT BY JOINING THE BASKETBALL TEAM.
IT'S NOT BY APOLO-GIZING.
IT'S BY DANCING MY HEART OUT.

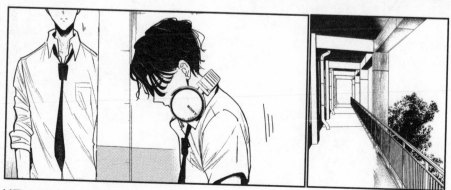

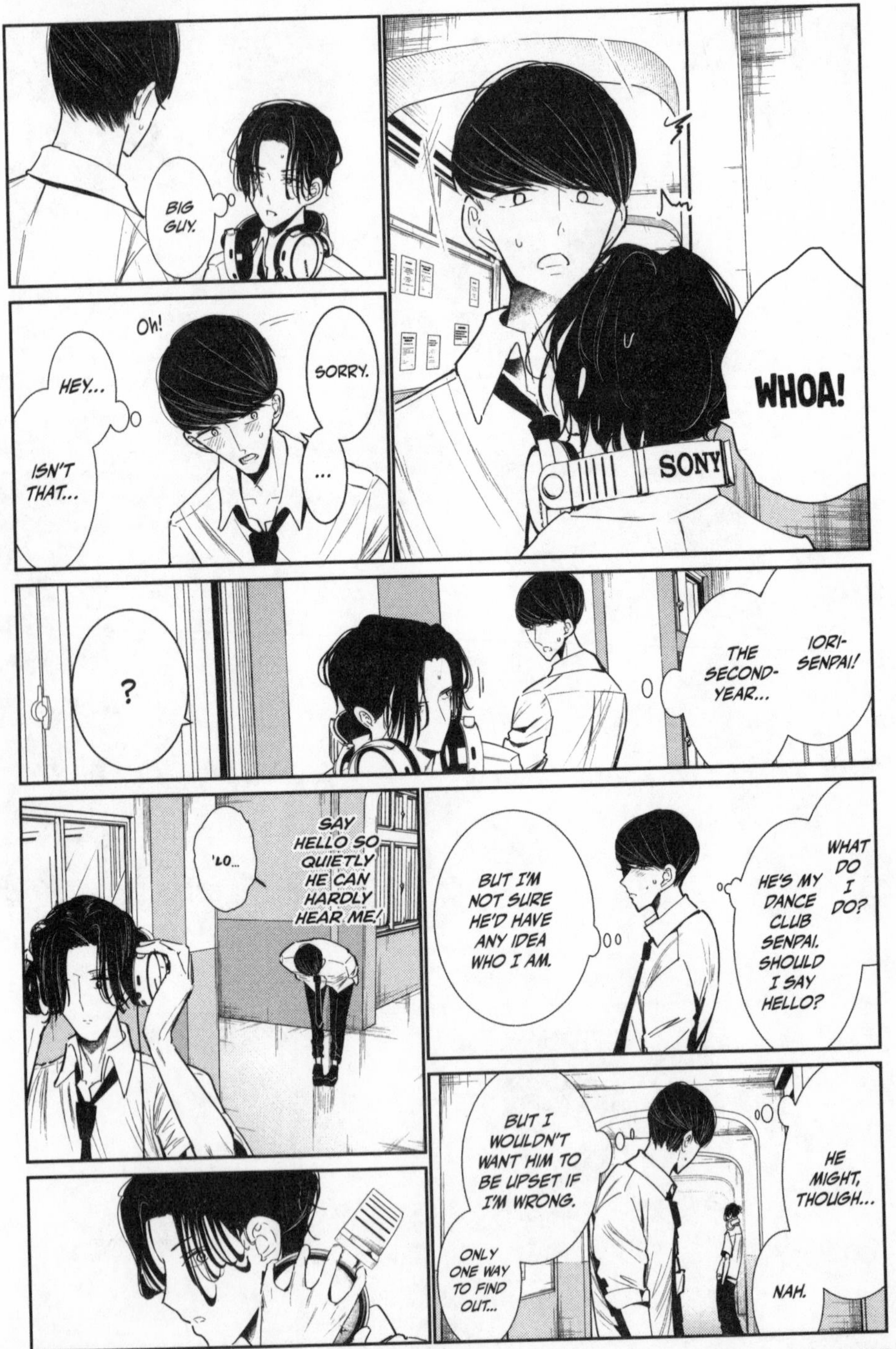
WHOA!
SONY
BIG GUY.
SORRY.
...
Oh!
HEY...
ISN'T THAT...
IORI-SENPAI!
THE SECOND-YEAR...
?
WHAT DO I DO?
HE'S MY DANCE CLUB SENPAI. SHOULD I SAY HELLO?
BUT I'M NOT SURE HE'D HAVE ANY IDEA WHO I AM.
HE MIGHT, THOUGH...
NAH.
BUT I WOULDN'T WANT HIM TO BE UPSET IF I'M WRONG.
ONLY ONE WAY TO FIND OUT...
'LO...
SAY HELLO SO QUIETLY HE CAN HARDLY HEAR ME!

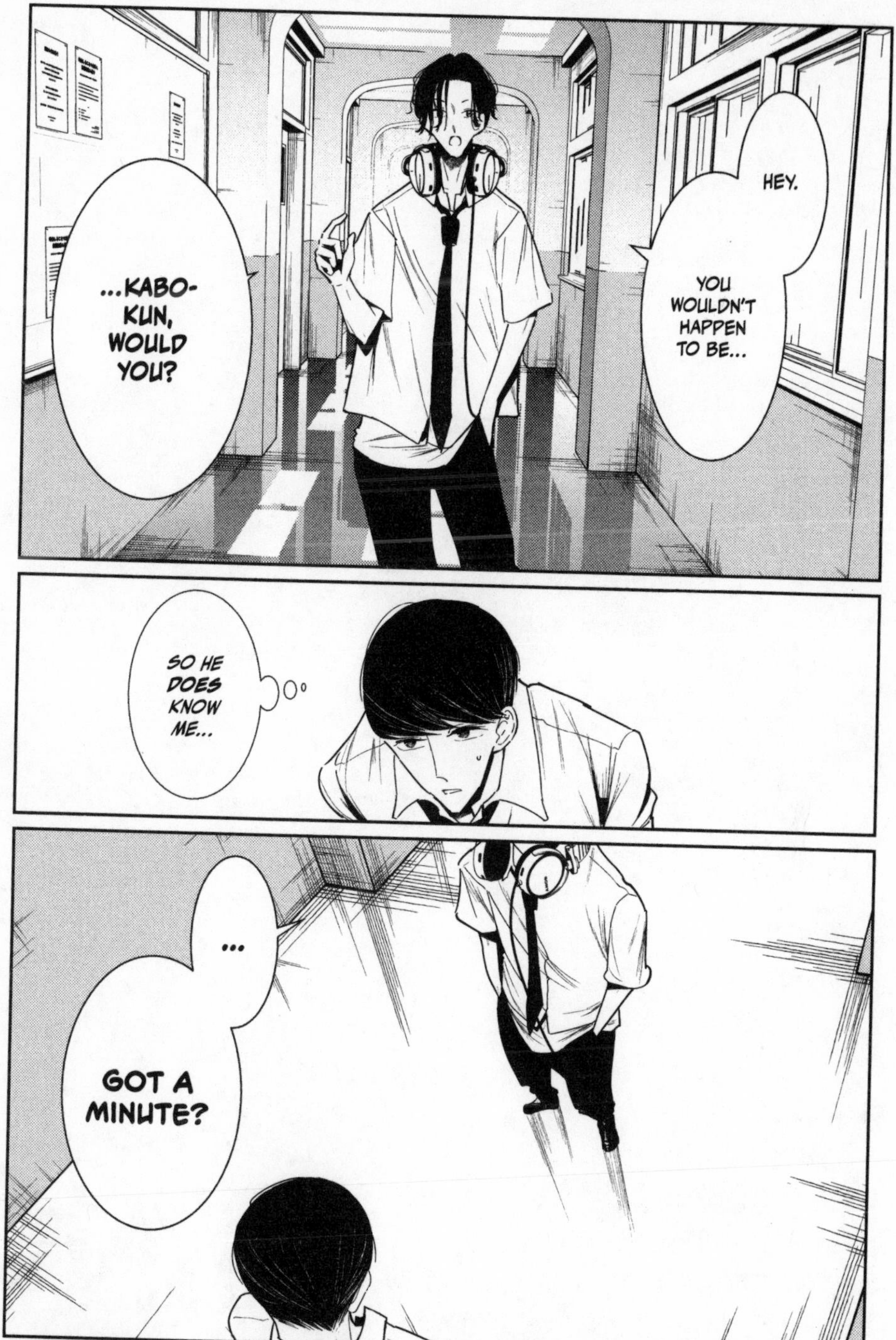
HEY.
YOU WOULDN'T HAPPEN TO BE...
...KABO-KUN, WOULD YOU?
SO HE DOES KNOW ME...
...
GOT A MINUTE?

Ch. 6: END

WANDANCE

Ch. 7: Feeling (Pt. 2)

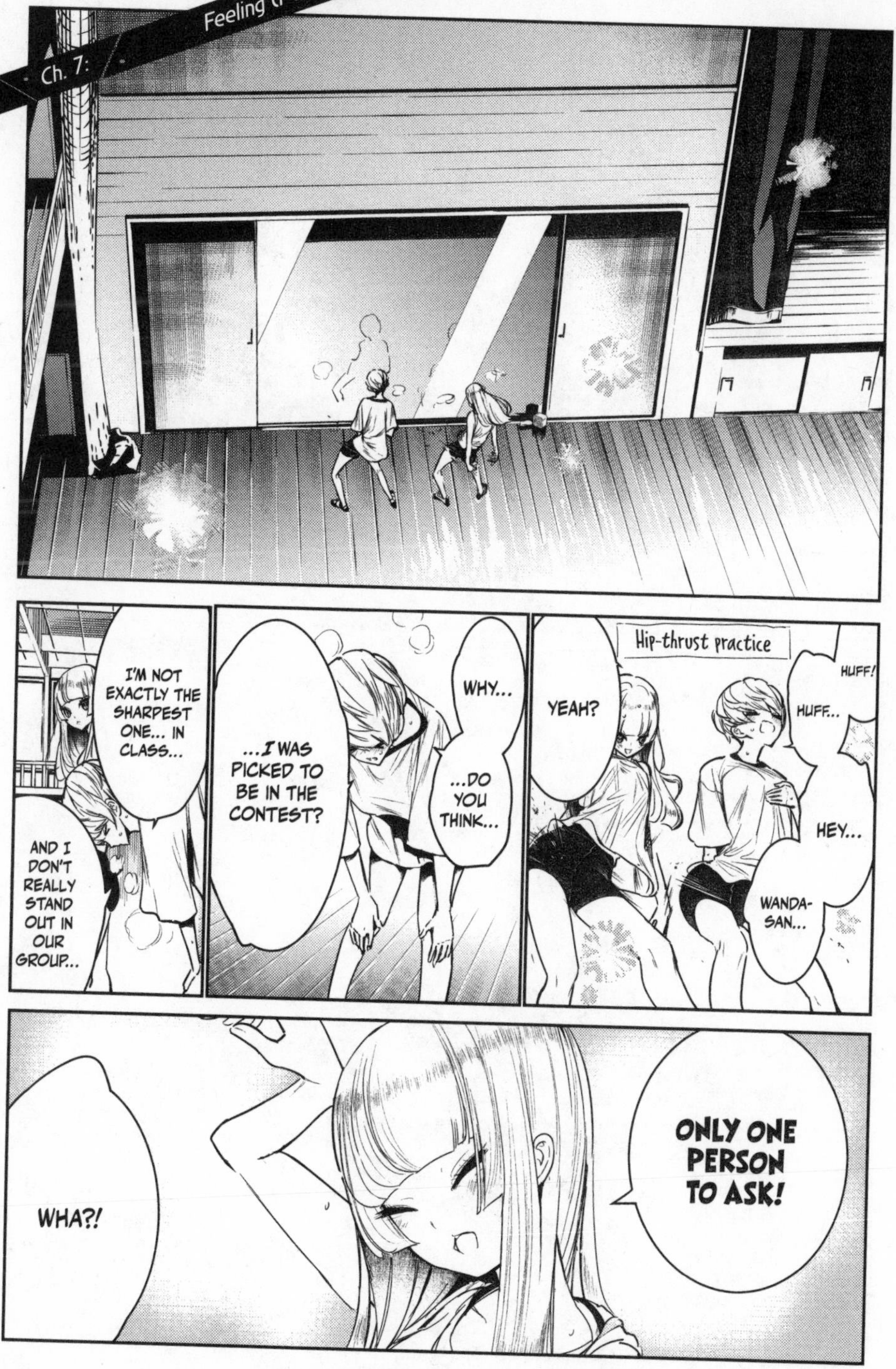
Hip-thrust practice
HUFF!
HUFF...
HEY...
WANDA-SAN...
YEAH?
WHY...
...DO YOU THINK...
...I WAS PICKED TO BE IN THE CONTEST?
I'M NOT EXACTLY THE SHARPEST ONE... IN CLASS...
AND I DON'T REALLY STAND OUT IN OUR GROUP...
ONLY ONE PERSON TO ASK!
WHA?!

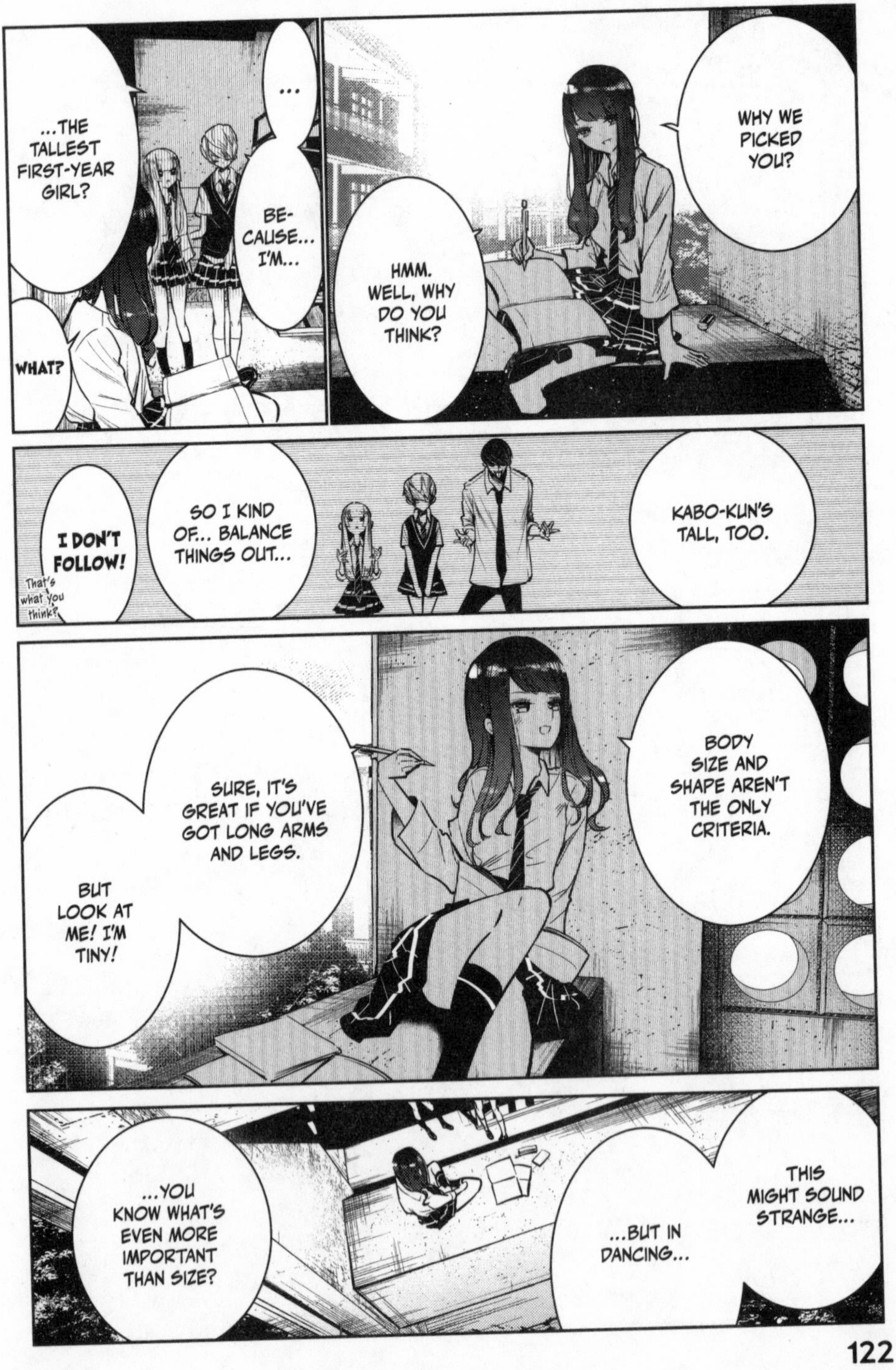
WHY WE PICKED YOU?
HMM. WELL, WHY DO YOU THINK?
...
BE-CAUSE... I'M...
...THE TALLEST FIRST-YEAR GIRL?
WHAT?
KABO-KUN'S TALL, TOO.
SO I KIND OF... BALANCE THINGS OUT...
I DON'T FOLLOW!
That's what you think?
BODY SIZE AND SHAPE AREN'T THE ONLY CRITERIA.
SURE, IT'S GREAT IF YOU'VE GOT LONG ARMS AND LEGS.
BUT LOOK AT ME! I'M TINY!
THIS MIGHT SOUND STRANGE...
...BUT IN DANCING...
...YOU KNOW WHAT'S EVEN MORE IMPORTANT THAN SIZE?

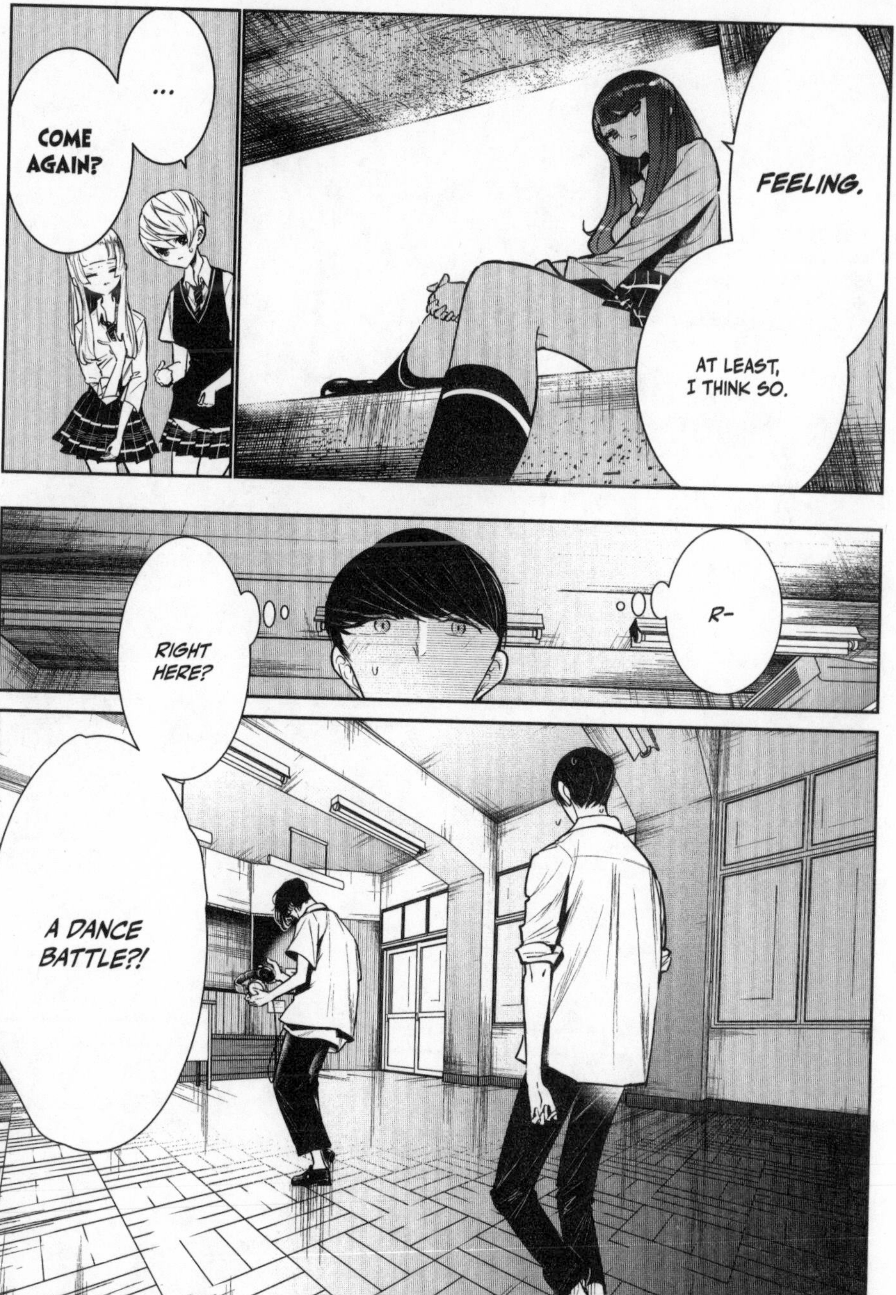
FEELING.
AT LEAST, I THINK SO.
...
COME AGAIN?
R-
RIGHT HERE?
A DANCE BATTLE?!

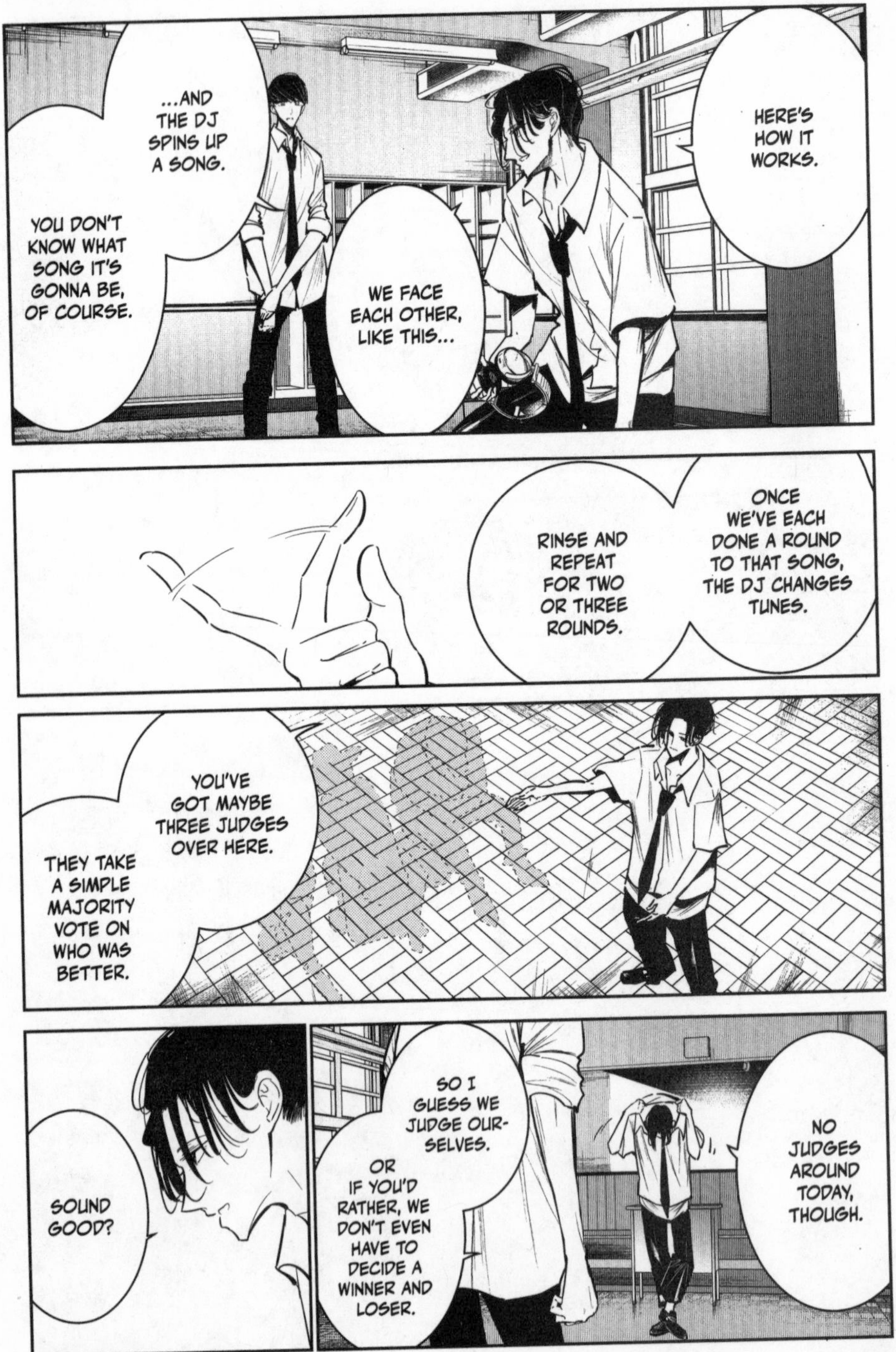
HERE'S HOW IT WORKS.
WE FACE EACH OTHER, LIKE THIS...
...AND THE DJ SPINS UP A SONG.
YOU DON'T KNOW WHAT SONG IT'S GONNA BE, OF COURSE.
ONCE WE'VE EACH DONE A ROUND TO THAT SONG, THE DJ CHANGES TUNES.
RINSE AND REPEAT FOR TWO OR THREE ROUNDS.
YOU'VE GOT MAYBE THREE JUDGES OVER HERE.
THEY TAKE A SIMPLE MAJORITY VOTE ON WHO WAS BETTER.
NO JUDGES AROUND TODAY, THOUGH.
SO I GUESS WE JUDGE OURSELVES.
OR IF YOU'D RATHER, WE DON'T EVEN HAVE TO DECIDE A WINNER AND LOSER.
SOUND GOOD?

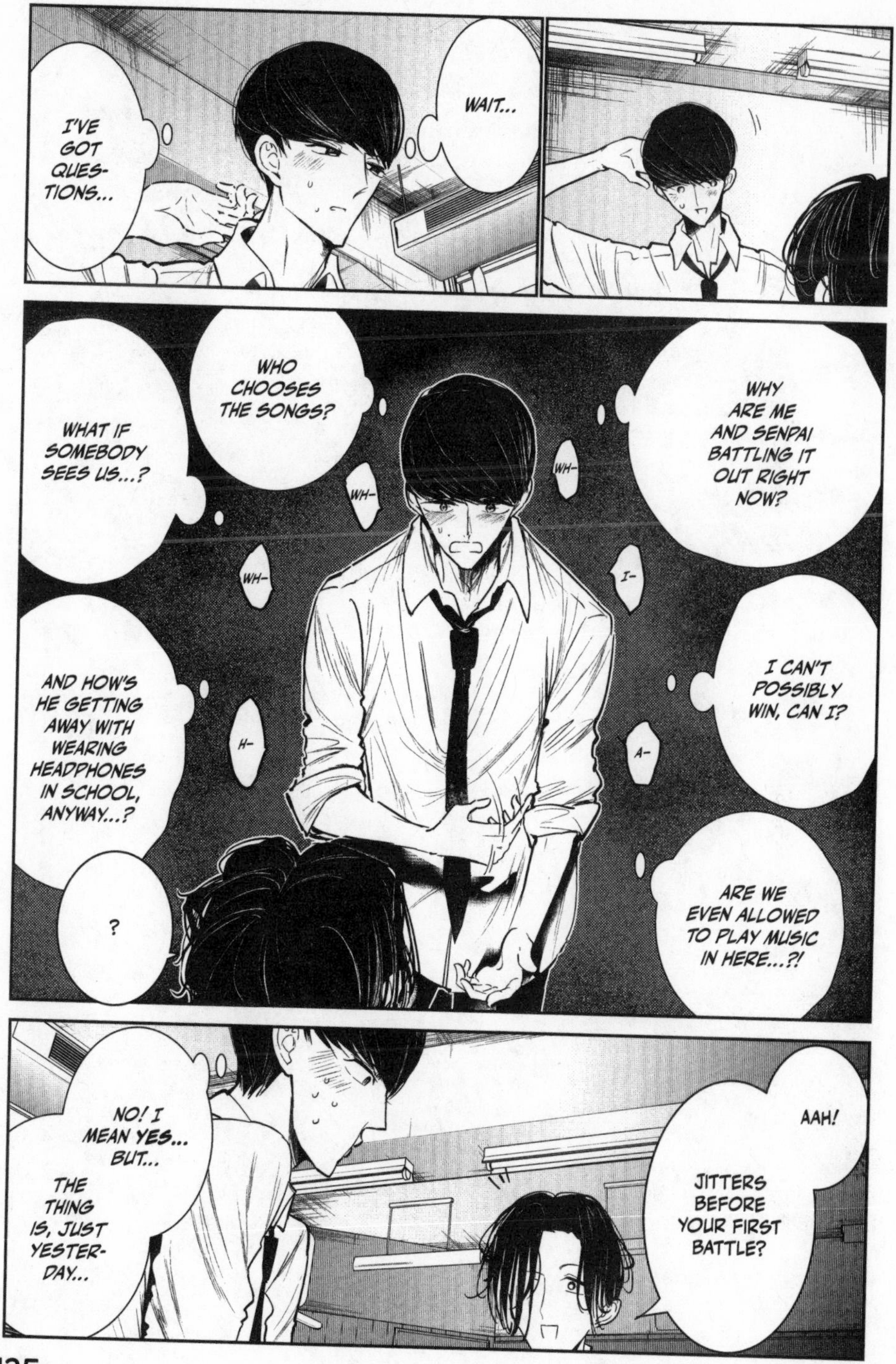
WAIT...
I'VE GOT QUES-TIONS...
WHY ARE ME AND SENPAI BATTLING IT OUT RIGHT NOW?
WH-
WHO CHOOSES THE SONGS?
WH-
WHAT IF SOMEBODY SEES US...?
I-
WH-
I CAN'T POSSIBLY WIN, CAN I?
A-
H-
AND HOW'S HE GETTING AWAY WITH WEARING HEADPHONES IN SCHOOL, ANYWAY...?
ARE WE EVEN ALLOWED TO PLAY MUSIC IN HERE...?!
?
AAH!
JITTERS BEFORE YOUR FIRST BATTLE?
NO! I MEAN YES... BUT...
THE THING IS, JUST YESTER-DAY...

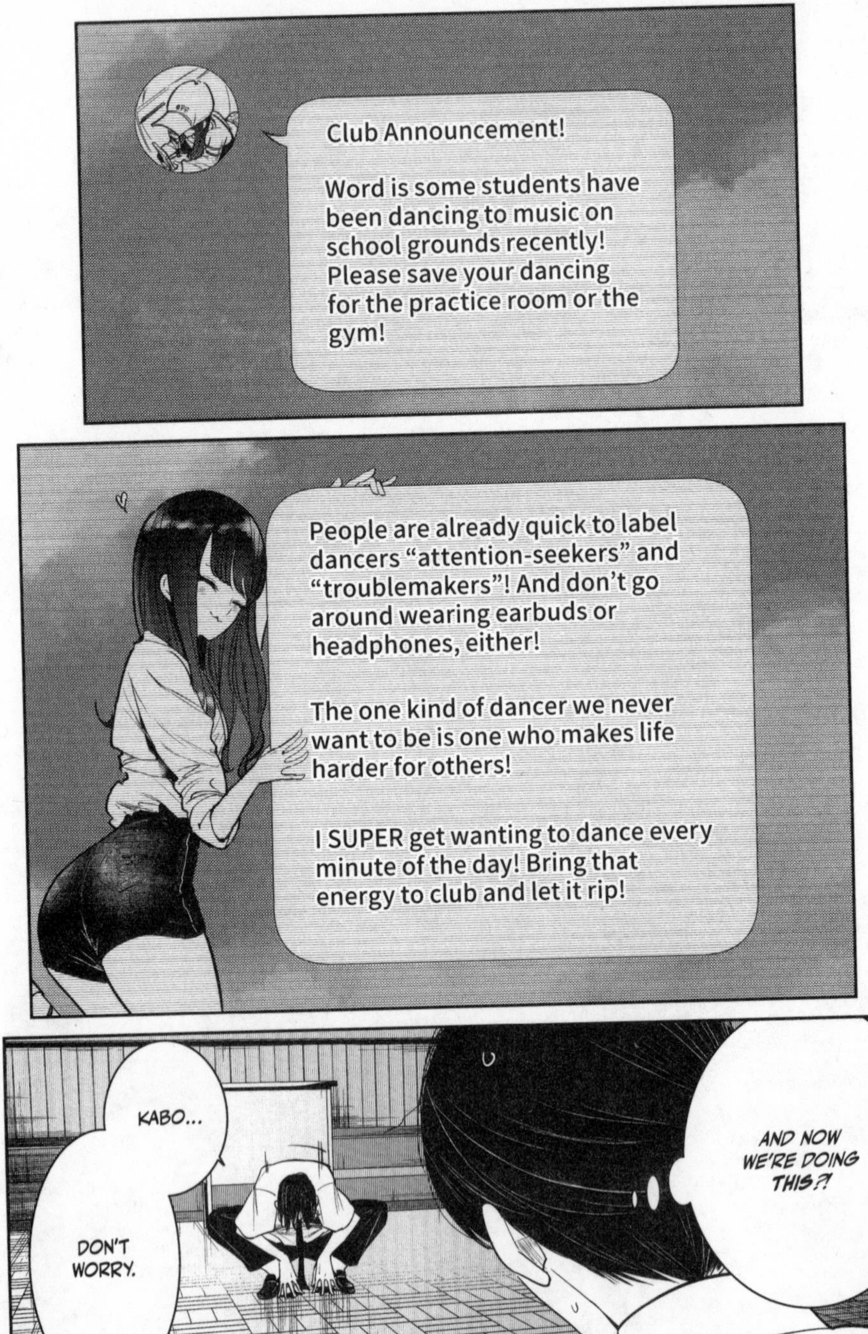
Club Announcement!
Word is some students have been dancing to music on school grounds recently! Please save your dancing for the practice room or the gym!
People are already quick to label dancers "attention-seekers" and "troublemakers"! And don't go around wearing earbuds or headphones, either!
The one kind of dancer we never want to be is one who makes life harder for others!
I SUPER get wanting to dance every minute of the day! Bring that energy to club and let it rip!
AND NOW WE'RE DOING THIS?!
KABO...
DON'T WORRY.

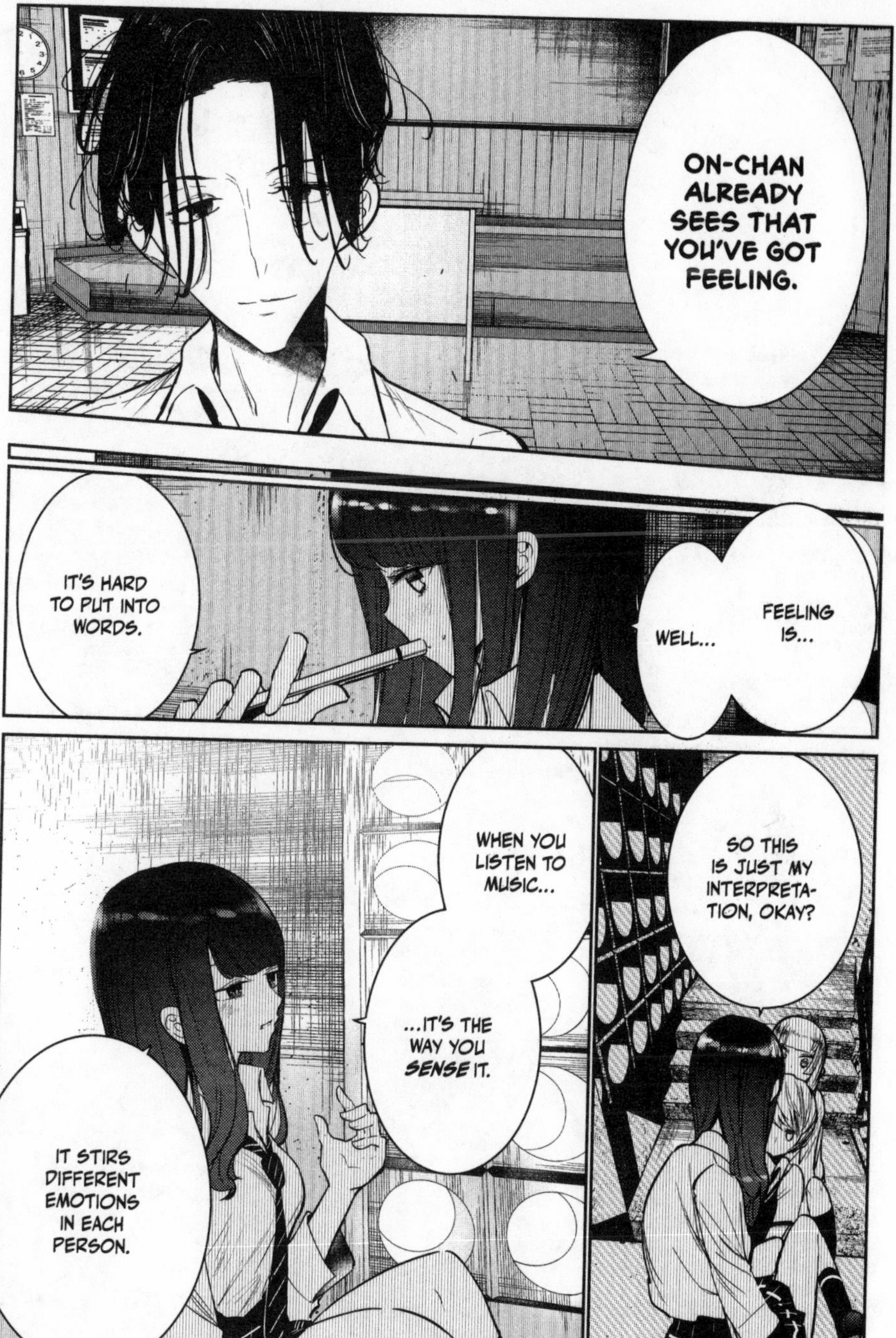
ON-CHAN ALREADY SEES THAT YOU'VE GOT FEELING.
FEELING IS...
WELL...
IT'S HARD TO PUT INTO WORDS.
SO THIS IS JUST MY INTERPRETATION, OKAY?
WHEN YOU LISTEN TO MUSIC...
...IT'S THE WAY YOU *SENSE* IT.
IT STIRS DIFFERENT EMOTIONS IN EACH PERSON.

TWO PEOPLE MIGHT LISTEN TO THE VERY SAME SONG...

...AND ONE OF THEM COULD THINK, "HMM..."

WHILE THE OTHER THINKS, "WOW! THAT'S OUTTA THIS WORLD!"

SOME SONGS MIGHT MAKE YOU NOSTALGIC...

...OR GIVE YOU A RUSH OF JOY.

THEY MIGHT GET YOU FIRED UP TO FIGHT.

IT'S DIFFERENT FOR EVERY-ONE, RIGHT?

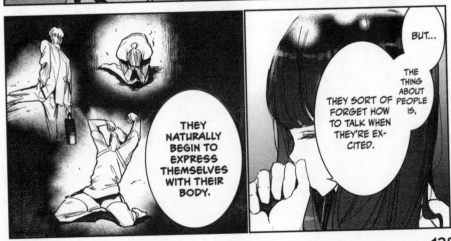

THE THING ABOUT PEOPLE IS,

BUT...

THEY SORT OF FORGET HOW TO TALK WHEN THEY'RE EX-CITED.

THEY NATURALLY BEGIN TO EXPRESS THEMSELVES WITH THEIR BODY.

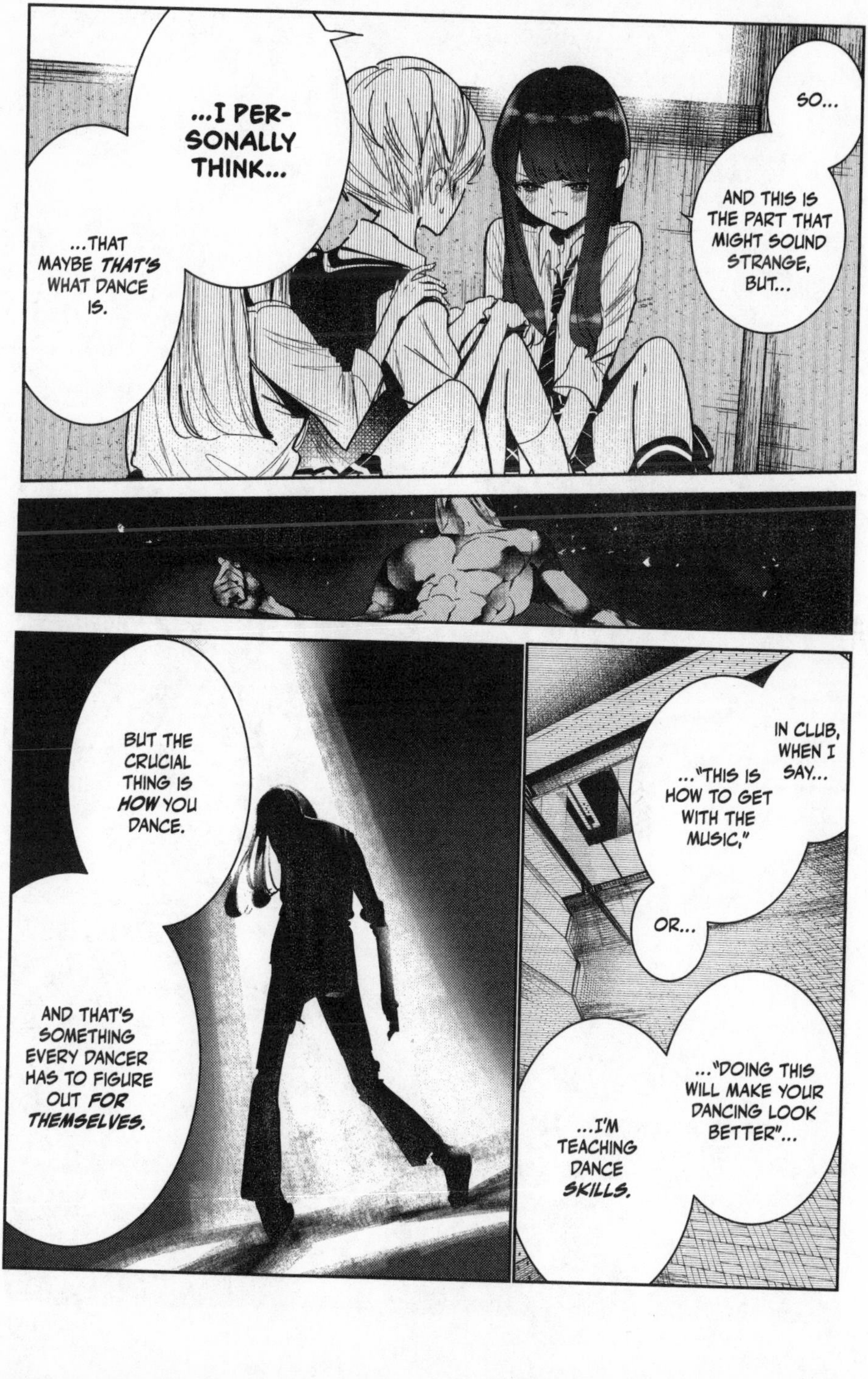
SO...
AND THIS IS THE PART THAT MIGHT SOUND STRANGE, BUT...
...I PERSONALLY THINK...
...THAT MAYBE *THAT'S* WHAT DANCE IS.
IN CLUB, WHEN I SAY...
..."THIS IS HOW TO GET WITH THE MUSIC,"
OR...
..."DOING THIS WILL MAKE YOUR DANCING LOOK BETTER"...
...I'M TEACHING DANCE *SKILLS*.
BUT THE CRUCIAL THING IS *HOW* YOU DANCE.
AND THAT'S SOMETHING EVERY DANCER HAS TO FIGURE OUT *FOR THEMSELVES*.

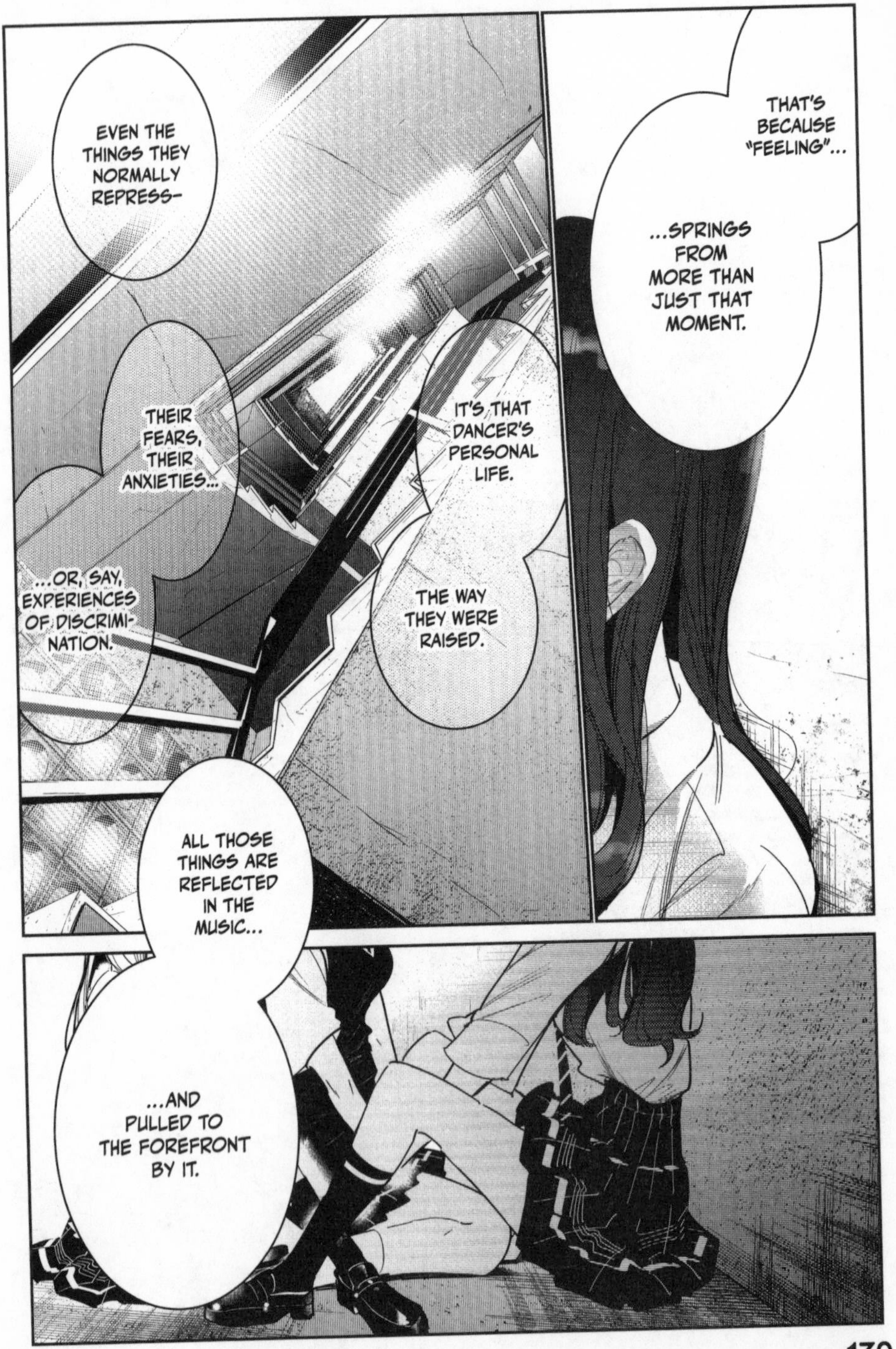
THAT'S BECAUSE "FEELING"...
...SPRINGS FROM MORE THAN JUST THAT MOMENT.
IT'S THAT DANCER'S PERSONAL LIFE.
THE WAY THEY WERE RAISED.
THEIR FEARS, THEIR ANXIETIES...
...OR, SAY, EXPERIENCES OF DISCRIMI-NATION.
EVEN THE THINGS THEY NORMALLY REPRESS–
ALL THOSE THINGS ARE REFLECTED IN THE MUSIC...
...AND PULLED TO THE FOREFRONT BY IT.

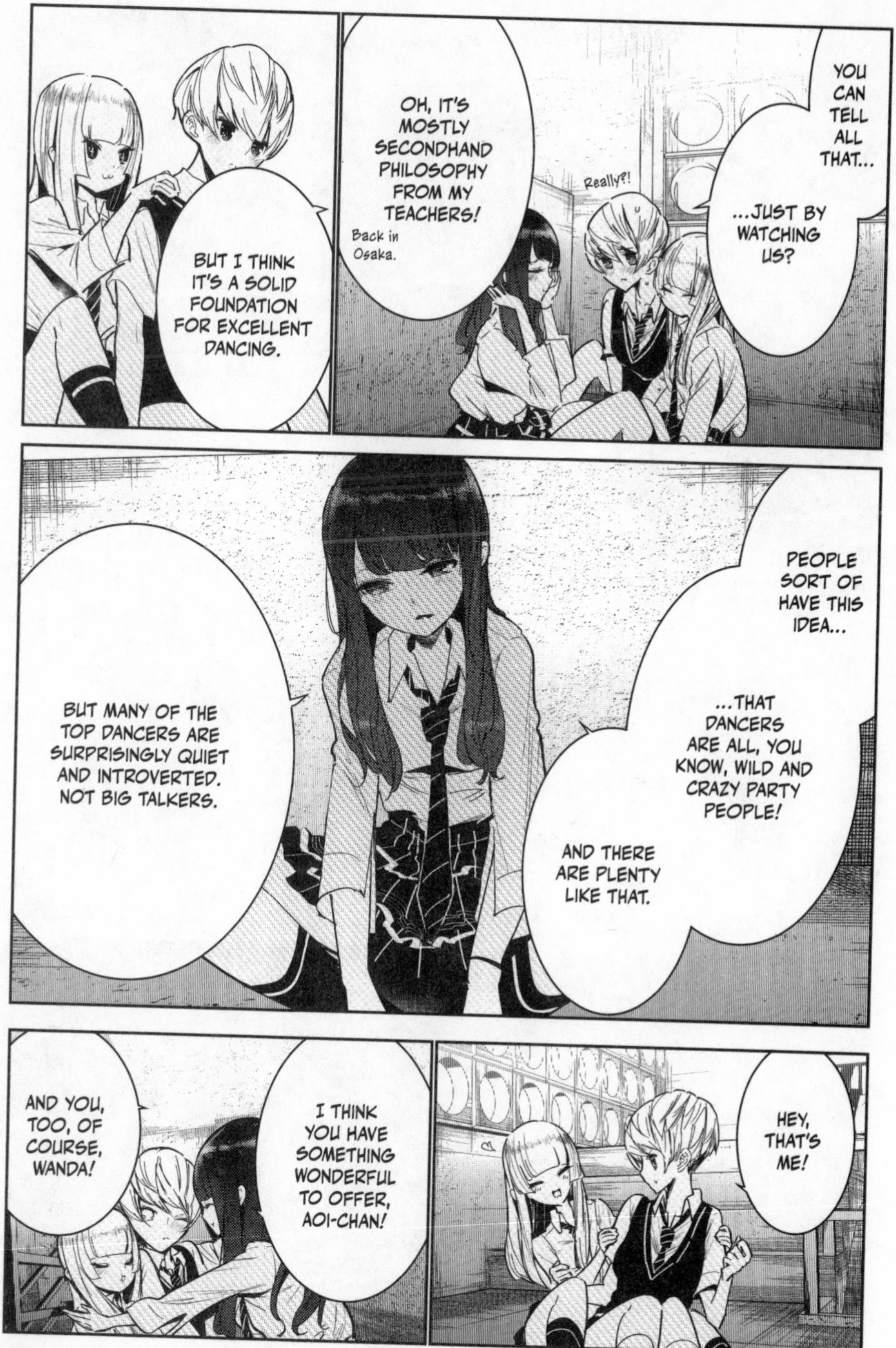
YOU CAN TELL ALL THAT...
...JUST BY WATCHING US?
Really?!
OH, IT'S MOSTLY SECONDHAND PHILOSOPHY FROM MY TEACHERS!
Back in Osaka.
BUT I THINK IT'S A SOLID FOUNDATION FOR EXCELLENT DANCING.
PEOPLE SORT OF HAVE THIS IDEA...
...THAT DANCERS ARE ALL, YOU KNOW, WILD AND CRAZY PARTY PEOPLE!
AND THERE ARE PLENTY LIKE THAT.
BUT MANY OF THE TOP DANCERS ARE SURPRISINGLY QUIET AND INTROVERTED. NOT BIG TALKERS.
HEY, THAT'S ME!
I THINK YOU HAVE SOMETHING WONDERFUL TO OFFER, AOI-CHAN!
AND YOU, TOO, OF COURSE, WANDA!

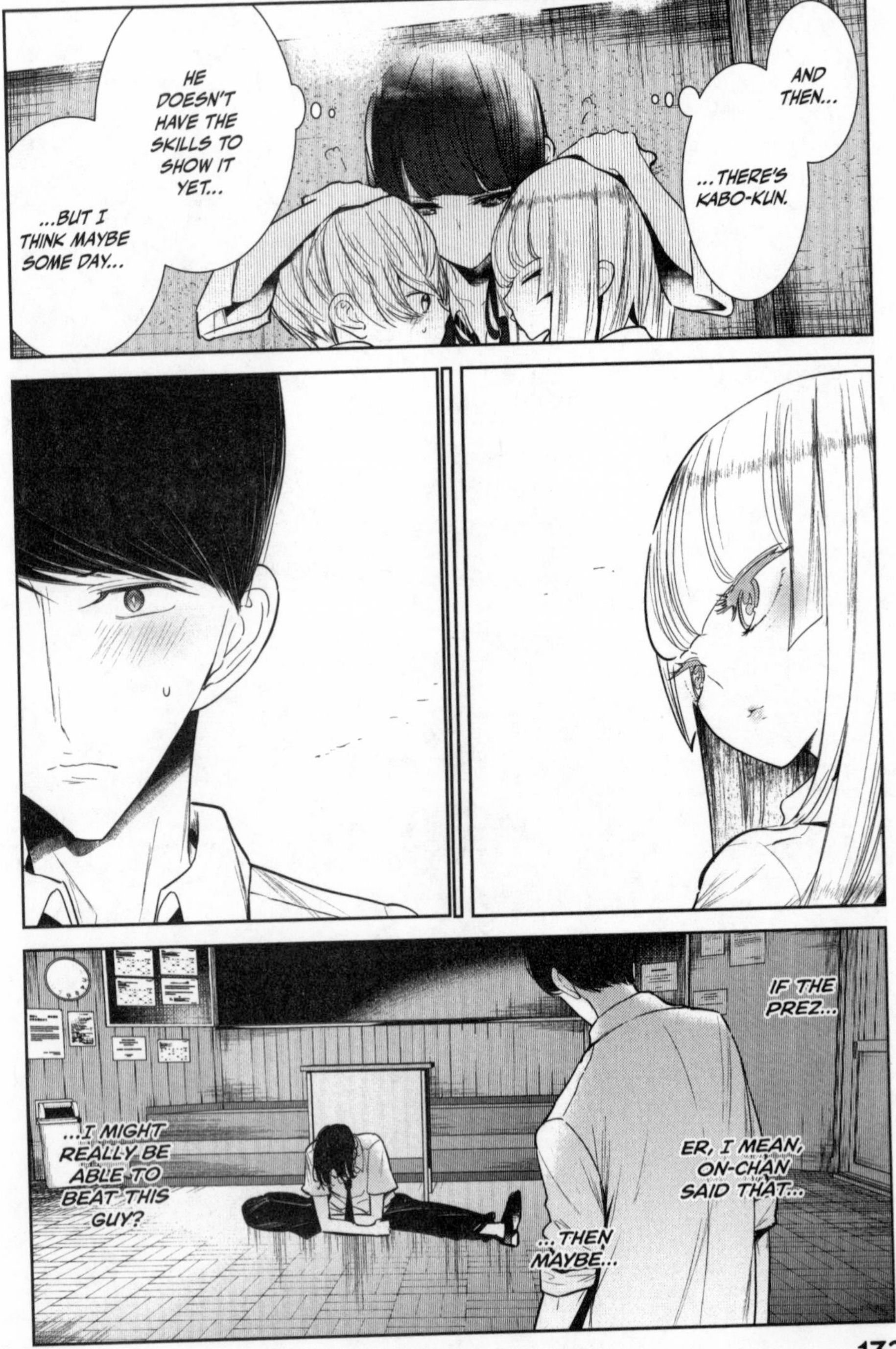
AND THEN...
...THERE'S KABO-KUN.
HE DOESN'T HAVE THE SKILLS TO SHOW IT YET...
...BUT I THINK MAYBE SOME DAY...
IF THE PREZ...
ER, I MEAN, ON-CHAN SAID THAT...
...THEN MAYBE...
...I MIGHT REALLY BE ABLE TO BEAT THIS GUY?

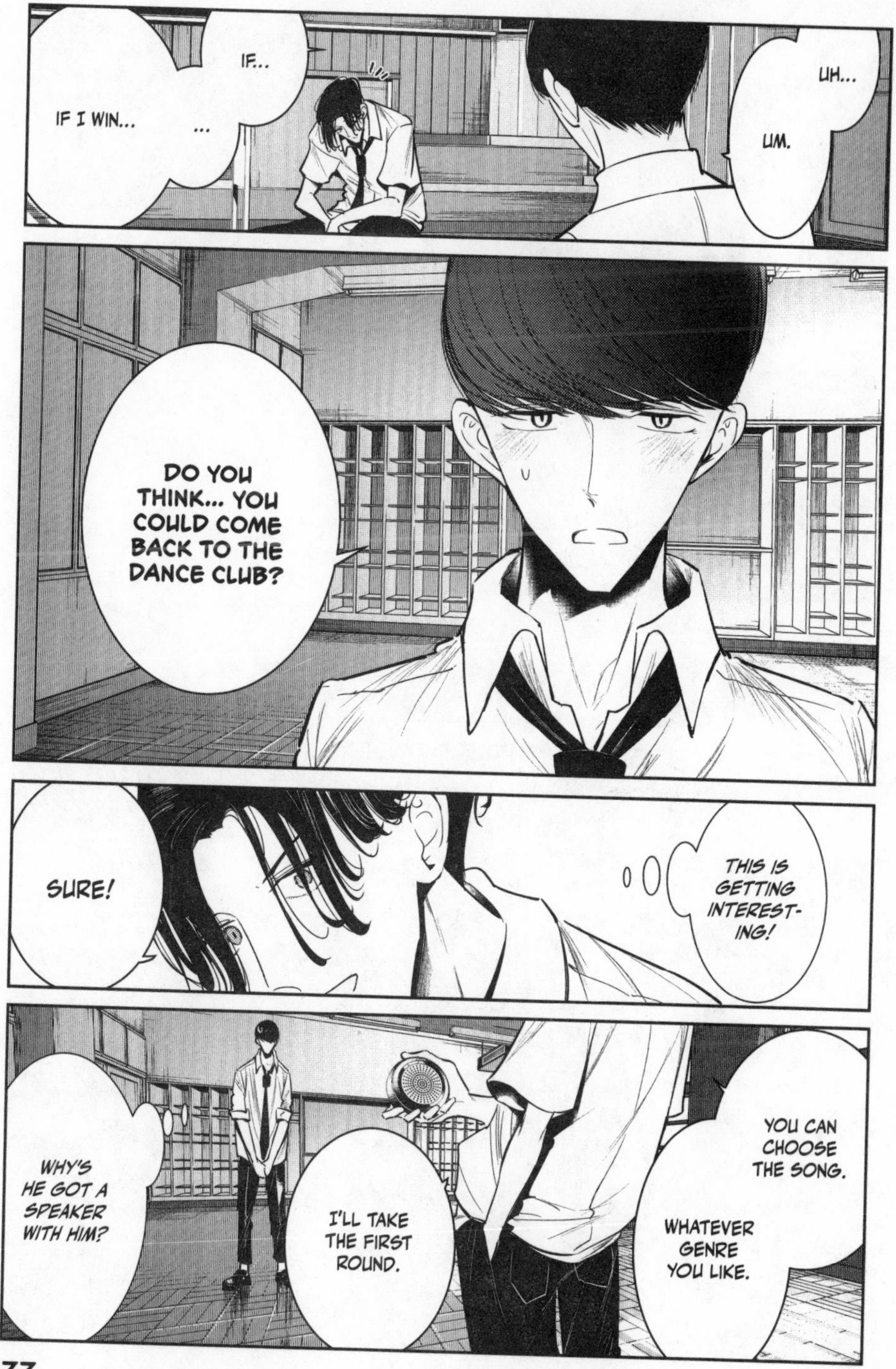
UH...
UM.
IF...
...
IF I WIN...
DO YOU THINK... YOU COULD COME BACK TO THE DANCE CLUB?
THIS IS GETTING INTEREST-ING!
SURE!
YOU CAN CHOOSE THE SONG.
WHATEVER GENRE YOU LIKE.
I'LL TAKE THE FIRST ROUND.
WHY'S HE GOT A SPEAKER WITH HIM?

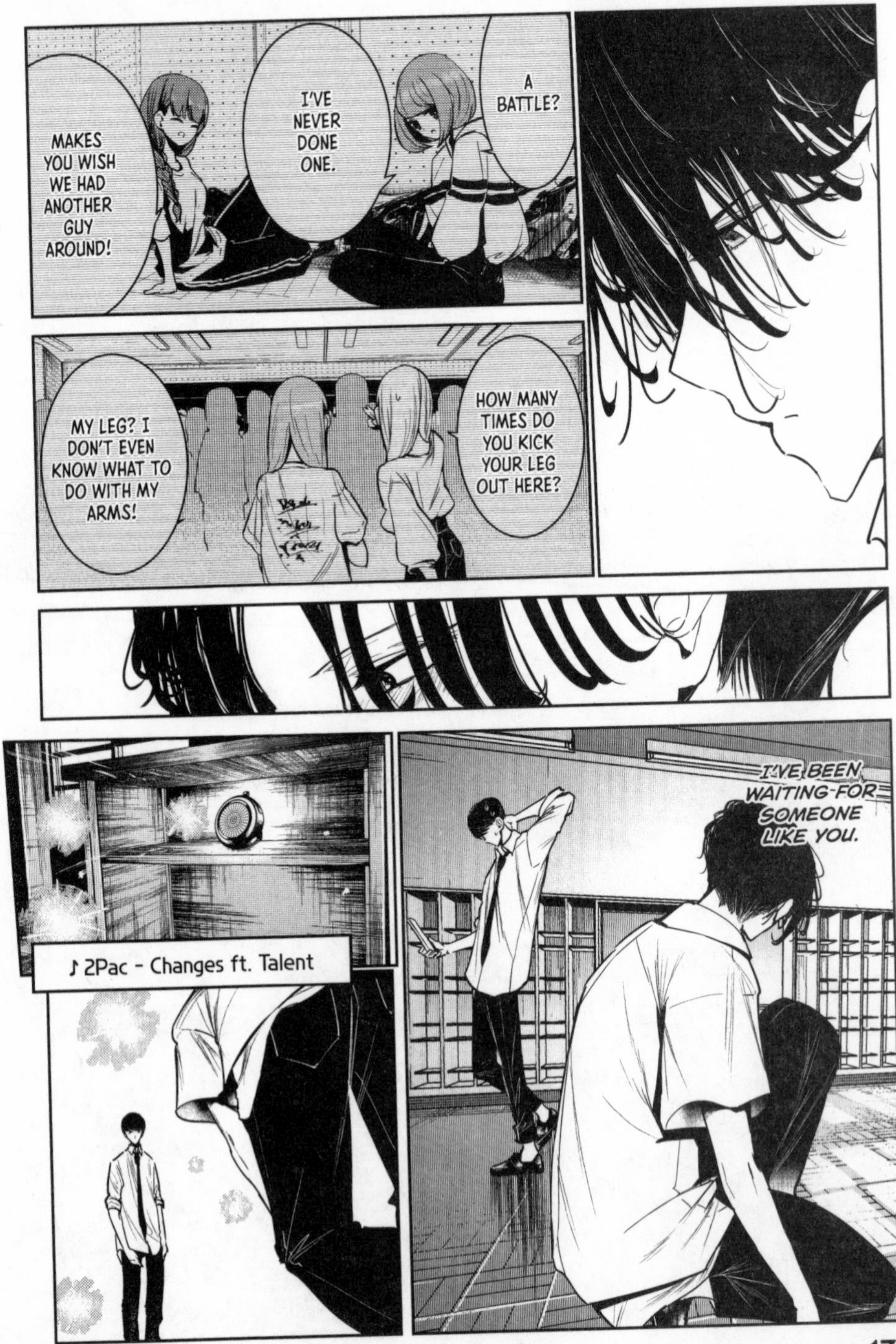
A BATTLE?
I'VE NEVER DONE ONE.
MAKES YOU WISH WE HAD ANOTHER GUY AROUND!
HOW MANY TIMES DO YOU KICK YOUR LEG OUT HERE?
MY LEG? I DON'T EVEN KNOW WHAT TO DO WITH MY ARMS!
I'VE BEEN WAITING FOR SOMEONE LIKE YOU.
♪ 2Pac - Changes ft. Talent

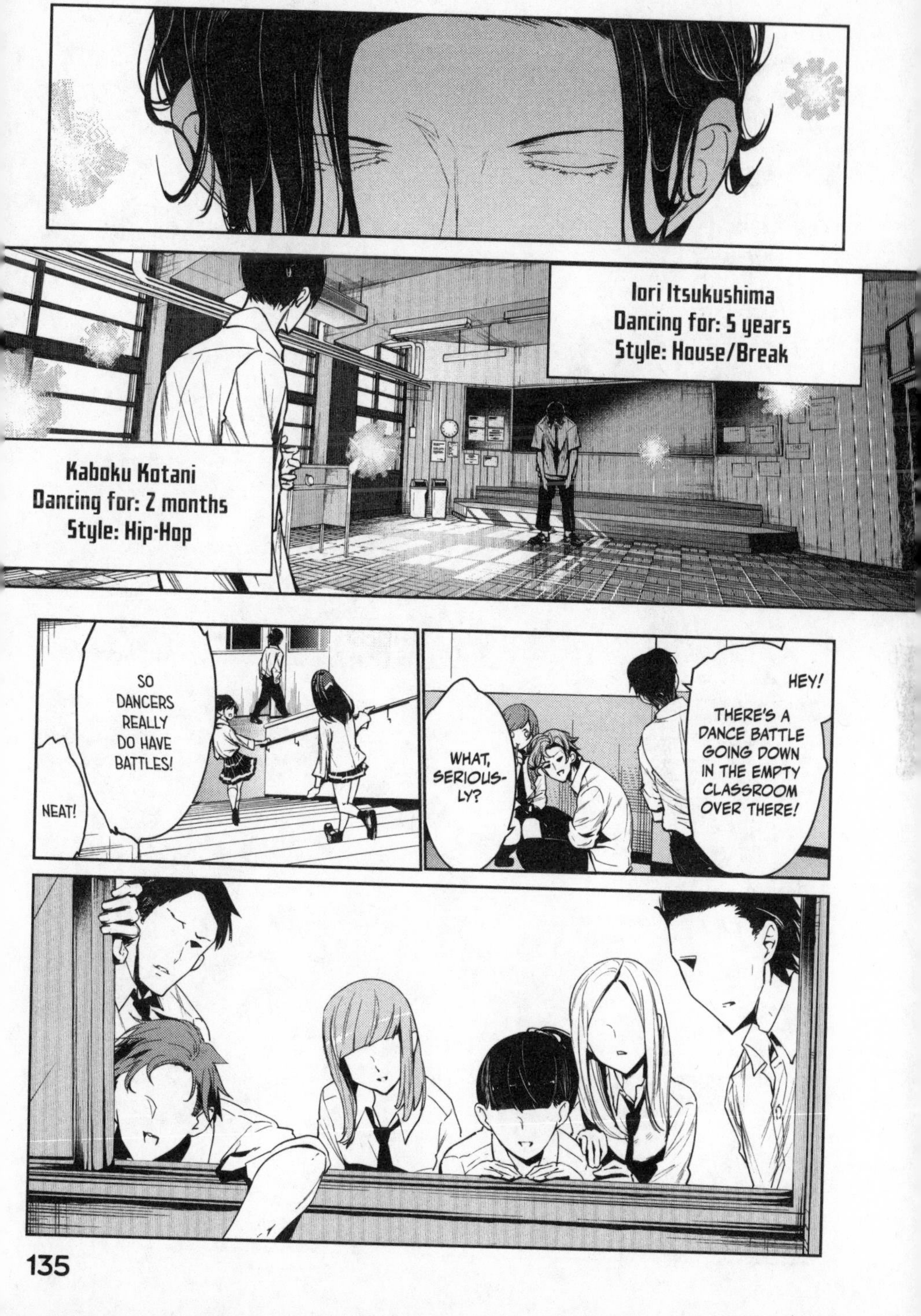
Iori Itsukushima
Dancing for: 5 years
Style: House/Break
Kaboku Kotani
Dancing for: 2 months
Style: Hip-Hop
HEY!
THERE'S A DANCE BATTLE GOING DOWN IN THE EMPTY CLASSROOM OVER THERE!
WHAT, SERIOUS-LY?
SO DANCERS REALLY DO HAVE BATTLES!
NEAT!

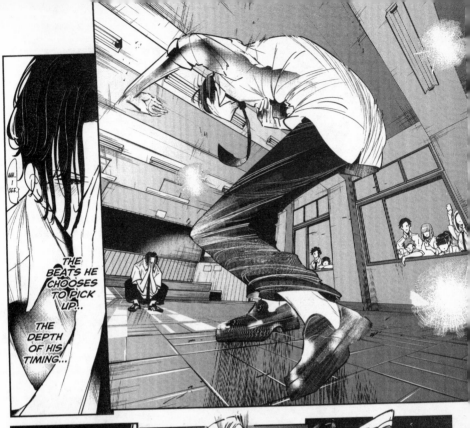

MAN, I SEE.

THE BEATS HE CHOOSES TO PICK UP...

THE DEPTH OF HIS TIMING...

HE REALLY IS HEARING THE MUSIC.

HE'S GOT THE RIGHT STUFF, NO DOUBT.

LOOK AT THAT CROWD!

YIKES ...

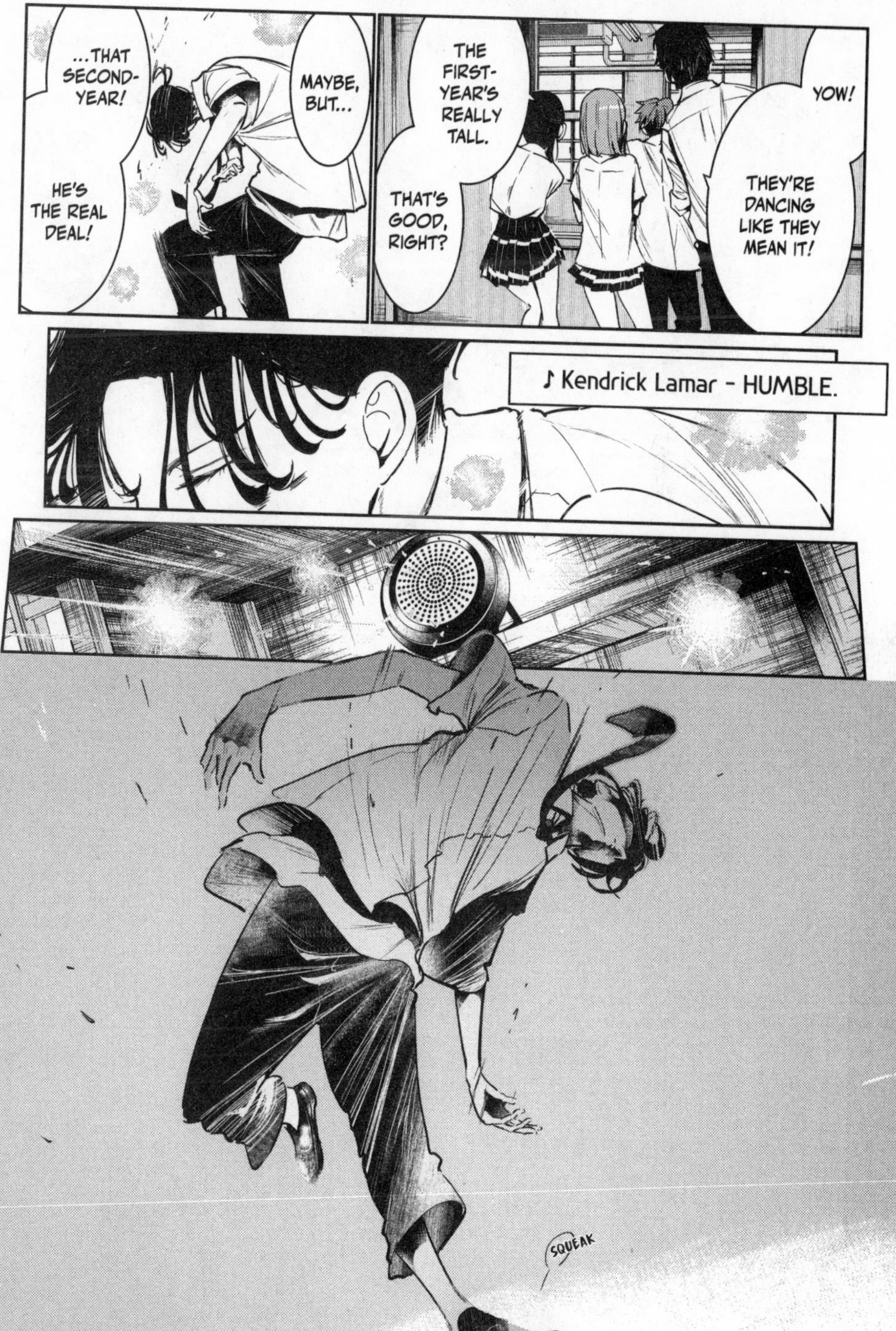
YOW!
THEY'RE DANCING LIKE THEY MEAN IT!
THE FIRST-YEAR'S REALLY TALL.
THAT'S GOOD, RIGHT?
MAYBE, BUT...
...THAT SECOND-YEAR!
HE'S THE REAL DEAL!
♪ Kendrick Lamar - HUMBLE.
SQUEAK

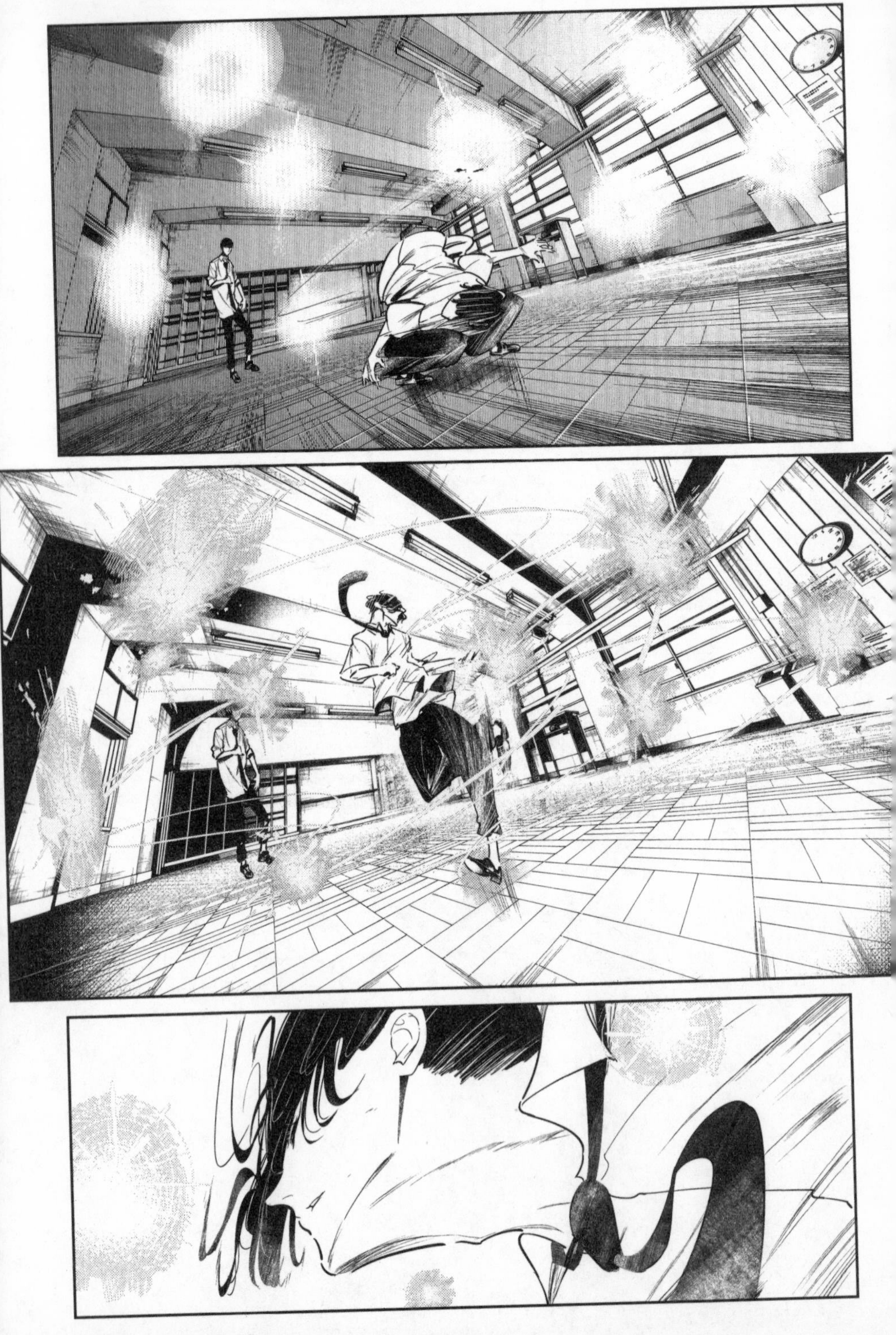

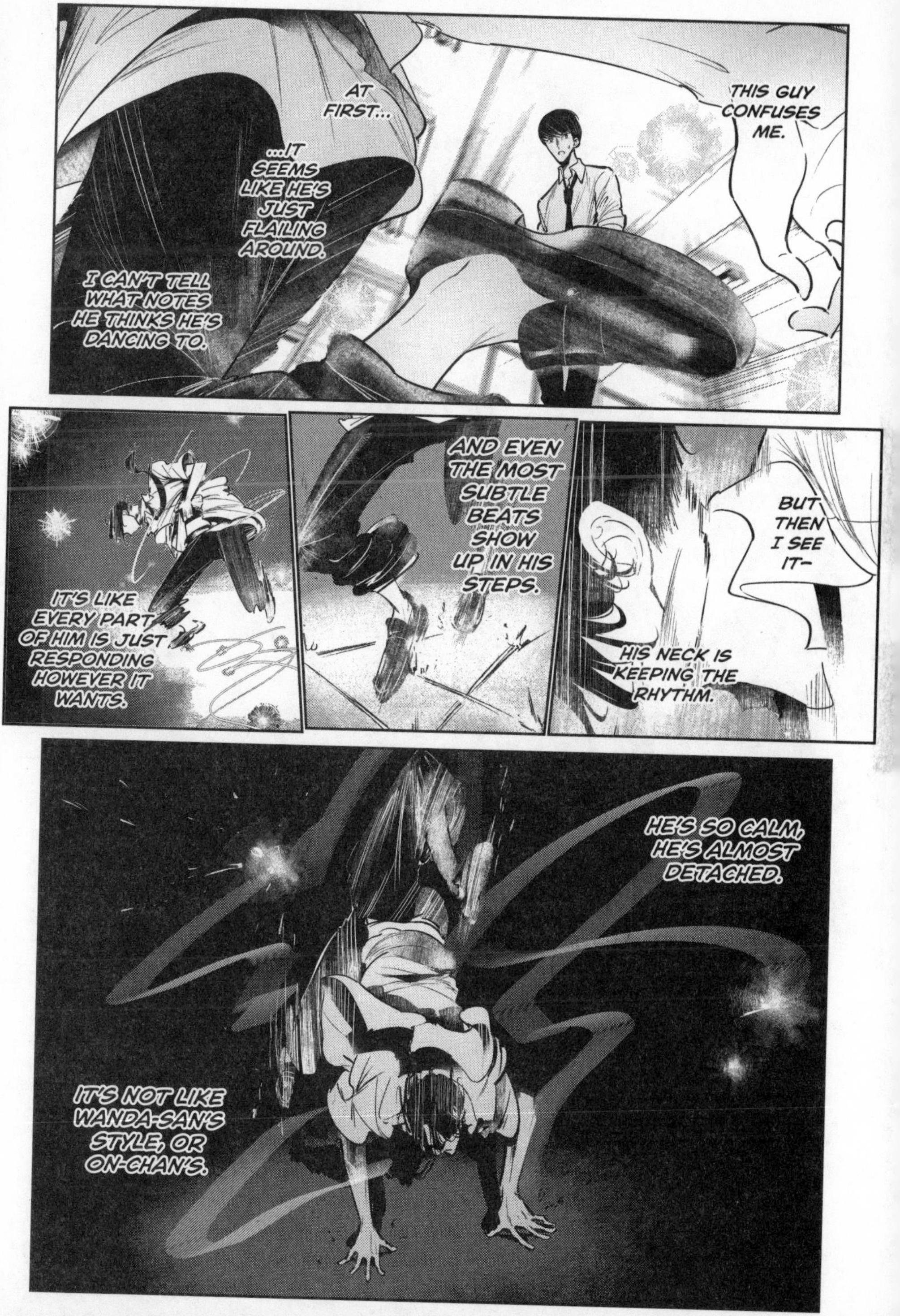
THIS GUY CONFUSES ME.
AT FIRST...
...IT SEEMS LIKE HE'S JUST FLAILING AROUND.
I CAN'T TELL WHAT NOTES HE THINKS HE'S DANCING TO.
BUT THEN I SEE IT–
HIS NECK IS KEEPING THE RHYTHM.
AND EVEN THE MOST SUBTLE BEATS SHOW UP IN HIS STEPS.
IT'S LIKE EVERY PART OF HIM IS JUST RESPONDING HOWEVER IT WANTS.
HE'S SO CALM, HE'S ALMOST DETACHED.
IT'S NOT LIKE WANDA-SAN'S STYLE, OR ON-CHAN'S.

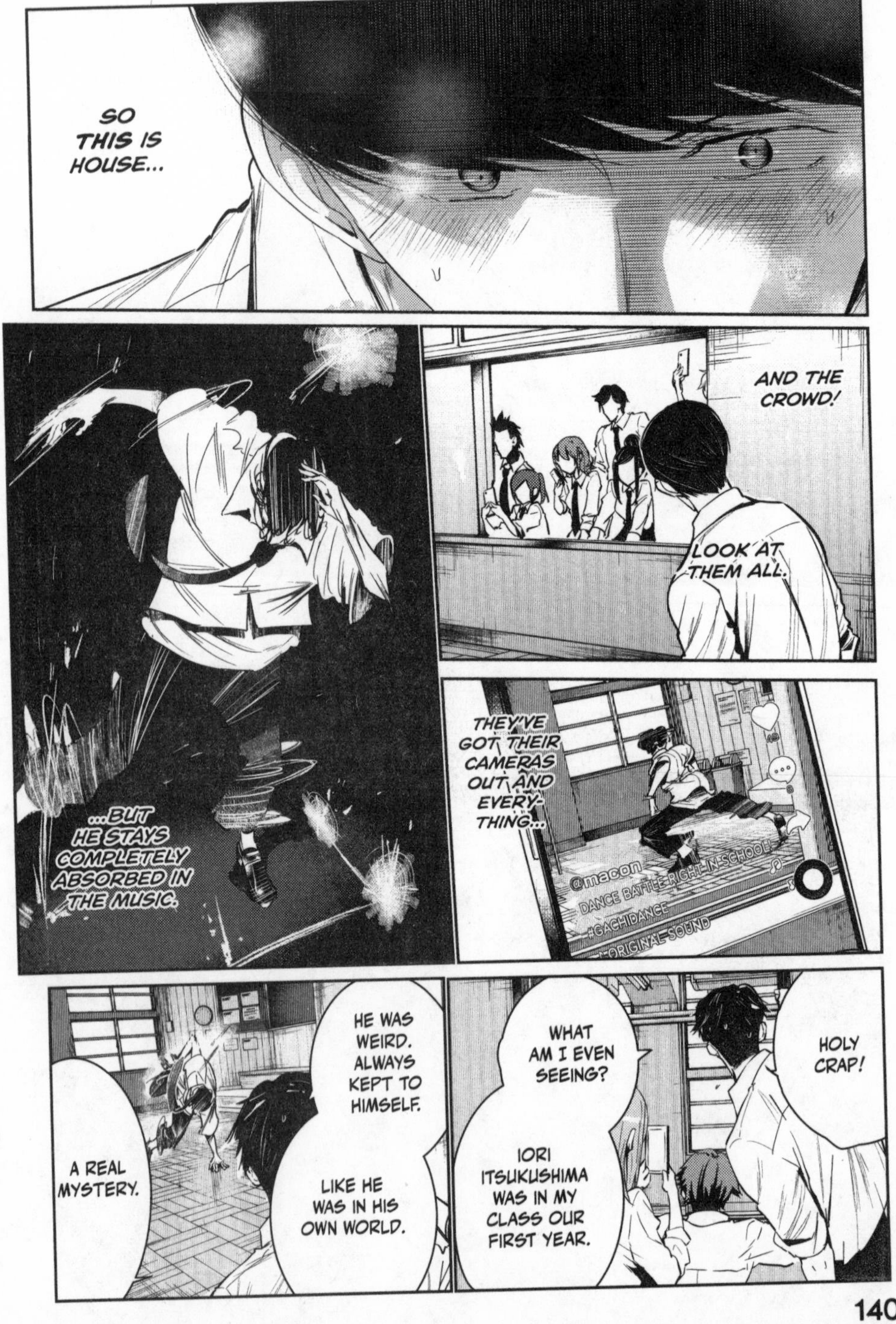
SO THIS IS HOUSE...
AND THE CROWD!
LOOK AT THEM ALL.
THEY'VE GOT THEIR CAMERAS OUT AND EVERYTHING...
@macon
DANCE BATTLE RIGHT IN SCHOOL!
#GACHIDANCE
ORIGINAL SOUND
...BUT HE STAYS COMPLETELY ABSORBED IN THE MUSIC.
HOLY CRAP!
WHAT AM I EVEN SEEING?
IORI ITSUKUSHIMA WAS IN MY CLASS OUR FIRST YEAR.
HE WAS WEIRD. ALWAYS KEPT TO HIMSELF.
LIKE HE WAS IN HIS OWN WORLD.
A REAL MYSTERY.

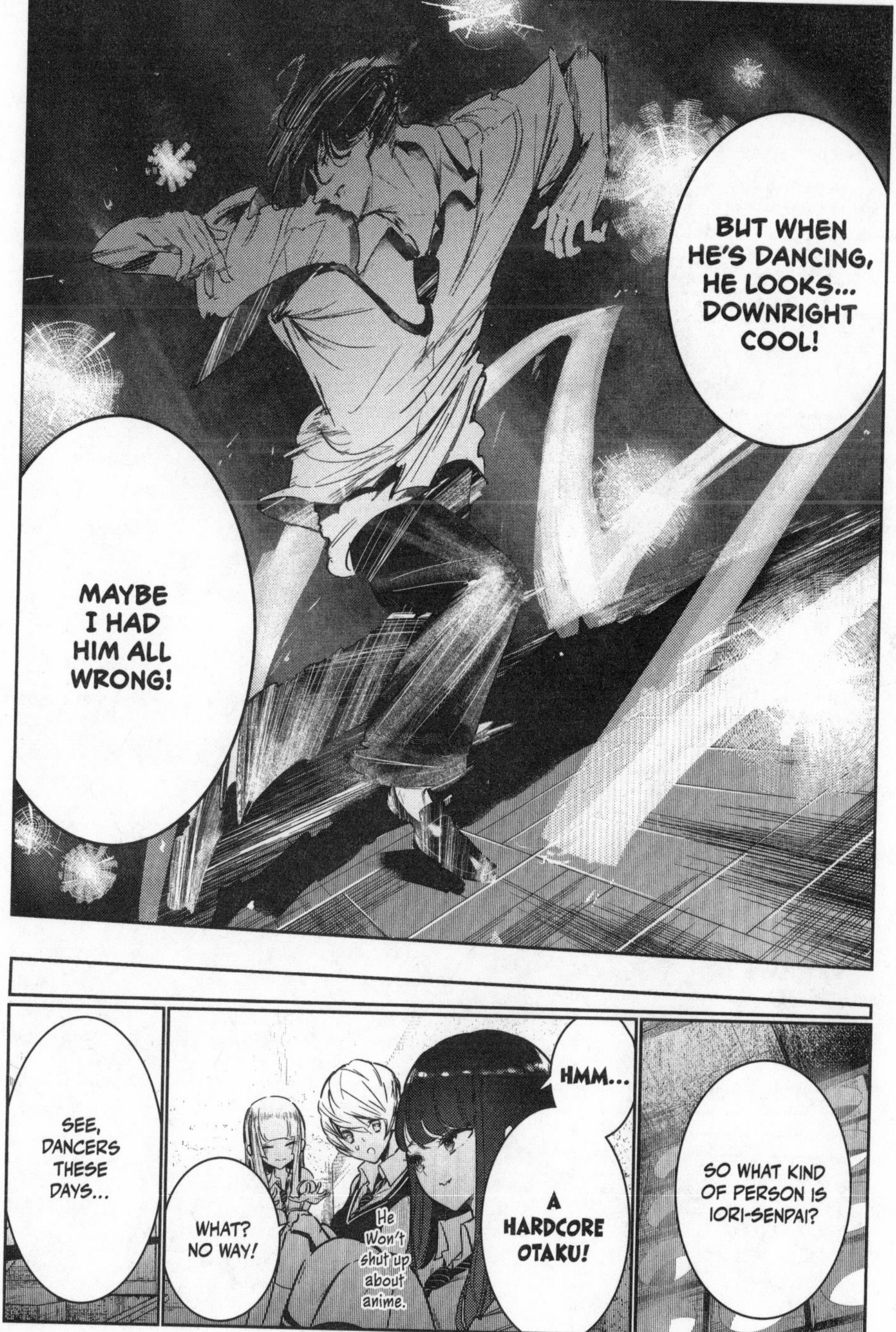
BUT WHEN HE'S DANCING, HE LOOKS... DOWNRIGHT COOL!
MAYBE I HAD HIM ALL WRONG!
SO WHAT KIND OF PERSON IS IORI-SENPAI?
HMM...
A HARDCORE OTAKU!
He won't shut up about anime.
WHAT? NO WAY!
SEE, DANCERS THESE DAYS...

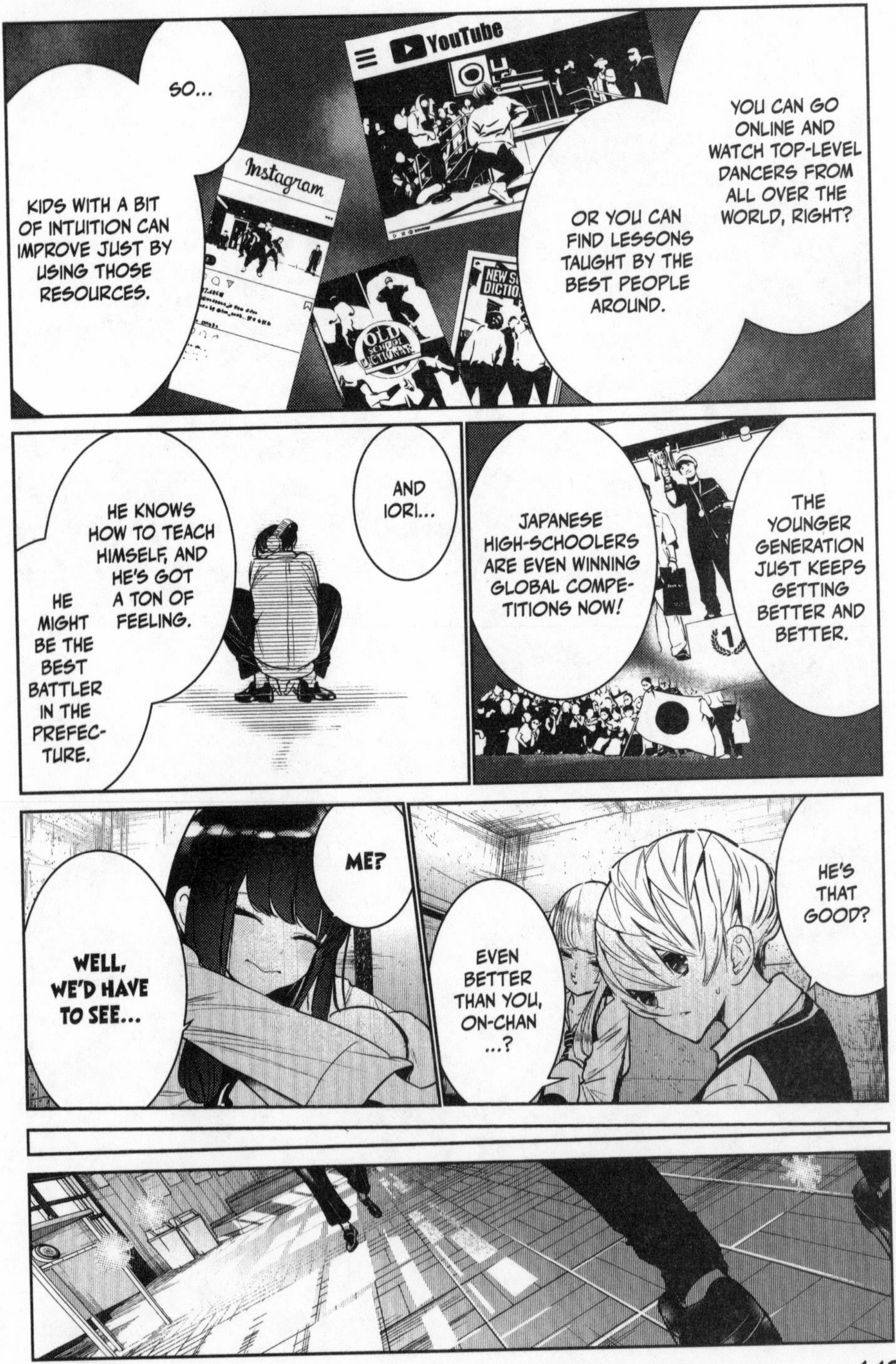
YOU CAN GO ONLINE AND WATCH TOP-LEVEL DANCERS FROM ALL OVER THE WORLD, RIGHT?
OR YOU CAN FIND LESSONS TAUGHT BY THE BEST PEOPLE AROUND.
YouTube
Instagram
SO...
KIDS WITH A BIT OF INTUITION CAN IMPROVE JUST BY USING THOSE RESOURCES.
THE YOUNGER GENERATION JUST KEEPS GETTING BETTER AND BETTER.
JAPANESE HIGH-SCHOOLERS ARE EVEN WINNING GLOBAL COMPETITIONS NOW!
AND IORI...
HE KNOWS HOW TO TEACH HIMSELF, AND HE'S GOT A TON OF FEELING.
HE MIGHT BE THE BEST BATTLER IN THE PREFECTURE.
HE'S THAT GOOD?
EVEN BETTER THAN YOU, ON-CHAN ...?
ME?
WELL, WE'D HAVE TO SEE...

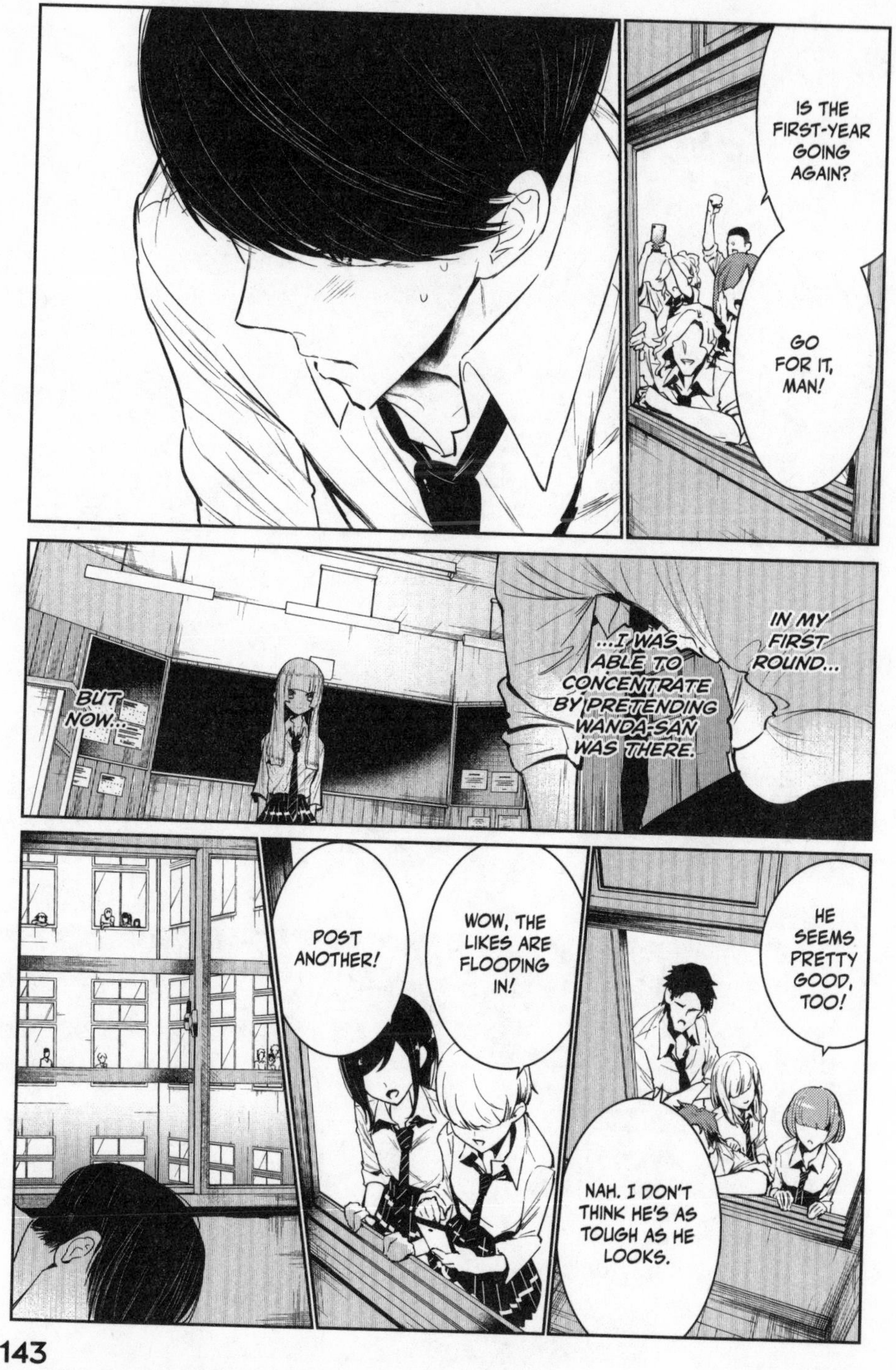
IS THE FIRST-YEAR GOING AGAIN?
GO FOR IT, MAN!
IN MY FIRST ROUND...
...I WAS ABLE TO CONCENTRATE BY PRETENDING WANDA-SAN WAS THERE.
BUT NOW...
HE SEEMS PRETTY GOOD, TOO!
NAH. I DON'T THINK HE'S AS TOUGH AS HE LOOKS.
WOW, THE LIKES ARE FLOODING IN!
POST ANOTHER!

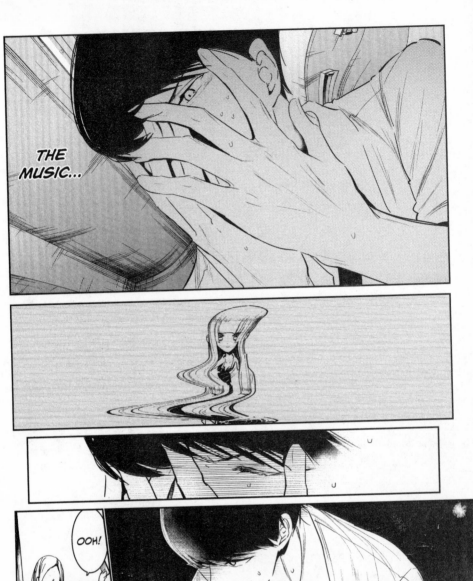

THE MUSIC...

OOH!

HERE HE GOES!

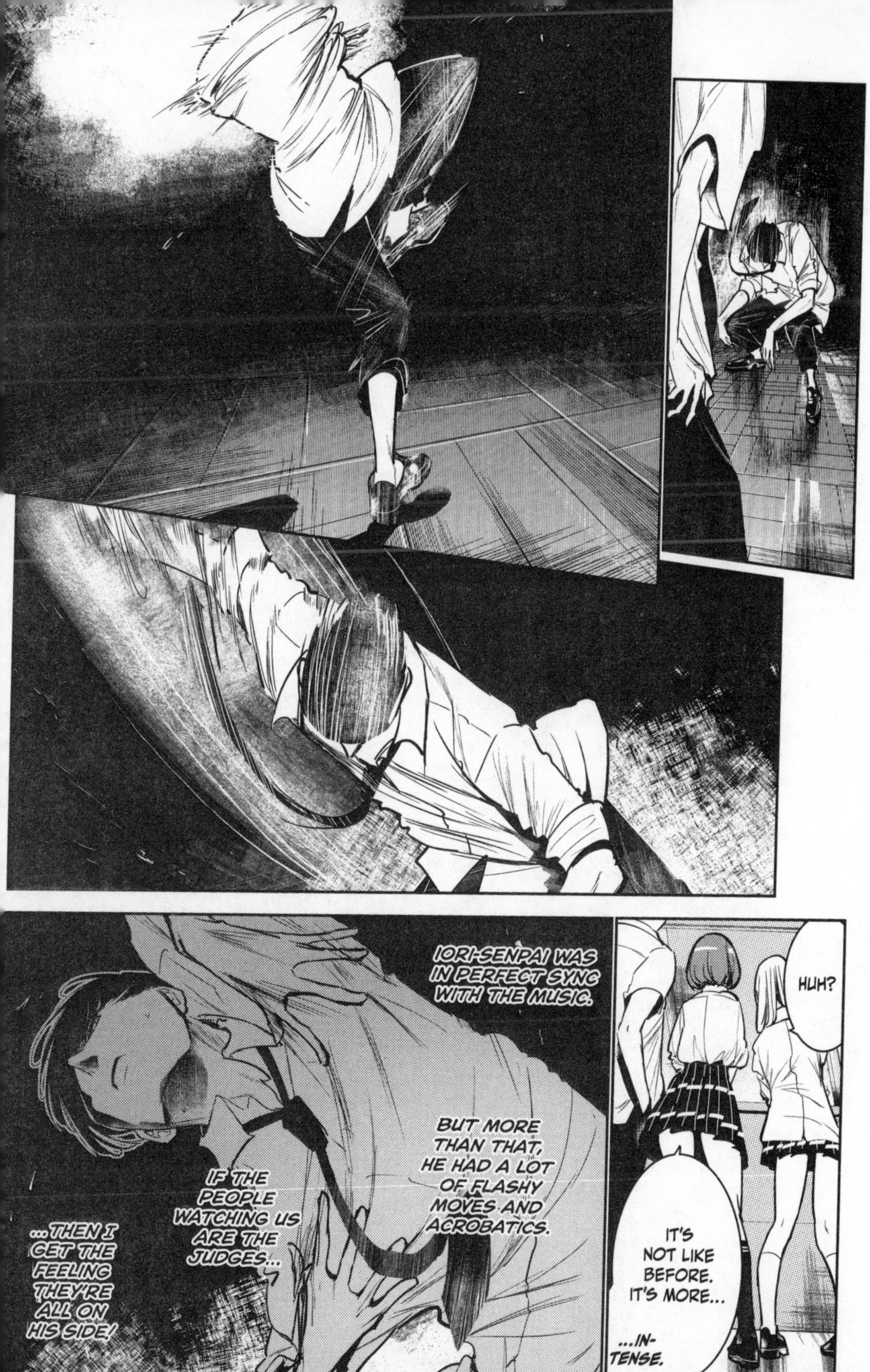
HUH?
IT'S NOT LIKE BEFORE. IT'S MORE...
...IN-TENSE.
IORI-SENPAI WAS IN PERFECT SYNC WITH THE MUSIC.
BUT MORE THAN THAT, HE HAD A LOT OF FLASHY MOVES AND ACROBATICS.
IF THE PEOPLE WATCHING US ARE THE JUDGES...
...THEN I GET THE FEELING THEY'RE ALL ON HIS SIDE!

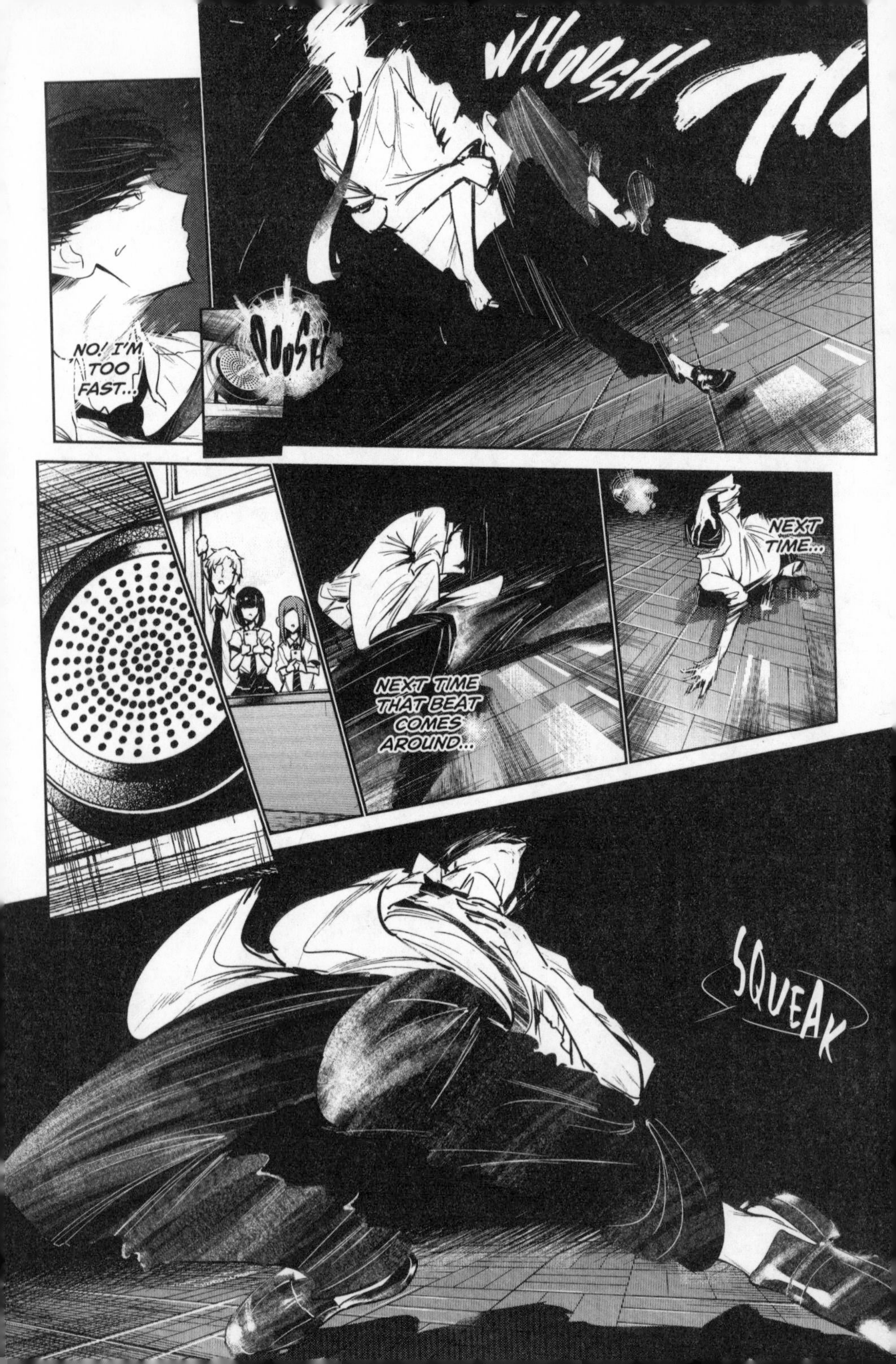
WHOOSH
POOSH
NO! I'M TOO FAST...
NEXT TIME...
NEXT TIME THAT BEAT COMES AROUND...
SQUEAK

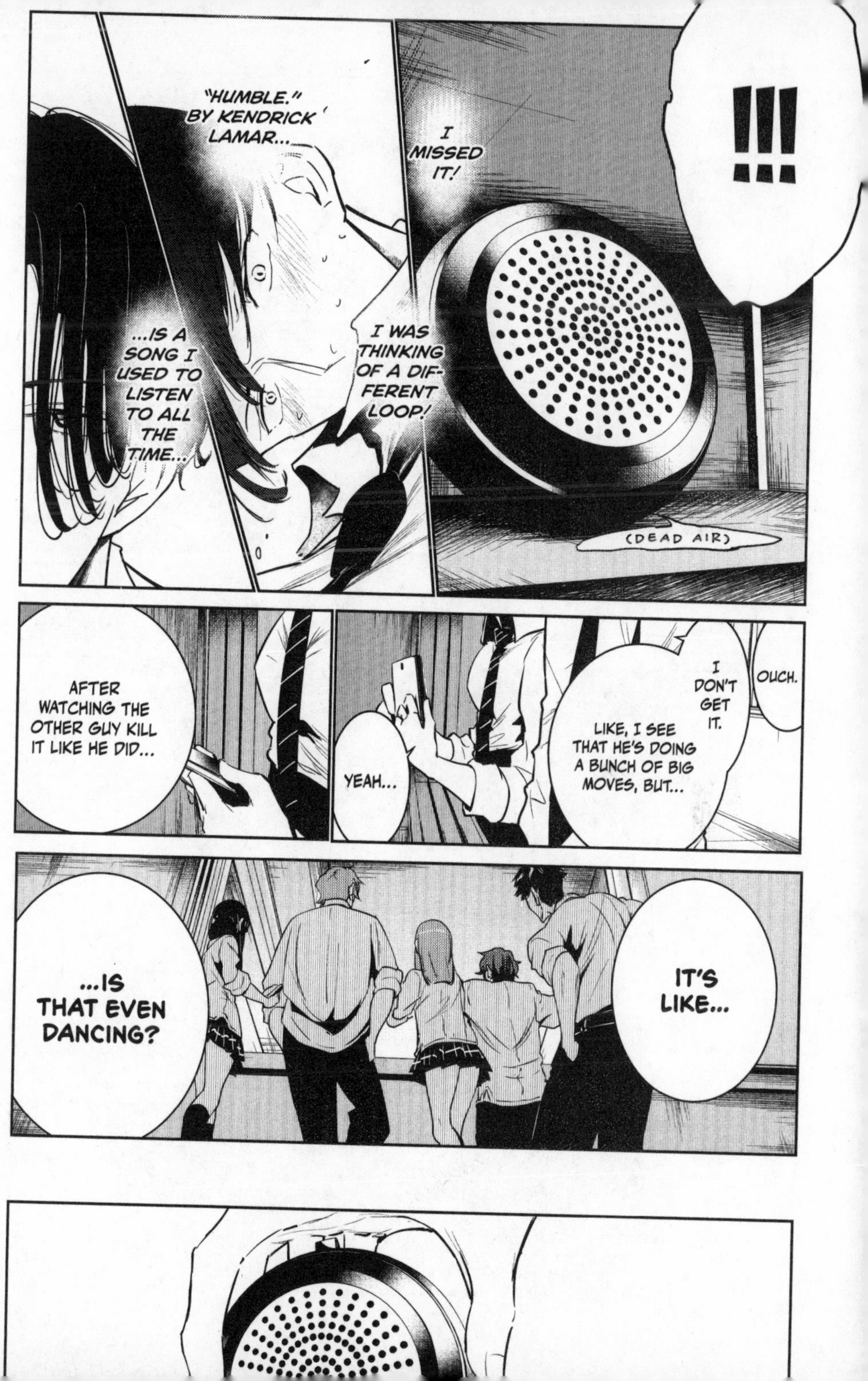
!!!
I MISSED IT!
I WAS THINKING OF A DIF- FERENT LOOP!
(DEAD AIR)
"HUMBLE." BY KENDRICK LAMAR...
...IS A SONG I USED TO LISTEN TO ALL THE TIME...
OUCH.
I DON'T GET IT.
LIKE, I SEE THAT HE'S DOING A BUNCH OF BIG MOVES, BUT...
YEAH...
AFTER WATCHING THE OTHER GUY KILL IT LIKE HE DID...
IT'S LIKE...
...IS THAT EVEN DANCING?

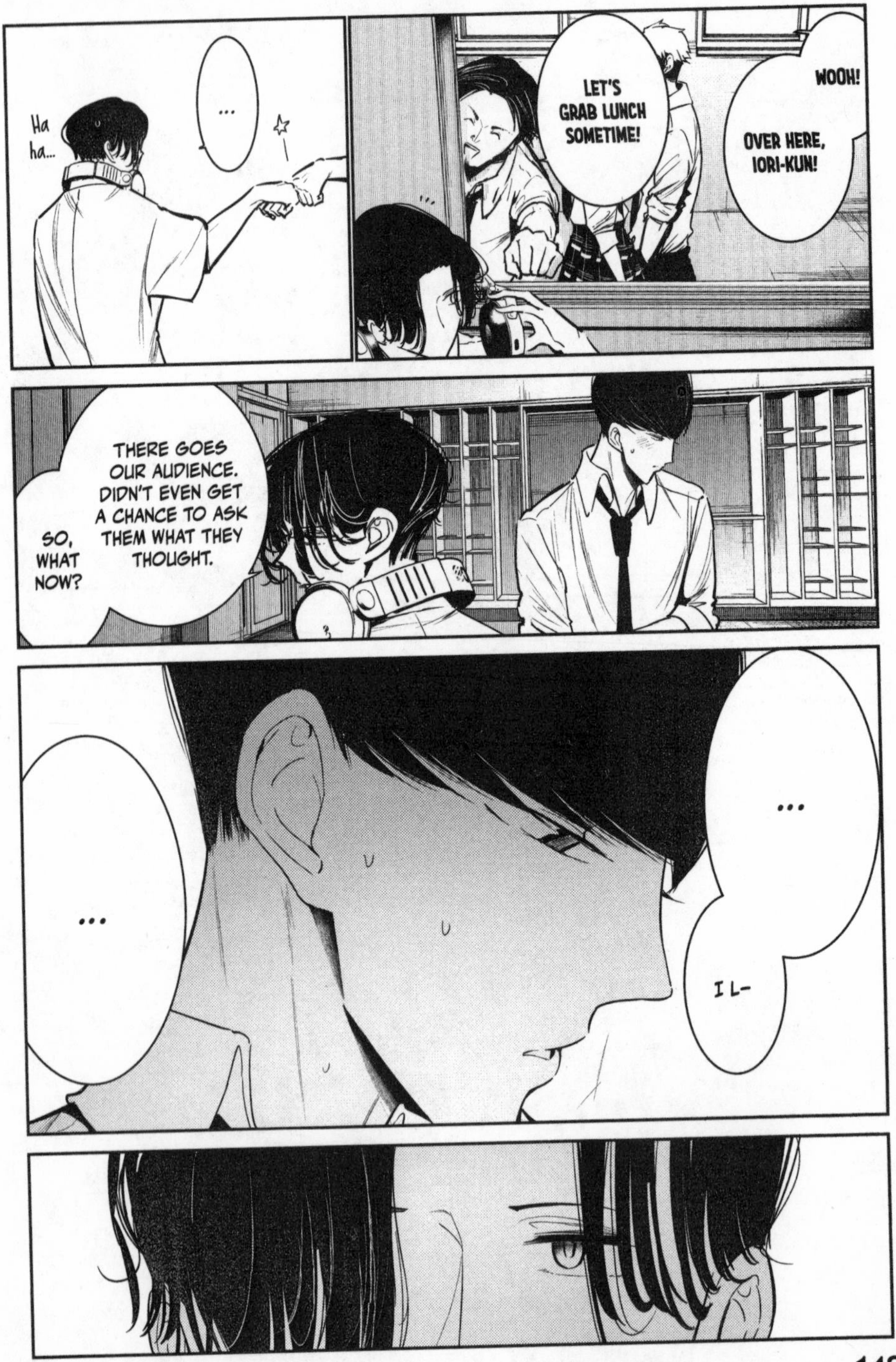
WOOH!
OVER HERE, IORI-KUN!
LET'S GRAB LUNCH SOMETIME!
...
Ha ha...
THERE GOES OUR AUDIENCE. DIDN'T EVEN GET A CHANCE TO ASK THEM WHAT THEY THOUGHT.
SO, WHAT NOW?
...
I L-
...

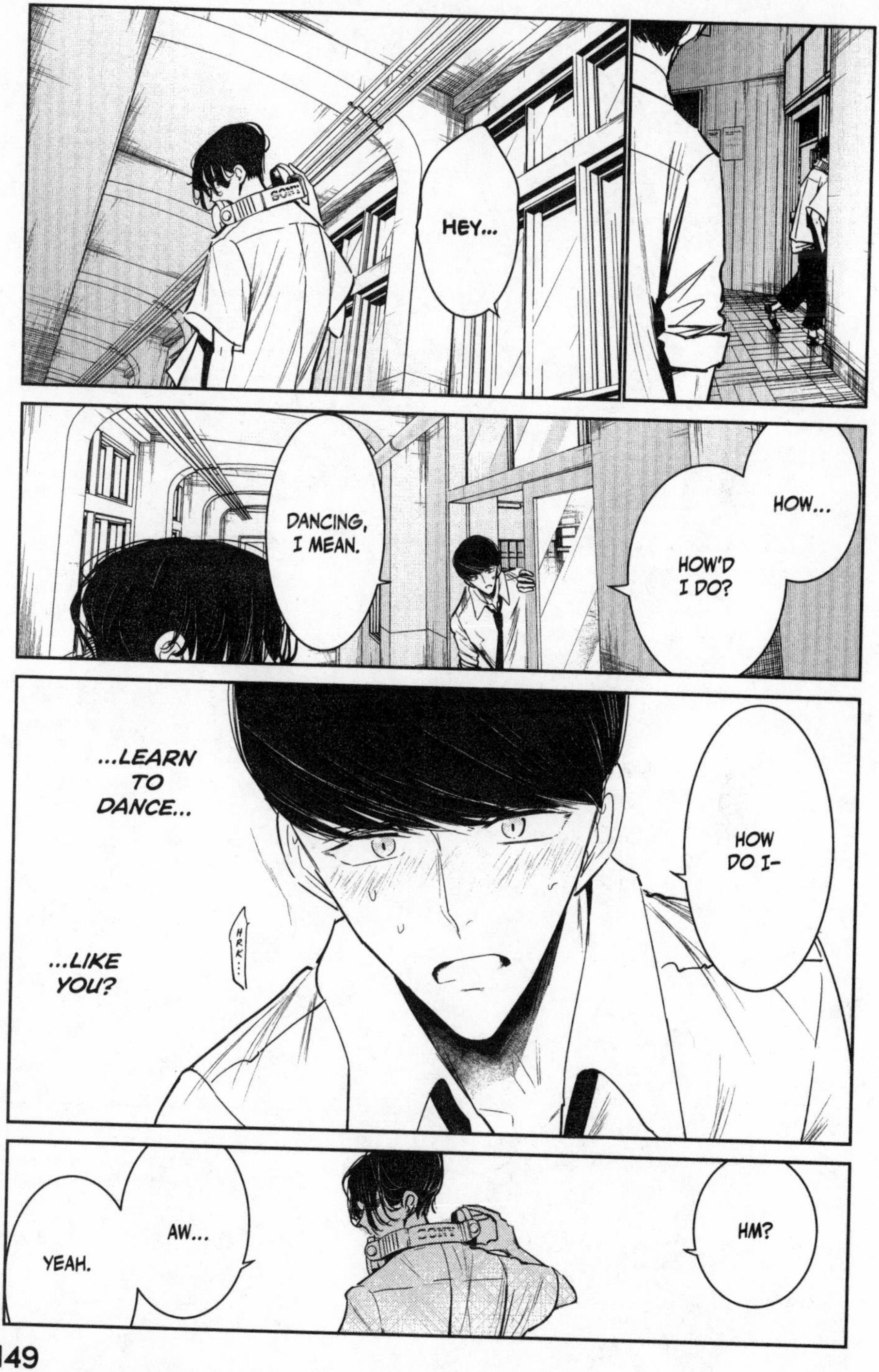
HEY...
HOW... HOW'D I DO?
DANCING, I MEAN.
HOW DO I-
...LEARN TO DANCE...
HRK...
...LIKE YOU?
HM?
AW... YEAH.

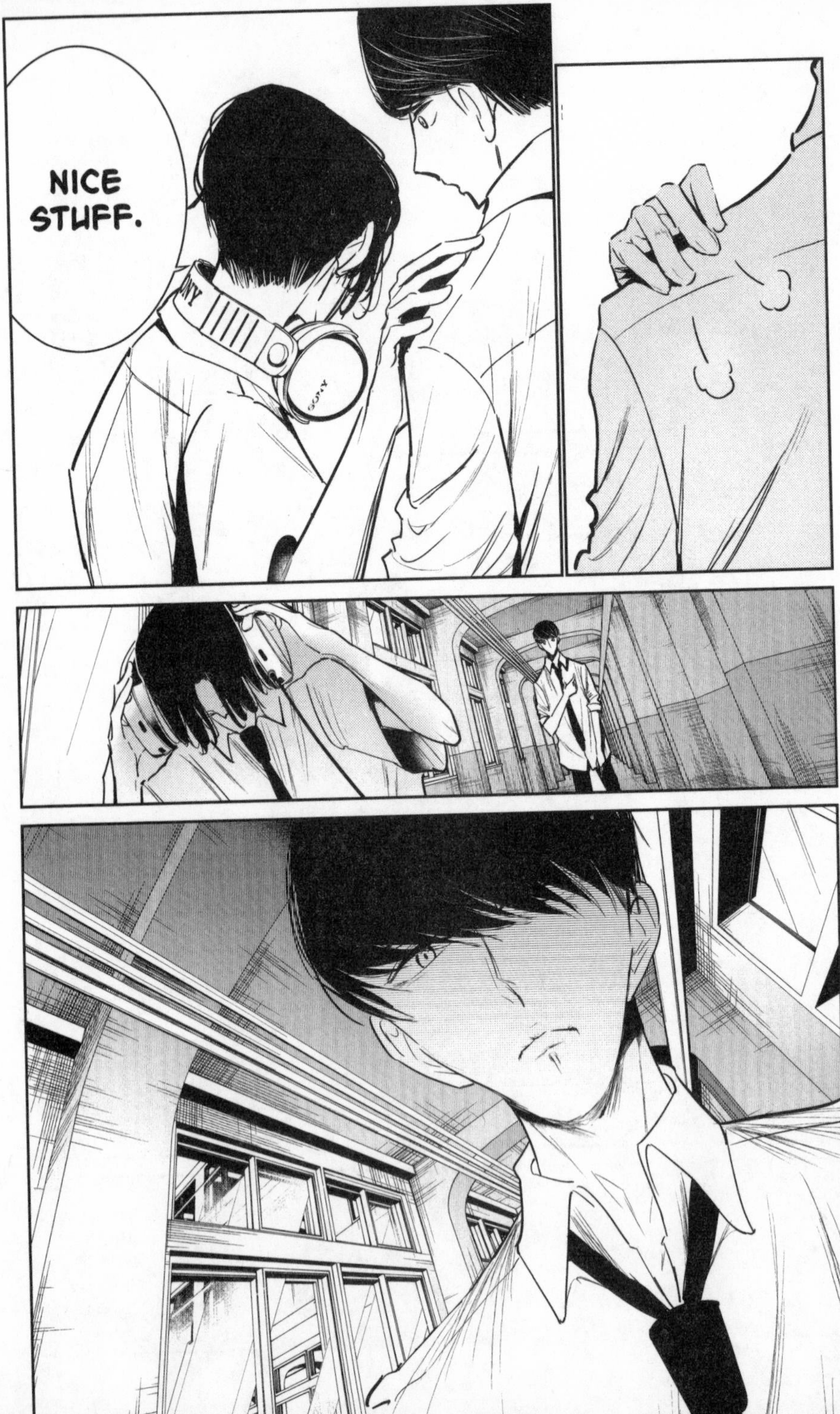
NICE STUFF.
SONY
SONY

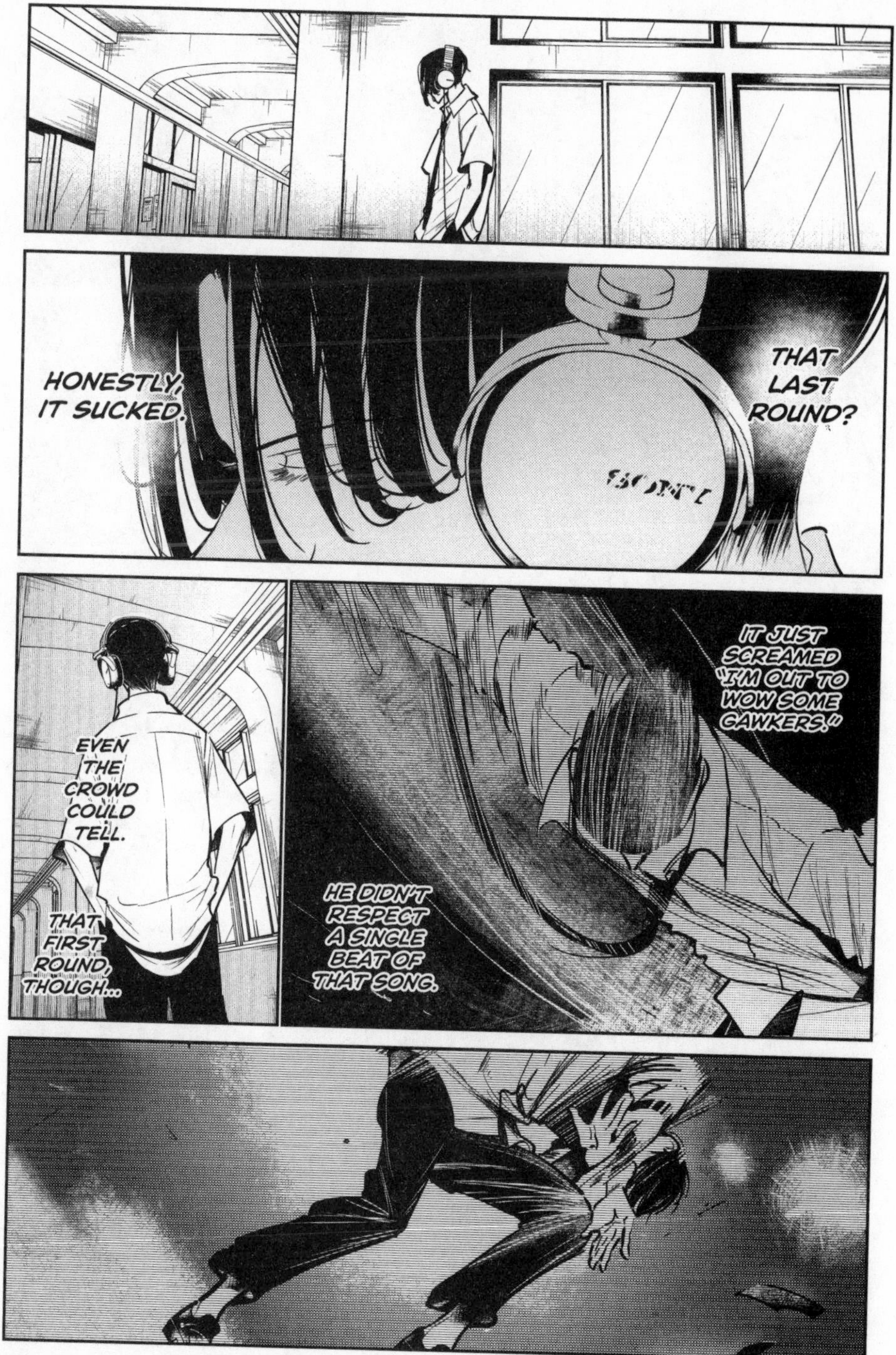
THAT LAST ROUND?
HONESTLY, IT SUCKED.
IT JUST SCREAMED "I'M OUT TO WOW SOME GAWKERS."
HE DIDN'T RESPECT A SINGLE BEAT OF THAT SONG.
EVEN THE CROWD COULD TELL.
THAT FIRST ROUND, THOUGH...

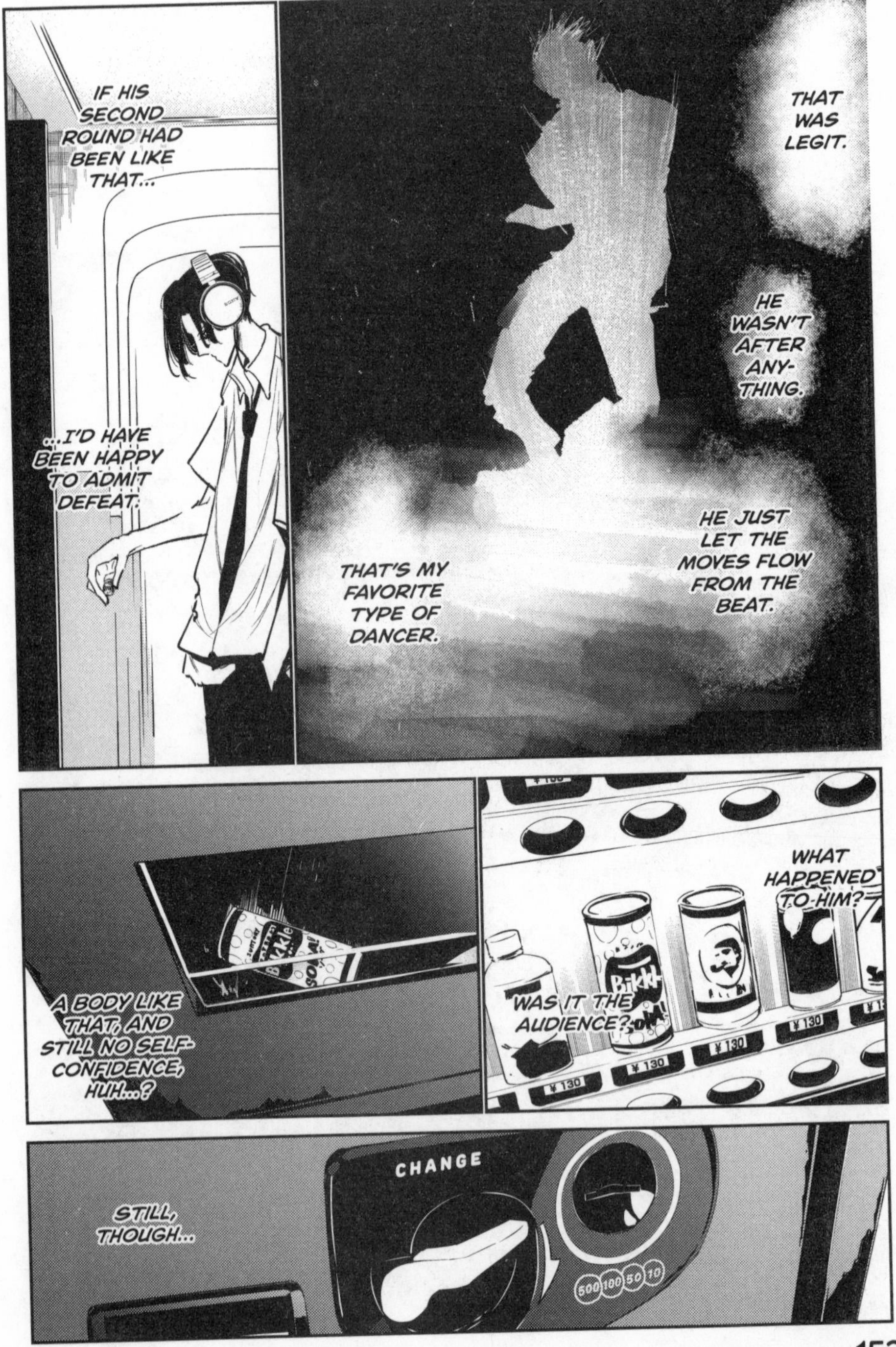
THAT WAS LEGIT.
HE WASN'T AFTER ANY-THING.
HE JUST LET THE MOVES FLOW FROM THE BEAT.
THAT'S MY FAVORITE TYPE OF DANCER.
IF HIS SECOND ROUND HAD BEEN LIKE THAT...
...I'D HAVE BEEN HAPPY TO ADMIT DEFEAT.
WHAT HAPPENED TO HIM?
WAS IT THE AUDIENCE?
¥130
A BODY LIKE THAT, AND STILL NO SELF-CONFIDENCE, HUH...?
CHANGE
STILL, THOUGH...
500 100 50 10

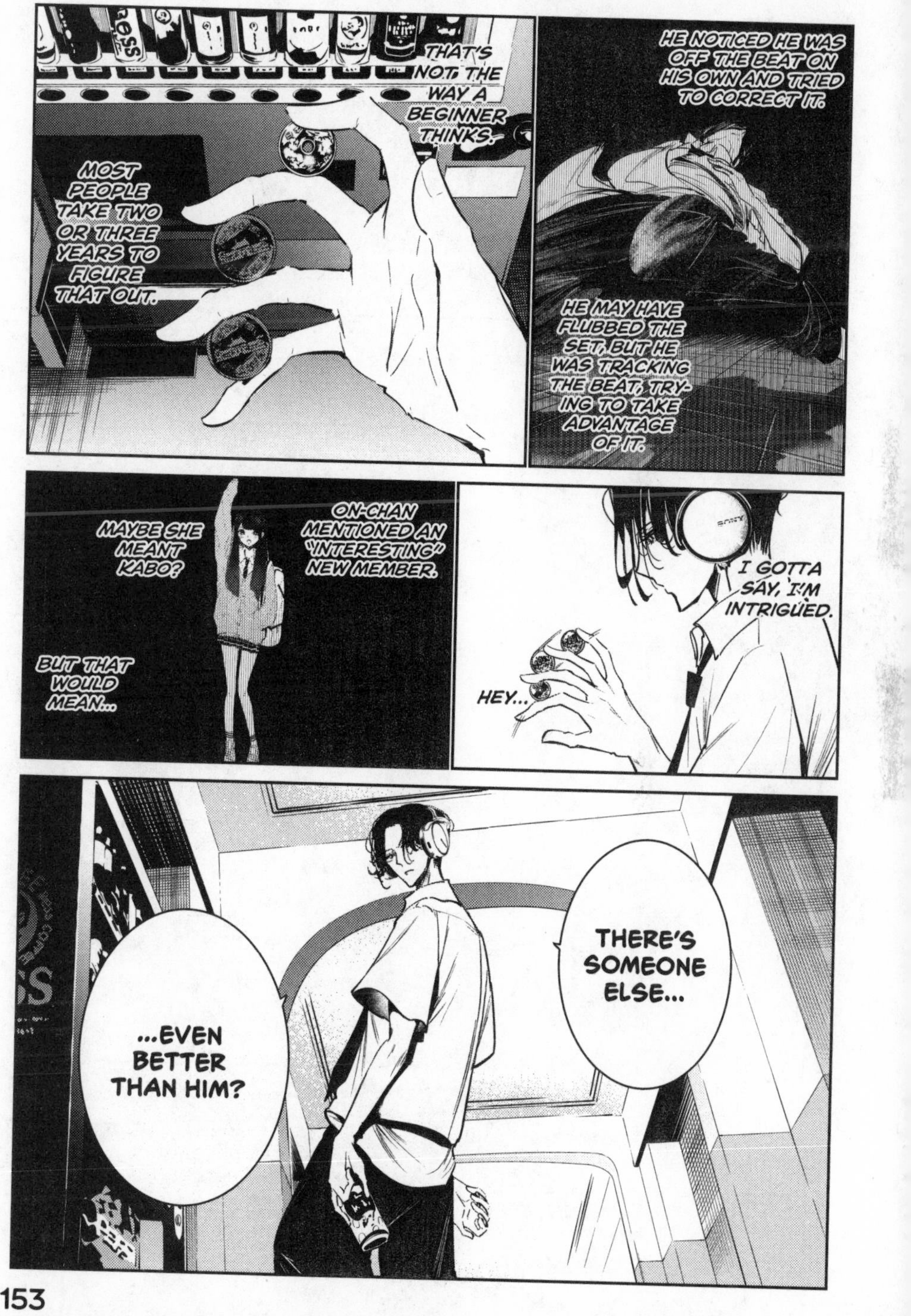
HE NOTICED HE WAS OFF THE BEAT ON HIS OWN AND TRIED TO CORRECT IT.
HE MAY HAVE FLUBBED THE SET, BUT HE WAS TRACKING THE BEAT, TRYING TO TAKE ADVANTAGE OF IT.
THAT'S NOT THE WAY A BEGINNER THINKS.
MOST PEOPLE TAKE TWO OR THREE YEARS TO FIGURE THAT OUT.
I GOTTA SAY, I'M INTRIGUED.
HEY...
ON-CHAN MENTIONED AN "INTERESTING" NEW MEMBER.
MAYBE SHE MEANT KABO?
BUT THAT WOULD MEAN...
THERE'S SOMEONE ELSE...
...EVEN BETTER THAN HIM?

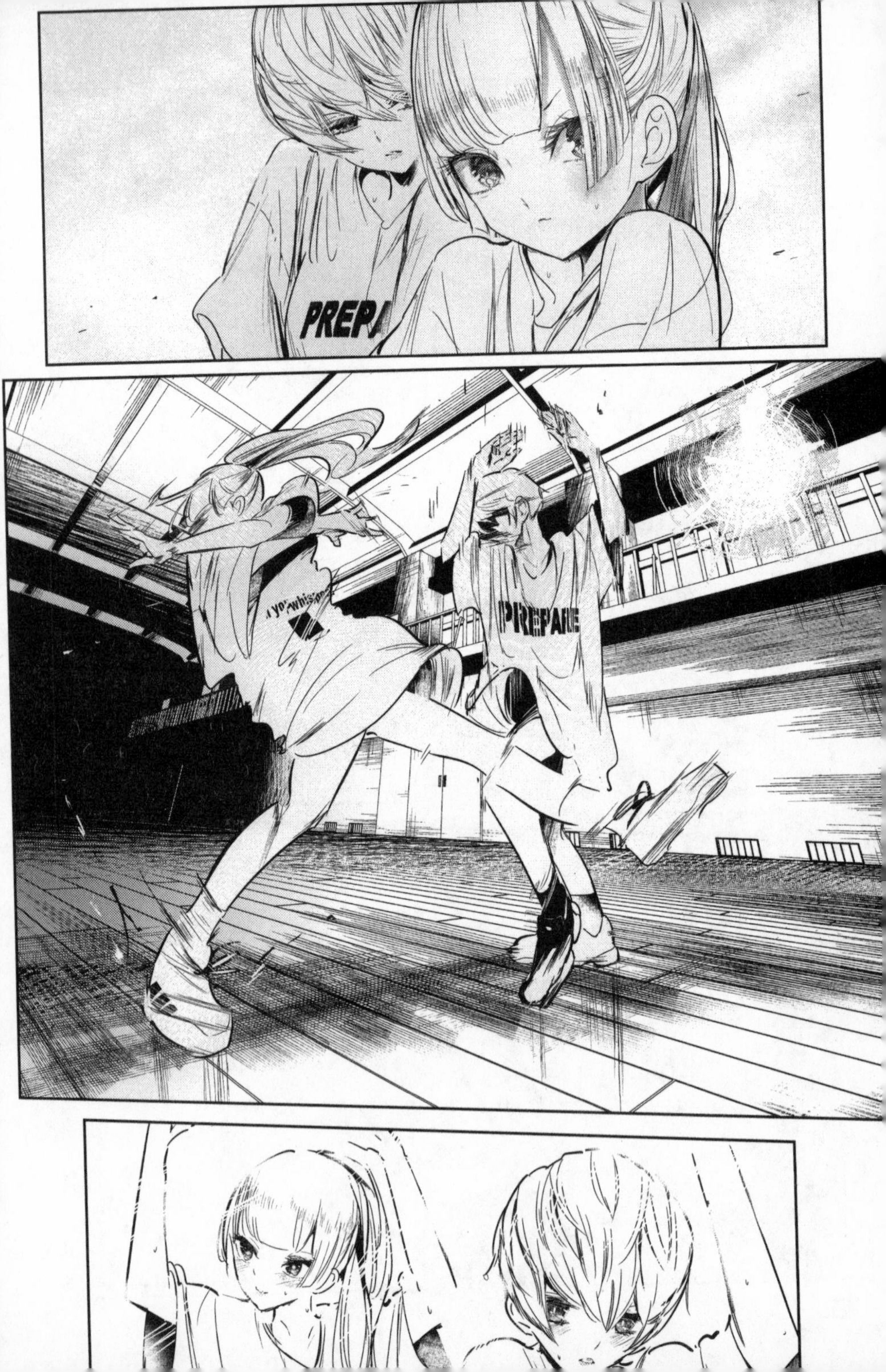
PREPA
PREPARE

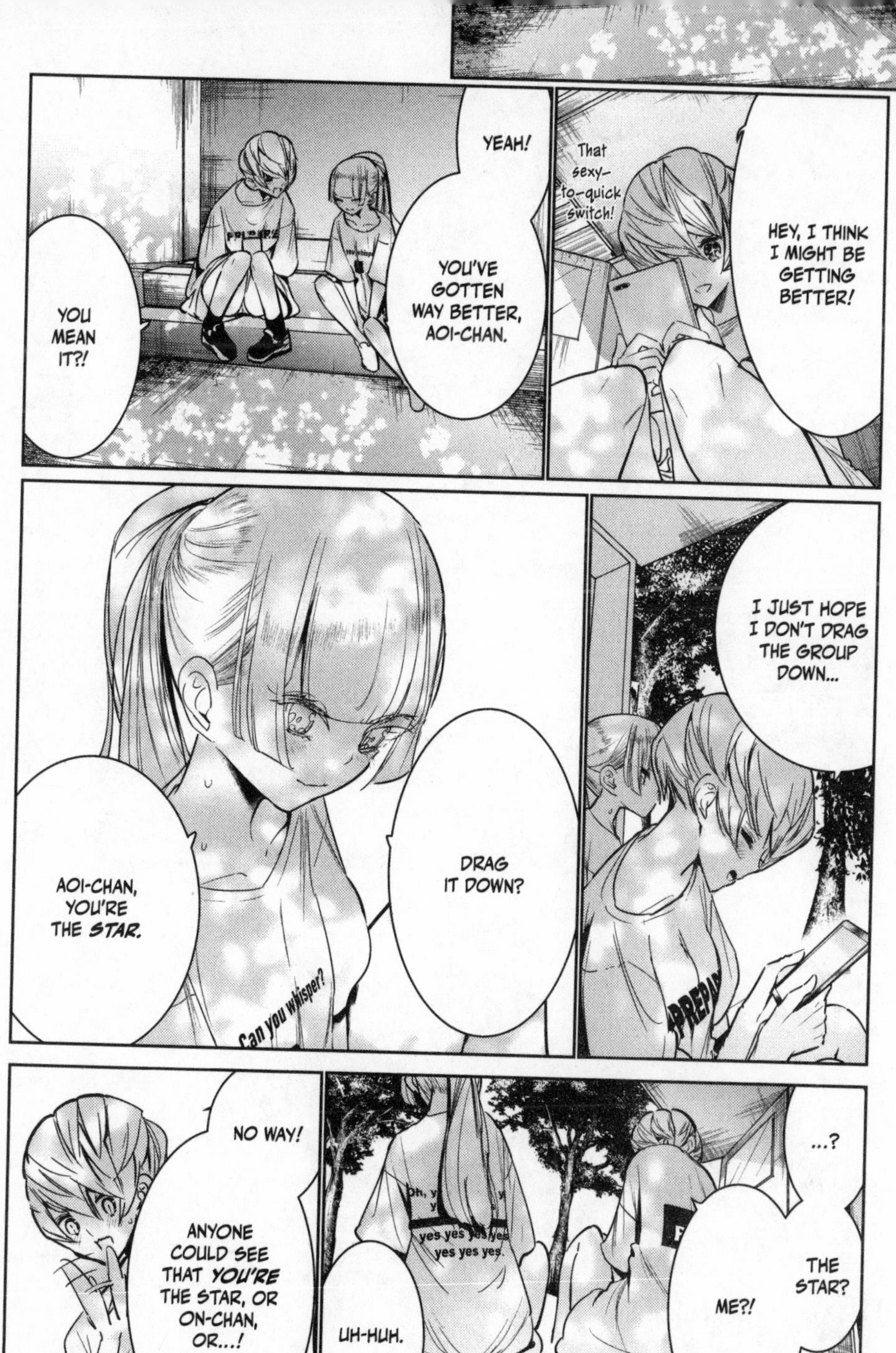
HEY, I THINK I MIGHT BE GETTING BETTER!
That sexy-to-quick switch!
YEAH!
YOU'VE GOTTEN WAY BETTER, AOI-CHAN.
YOU MEAN IT?!
I JUST HOPE I DON'T DRAG THE GROUP DOWN...
DRAG IT DOWN?
AOI-CHAN, YOU'RE THE STAR.
...?
THE STAR?
ME?!
UH-HUH.
NO WAY!
ANYONE COULD SEE THAT YOU'RE THE STAR, OR ON-CHAN, OR...!

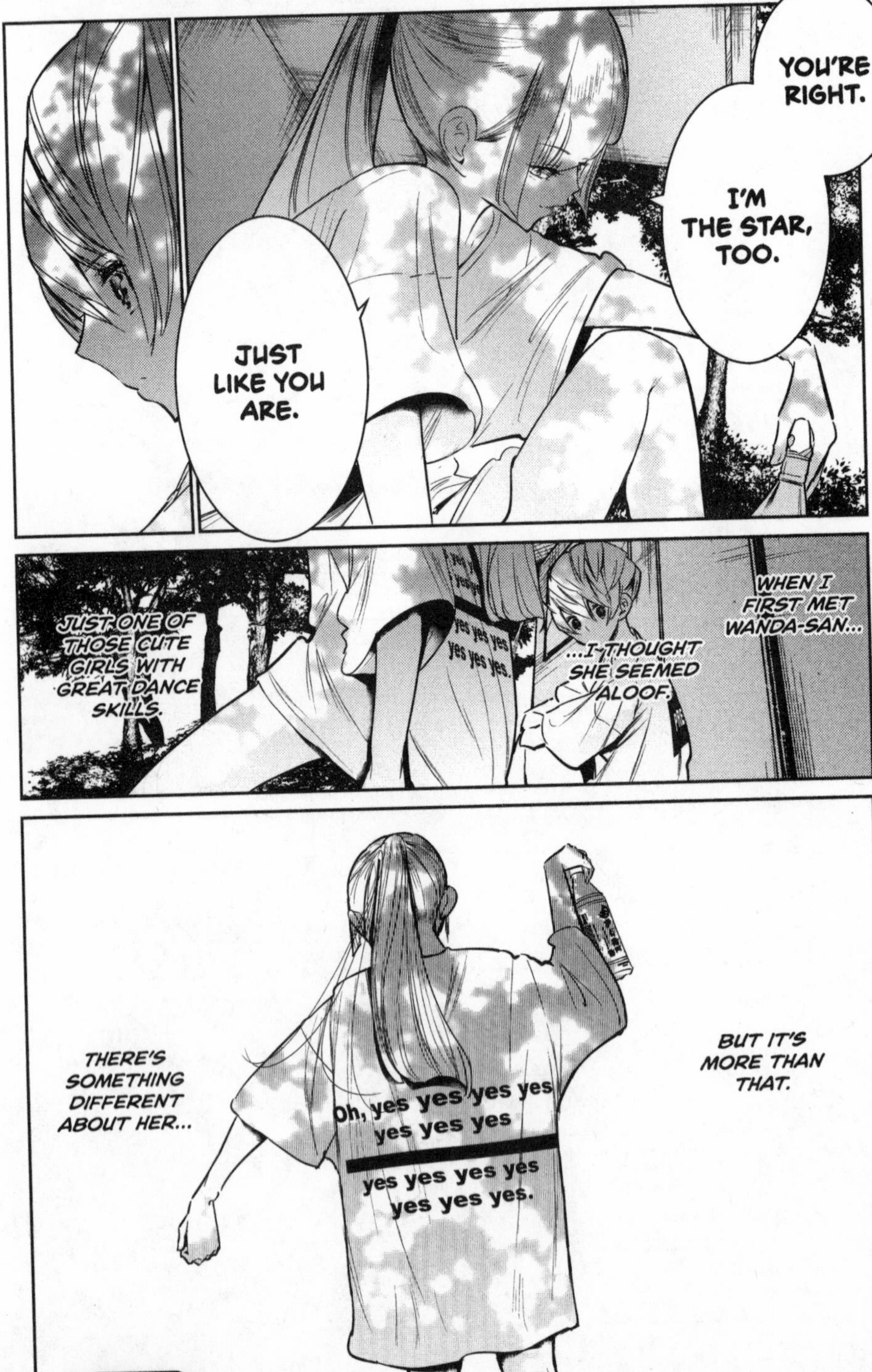
YOU'RE RIGHT.
I'M THE STAR, TOO.
JUST LIKE YOU ARE.
WHEN I FIRST MET WANDA-SAN...
...I THOUGHT SHE SEEMED ALOOF.
yes yes yes yes yes yes.
JUST ONE OF THOSE CUTE GIRLS WITH GREAT DANCE SKILLS.
BUT IT'S MORE THAN THAT.
Oh, yes yes yes yes yes yes yes
yes yes yes yes yes yes yes.
THERE'S SOMETHING DIFFERENT ABOUT HER...
Ch. 7: END

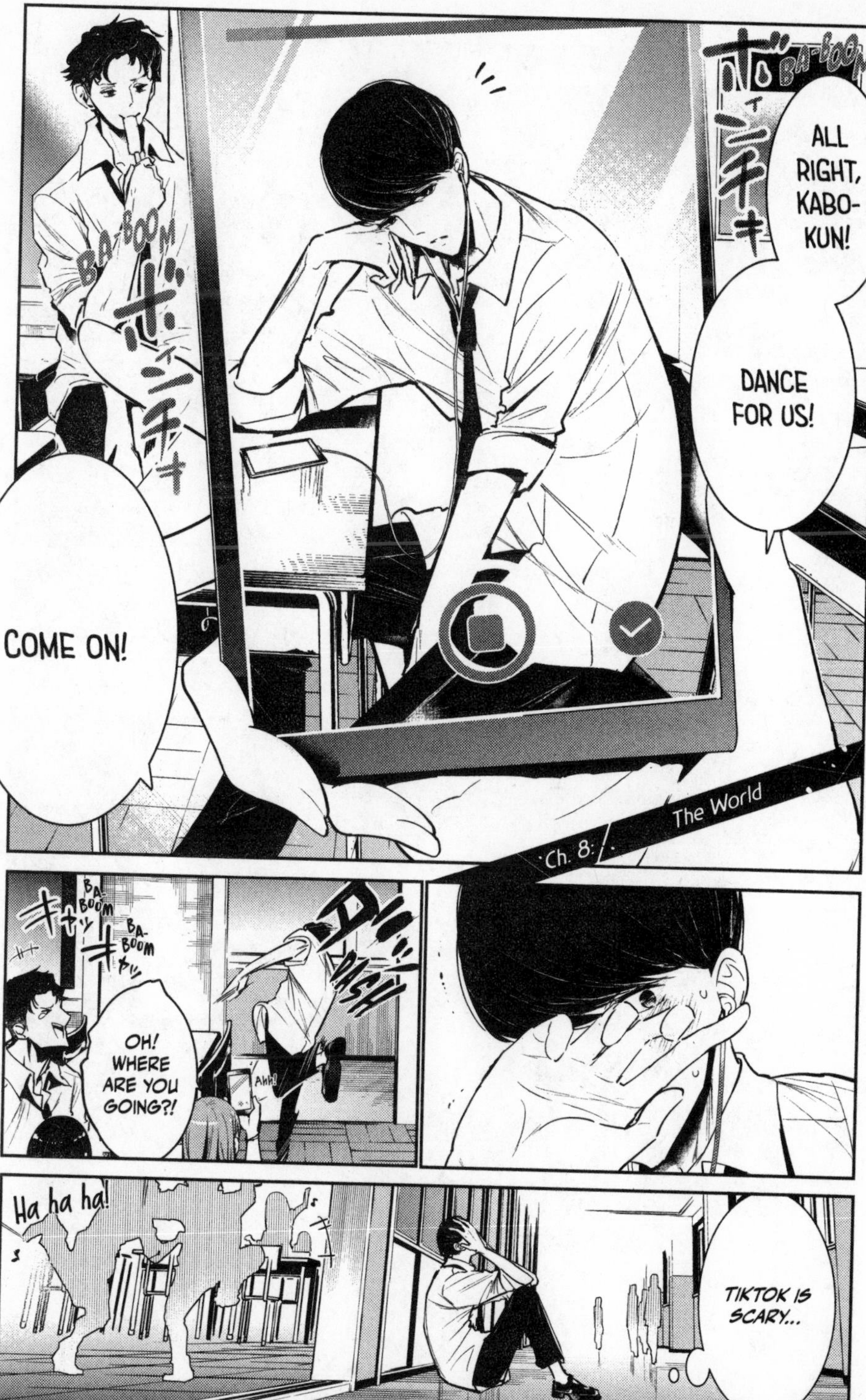
BA-BOOM
ALL RIGHT, KABO-KUN!
DANCE FOR US!
BA-BOOM
COME ON!
Ch. 8: The World
DASH
BA-BOOM
BA-BOOM
OH! WHERE ARE YOU GOING?!
AHH!
TIKTOK IS SCARY...
Ha ha ha!

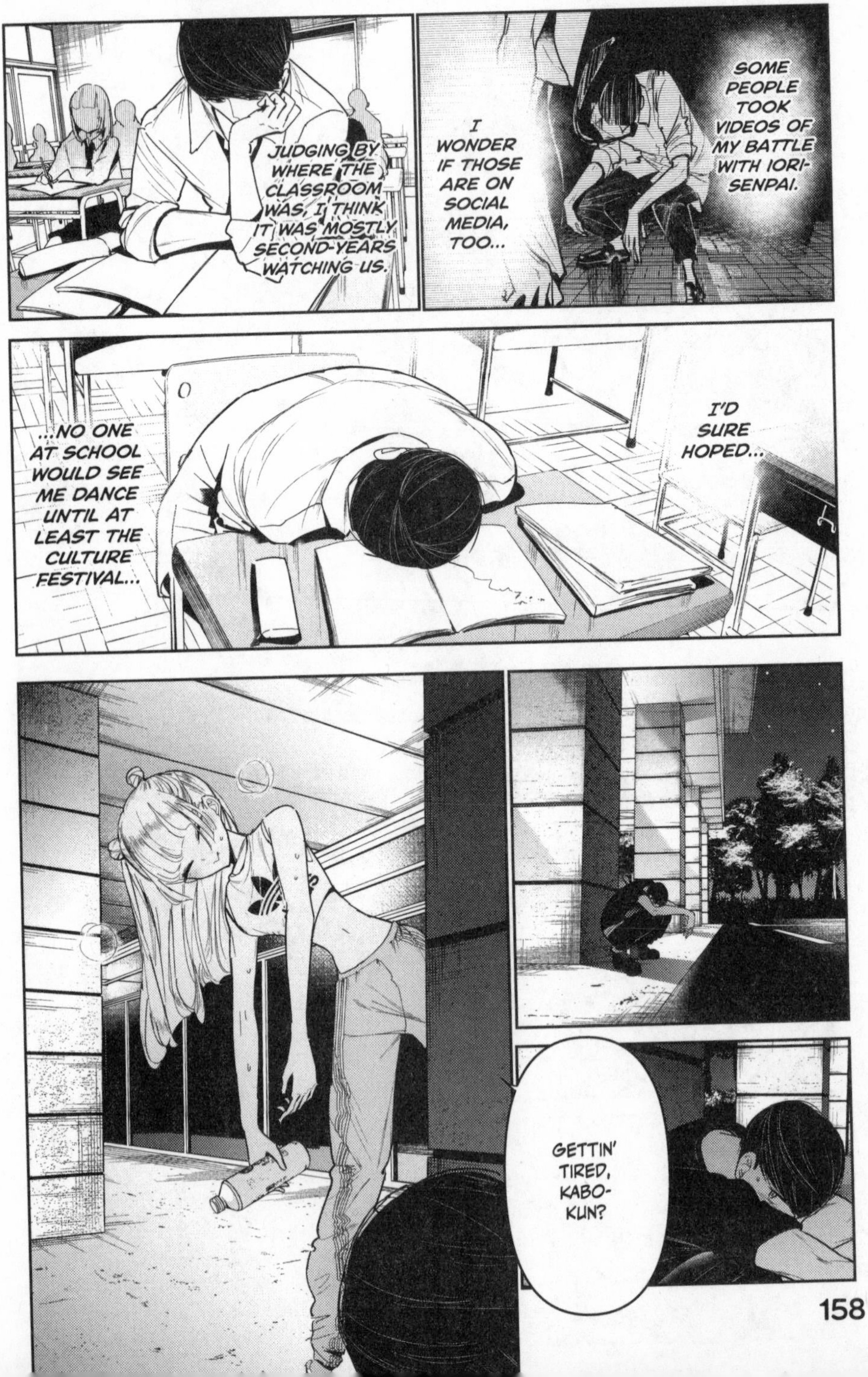
SOME PEOPLE TOOK VIDEOS OF MY BATTLE WITH IORI-SENPAI.
I WONDER IF THOSE ARE ON SOCIAL MEDIA, TOO...
JUDGING BY WHERE THE CLASSROOM WAS, I THINK IT WAS MOSTLY SECOND-YEARS WATCHING US.
I'D SURE HOPED...
...NO ONE AT SCHOOL WOULD SEE ME DANCE UNTIL AT LEAST THE CULTURE FESTIVAL...
GETTIN' TIRED, KABO-KUN?

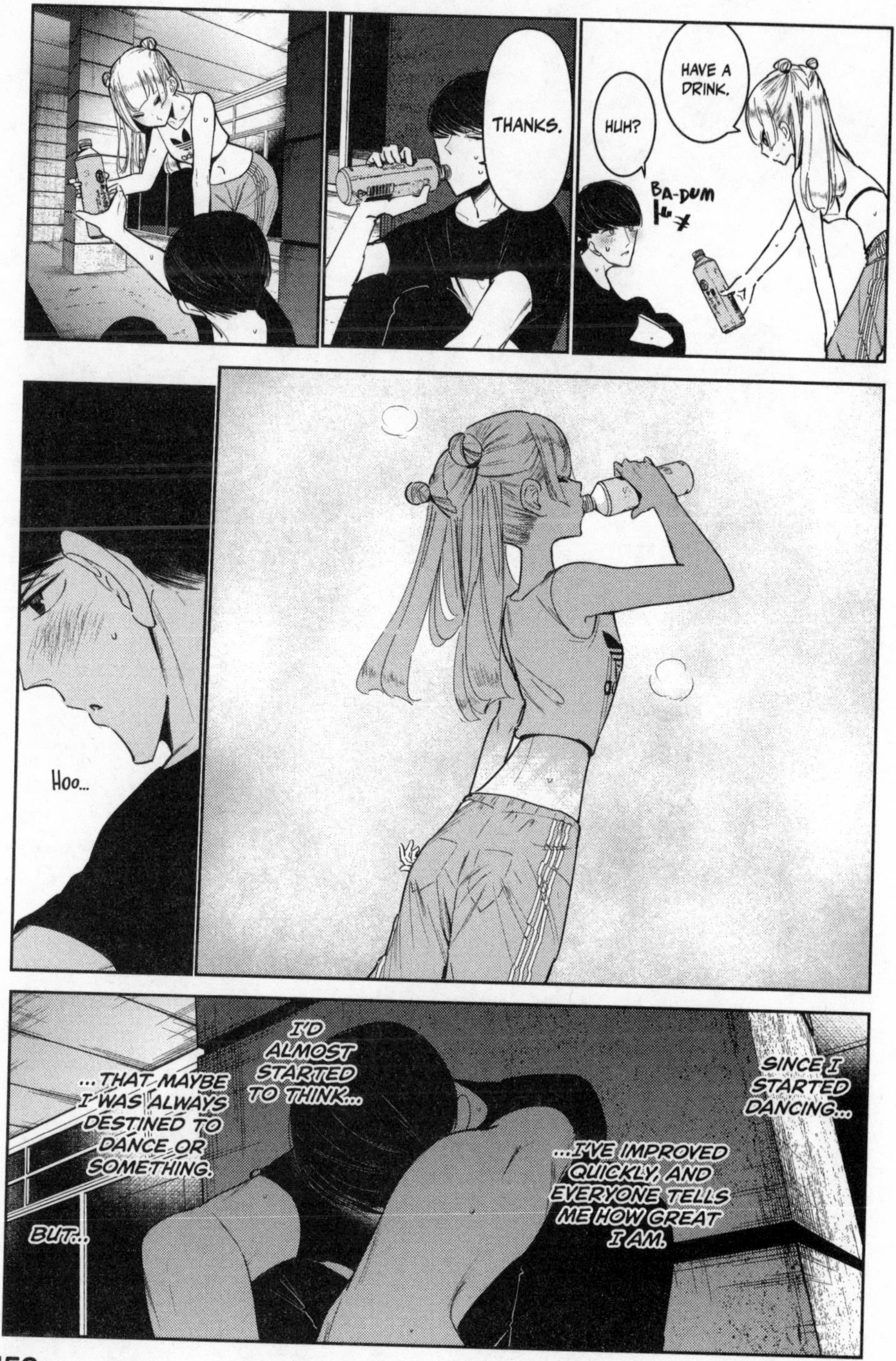
HAVE A DRINK.
HUH?
BA-DUM
THANKS.
Hoo...
SINCE I STARTED DANCING...
...I'VE IMPROVED QUICKLY, AND EVERYONE TELLS ME HOW GREAT I AM.
I'D ALMOST STARTED TO THINK...
...THAT MAYBE I WAS ALWAYS DESTINED TO DANCE OR SOMETHING.
BUT...

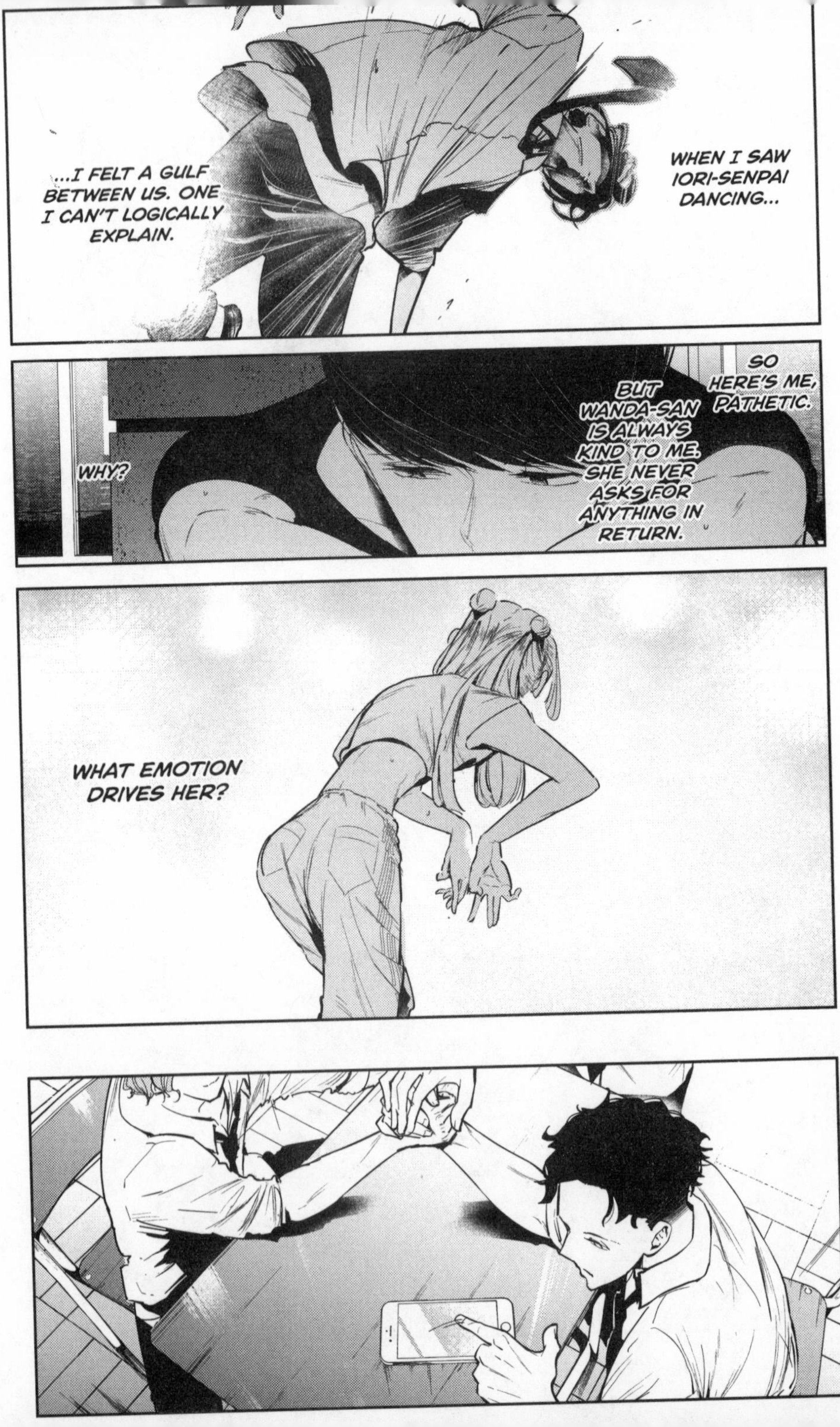
WHEN I SAW IORI-SENPAI DANCING...
...I FELT A GULF BETWEEN US. ONE I CAN'T LOGICALLY EXPLAIN.
SO HERE'S ME, PATHETIC.
BUT WANDA-SAN IS ALWAYS KIND TO ME. SHE NEVER ASKS FOR ANYTHING IN RETURN.
WHY?
WHAT EMOTION DRIVES HER?

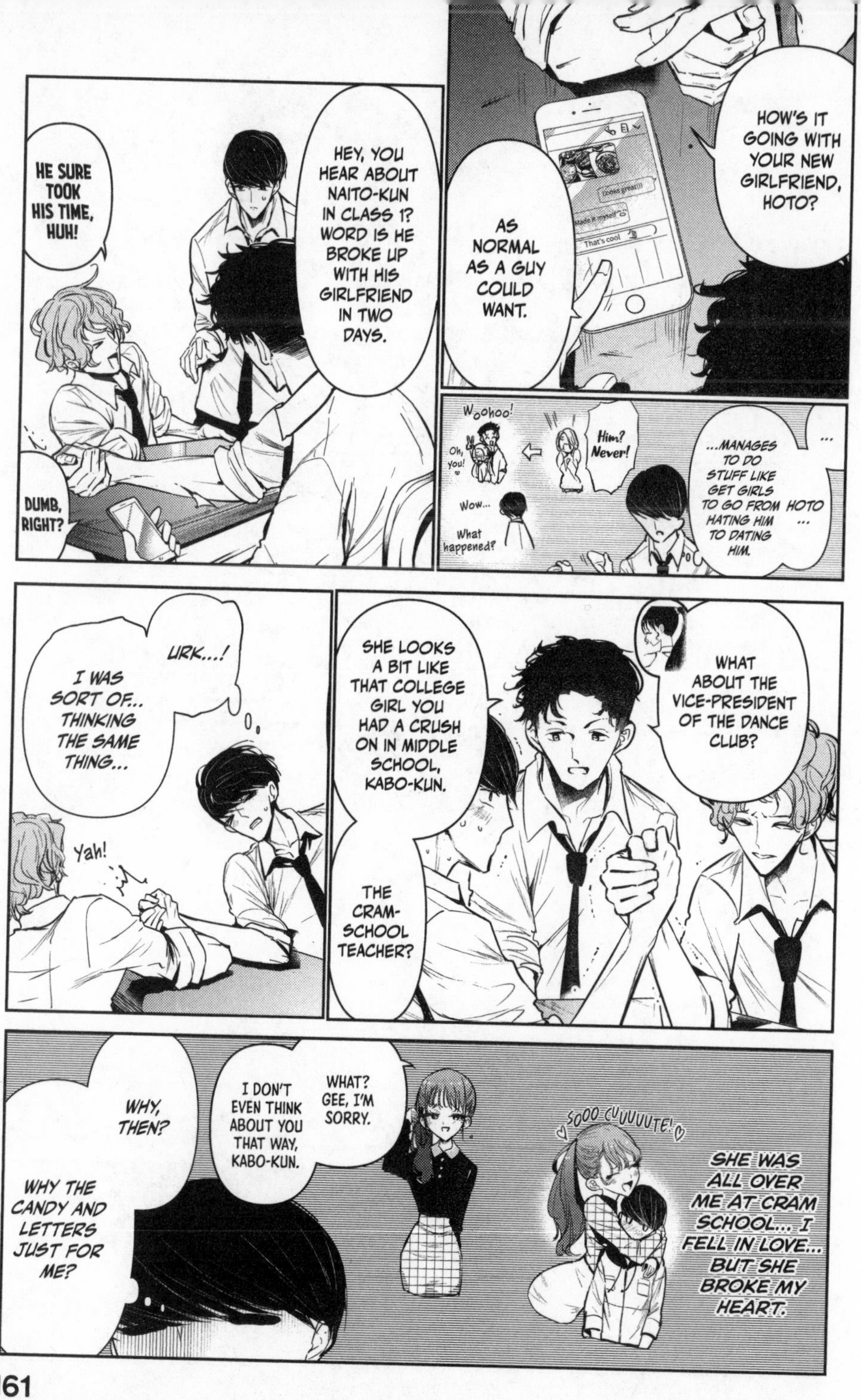
HOW'S IT GOING WITH YOUR NEW GIRLFRIEND, HOTO?
Looks great!!
That's cool
AS NORMAL AS A GUY COULD WANT.
...
...MANAGES TO DO STUFF LIKE GET GIRLS TO GO FROM HATING HIM TO DATING HIM.
HOTO ...
Him? Never!
Woohoo!
Oh, you!
Wow...
What happened?
HEY, YOU HEAR ABOUT NAITO-KUN IN CLASS 1? WORD IS HE BROKE UP WITH HIS GIRLFRIEND IN TWO DAYS.
HE SURE TOOK HIS TIME, HUH!
DUMB, RIGHT?
WHAT ABOUT THE VICE-PRESIDENT OF THE DANCE CLUB?
SHE LOOKS A BIT LIKE THAT COLLEGE GIRL YOU HAD A CRUSH ON IN MIDDLE SCHOOL, KABO-KUN.
THE CRAM-SCHOOL TEACHER?
URK...!
I WAS SORT OF... THINKING THE SAME THING...
Yah!
SHE WAS ALL OVER ME AT CRAM SCHOOL... I FELL IN LOVE... BUT SHE BROKE MY HEART.
SOOO CUUUUTE!
WHAT? GEE, I'M SORRY.
I DON'T EVEN THINK ABOUT YOU THAT WAY, KABO-KUN.
WHY, THEN?
WHY THE CANDY AND LETTERS JUST FOR ME?

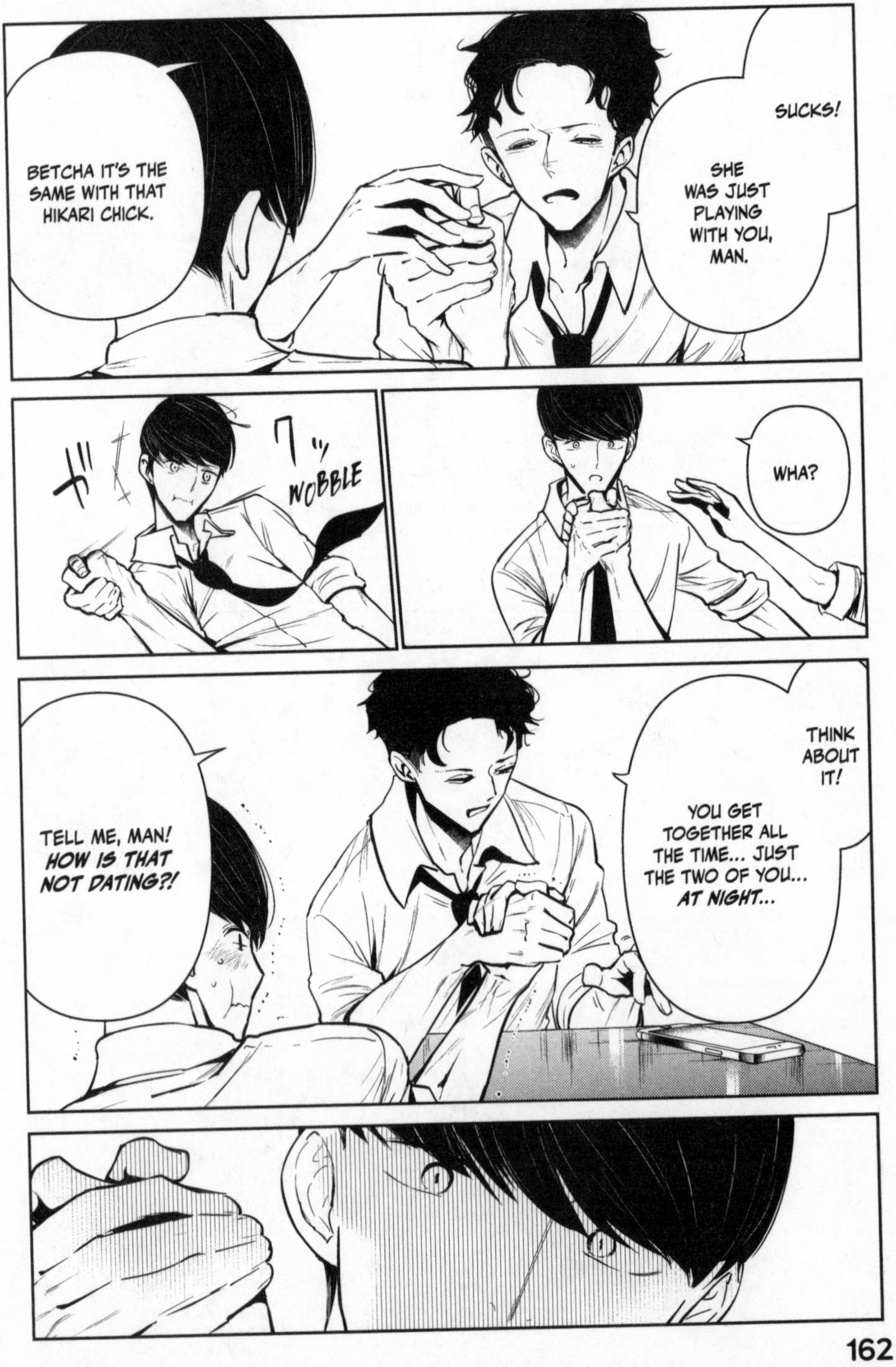
SUCKS!
SHE WAS JUST PLAYING WITH YOU, MAN.
BETCHA IT'S THE SAME WITH THAT HIKARI CHICK.
WHA?
ワッ
WOBBLE
ガ
THINK ABOUT IT!
YOU GET TOGETHER ALL THE TIME... JUST THE TWO OF YOU... AT NIGHT...
TELL ME, MAN! HOW IS THAT NOT DATING?!

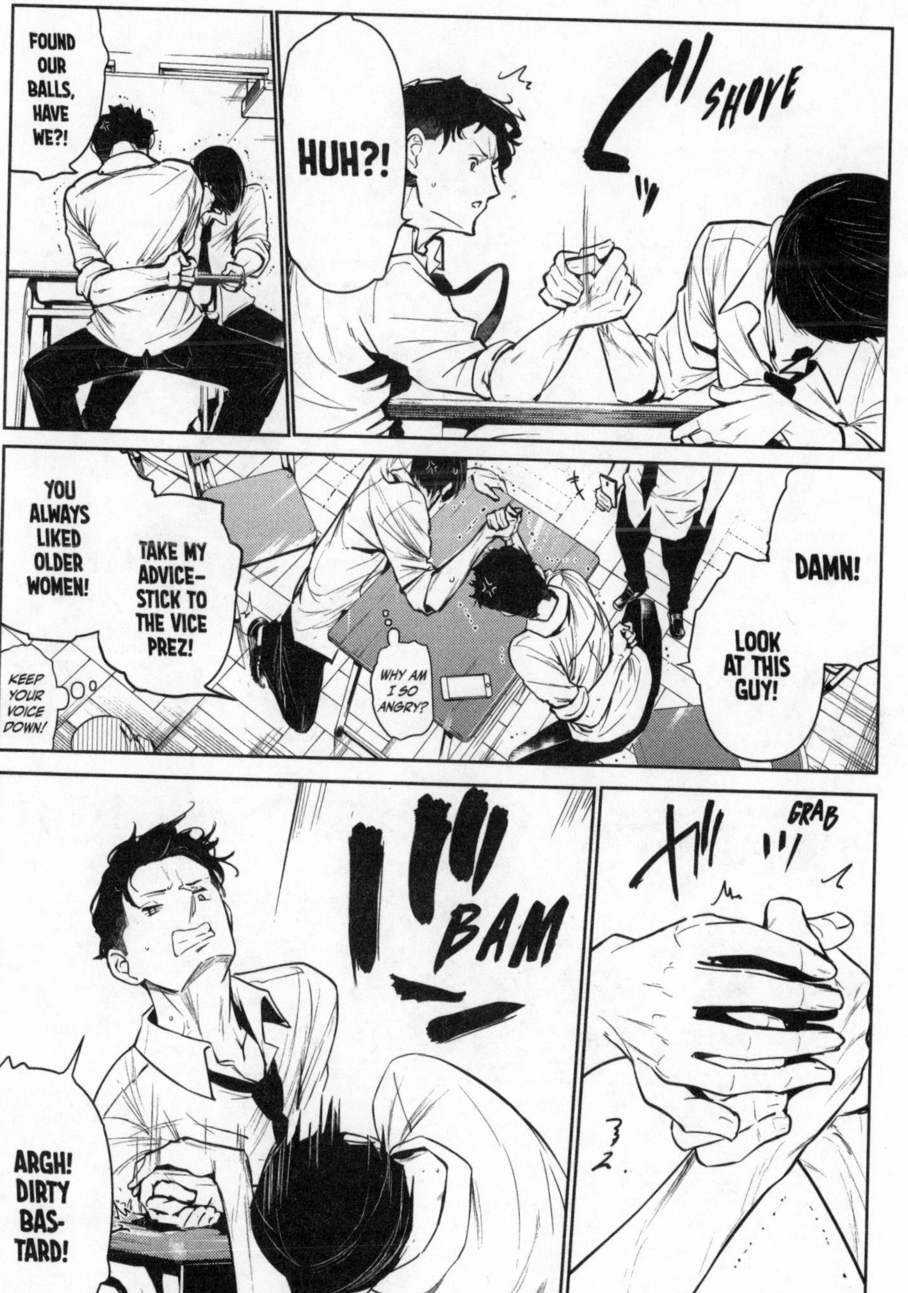
SHOVE
HUH?!
FOUND OUR BALLS, HAVE WE?!
DAMN!
LOOK AT THIS GUY!
WHY AM I SO ANGRY?
TAKE MY ADVICE- STICK TO THE VICE PREZ!
YOU ALWAYS LIKED OLDER WOMEN!
KEEP YOUR VOICE DOWN!
GRAB
BAM
ARGH! DIRTY BAS- TARD!

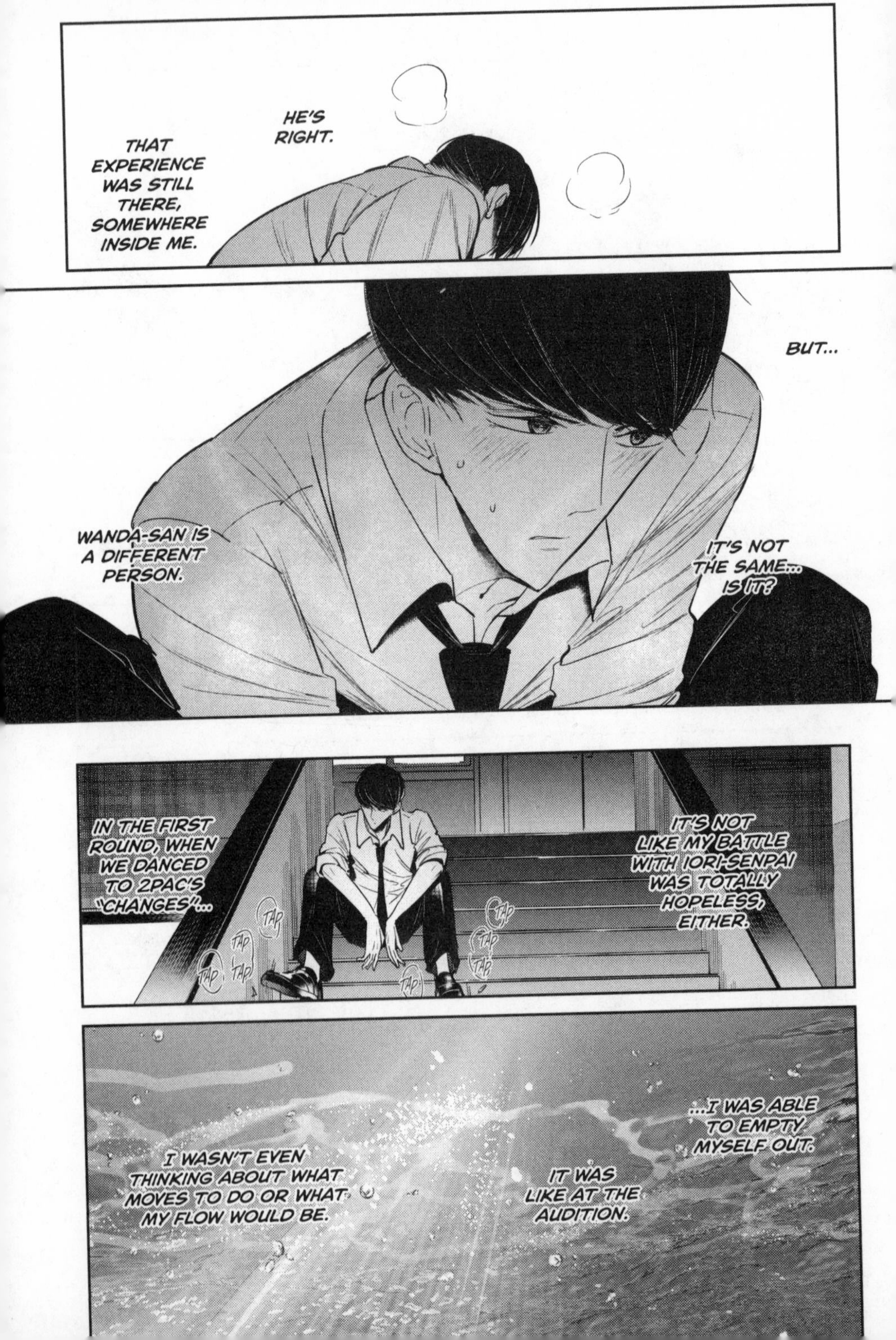
HE'S RIGHT.
THAT EXPERIENCE WAS STILL THERE, SOMEWHERE INSIDE ME.
BUT...
IT'S NOT THE SAME... IS IT?
WANDA-SAN IS A DIFFERENT PERSON.
IT'S NOT LIKE MY BATTLE WITH IORI-SENPAI WAS TOTALLY HOPELESS, EITHER.
TAP TAP TAP
IN THE FIRST ROUND, WHEN WE DANCED TO 2PAC'S "CHANGES"...
TAP TAP TAP TAP
...I WAS ABLE TO EMPTY MYSELF OUT.
IT WAS LIKE AT THE AUDITION.
I WASN'T EVEN THINKING ABOUT WHAT MOVES TO DO OR WHAT MY FLOW WOULD BE.

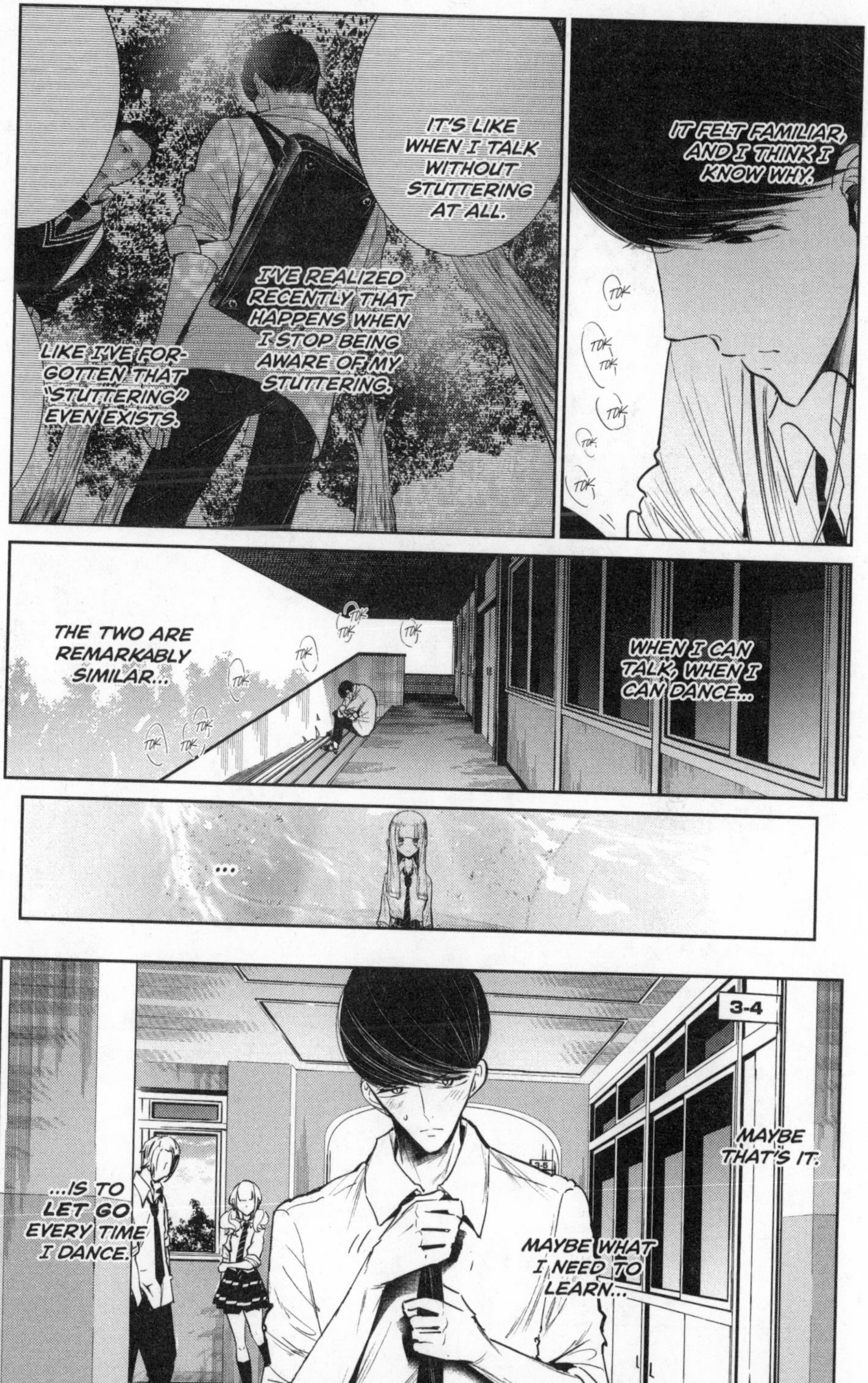
IT FELT FAMILIAR, AND I THINK I KNOW WHY.
TOK
TOK TOK
TOK
TOK
TOK
IT'S LIKE WHEN I TALK WITHOUT STUTTERING AT ALL.
I'VE REALIZED RECENTLY THAT HAPPENS WHEN I STOP BEING AWARE OF MY STUTTERING.
LIKE I'VE FOR-GOTTEN THAT "STUTTERING" EVEN EXISTS.
WHEN I CAN TALK, WHEN I CAN DANCE...
TOK TOK
TOK
TOK
TOK
THE TWO ARE REMARKABLY SIMILAR...
TOK TOK
TOK
...
3-4
MAYBE THAT'S IT.
MAYBE WHAT I NEED TO LEARN...
...IS TO LET GO EVERY TIME I DANCE.

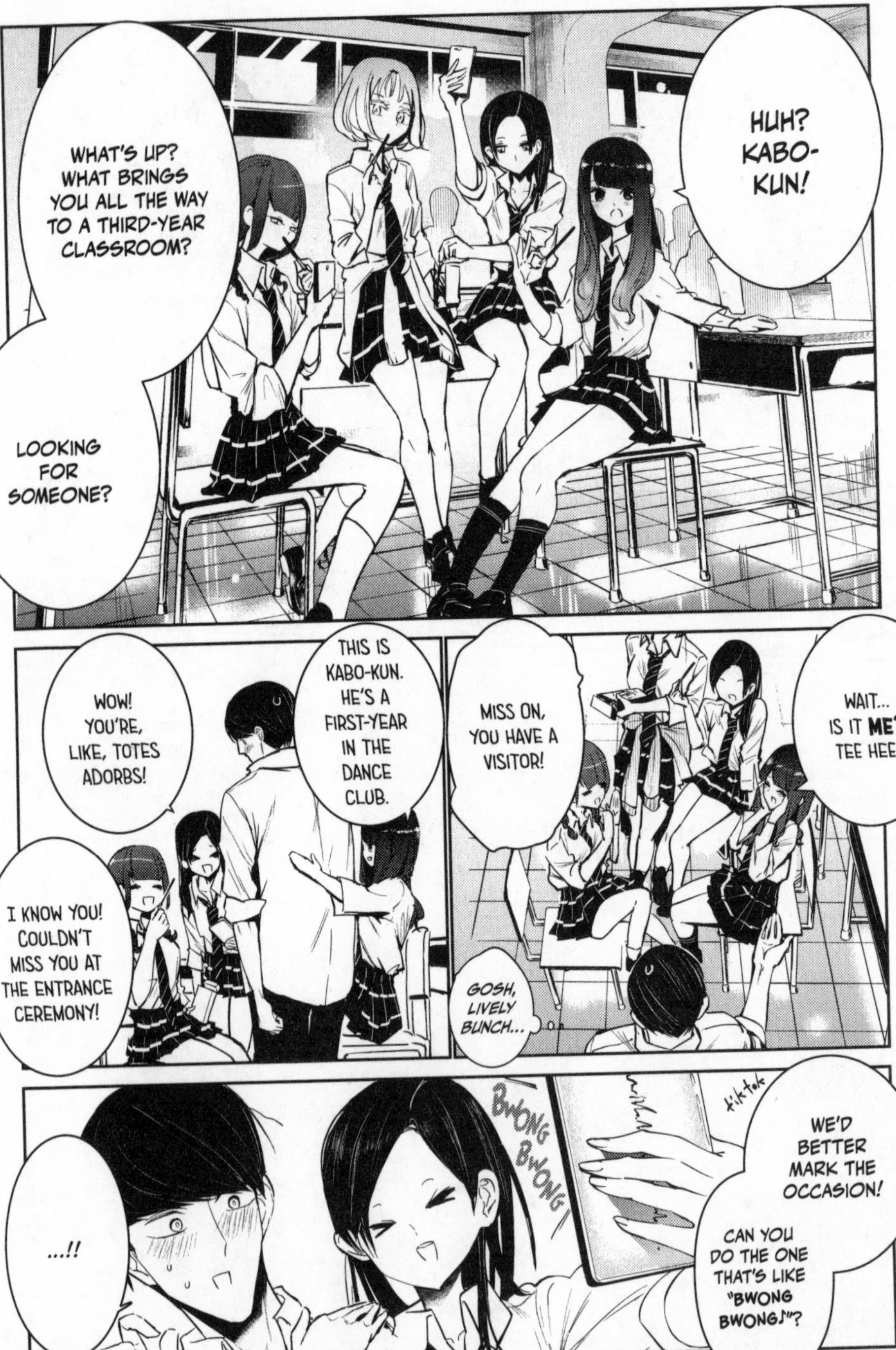
HUH? KABO-KUN!
WHAT'S UP? WHAT BRINGS YOU ALL THE WAY TO A THIRD-YEAR CLASSROOM?
LOOKING FOR SOMEONE?
WAIT... IS IT ME? TEE HEE!
MISS ON, YOU HAVE A VISITOR!
GOSH, LIVELY BUNCH...
THIS IS KABO-KUN. HE'S A FIRST-YEAR IN THE DANCE CLUB.
WOW! YOU'RE, LIKE, TOTES ADORBS!
I KNOW YOU! COULDN'T MISS YOU AT THE ENTRANCE CEREMONY!
WE'D BETTER MARK THE OCCASION!
CAN YOU DO THE ONE THAT'S LIKE "BWONG BWONG♪"?
BWONG BWONG
...!!

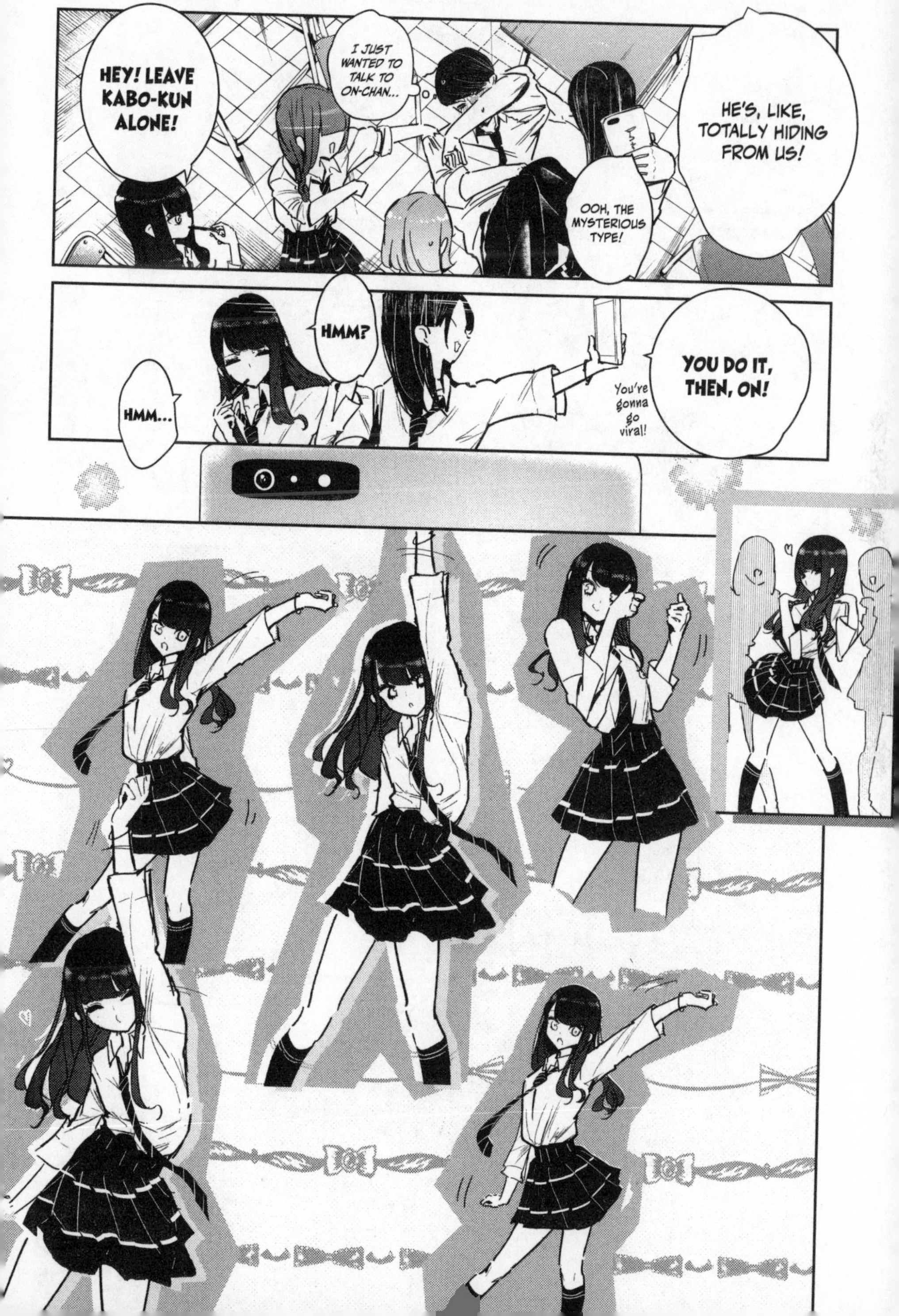
HE'S, LIKE, TOTALLY HIDING FROM US!
OOH, THE MYSTERIOUS TYPE!
I JUST WANTED TO TALK TO ON-CHAN...
HEY! LEAVE KABO-KUN ALONE!
YOU DO IT, THEN, ON!
You're gonna go viral!
HMM?
HMM...

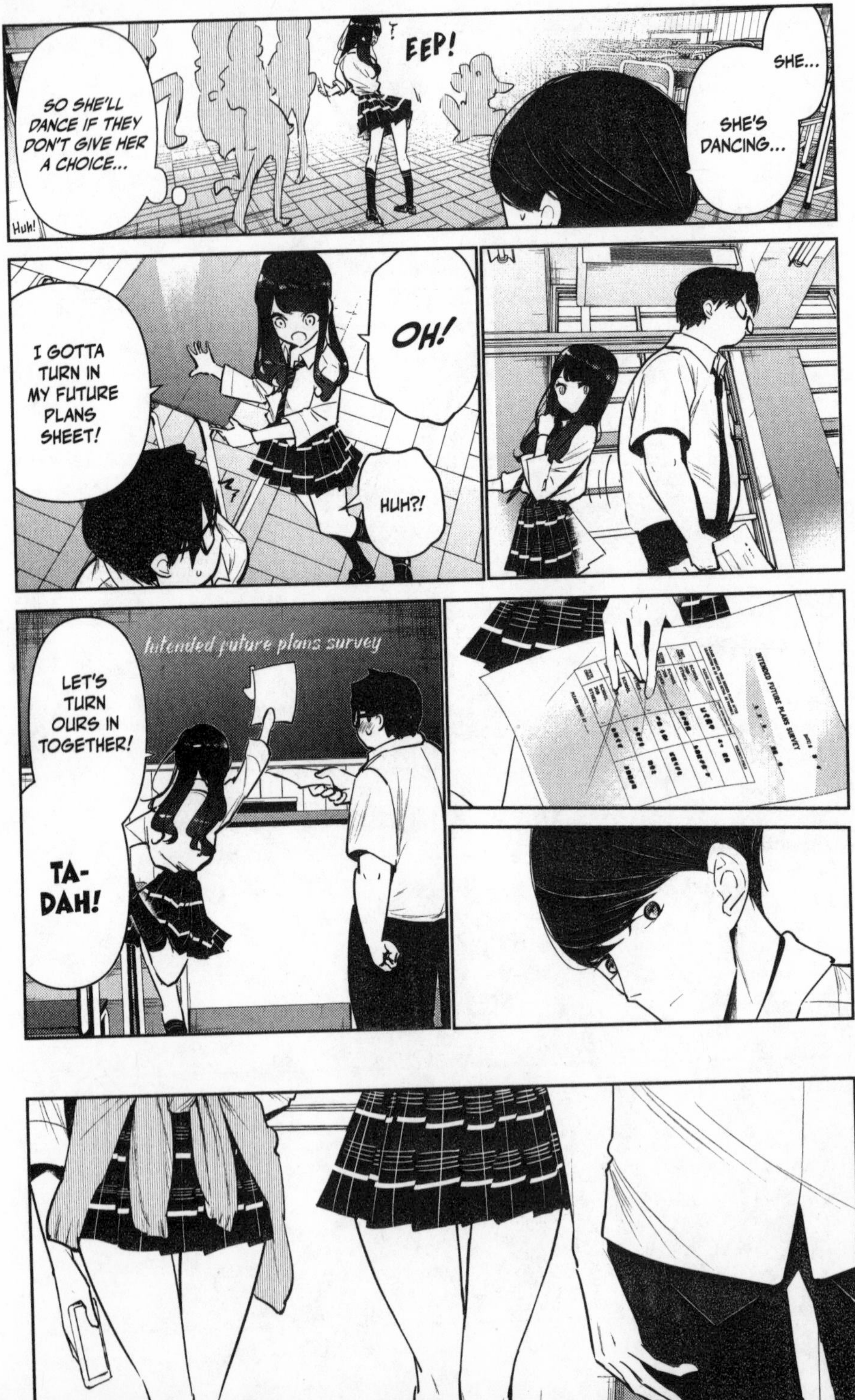
SHE...
SHE'S DANCING...
EEP!
SO SHE'LL DANCE IF THEY DON'T GIVE HER A CHOICE...
Huh!
OH!
I GOTTA TURN IN MY FUTURE PLANS SHEET!
HUH?!
INTENDED FUTURE PLANS SURVEY
Intended future plans survey
LET'S TURN OURS IN TOGETHER!
TA-DAH!

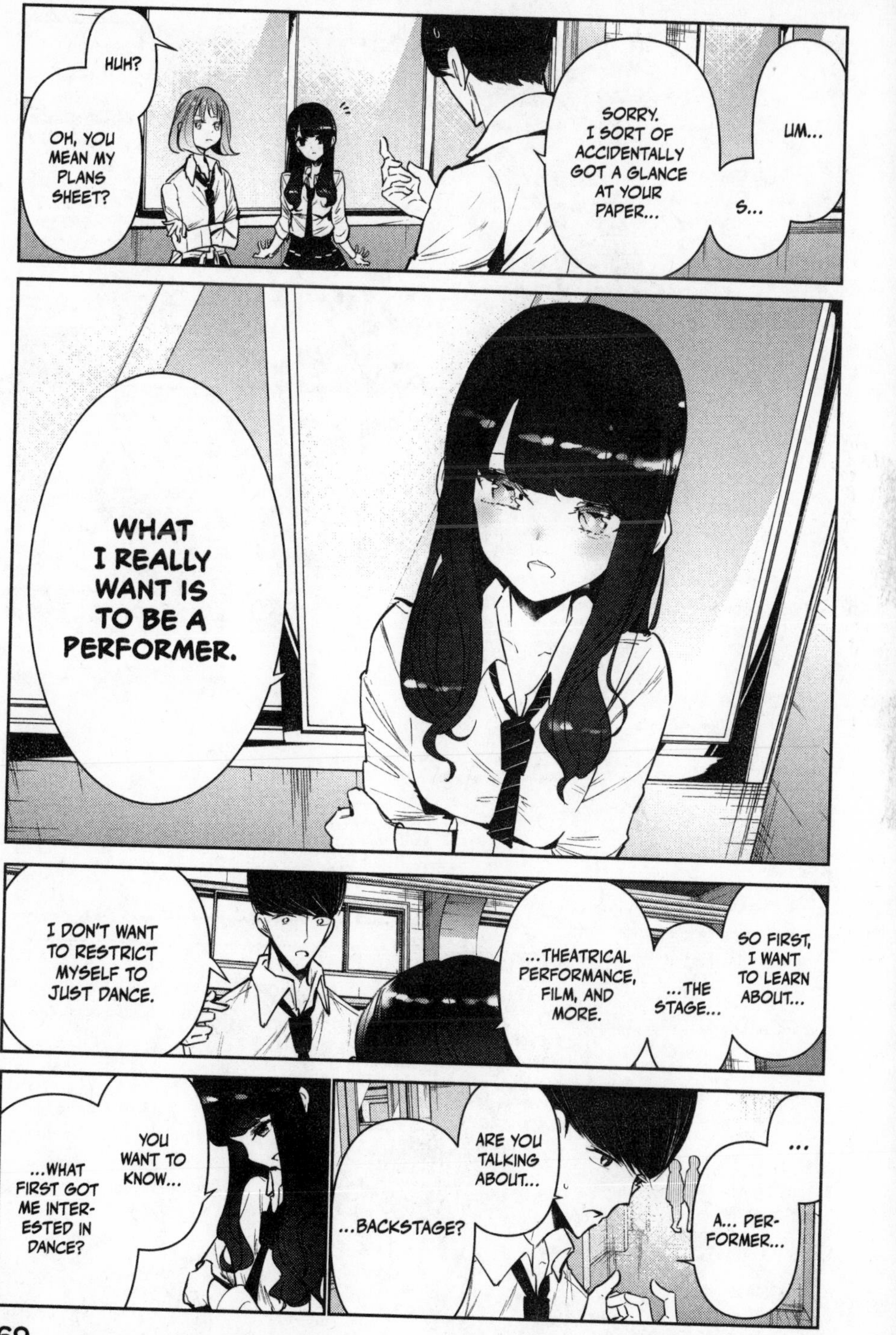
UM...
S...
SORRY. I SORT OF ACCIDENTALLY GOT A GLANCE AT YOUR PAPER...
HUH?
OH, YOU MEAN MY PLANS SHEET?
WHAT I REALLY WANT IS TO BE A PERFORMER.
SO FIRST, I WANT TO LEARN ABOUT...
...THE STAGE...
...THEATRICAL PERFORMANCE, FILM, AND MORE.
I DON'T WANT TO RESTRICT MYSELF TO JUST DANCE.
...
A... PER-FORMER...
ARE YOU TALKING ABOUT...
...BACKSTAGE?
YOU WANT TO KNOW...
...WHAT FIRST GOT ME INTER-ESTED IN DANCE?

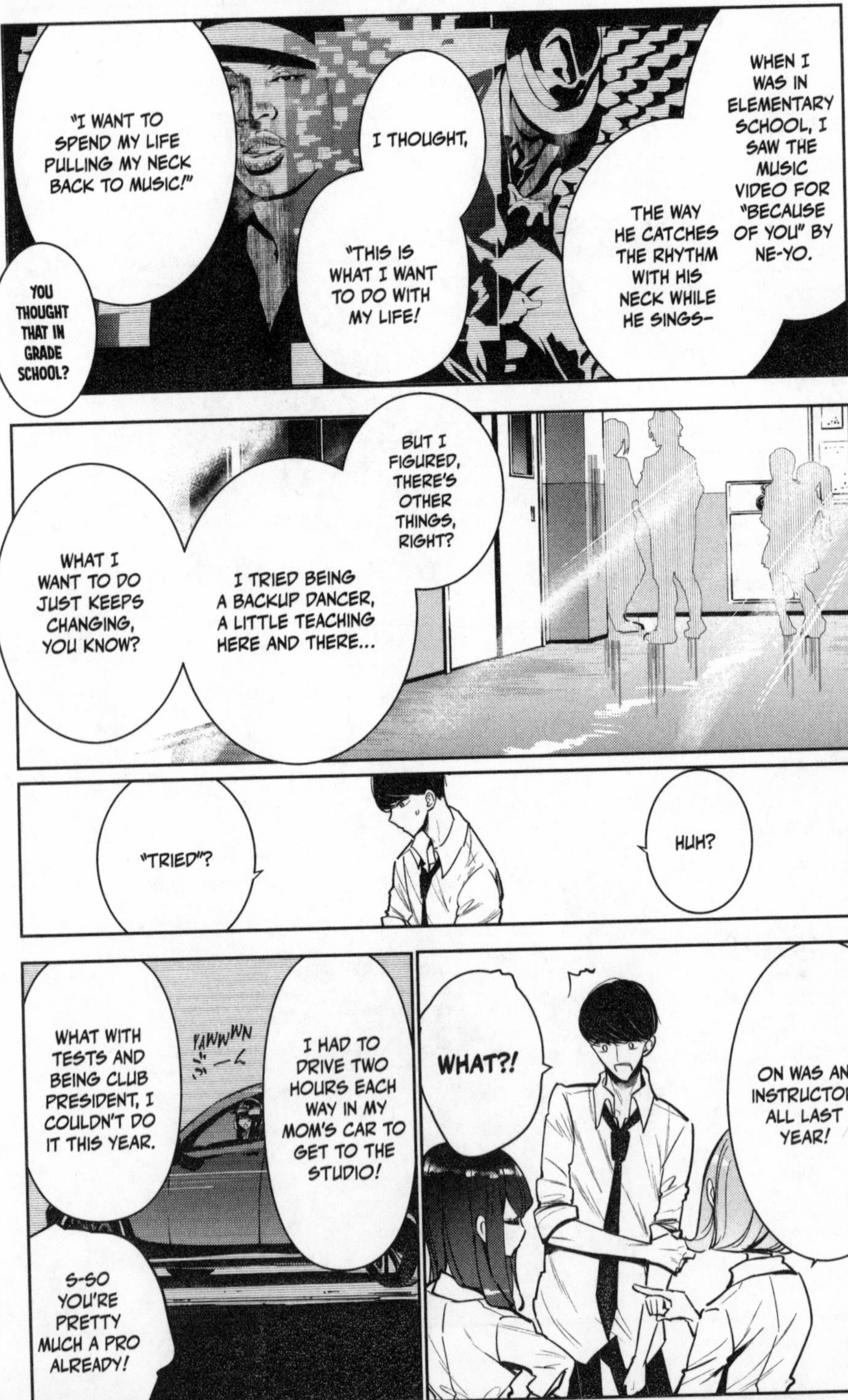
WHEN I WAS IN ELEMENTARY SCHOOL, I SAW THE MUSIC VIDEO FOR "BECAUSE OF YOU" BY NE-YO.
THE WAY HE CATCHES THE RHYTHM WITH HIS NECK WHILE HE SINGS-
I THOUGHT,
"THIS IS WHAT I WANT TO DO WITH MY LIFE!
"I WANT TO SPEND MY LIFE PULLING MY NECK BACK TO MUSIC!"
YOU THOUGHT THAT IN GRADE SCHOOL?
BUT I FIGURED, THERE'S OTHER THINGS, RIGHT?
I TRIED BEING A BACKUP DANCER, A LITTLE TEACHING HERE AND THERE...
WHAT I WANT TO DO JUST KEEPS CHANGING, YOU KNOW?
HUH?
"TRIED"?
ON WAS AN INSTRUCTOR ALL LAST YEAR!
WHAT?!
I HAD TO DRIVE TWO HOURS EACH WAY IN MY MOM'S CAR TO GET TO THE STUDIO!
YAWWWN
WHAT WITH TESTS AND BEING CLUB PRESIDENT, I COULDN'T DO IT THIS YEAR.
S-SO YOU'RE PRETTY MUCH A PRO ALREADY!

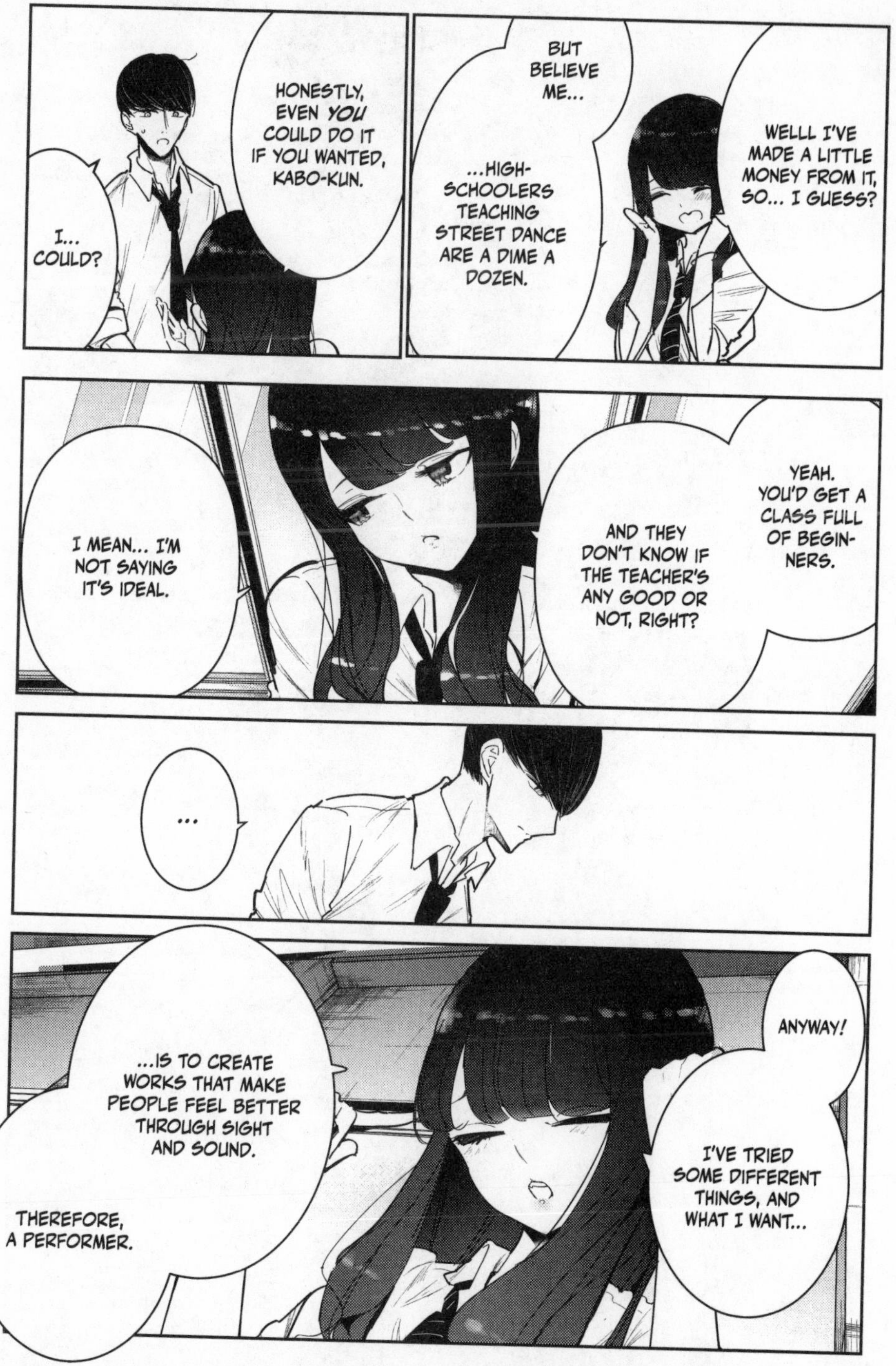
WELLL I'VE MADE A LITTLE MONEY FROM IT, SO... I GUESS?
BUT BELIEVE ME...
...HIGH-SCHOOLERS TEACHING STREET DANCE ARE A DIME A DOZEN.
HONESTLY, EVEN *YOU* COULD DO IT IF YOU WANTED, KABO-KUN.
I... COULD?
YEAH. YOU'D GET A CLASS FULL OF BEGIN-NERS.
AND THEY DON'T KNOW IF THE TEACHER'S ANY GOOD OR NOT, RIGHT?
I MEAN... I'M NOT SAYING IT'S IDEAL.
...
ANYWAY!
I'VE TRIED SOME DIFFERENT THINGS, AND WHAT I WANT...
...IS TO CREATE WORKS THAT MAKE PEOPLE FEEL BETTER THROUGH SIGHT AND SOUND.
THEREFORE, A PERFORMER.

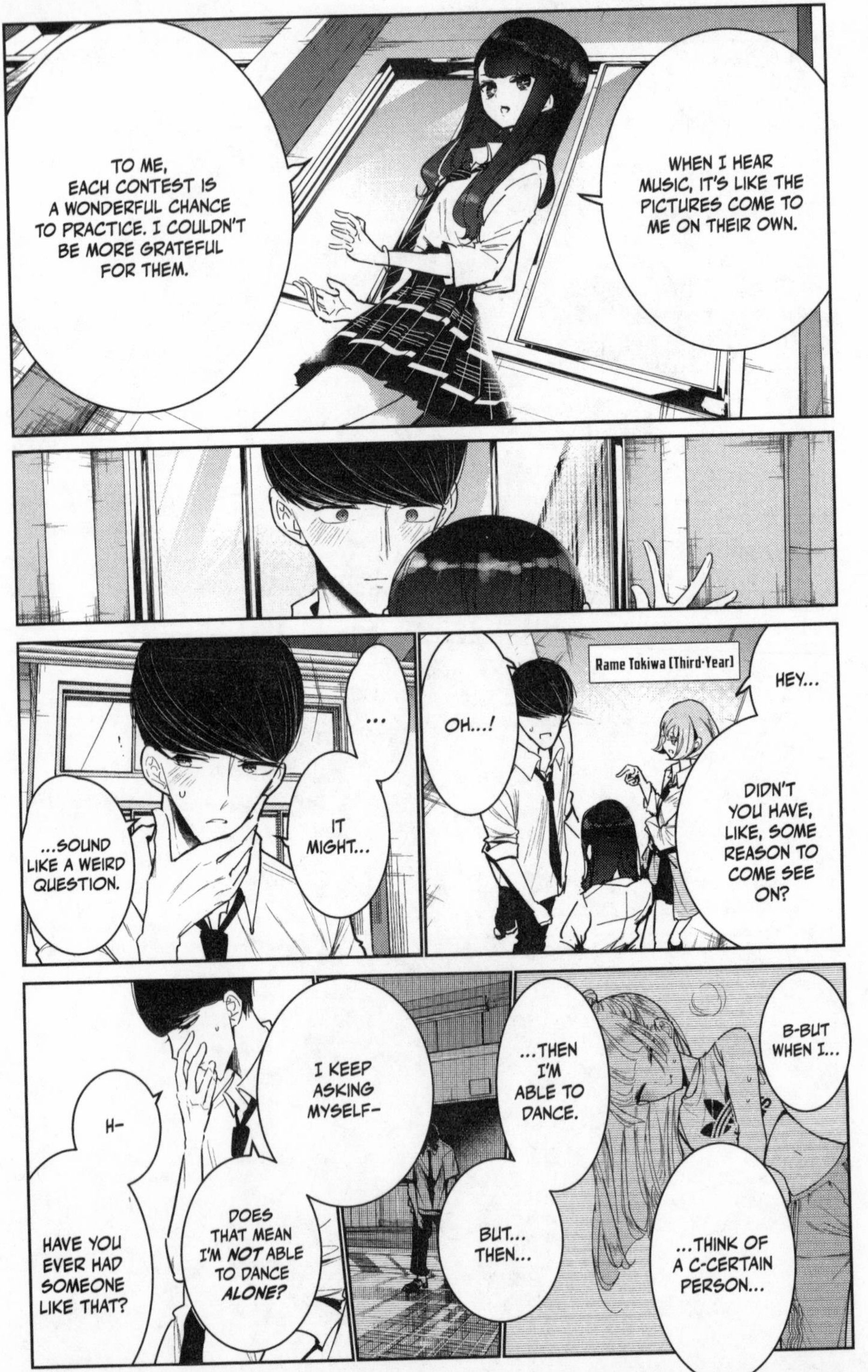
WHEN I HEAR MUSIC, IT'S LIKE THE PICTURES COME TO ME ON THEIR OWN.
TO ME, EACH CONTEST IS A WONDERFUL CHANCE TO PRACTICE. I COULDN'T BE MORE GRATEFUL FOR THEM.
Rame Tokiwa [Third-Year]
HEY...
DIDN'T YOU HAVE, LIKE, SOME REASON TO COME SEE ON?
OH...!
...
IT MIGHT...
...SOUND LIKE A WEIRD QUESTION.
B-BUT WHEN I...
...THINK OF A C-CERTAIN PERSON...
...THEN I'M ABLE TO DANCE.
BUT... THEN...
I KEEP ASKING MYSELF-
DOES THAT MEAN I'M *NOT* ABLE TO DANCE *ALONE?*
H-
HAVE YOU EVER HAD SOMEONE LIKE THAT?

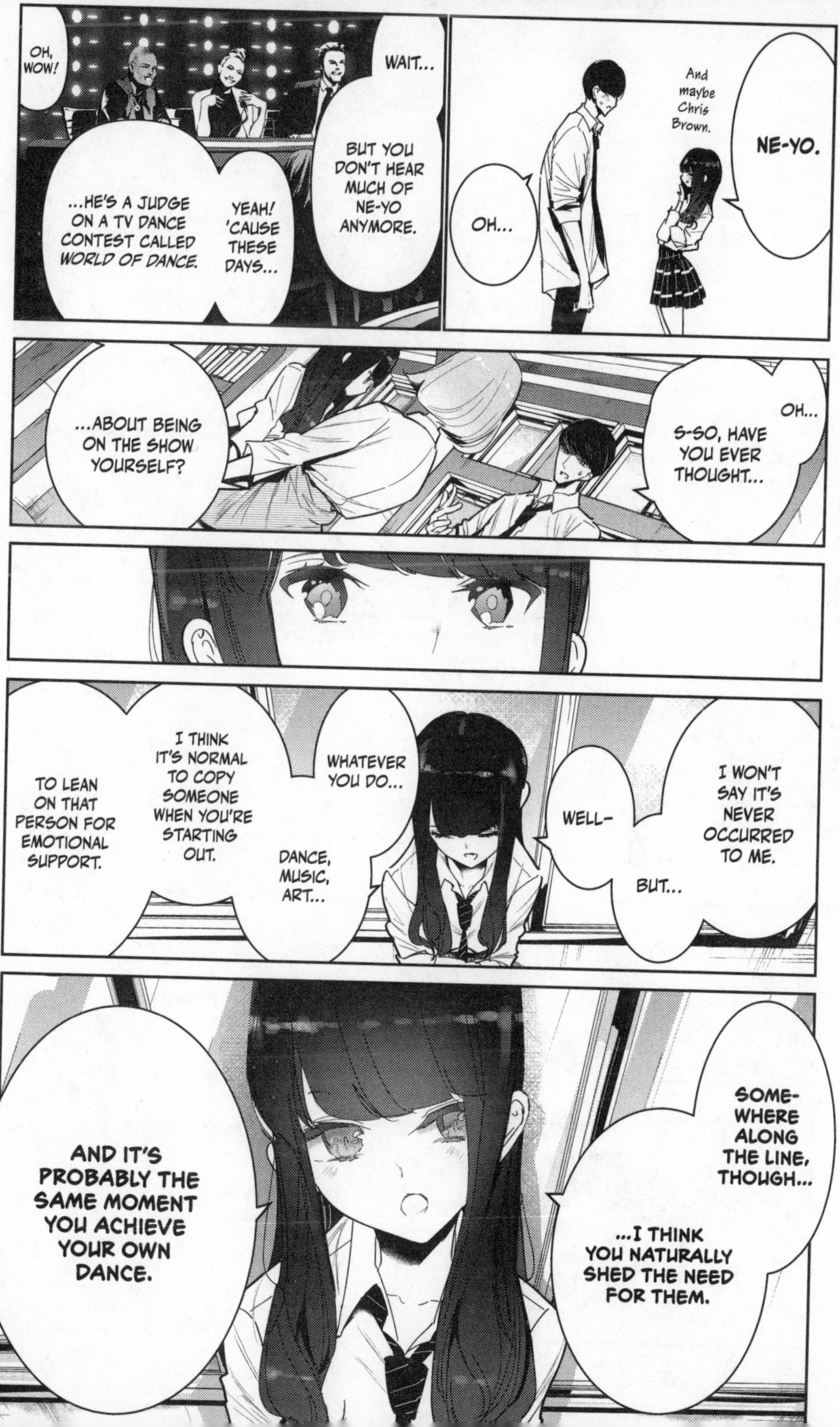
NE-YO.
And maybe Chris Brown.
OH...
WAIT...
BUT YOU DON'T HEAR MUCH OF NE-YO ANYMORE.
YEAH! 'CAUSE THESE DAYS...
...HE'S A JUDGE ON A TV DANCE CONTEST CALLED WORLD OF DANCE.
OH, WOW!
OH...
S-SO, HAVE YOU EVER THOUGHT...
...ABOUT BEING ON THE SHOW YOURSELF?
I WON'T SAY IT'S NEVER OCCURRED TO ME.
BUT...
WELL-
WHATEVER YOU DO...
DANCE, MUSIC, ART...
I THINK IT'S NORMAL TO COPY SOMEONE WHEN YOU'RE STARTING OUT.
TO LEAN ON THAT PERSON FOR EMOTIONAL SUPPORT.
SOME-WHERE ALONG THE LINE, THOUGH...
...I THINK YOU NATURALLY SHED THE NEED FOR THEM.
AND IT'S PROBABLY THE SAME MOMENT YOU ACHIEVE YOUR OWN DANCE.

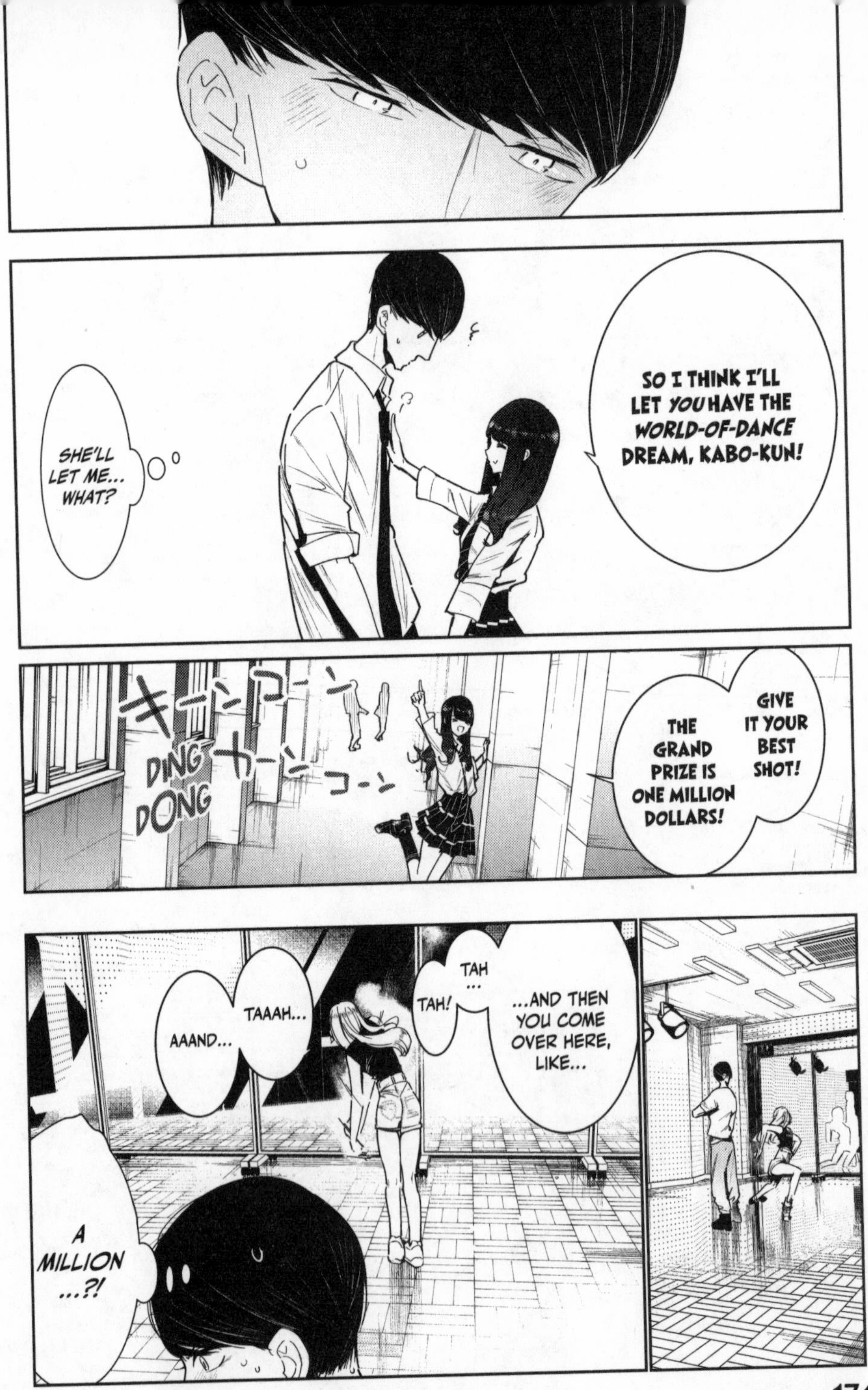
SO I THINK I'LL LET YOU HAVE THE WORLD-OF-DANCE DREAM, KABO-KUN!
SHE'LL LET ME... WHAT?
GIVE IT YOUR BEST SHOT!
THE GRAND PRIZE IS ONE MILLION DOLLARS!
キーンコーンカーンコーン
DING DONG
...AND THEN YOU COME OVER HERE, LIKE...
TAH ... TAH!
TAAAH...
AAAND...
A MILLION ...?!

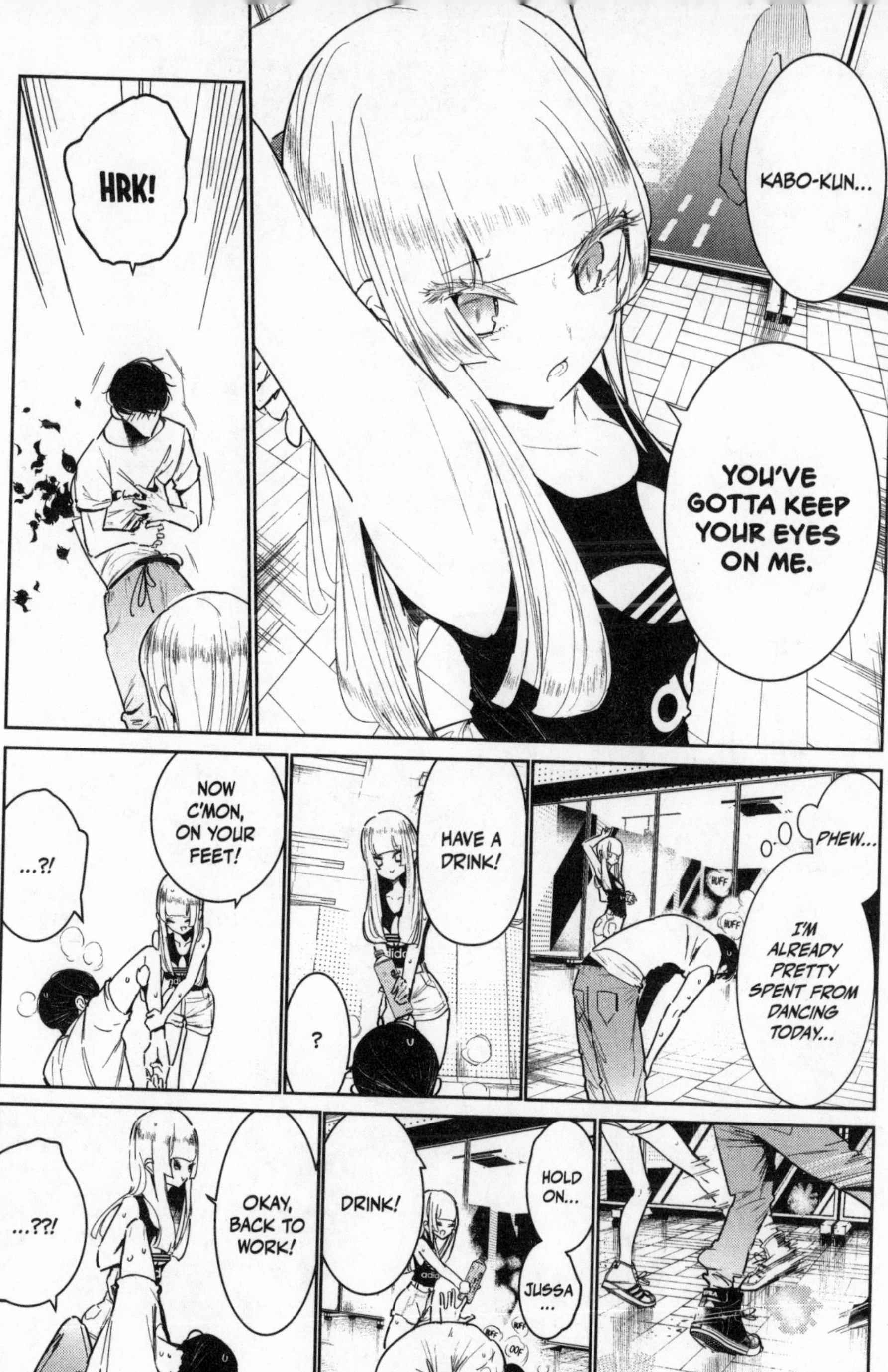
KABO-KUN...
YOU'VE GOTTA KEEP YOUR EYES ON ME.
HRK!
PHEW...
HUFF
HUFF
I'M ALREADY PRETTY SPENT FROM DANCING TODAY...
HAVE A DRINK!
?
NOW C'MON, ON YOUR FEET!
...?!
HOLD ON...
DRINK!
JUSSA...
HUFF
HUFF
OOF
OKAY, BACK TO WORK!
...??!

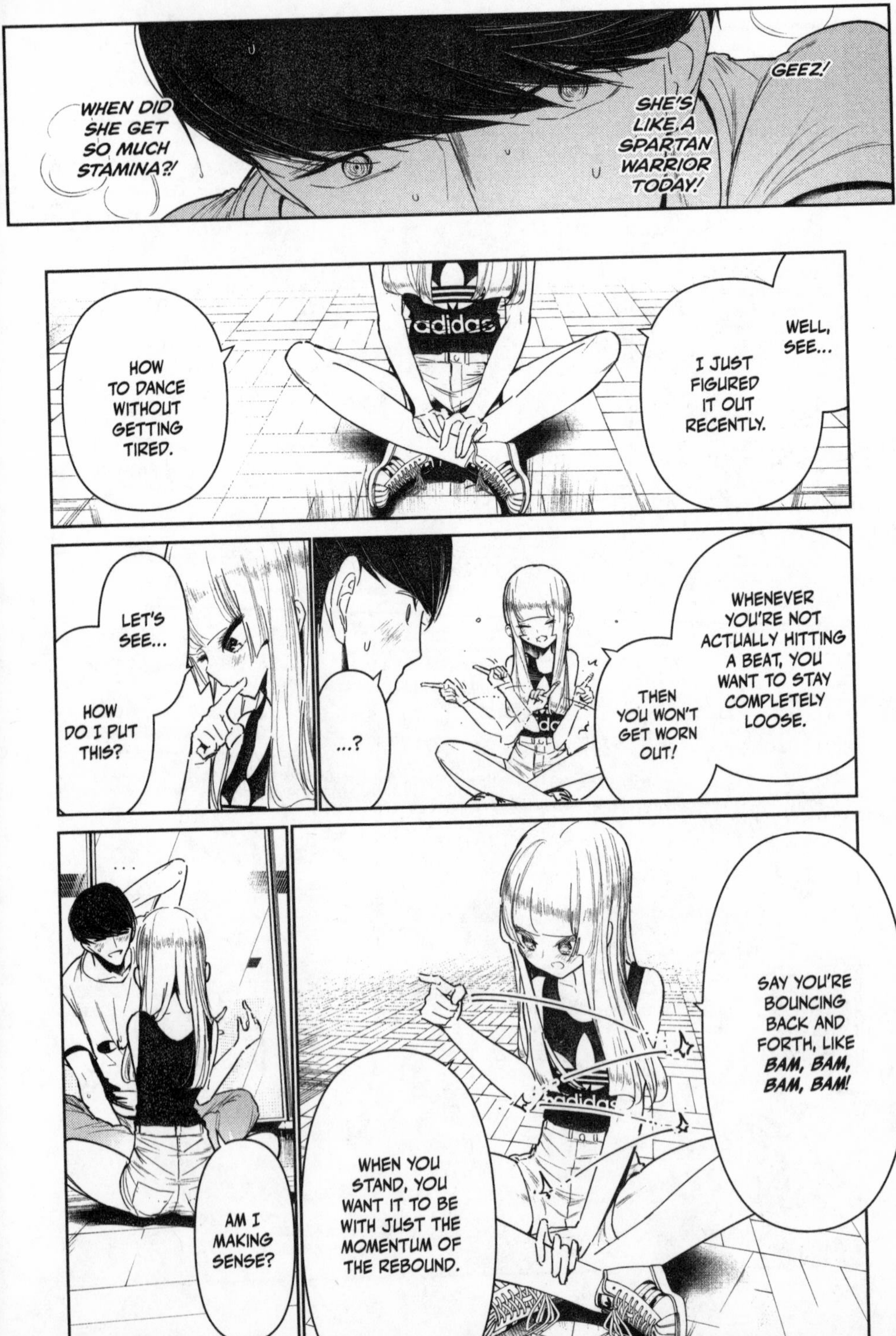
GEEZ!
SHE'S LIKE A SPARTAN WARRIOR TODAY!
WHEN DID SHE GET SO MUCH STAMINA?!
WELL, SEE...
I JUST FIGURED IT OUT RECENTLY.
HOW TO DANCE WITHOUT GETTING TIRED.
WHENEVER YOU'RE NOT ACTUALLY HITTING A BEAT, YOU WANT TO STAY COMPLETELY LOOSE.
THEN YOU WON'T GET WORN OUT!
...?
LET'S SEE...
HOW DO I PUT THIS?
SAY YOU'RE BOUNCING BACK AND FORTH, LIKE *BAM, BAM, BAM, BAM!*
WHEN YOU STAND, YOU WANT IT TO BE WITH JUST THE MOMENTUM OF THE REBOUND.
...
AM I MAKING SENSE?

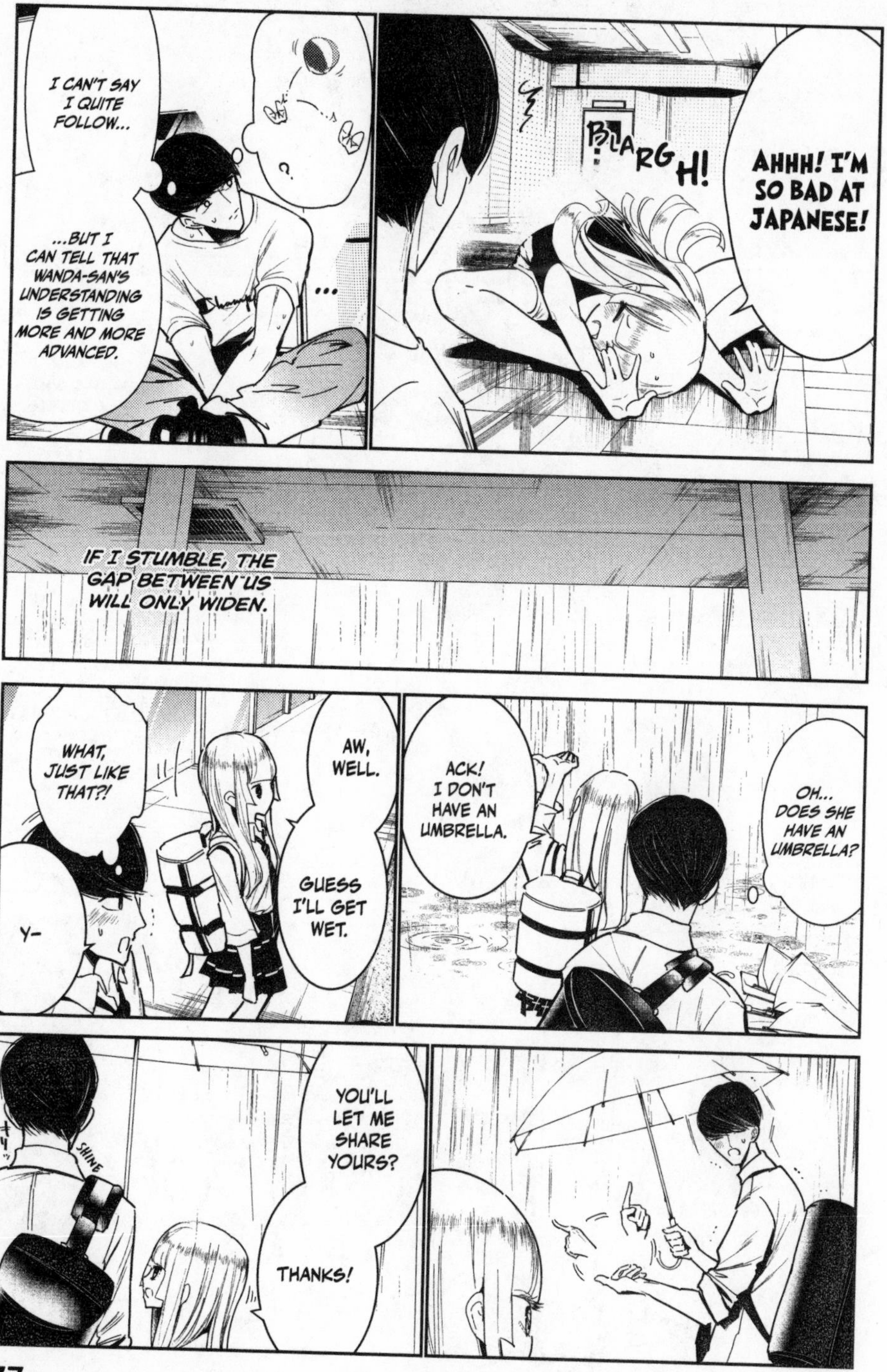
BLARGH!
AHHH! I'M SO BAD AT JAPANESE!
...
I CAN'T SAY I QUITE FOLLOW...
...BUT I CAN TELL THAT WANDA-SAN'S UNDERSTANDING IS GETTING MORE AND MORE ADVANCED.
IF I STUMBLE, THE GAP BETWEEN US WILL ONLY WIDEN.
OH... DOES SHE HAVE AN UMBRELLA?
ACK! I DON'T HAVE AN UMBRELLA.
AW, WELL.
GUESS I'LL GET WET.
WHAT, JUST LIKE THAT?!
Y-
YOU'LL LET ME SHARE YOURS?
THANKS!
キリッ
SHINE

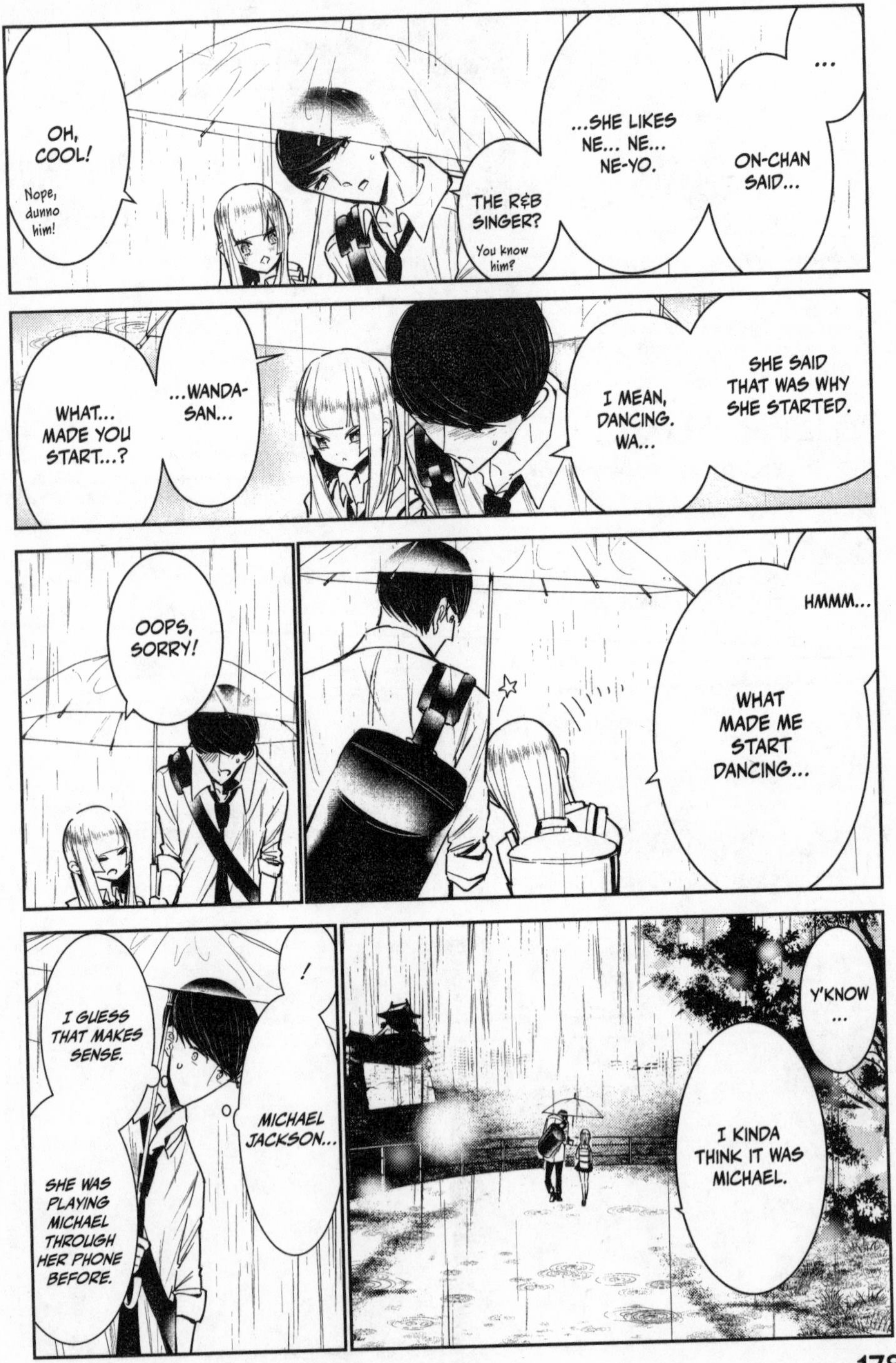
...
ON-CHAN SAID...
...SHE LIKES NE... NE... NE-YO.
THE R&B SINGER?
You know him?
OH, COOL!
Nope, dunno him!
SHE SAID THAT WAS WHY SHE STARTED.
I MEAN, DANCING. WA...
...WANDA-SAN...
WHAT... MADE YOU START...?
HMMM...
WHAT MADE ME START DANCING...
OOPS, SORRY!
Y'KNOW...
I KINDA THINK IT WAS MICHAEL.
!
MICHAEL JACKSON...
I GUESS THAT MAKES SENSE.
SHE WAS PLAYING MICHAEL THROUGH HER PHONE BEFORE.

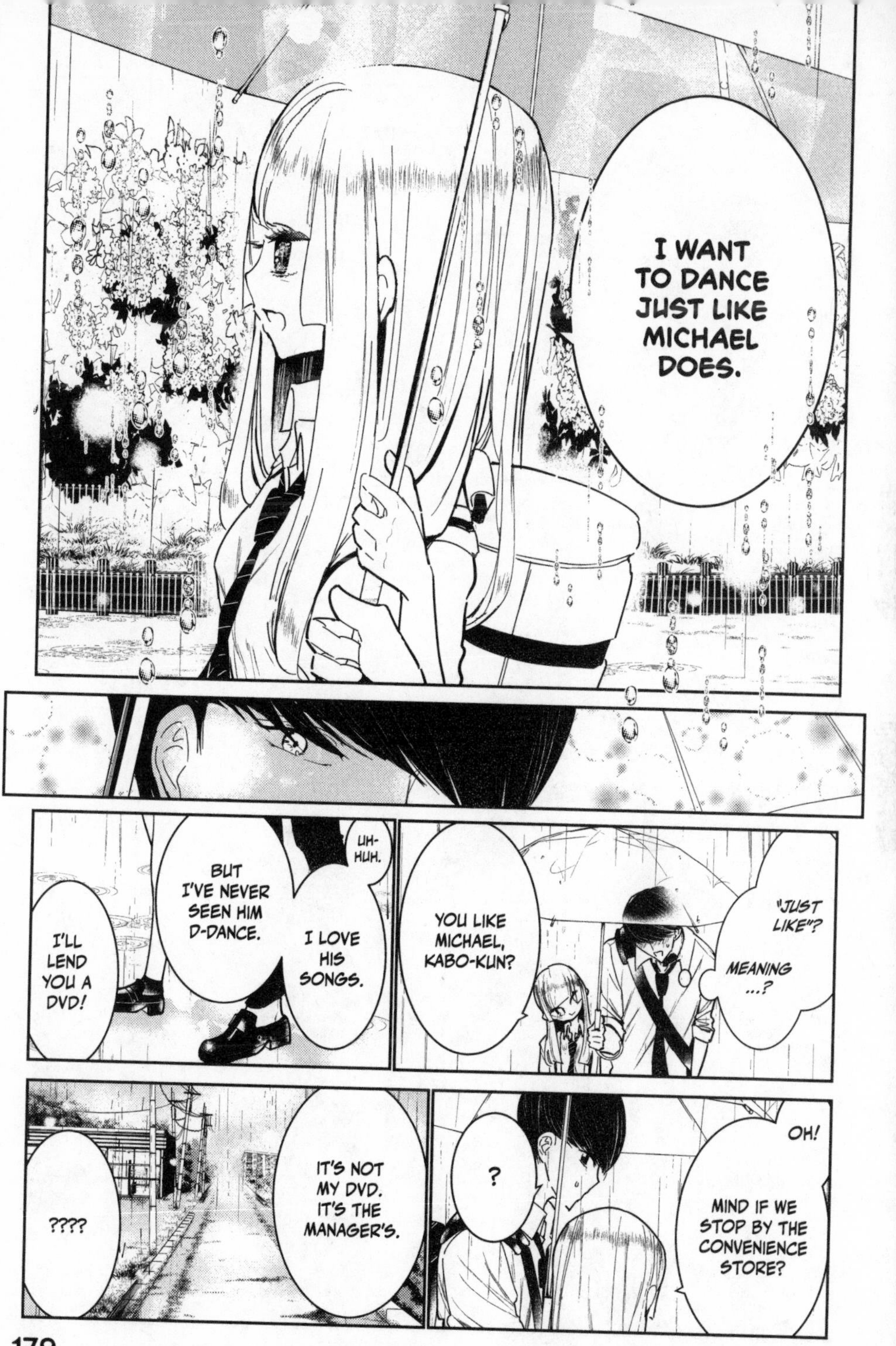
I WANT TO DANCE JUST LIKE MICHAEL DOES.
"JUST LIKE"?
MEANING ...?
YOU LIKE MICHAEL, KABO-KUN?
UH-HUH.
I LOVE HIS SONGS.
BUT I'VE NEVER SEEN HIM D-DANCE.
I'LL LEND YOU A DVD!
OH!
MIND IF WE STOP BY THE CONVENIENCE STORE?
?
IT'S NOT MY DVD. IT'S THE MANAGER'S.
????

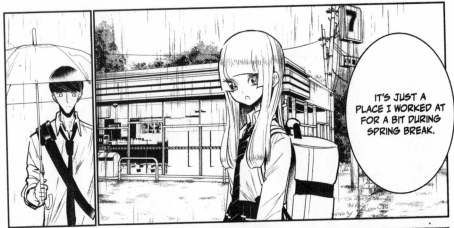

IT'S JUST A PLACE I WORKED AT FOR A BIT DURING SPRING BREAK.
WHO'S THIS, YOUR BOYFRIEND?
I LIKE HIM! THE MANLY TYPE.

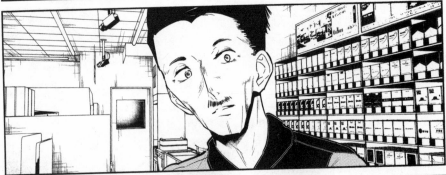

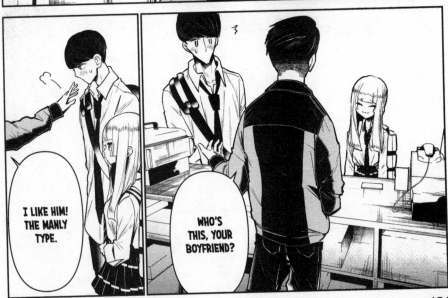

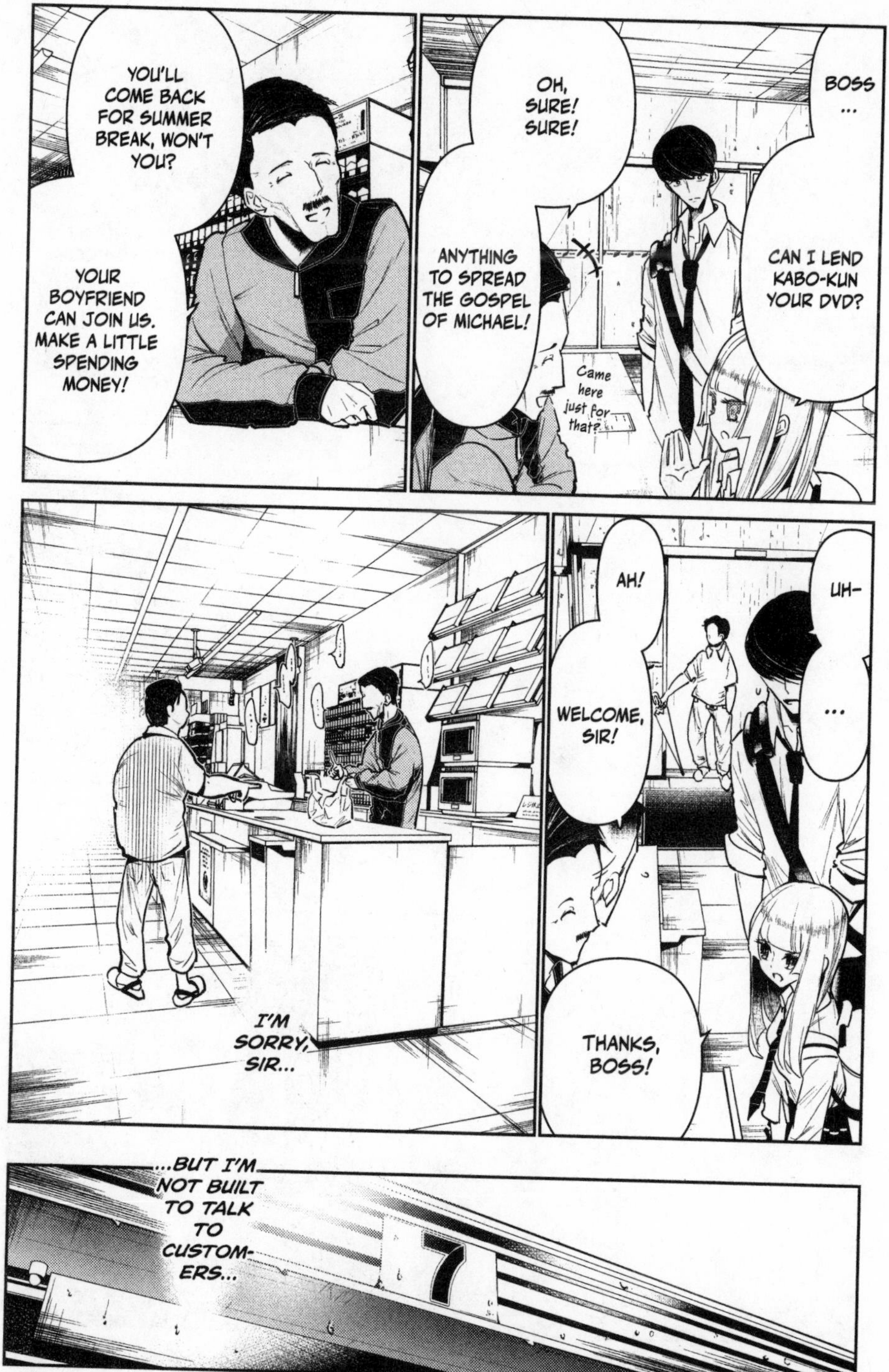
BOSS...
CAN I LEND KABO-KUN YOUR DVD?
OH, SURE! SURE!
ANYTHING TO SPREAD THE GOSPEL OF MICHAEL!
Came here just for that?
YOU'LL COME BACK FOR SUMMER BREAK, WON'T YOU?
YOUR BOYFRIEND CAN JOIN US. MAKE A LITTLE SPENDING MONEY!
UH-
...
AH!
WELCOME, SIR!
THANKS, BOSS!
I'M SORRY, SIR...
...BUT I'M NOT BUILT TO TALK TO CUSTOMERS...
7

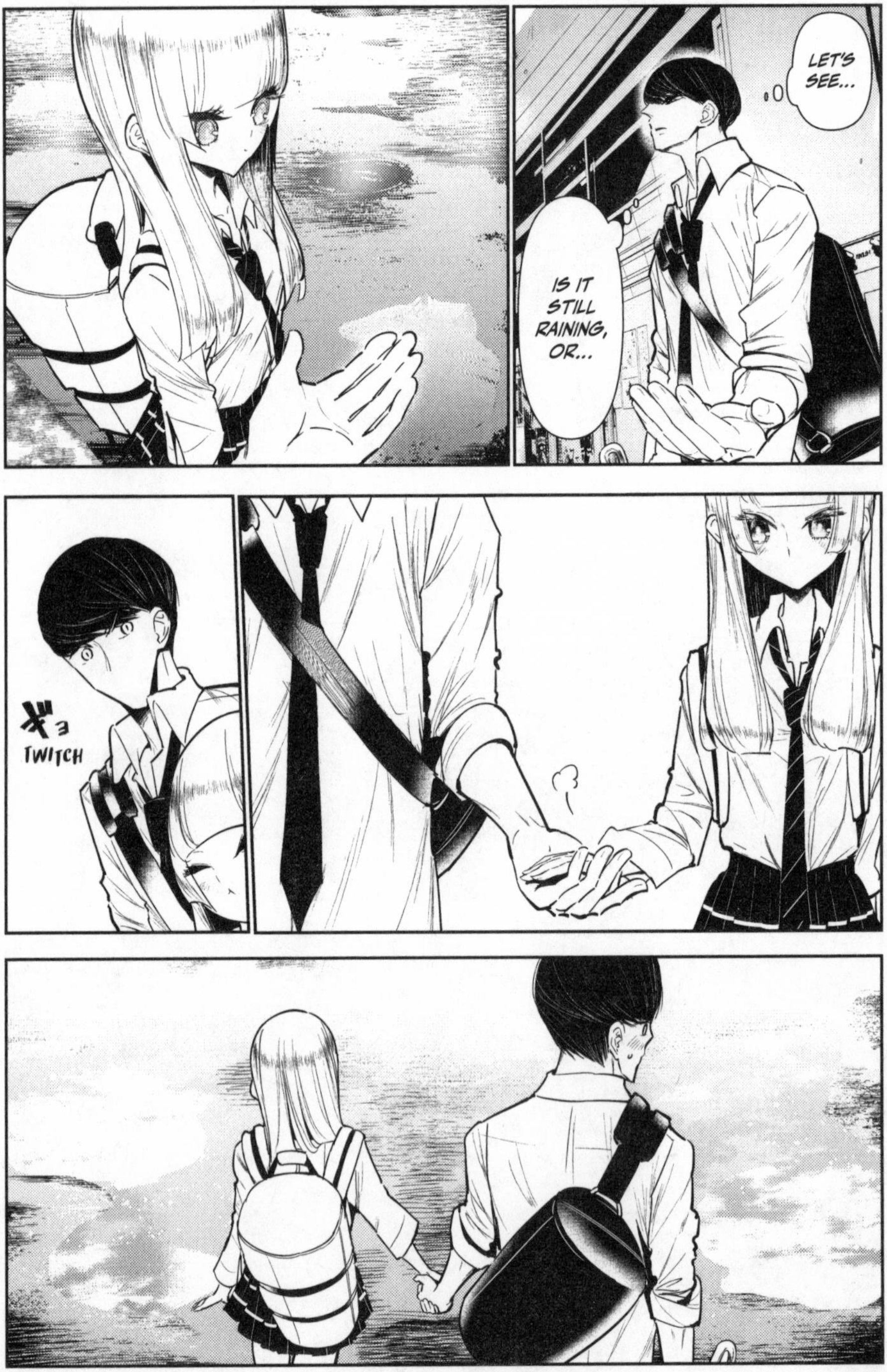
LET'S SEE...
IS IT STILL RAINING, OR...
ギョ
TWITCH

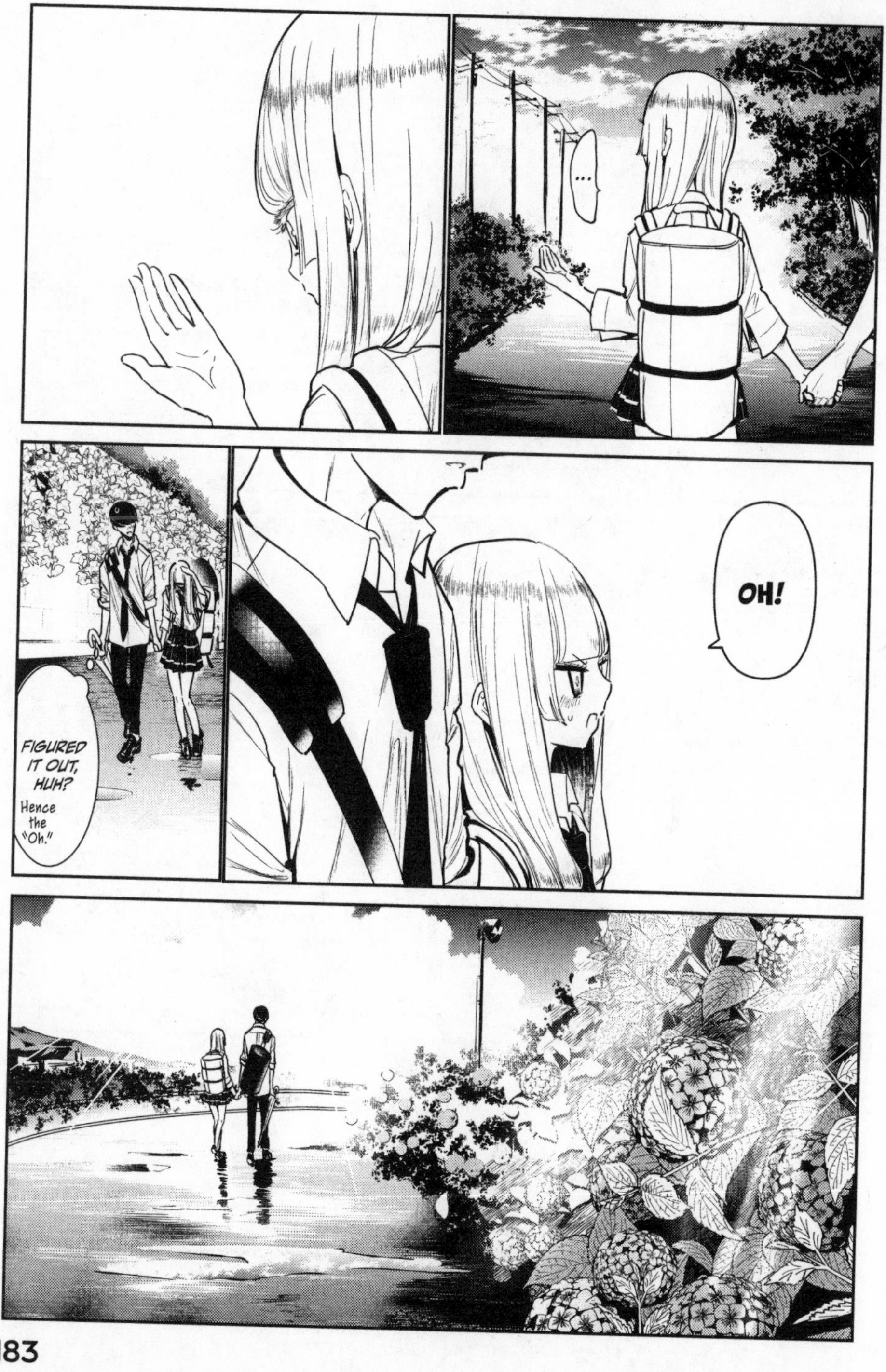
...
OH!
FIGURED IT OUT, HUH?
Hence the "Oh."

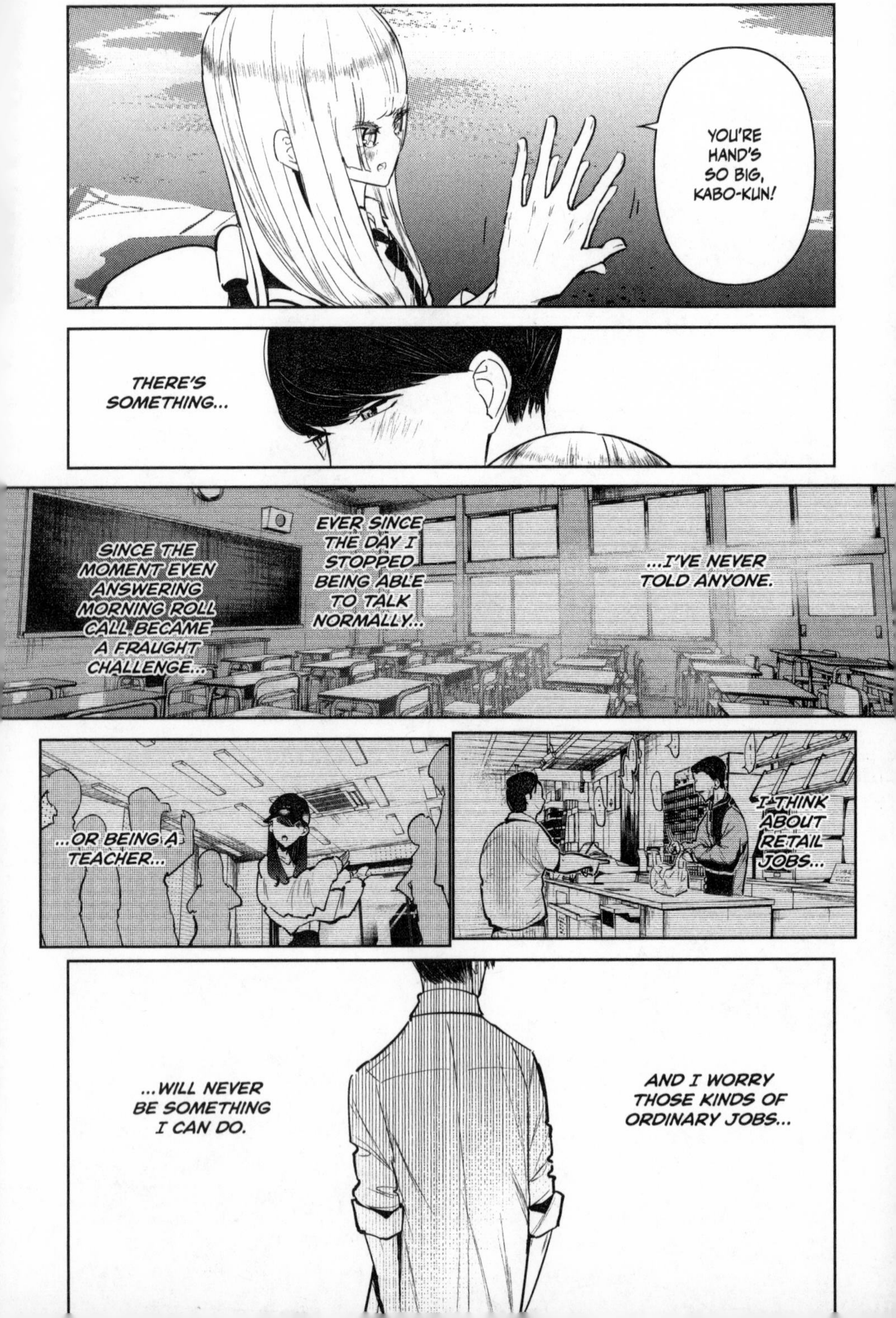
YOU'RE HAND'S SO BIG, KABO-KUN!
THERE'S SOMETHING...
...I'VE NEVER TOLD ANYONE.
EVER SINCE THE DAY I STOPPED BEING ABLE TO TALK NORMALLY...
SINCE THE MOMENT EVEN ANSWERING MORNING ROLL CALL BECAME A FRAUGHT CHALLENGE...
I THINK ABOUT RETAIL JOBS...
...OR BEING A TEACHER...
AND I WORRY THOSE KINDS OF ORDINARY JOBS...
...WILL NEVER BE SOMETHING I CAN DO.

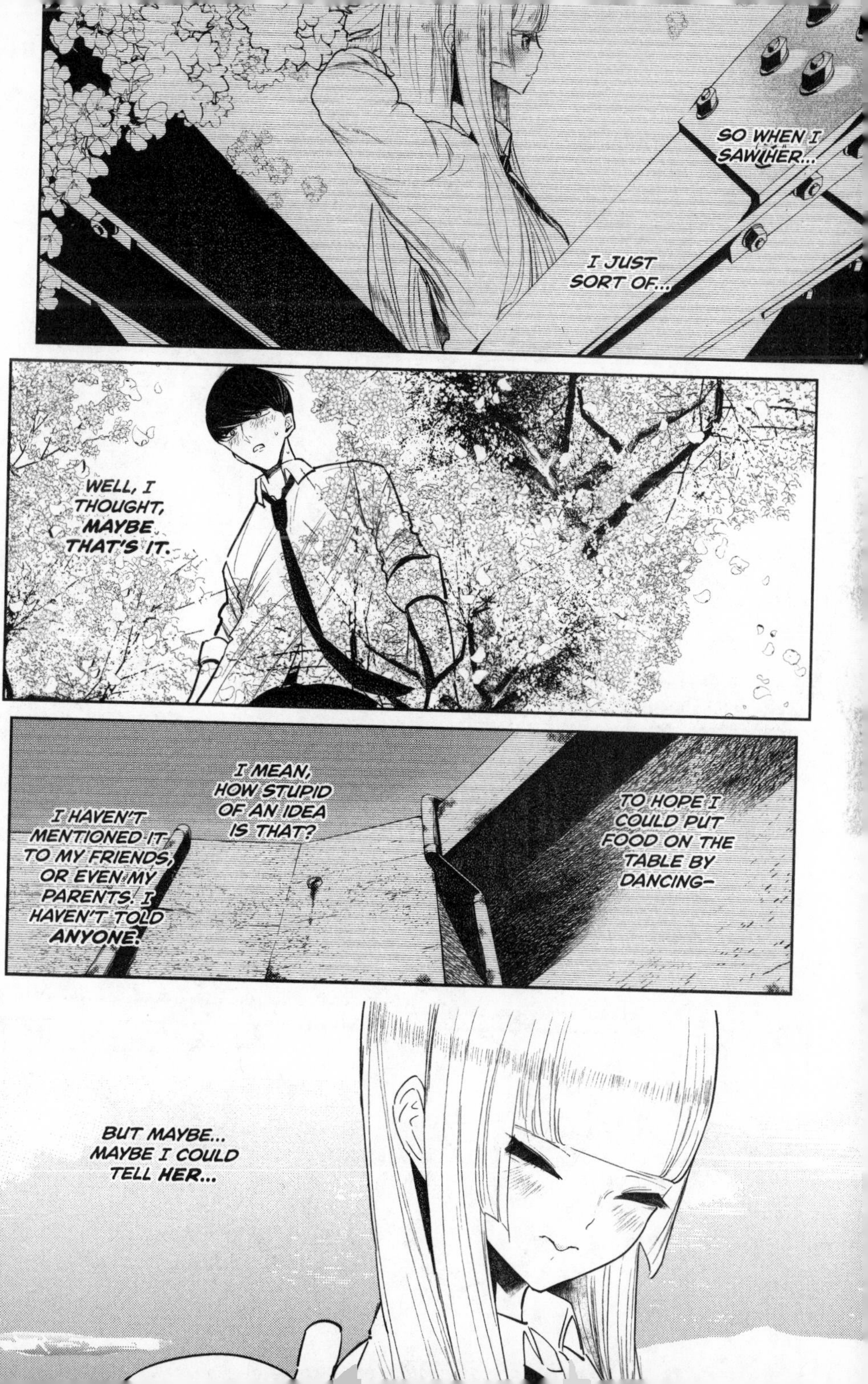
SO WHEN I SAW HER...
I JUST SORT OF...
WELL, I THOUGHT, **MAYBE** THAT'S IT.
TO HOPE I COULD PUT FOOD ON THE TABLE BY DANCING–
I MEAN, HOW STUPID OF AN IDEA IS THAT?
I HAVEN'T MENTIONED IT TO MY FRIENDS, OR EVEN MY PARENTS. I HAVEN'T TOLD **ANYONE**.
BUT MAYBE... MAYBE I COULD TELL **HER**...

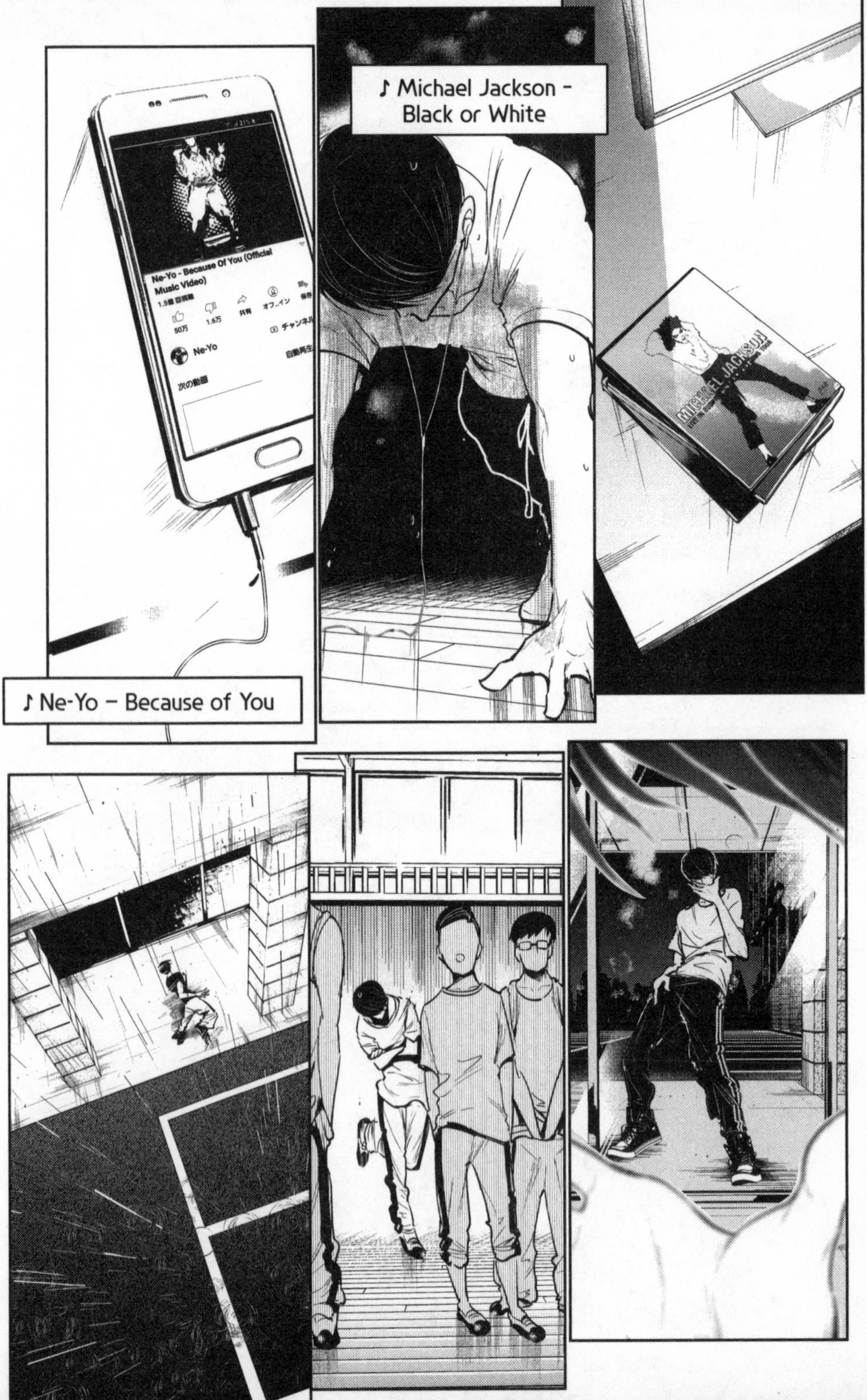
MICHAEL JACKSON
♪ Michael Jackson - Black or White
Ne-Yo - Because Of You (Official Music Video)
Ne-Yo
次の動画
♪ Ne-Yo – Because of You

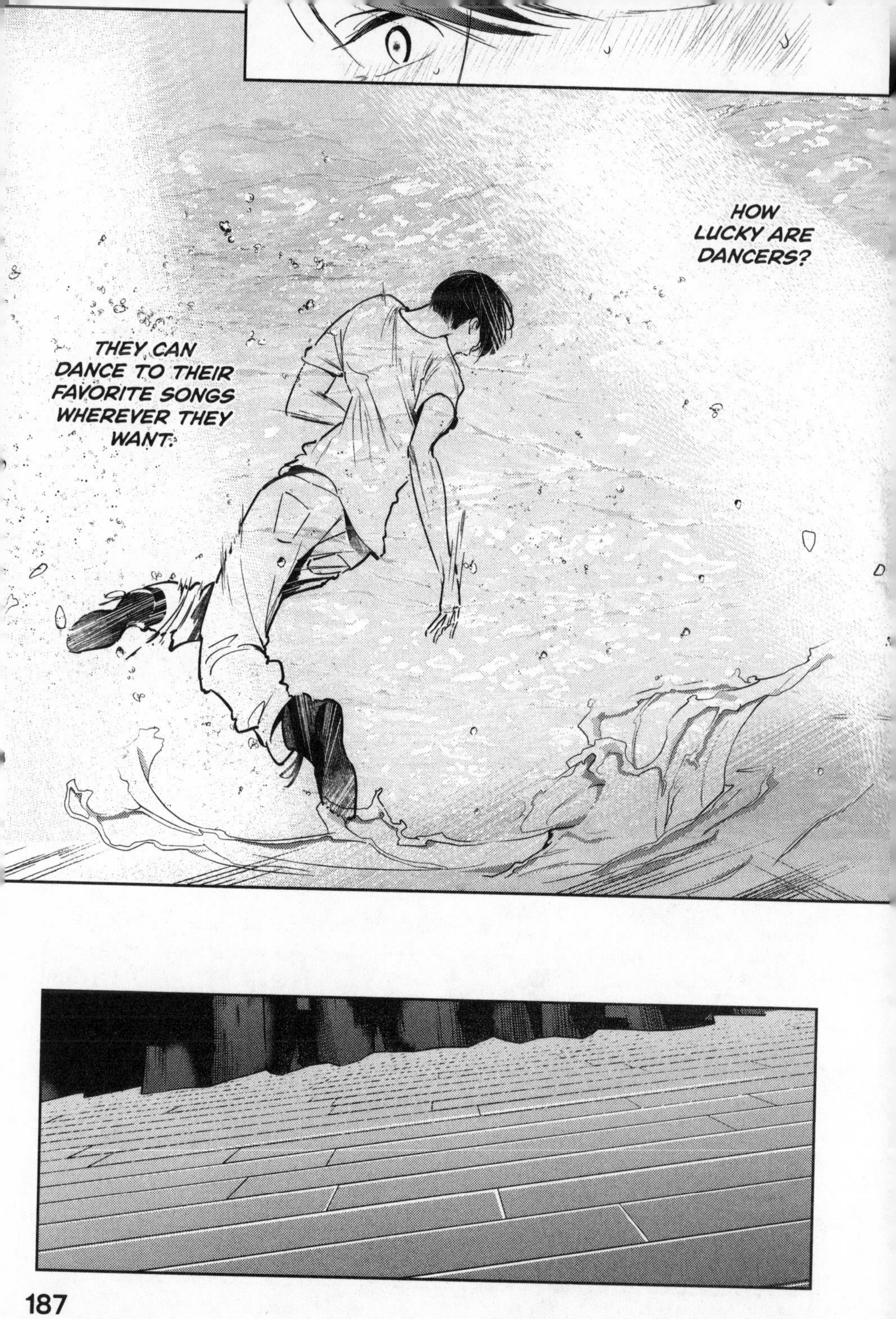
HOW LUCKY ARE DANCERS?
THEY CAN DANCE TO THEIR FAVORITE SONGS WHEREVER THEY WANT.

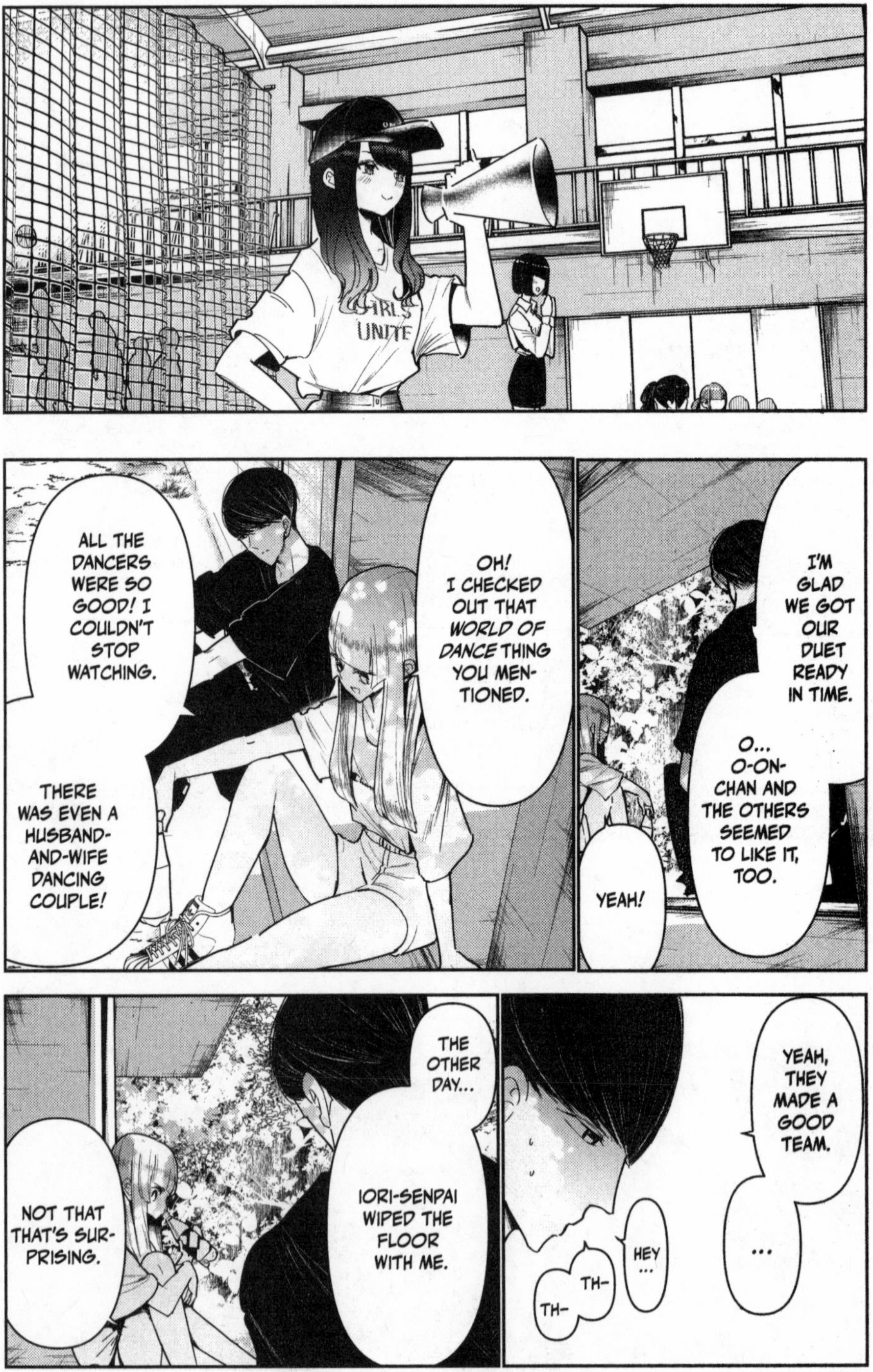
GIRLS UNITE
I'M GLAD WE GOT OUR DUET READY IN TIME.
O... O-ON-CHAN AND THE OTHERS SEEMED TO LIKE IT, TOO.
YEAH!
OH! I CHECKED OUT THAT *WORLD OF DANCE* THING YOU MENTIONED.
ALL THE DANCERS WERE SO GOOD! I COULDN'T STOP WATCHING.
THERE WAS EVEN A HUSBAND-AND-WIFE DANCING COUPLE!
YEAH, THEY MADE A GOOD TEAM.
...
HEY...
TH-
TH-
THE OTHER DAY...
IORI-SENPAI WIPED THE FLOOR WITH ME.
NOT THAT THAT'S SURPRISING.

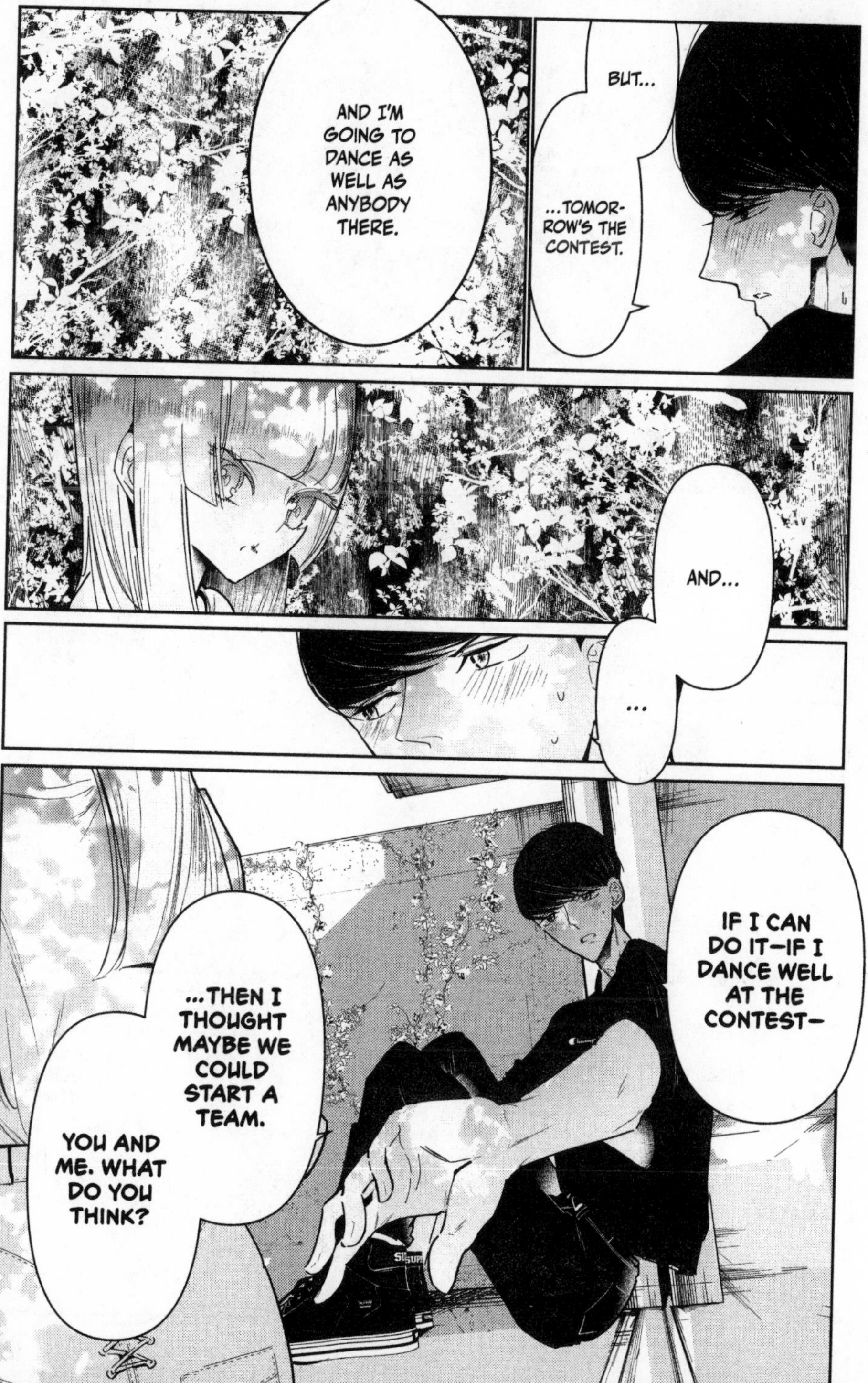
BUT...
...TOMORROW'S THE CONTEST.
AND I'M GOING TO DANCE AS WELL AS ANYBODY THERE.
AND...
...
IF I CAN DO IT—IF I DANCE WELL AT THE CONTEST—
...THEN I THOUGHT MAYBE WE COULD START A TEAM.
YOU AND ME. WHAT DO YOU THINK?

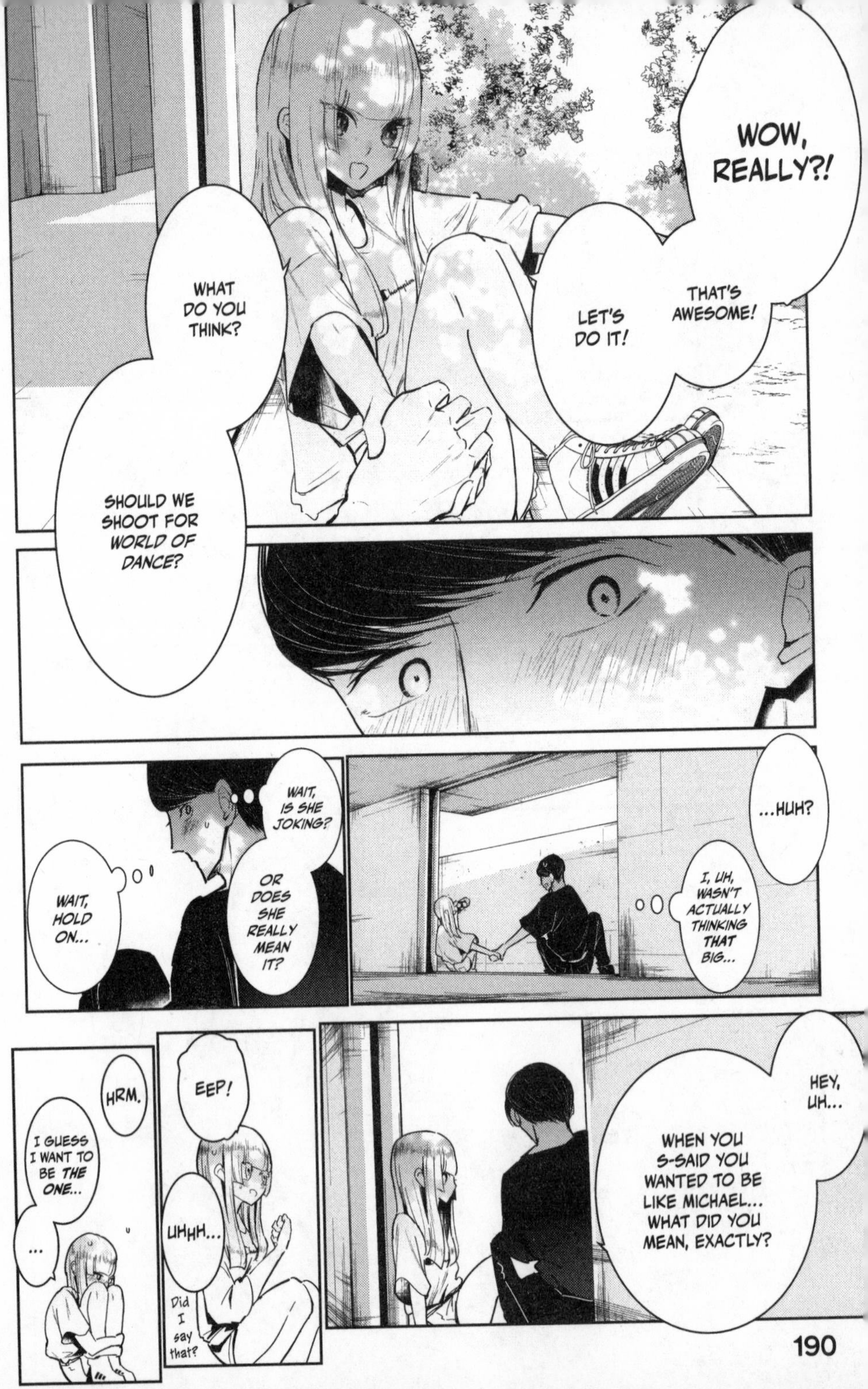

WOW, REALLY?!
THAT'S AWESOME!
LET'S DO IT!
WHAT DO YOU THINK?
SHOULD WE SHOOT FOR WORLD OF DANCE?
...HUH?
I, UH, WASN'T ACTUALLY THINKING THAT BIG...
WAIT, IS SHE JOKING?
OR DOES SHE REALLY MEAN IT?
WAIT, HOLD ON...
HEY, UH...
WHEN YOU S-SAID YOU WANTED TO BE LIKE MICHAEL... WHAT DID YOU MEAN, EXACTLY?
EEP!
UHHH...
Did I say that?
HRM.
I GUESS I WANT TO BE THE ONE...
...

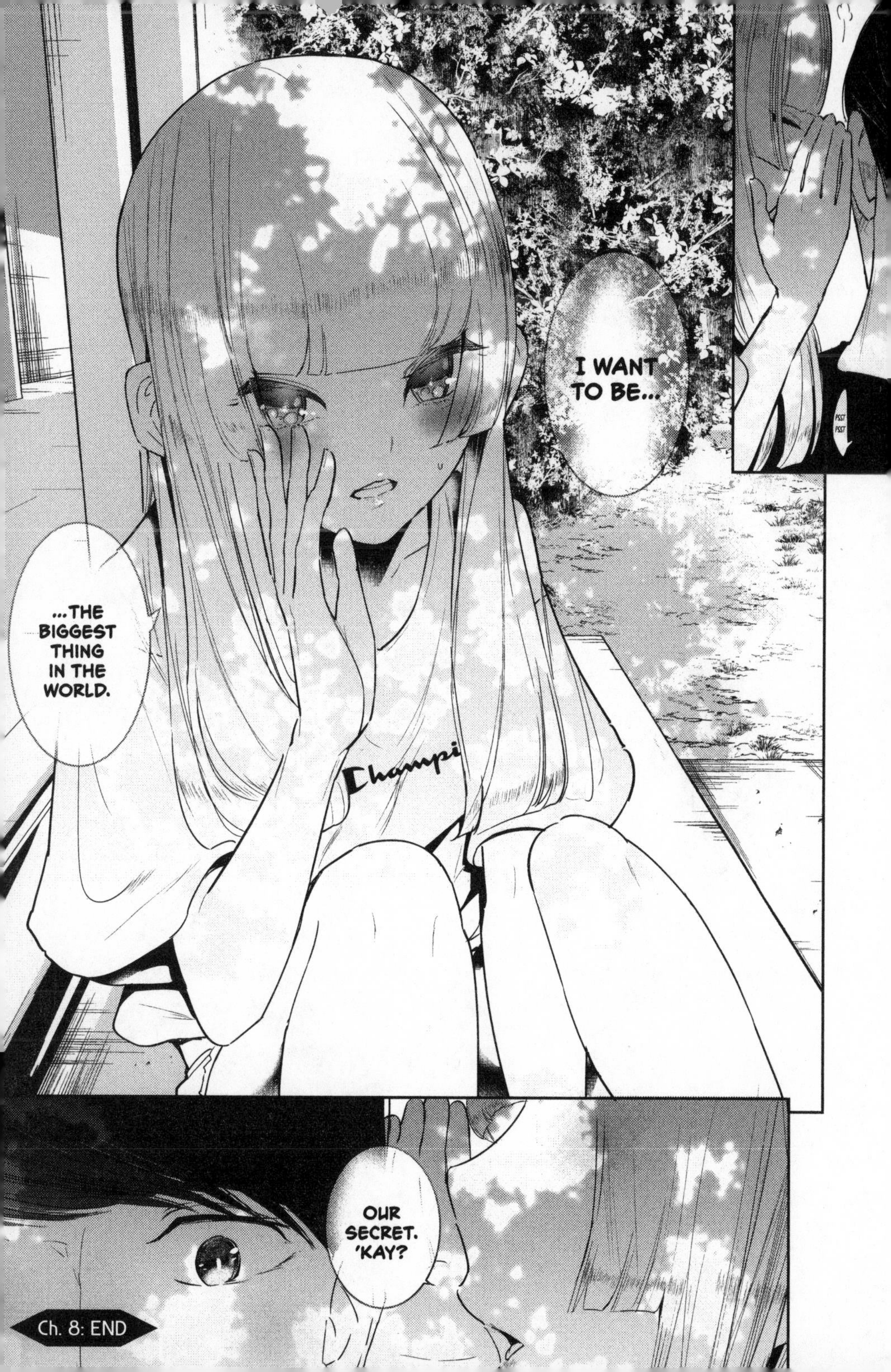
PSST PSST
I WANT TO BE...
...THE BIGGEST THING IN THE WORLD.
OUR SECRET. 'KAY?
Ch. 8: END

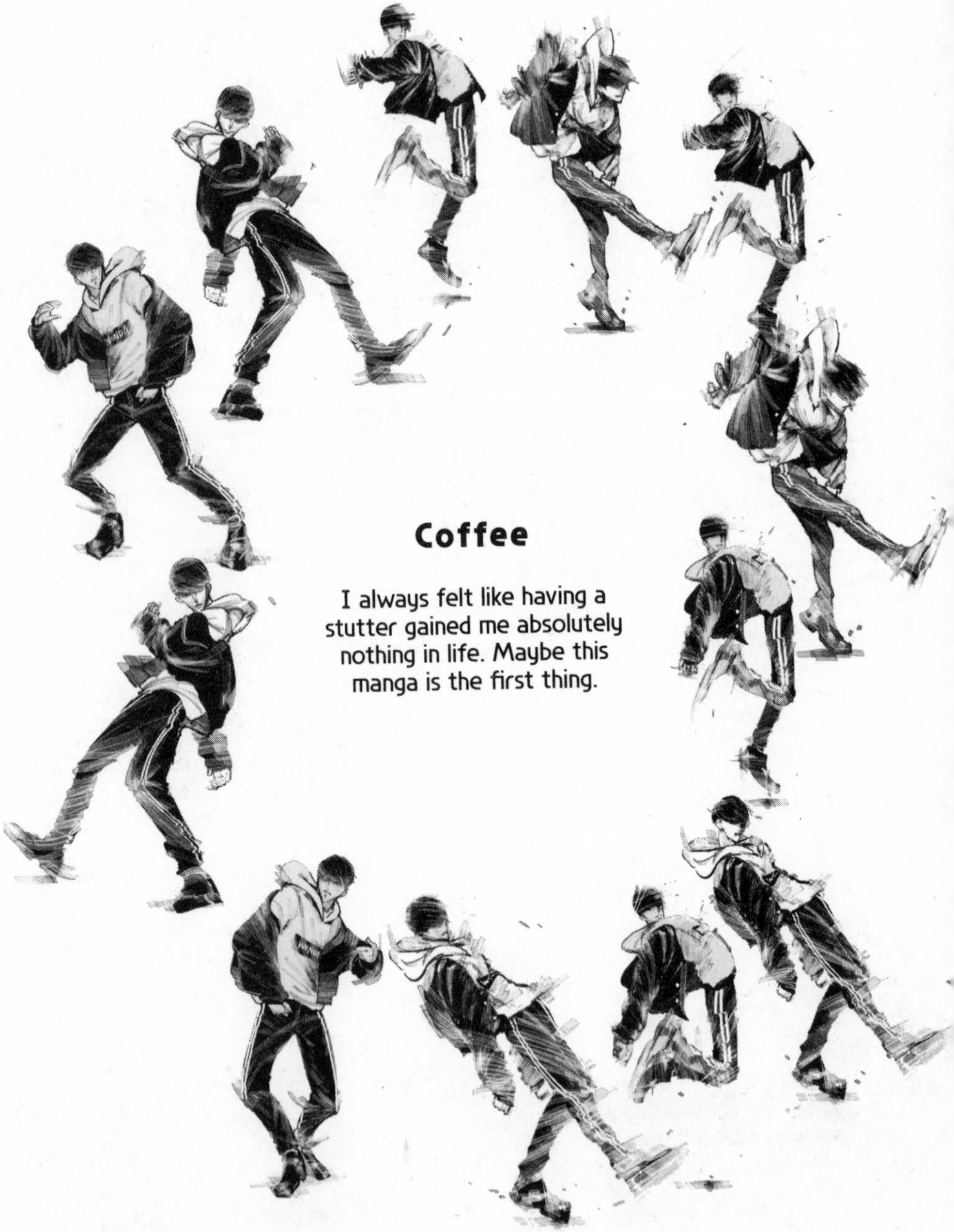

Coffee

I always felt like having a stutter gained me absolutely nothing in life. Maybe this manga is the first thing.

translation notes

Early-Modern Japanese Popular Music, page 7

The word *kayoukyoku* (which combines three different kanji which all essentially mean “song”) is a genre of Japanese pop music with its origins in the late 1920s (the beginning of the Showa era). As the genre evolved over time, and especially as several major female singers became prominent in the 1980s, *kayoukyoku* came to form the basis of the J-Pop genre.

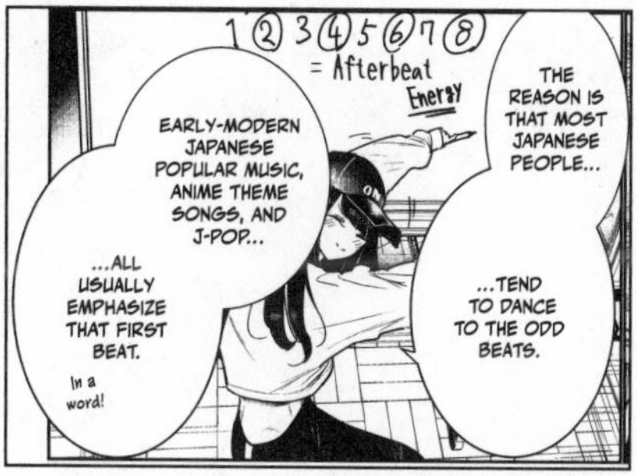
1 2 3 4 5 6 7 8
= Afterbeat
Energy
THE REASON IS THAT MOST JAPANESE PEOPLE...
...TEND TO DANCE TO THE ODD BEATS.
EARLY-MODERN JAPANESE POPULAR MUSIC, ANIME THEME SONGS, AND J-POP...
...ALL USUALLY EMPHASIZE THAT FIRST BEAT.
In a word!

Yanyan Tsukebo, page 90

This is a real snack product in Japan. The container is split into compartments, one of which contains biscuit sticks, while the others contain frosting in which to dip the biscuits. The panda character on the container appears to be saying *“choco kuriimu”* (chocolate frosting), an abbreviated version of what the character says on the actual packaging, *“choco kuriimu wo tsukeru to oishii yo!”* (“Put chocolate frosting on [the sticks]–it’s delicious!”) The actual product name, “tsukebo,” could be loosely translated as “dipping sticks.”

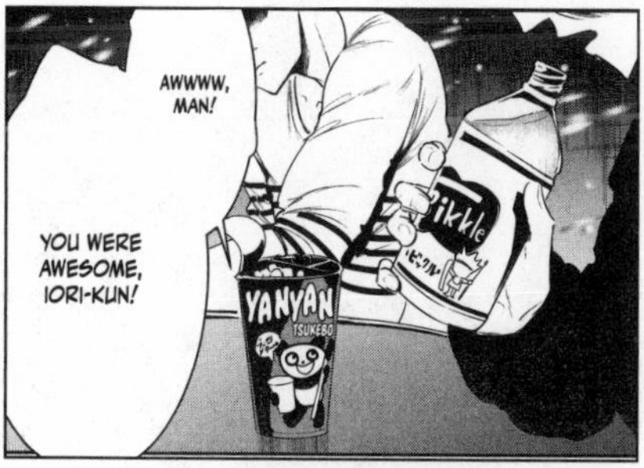
Bikkle
AWWWW, MAN!
YOU WERE AWESOME, IORI-KUN!
YANYAN
TSUKEBO

Bikkle, page 91

Like Tsukebo, Bikkle is also a real product, a yogurt-based drink with a distinctive sweet flavor.

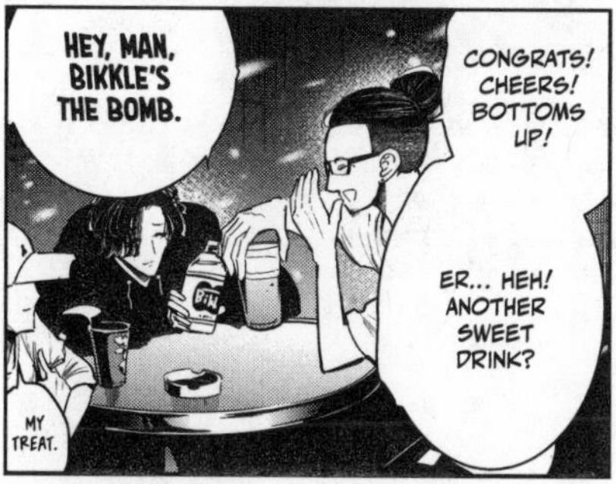
CONGRATS! CHEERS! BOTTOMS UP!
HEY, MAN, BIKKLE'S THE BOMB.
ER... HEH! ANOTHER SWEET DRINK?
MY TREAT.

Coins, page 153

In this panel, Iori is holding a 5-yen coin (the uppermost one, with a hole in it) and two 10-yen coins. The total is equivalent to approximately 25 cents USD.

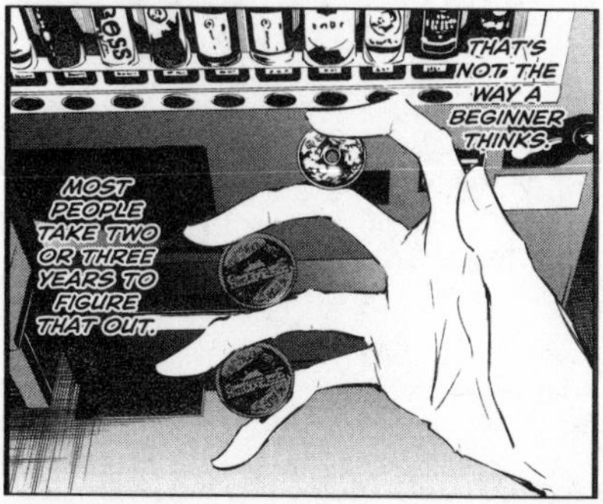
THAT'S NOT THE WAY A BEGINNER THINKS.
MOST PEOPLE TAKE TWO OR THREE YEARS TO FIGURE THAT OUT.

translation notes

Bwong Bwong, page 166-167

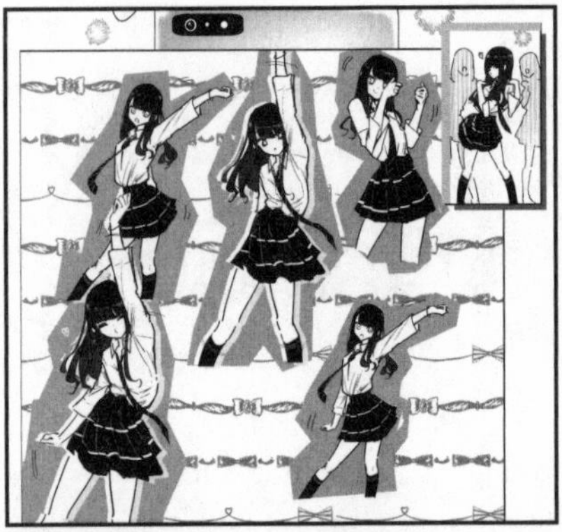

This seems to be a reference to "Hey Julie," a music clip/ dance meme that was viral on TikTok in 2019, the year *Wandance* volume 2 was published in Japan.

Future Plans Sheet, page 168

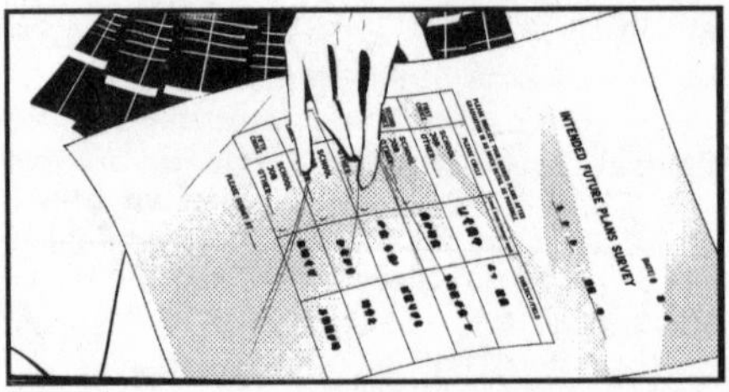
INTENDED FUTURE PLANS SURVEY

As a third-year, On is in her last year of high school. The *shinro kibou chousa* ("desired progression survey") sheet she turns in here is a standard worksheet for students in their last year of high school to help them think about where they want to go next (such as going to college or entering the workforce) and to let teachers know what students are planning.

World of Dance, page 173

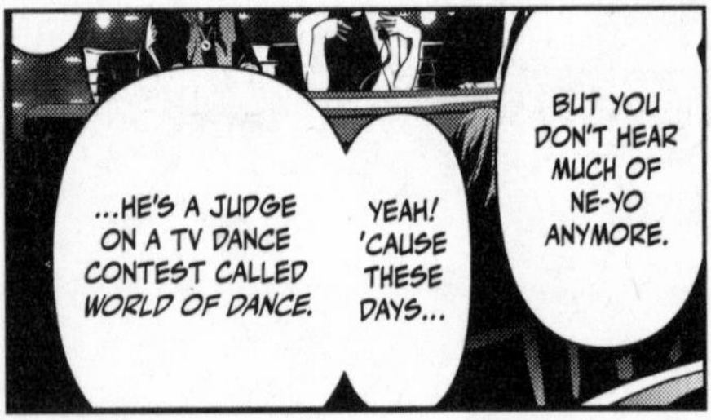
BUT YOU DON'T HEAR MUCH OF NE-YO ANYMORE.
YEAH! 'CAUSE THESE DAYS...
...HE'S A JUDGE ON A TV DANCE CONTEST CALLED *WORLD OF DANCE.*

World of Dance was a televised competition in which solo acts and groups competed in front of a panel of judges for a grand prize of one million dollars. It first aired in 2017, and was cancelled in March 2021 after running for four seasons.

A SMART, NEW ROMANTIC COMEDY FOR FANS OF *SHORTCAKE CAKE* AND *TERRACE HOUSE!*

KC
KODANSHA
COMICS

A romance manga starring high school girl Meeko, who learns to live on her own in a boarding house whose living room is home to the odd (but handsome) Matsunaga-san. She begins to adjust to her new life away from her parents, but Meeko soon learns that no matter how far away from home she is, she's still a young girl at heart — especially when she finds herself falling for Matsunaga-san.

PERFECT WORLD

Rie Aruga

A TOUCHING NEW SERIES ABOUT LOVE AND COPING WITH DISABILITY

An office party reunites Tsugumi with her high school crush Itsuki. He's realized his dream of becoming an architect, but along the way, he experienced a spinal injury that put him in a wheelchair. Now Tsugumi's rekindled feelings will butt up against prejudices she never considered — and Itsuki will have to decide if he's ready to let someone into his heart...

"Depicts with great delicacy and courage the difficulties some with disabilities experience getting involved in romantic relationships... Rie Aruga refuses to romanticize, pushing her heroine to face the reality of disability. She invites her readers to the same tasks of empathy, knowledge and recognition."
—Slate.fr

"An important entry [in manga romance]... The emotional core of both plot and characters indicates thoughtfulness... [Aruga's] research is readily apparent in the text and artwork, making this feel like a real story."
—Anime News Network

Something's Wrong With Us

NATSUMI ANDO

The dark, psychological, sexy shojo series readers have been waiting for!

A spine-chilling and steamy romance between a Japanese sweets maker and the man who framed her mother for murder!

Following in her mother's footsteps, Nao became a traditional Japanese sweets maker, and with unparalleled artistry and a bright attitude, she gets an offer to work at a world-class confectionary company. But when she meets the young, handsome owner, she recognizes his cold stare...

Young characters and steampunk setting, like *Howl's Moving Castle* and *Battle Angel Alita*

Beyond the Clouds © 2018 Nicke / Ki-oon

A boy with a talent for machines and a mysterious girl whose wings he's fixed will take you beyond the clouds! In the tradition of the high-flying, resonant adventure stories of Studio Ghibli comes a gorgeous tale about the longing of young hearts for adventure and friendship!

The art-deco cyberpunk classic from the creators of *xxxHOLiC* and *Cardcaptor Sakura!*

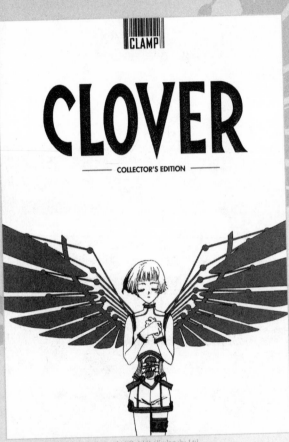

CLOVER © CLAMP-ShigatsuTsuitachi CO.,LTD./Kodansha Ltd.

Su was born into a bleak future, where the government keeps tight control over children with magical powers—codenamed "Clovers." With Su being the only "four-leaf" Clover in the world, she has been kept isolated nearly her whole life. Can ex-military agent Kazuhiko deliver her to the happiness she seeks? Experience the complete series in this hardcover edition, which also includes over twenty pages of ravishing color art!

KC
KODANSHA
COMICS

The beloved characters from *Cardcaptor Sakura* return in a brand new, reimagined fantasy adventure!

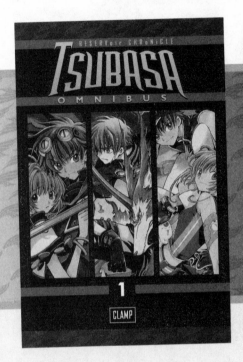

"[*Tsubasa*] takes readers on a fantastic ride that only gets more exhilarating with each successive chapter." —Anime News Network

In the Kingdom of Clow, an archaeological dig unleashes an incredible power, causing Princess Sakura to lose her memories. To save her, her childhood friend Syaoran must follow the orders of the Dimension Witch and travel alongside Kurogane, an unrivaled warrior; Fai, a powerful magician; and Mokona, a curiously strange creature, to retrieve Sakura's dispersed memories!

"Clever, sassy, and original....*xxxHOLiC* has the inherent hallmarks of a runaway hit."
—NewType magazine

Beautifully seductive artwork and uniquely Japanese depictions of the supernatural will hypnotize CLAMP fans!

xxxHOLiC © CLAMP-ShigatsuTsuitachi CO.,LTD./Kodansha Ltd.
xxxHOLiC Rei © CLAMP-ShigatsuTsuitachi CO.,LTD./Kodansha Ltd.

Kimihiro Watanuki is haunted by visions of ghosts and spirits. He seeks help from a mysterious woman named Yuko, who claims she can help. However, Watanuki must work for Yuko in order to pay for her aid. Soon Watanuki finds himself employed in Yuko's shop, where he sees things and meets customers that are stranger than anything he could have ever imagined.

KC
KODANSHA COMICS

MAGIC ● KNIGHT RAYEARTH

25TH ANNIVERSARY EDITION

CLAMP

A BELOVED CLASSIC MAKES ITS STUNNING RETURN IN THIS GORGEOUS, LIMITED EDITION BOX SET!

This tale of three Tokyo teenagers who cross through a magical portal and become the champions of another world is a modern manga classic. The box set includes three volumes of manga covering the entire first series of *Magic Knight Rayearth*, plus the series's super-rare full-color art book companion, all printed at a larger size than ever before on premium paper, featuring a newly-revised translation and lettering, and exquisite foil-stamped covers.

A strictly limited edition, this will be gone in a flash!

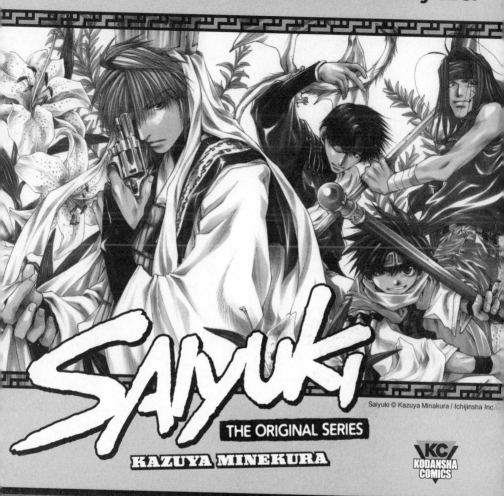

The adorable new odd-couple cat comedy manga from the creator of the beloved *Chi's Sweet Home*, in full color!

Sue & Tai-chan

Konami Kanata

Sue is an aging housecat who's looking forward to living out her life in peace... but her plans change when the mischievous black tomcat Tai-chan enters the picture! Hey! Sue never signed up to be a catsitter! *Sue & Tai-chan* is the latest from the reigning meow-narch of cute kitty comics, Konami Kanata.

KC KODANSHA COMICS

THE MAGICAL GIRL CLASSIC THAT BROUGHT A GENERATION OF READERS TO MANGA, NOW BACK IN A DEFINITIVE, HARDCOVER COLLECTOR'S EDITION!

CARDCAPTOR SAKURA
COLLECTOR'S EDITION
C L A M P

Ten-year-old Sakura Kinomoto lives a pretty normal life with her older brother, Tōya, and widowed father, Fujitaka—until the day she discovers a strange book in her father's library, and her life takes a magical turn...

- A deluxe large-format hardcover edition of CLAMP's shojo manga classic
- All-new foil-stamped cover art on each volume
- Comes with exclusive collectible art card

KC
KODANSHA COMICS

THE WORLD OF CLAMP!

Cardcaptor Sakura
Collector's Edition

Cardcaptor Sakura:
Clear Card

Magic Knight Rayearth
25th Anniversary Box Set

Chobits

TSUBASA Omnibus

TSUBASA WoRLD CHRoNiCLE

xxxHOLiC Omnibus

xxxHOLiC Rei

CLOVER Collector's Edition

Kodansha Comics welcomes you to explore the expansive world of CLAMP, the all-female artist collective that has produced some of the most acclaimed manga of the century. Our growing catalog includes icons like *Cardcaptor Sakura* and *Magic Knight Rayearth*, each crafted with CLAMP's one-of-a-kind style and characters!

A Kodansha Trade Paperback Original

Wandance 2 copyright © 2019 Coffee
English translation copyright © 2022 Coffee

Published in the United States by
Kodansha USA Publishing, LLC, New York.

Publication rights for this English edition arranged through Kodansha Ltd., Tokyo.

First published in Japan in 2019 by Kodansha Ltd., Tokyo.

ISBN 978-1-64651-516-5

Printed in the United States of America.

9 8 7 6 5 4 3 2 1

Translation: Kevin Steinbach
Lettering: Nicole Roderick
Editing: Tiff Joshua TJ Ferentini
Kodansha USA Publishing edition cover design by Adam Del Re

Publisher: Kiichiro Sugawara

Director of Publishing Services: Ben Applegate
Director of Publishing Operations: Dave Barrett
Associate Director of Publishing Operations: Stephen Pakula
Publishing Services Managing Editors: Alanna Ruse, Madison Salters
Senior Production Manager: Angela Zurlo

KODANSHA.US

 KODANSHA